volume 3

ASADORA!

NAOKI URASAWA

Chapter 17	A Slight Possibility	003
Chapter 18	Five Rings	027
Chapter 19	Things You Can't Say	053
Chapter 20	The Search Begins	077
Chapter 21	Letters	103
Chapter 22	Just a Fighter Plane	129
Chapter 23	Kinuyo's Wrath	155

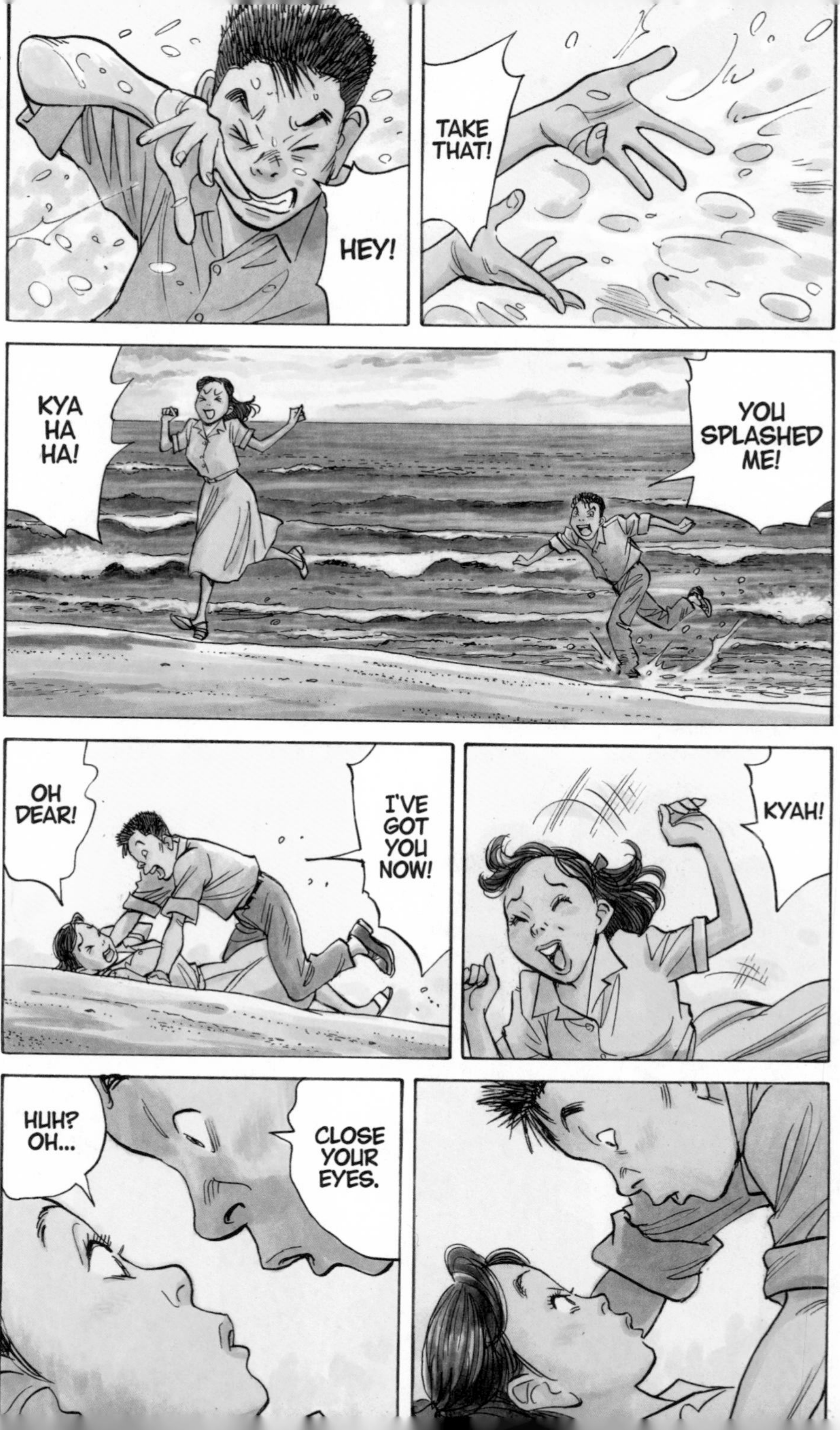
TAKE THAT!
HEY!
YOU SPLASHED ME!
KYA HA HA!
KYAH!
I'VE GOT YOU NOW!
OH DEAR!
CLOSE YOUR EYES.
HUH? OH...

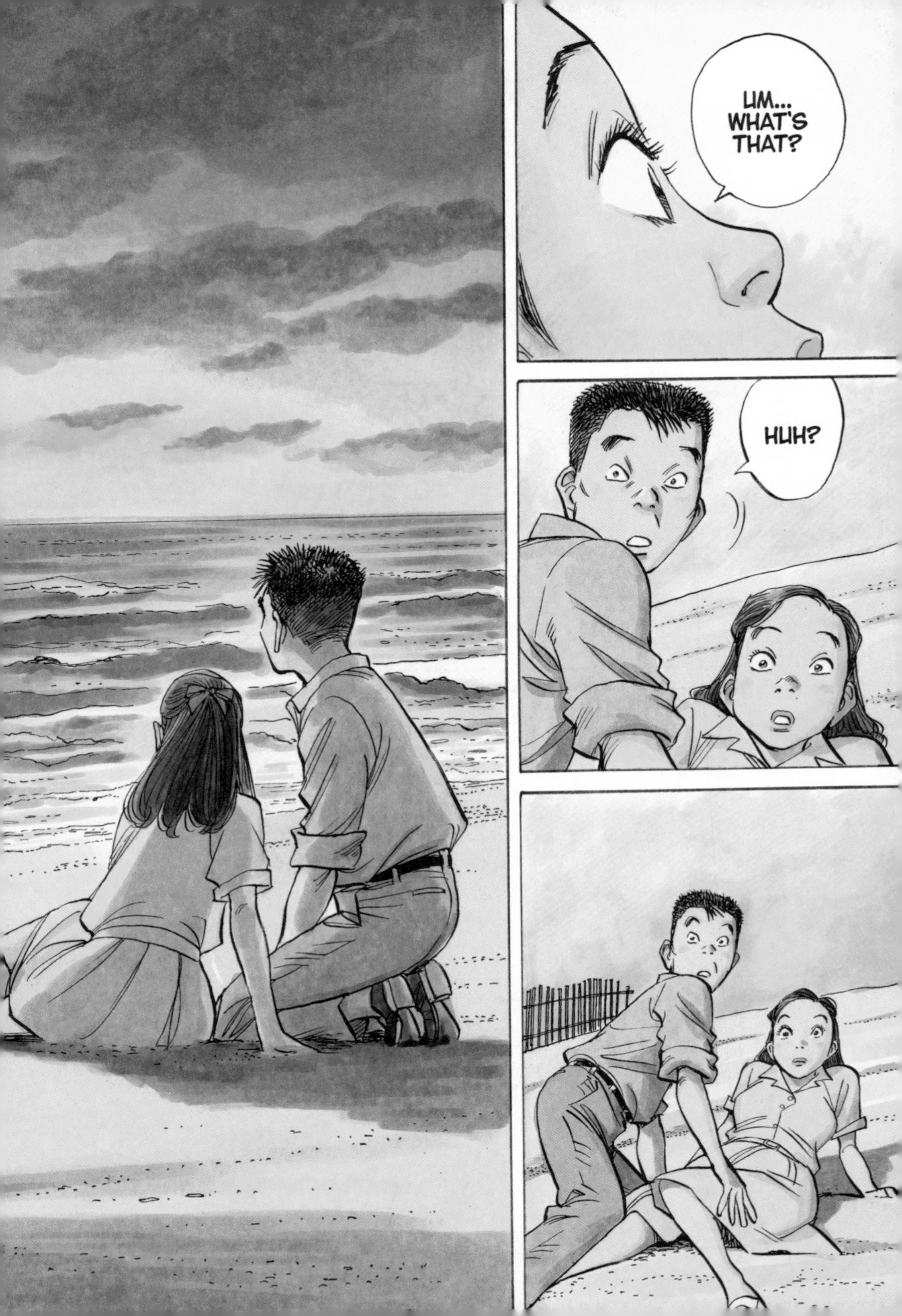
UM... WHAT'S THAT?
HUH?

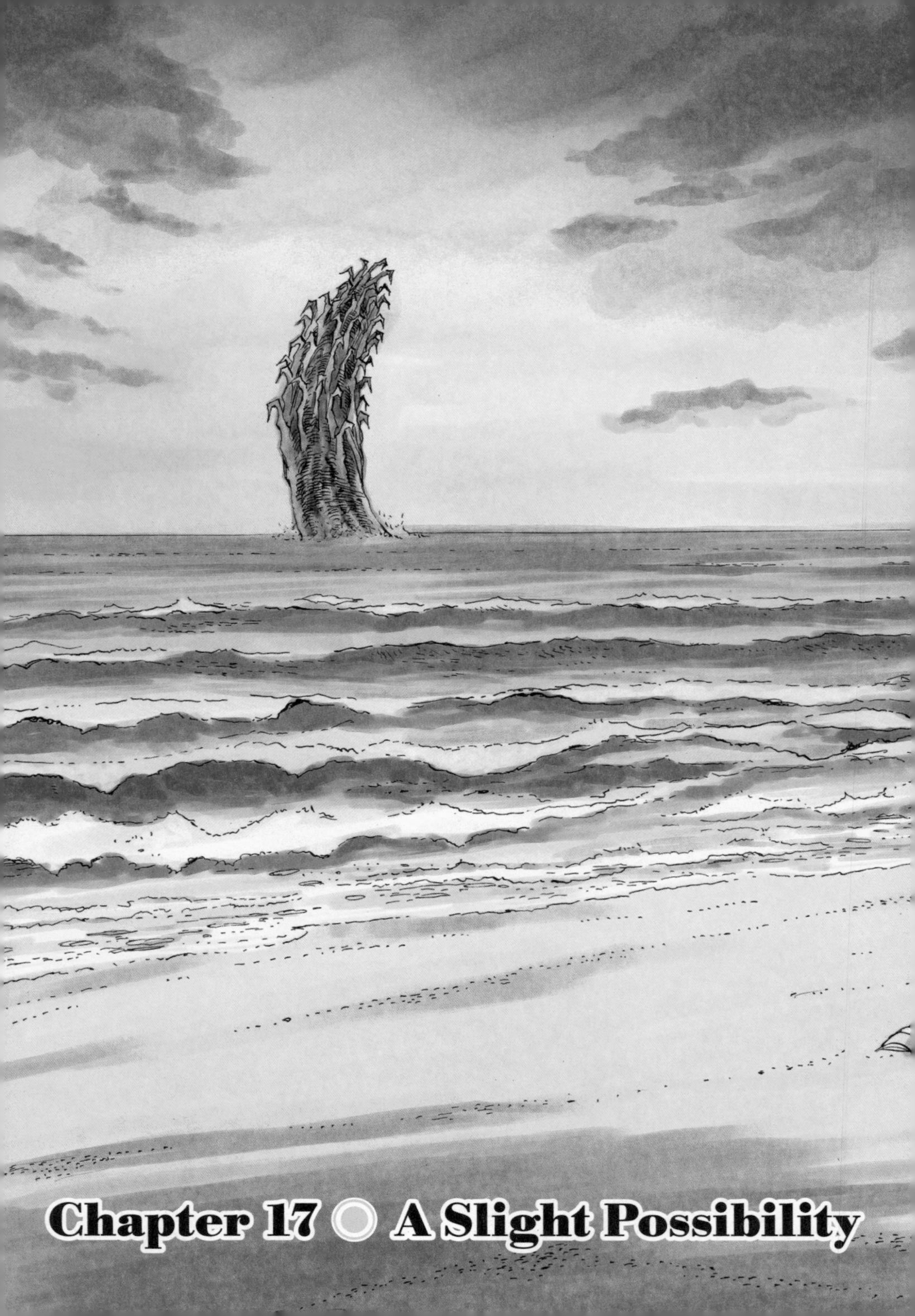

Chapter 17 ◯ A Slight Possibility

ASADORA!

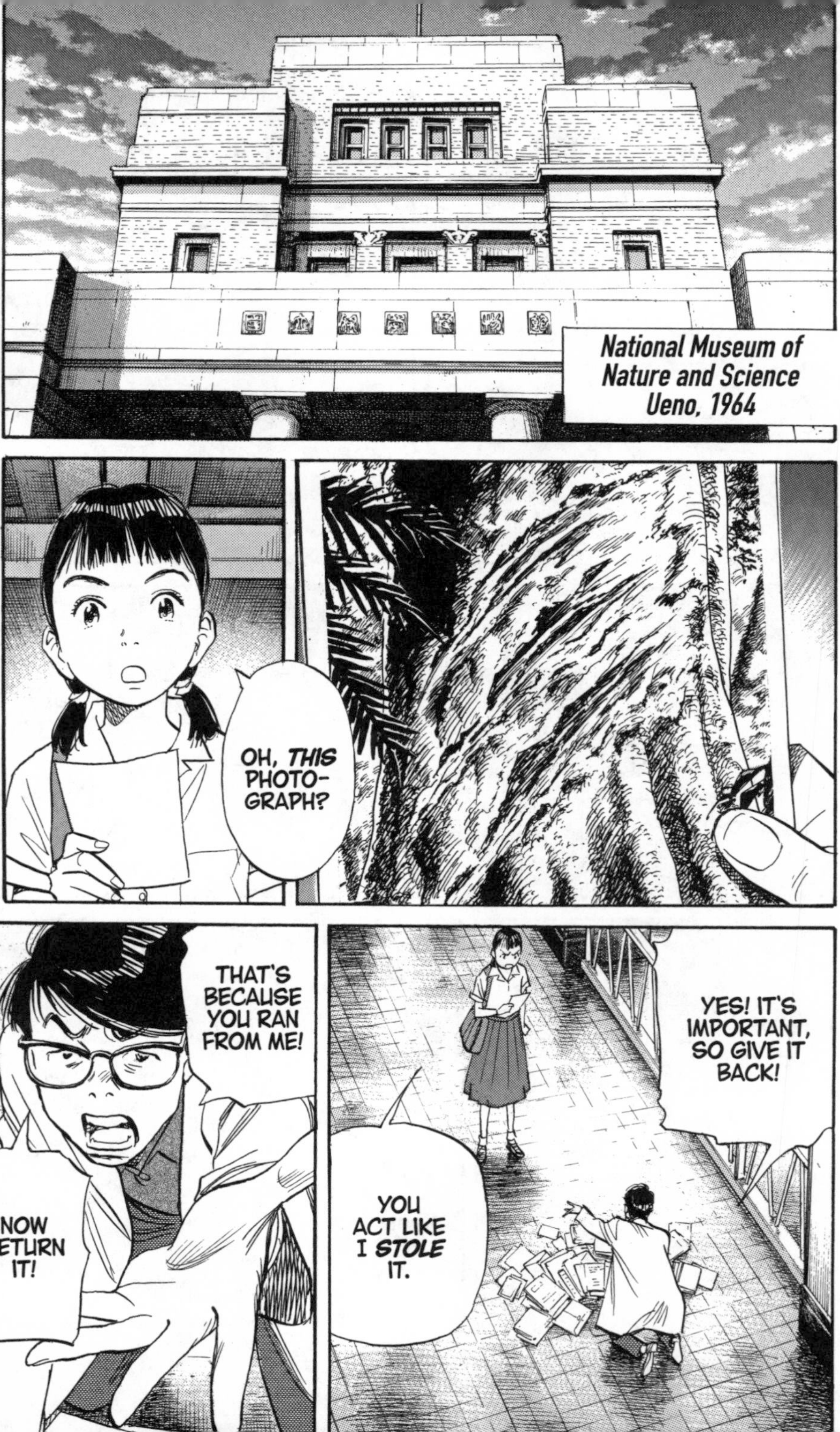
National Museum of Nature and Science Ueno, 1964
OH, *THIS* PHOTOGRAPH?
YES! IT'S IMPORTANT, SO GIVE IT BACK!
YOU ACT LIKE I *STOLE* IT.
THAT'S BECAUSE YOU RAN FROM ME!
NOW RETURN IT!

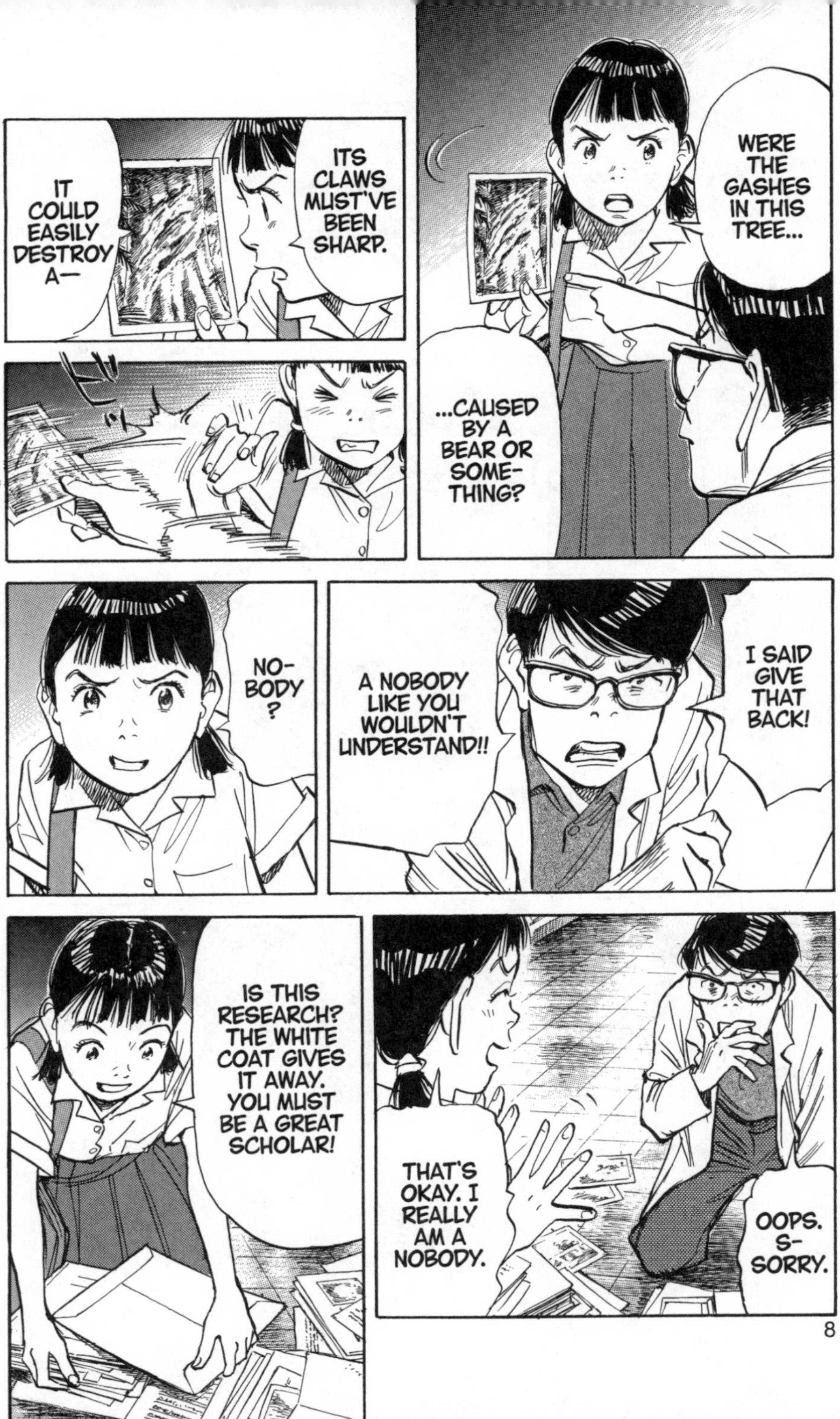
WERE THE GASHES IN THIS TREE...
...CAUSED BY A BEAR OR SOME-THING?
ITS CLAWS MUST'VE BEEN SHARP.
IT COULD EASILY DESTROY A—
I SAID GIVE THAT BACK!
A NOBODY LIKE YOU WOULDN'T UNDERSTAND!!
NO-BODY?
OOPS. S-SORRY.
THAT'S OKAY. I REALLY AM A NOBODY.
IS THIS RESEARCH? THE WHITE COAT GIVES IT AWAY. YOU MUST BE A GREAT SCHOLAR!

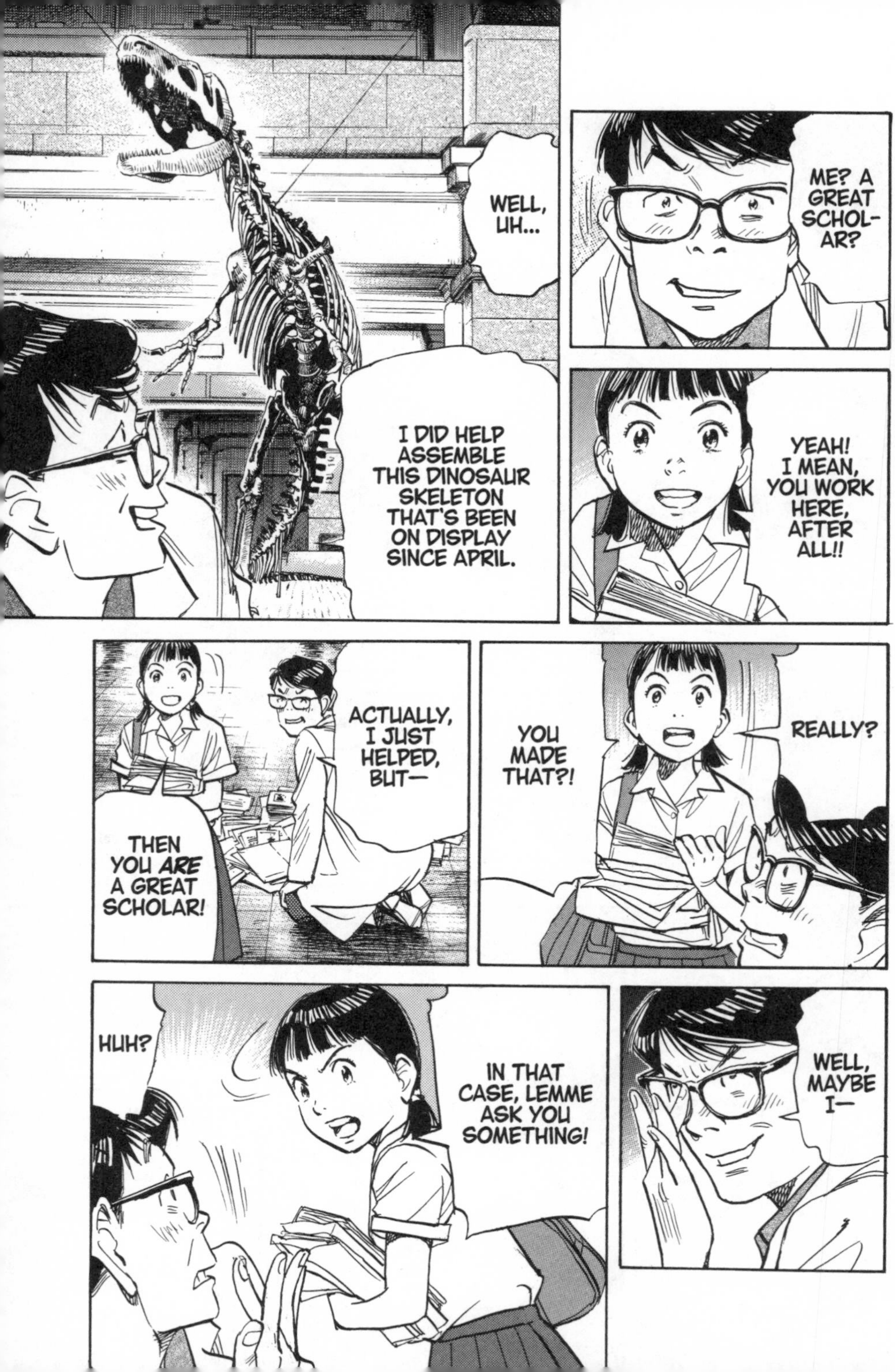
ME? A GREAT SCHOL-AR?
YEAH! I MEAN, YOU WORK HERE, AFTER ALL!!
WELL, UH...
I DID HELP ASSEMBLE THIS DINOSAUR SKELETON THAT'S BEEN ON DISPLAY SINCE APRIL.
REALLY?
YOU MADE THAT?!
ACTUALLY, I JUST HELPED, BUT—
THEN YOU *ARE* A GREAT SCHOLAR!
WELL, MAYBE I—
IN THAT CASE, LEMME ASK YOU SOMETHING!
HUH?

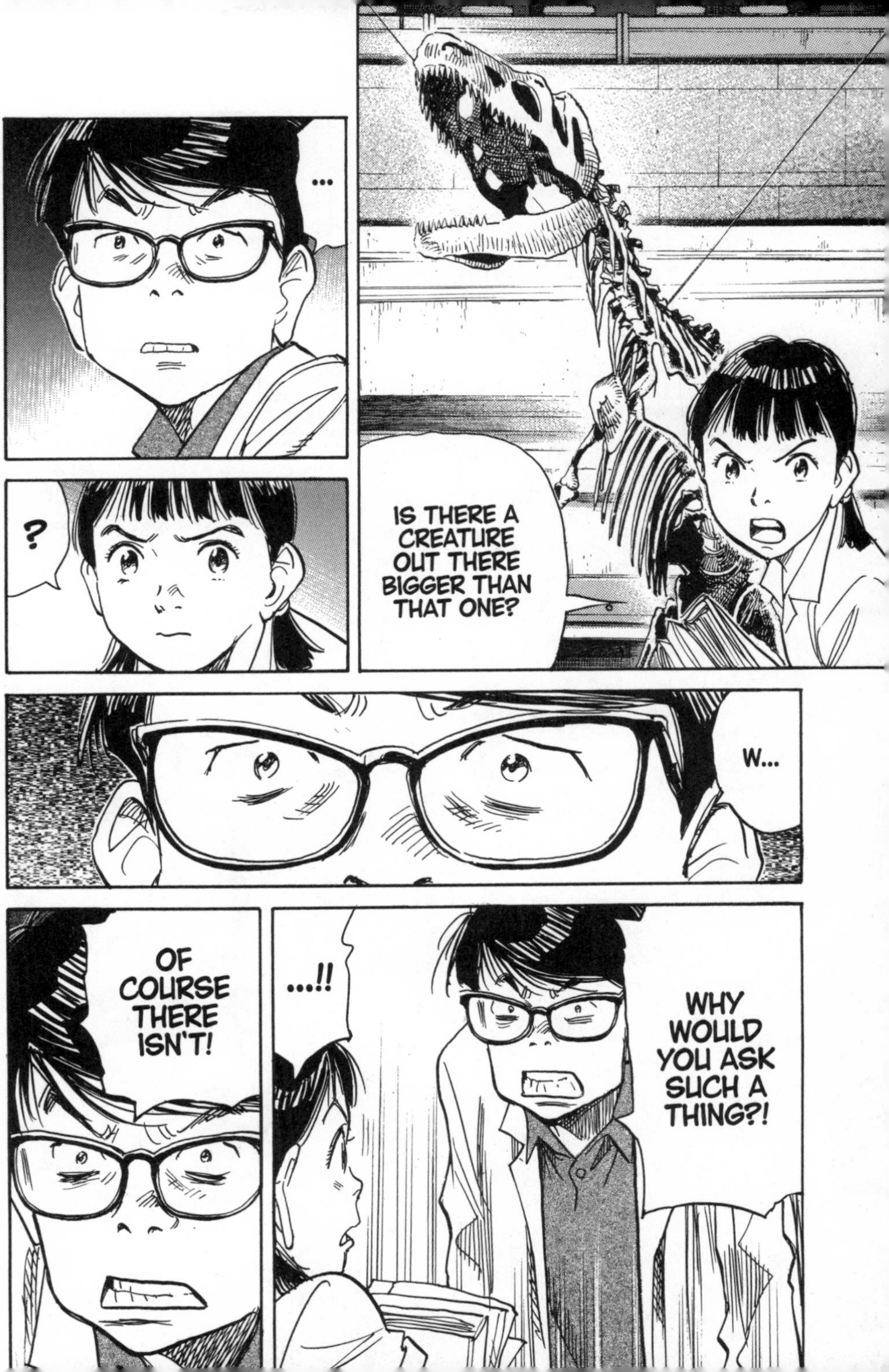
IS THERE A CREATURE OUT THERE BIGGER THAN THAT ONE?
...
?
W...
WHY WOULD YOU ASK SUCH A THING?!
...!!
OF COURSE THERE ISN'T!

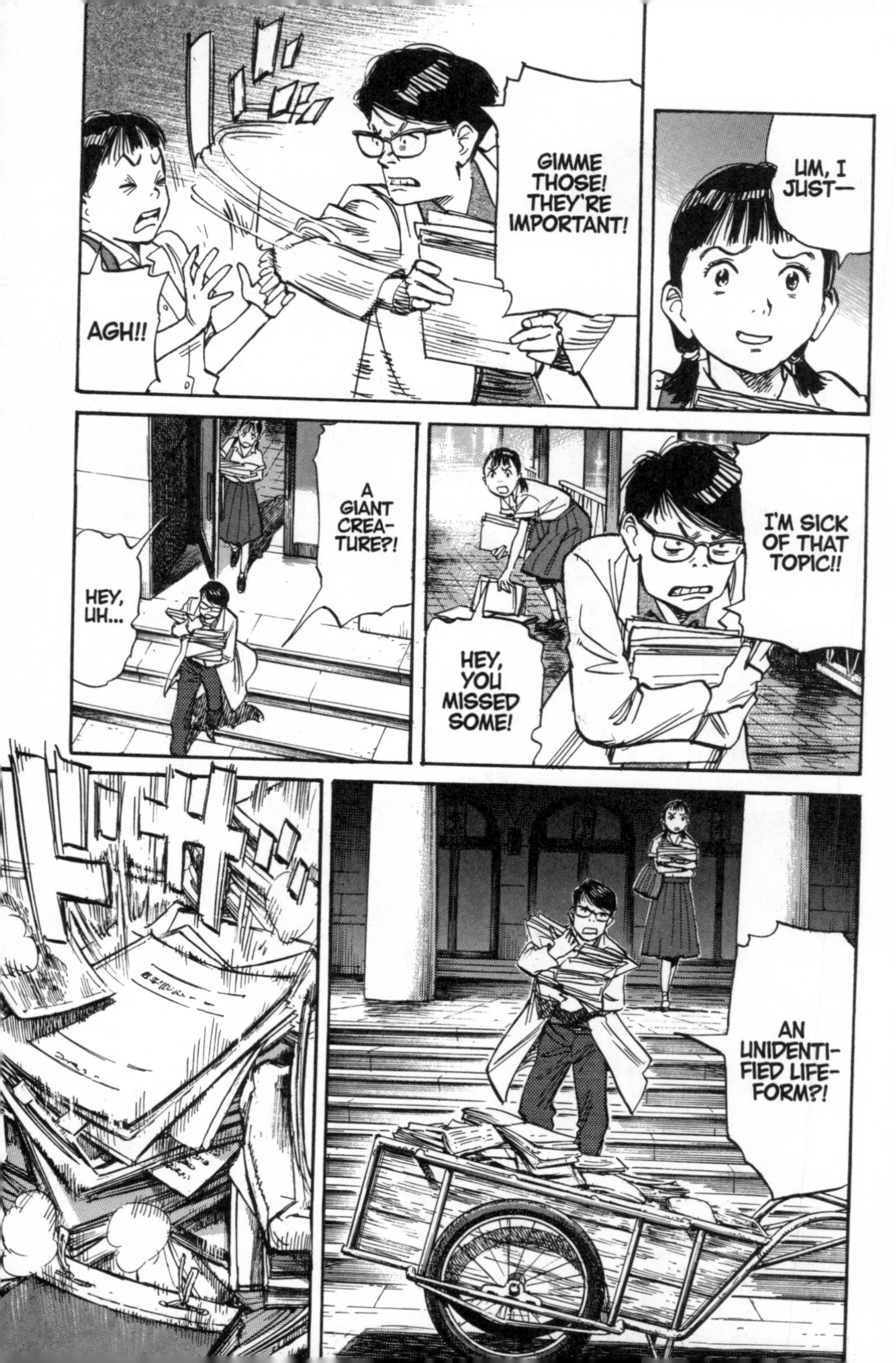
UM, I JUST—
GIMME THOSE! THEY'RE IMPORTANT!
AGH!!
I'M SICK OF THAT TOPIC!!
HEY, YOU MISSED SOME!
A GIANT CREA-TURE?!
HEY, UH...
AN UNIDENTI-FIED LIFE-FORM?!
ドサッ

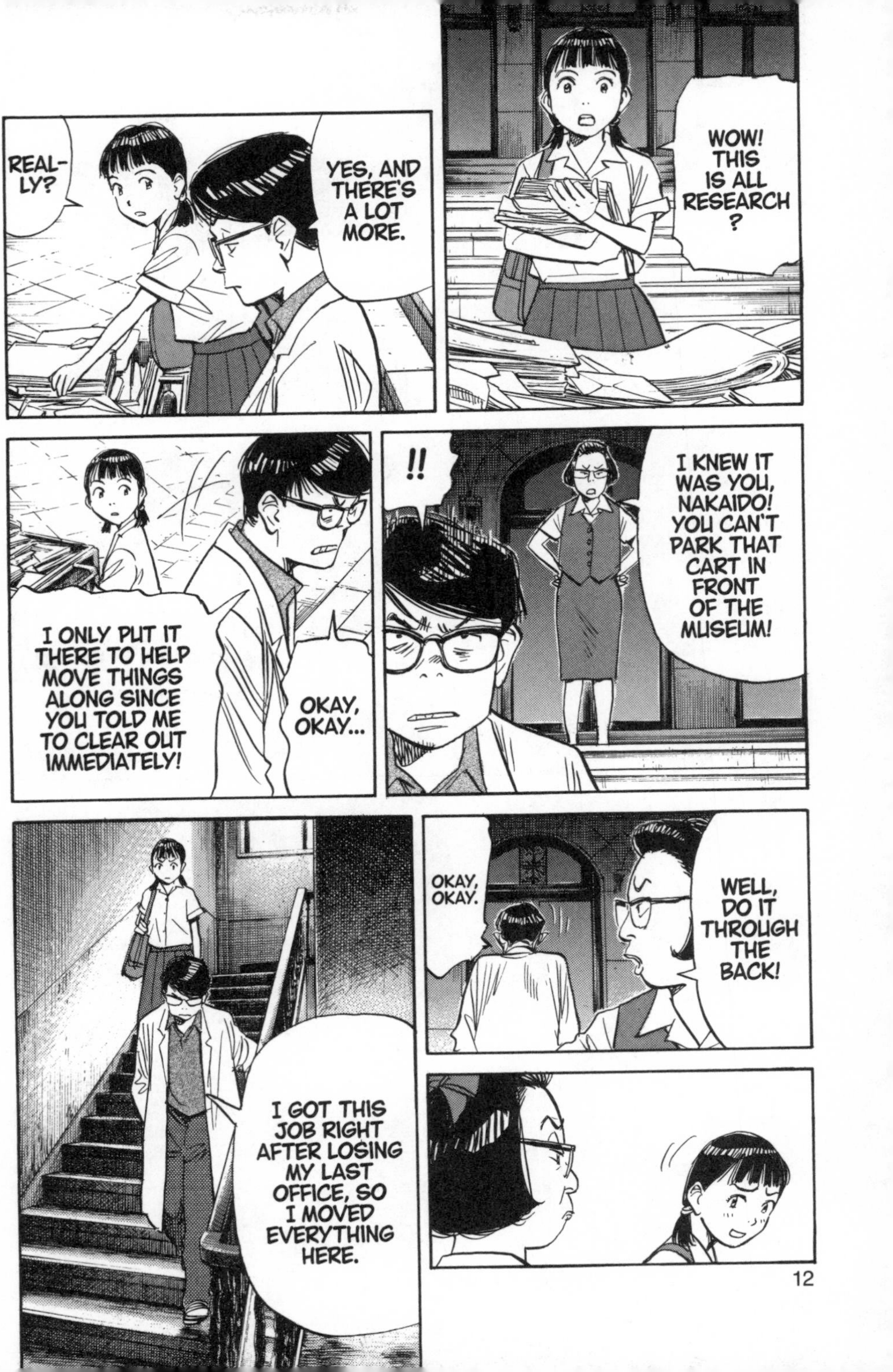
WOW! THIS IS ALL RESEARCH ?
YES, AND THERE'S A LOT MORE.
REAL-LY?
I KNEW IT WAS YOU, NAKAIDO! YOU CAN'T PARK THAT CART IN FRONT OF THE MUSEUM!
!!
OKAY, OKAY...
I ONLY PUT IT THERE TO HELP MOVE THINGS ALONG SINCE YOU TOLD ME TO CLEAR OUT IMMEDIATELY!
WELL, DO IT THROUGH THE BACK!
OKAY, OKAY.
I GOT THIS JOB RIGHT AFTER LOSING MY LAST OFFICE, SO I MOVED EVERYTHING HERE.

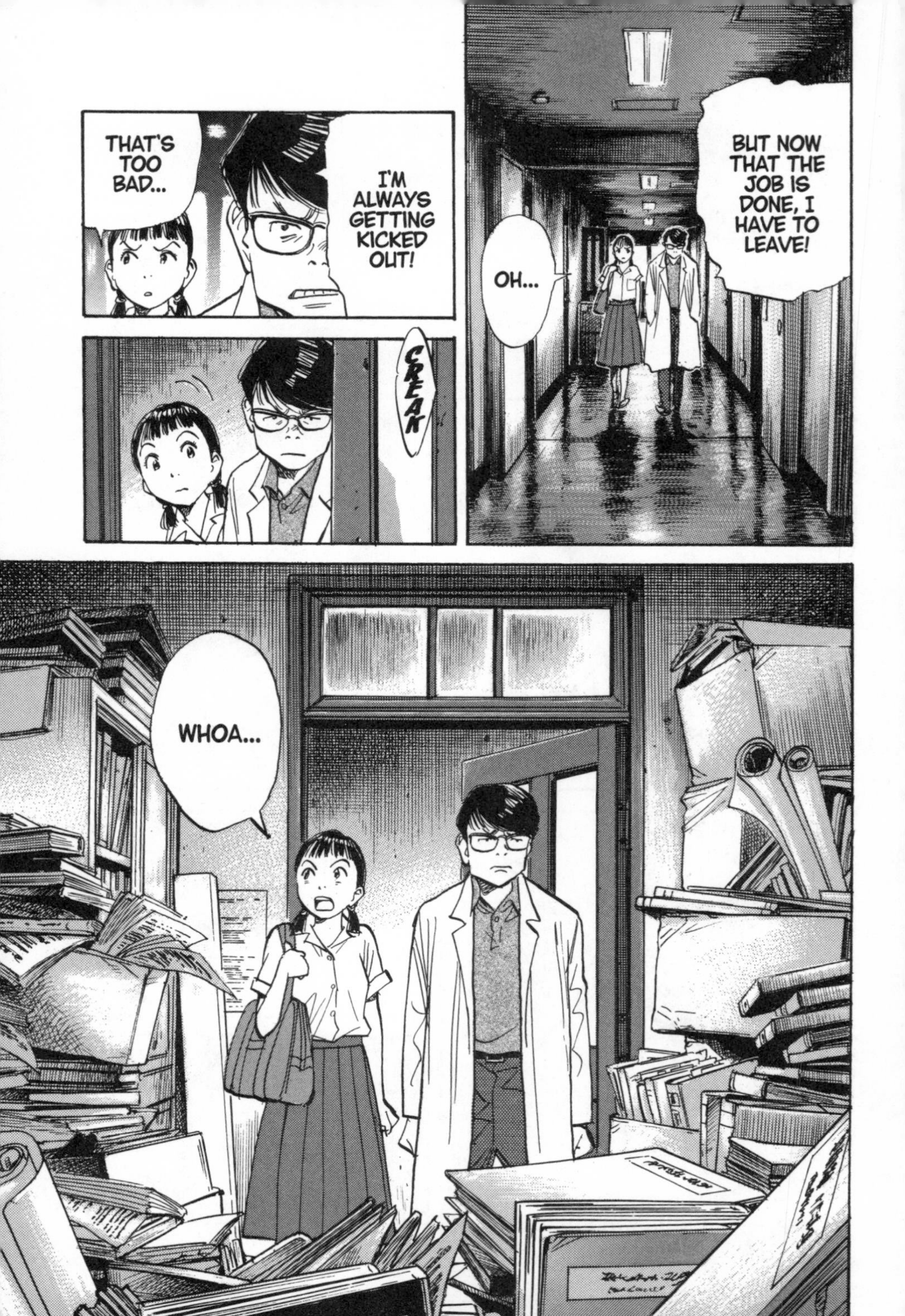
BUT NOW THAT THE JOB IS DONE, I HAVE TO LEAVE!
OH...
I'M ALWAYS GETTING KICKED OUT!
THAT'S TOO BAD...
CREAK
WHOA...

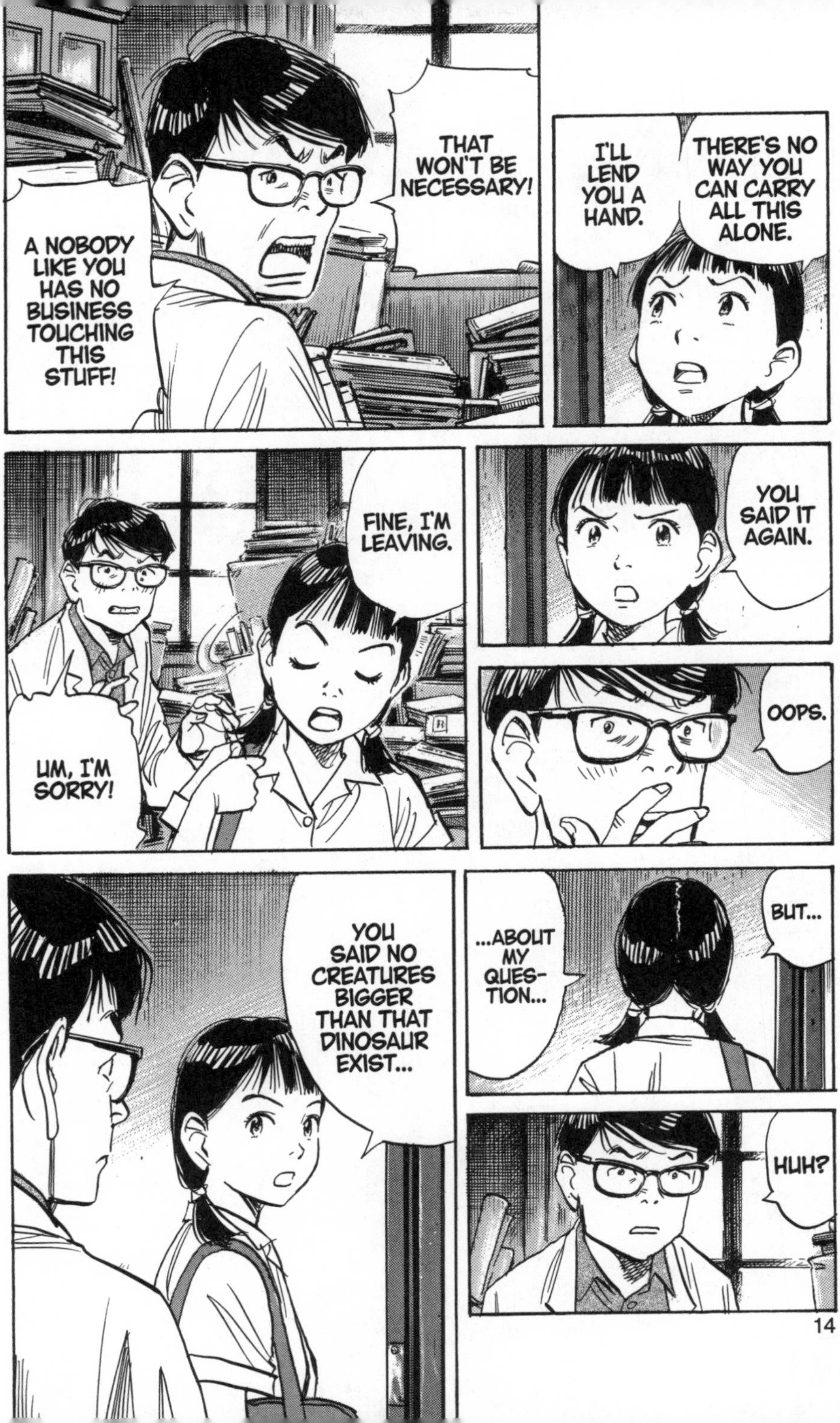
THERE'S NO WAY YOU CAN CARRY ALL THIS ALONE.
I'LL LEND YOU A HAND.
THAT WON'T BE NECESSARY!
A NOBODY LIKE YOU HAS NO BUSINESS TOUCHING THIS STUFF!
YOU SAID IT AGAIN.
OOPS.
FINE, I'M LEAVING.
UM, I'M SORRY!
BUT...
...ABOUT MY QUES-TION...
HUH?
YOU SAID NO CREATURES BIGGER THAN THAT DINOSAUR EXIST...

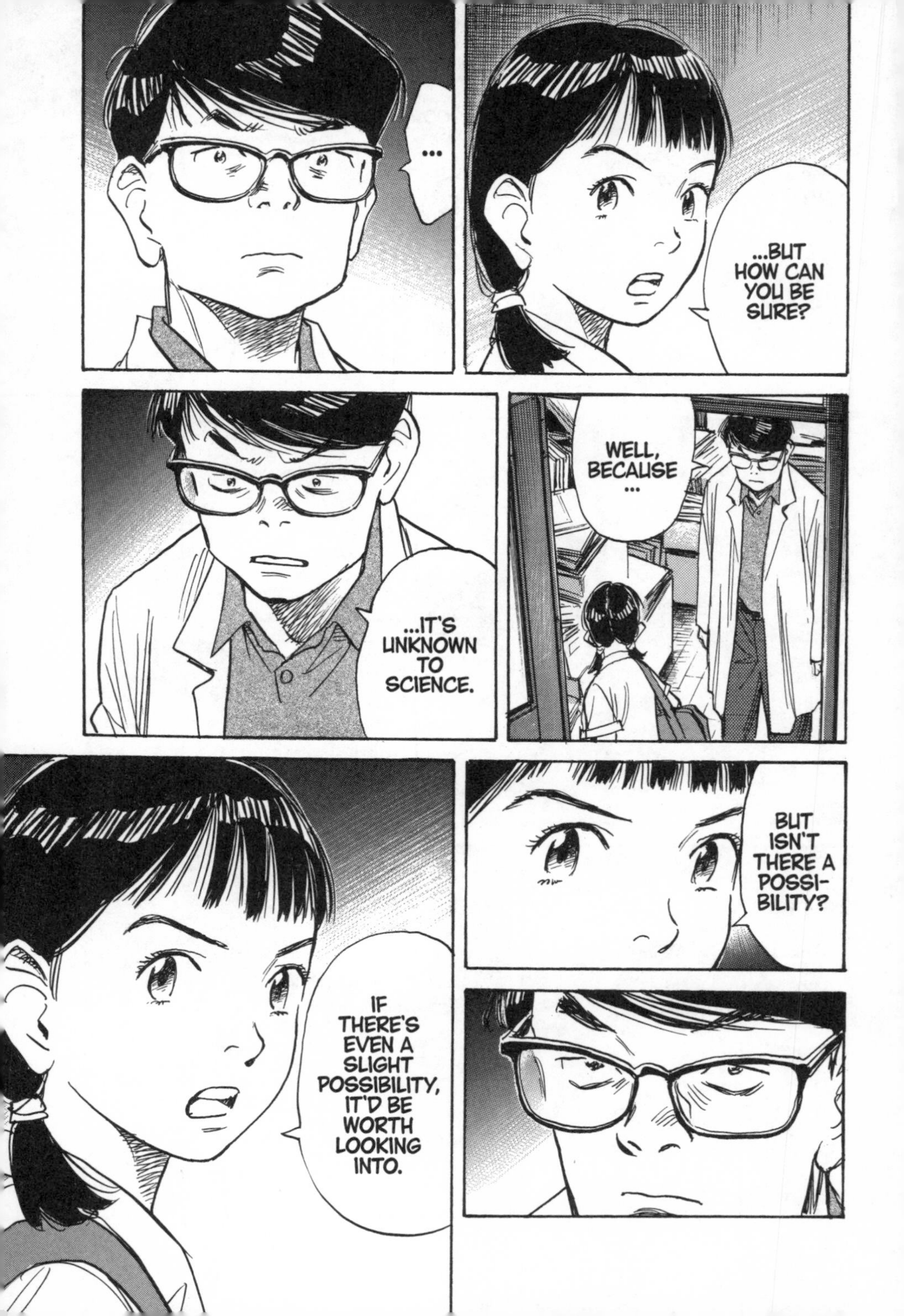
...BUT HOW CAN YOU BE SURE?
...
WELL, BECAUSE ...
...IT'S UNKNOWN TO SCIENCE.
BUT ISN'T THERE A POSSI- BILITY?
IF THERE'S EVEN A SLIGHT POSSIBILITY, IT'D BE WORTH LOOKING INTO.

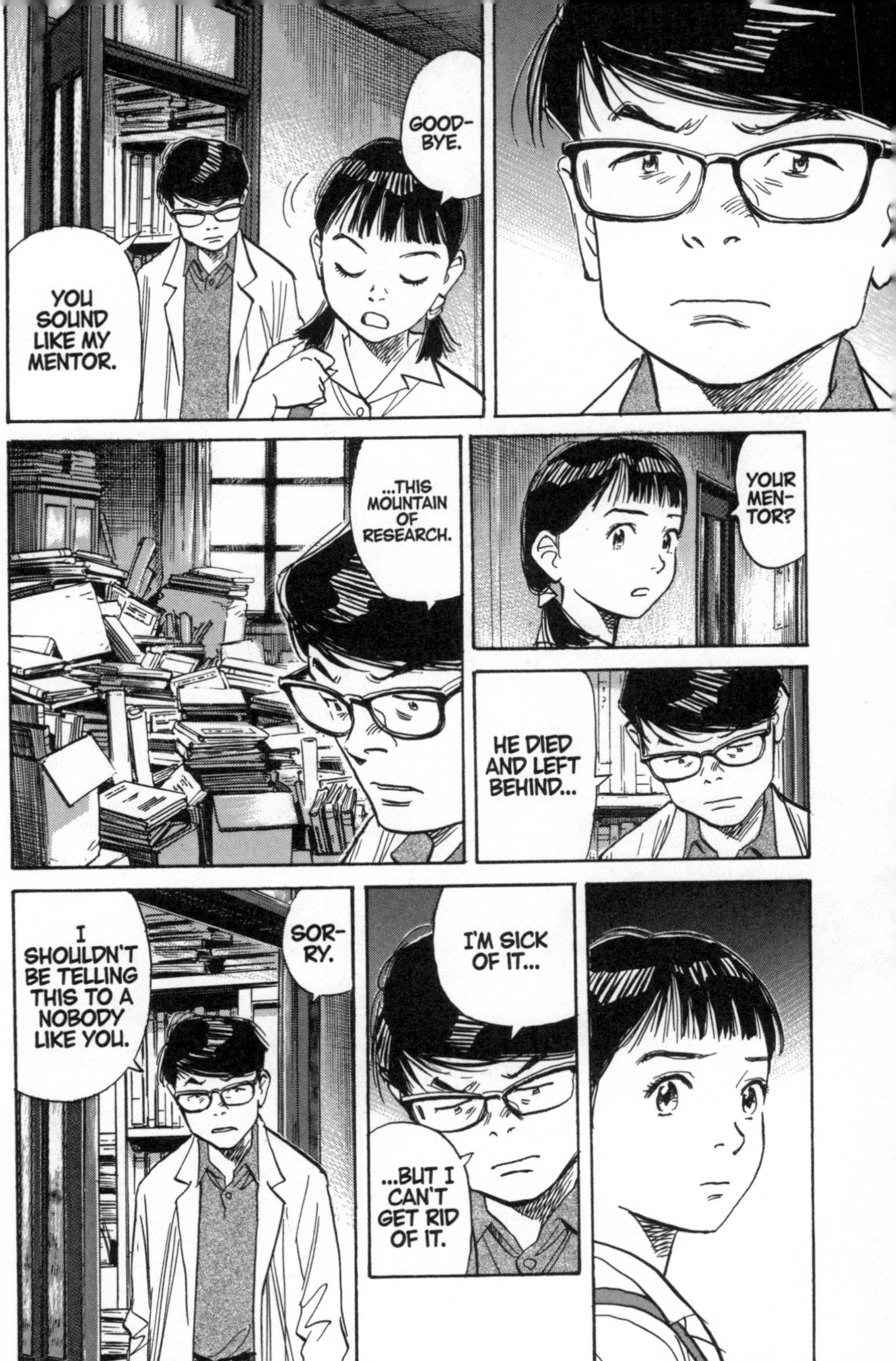
GOOD-BYE.
YOU SOUND LIKE MY MENTOR.
YOUR MEN-TOR?
HE DIED AND LEFT BEHIND...
...THIS MOUNTAIN OF RESEARCH.
I'M SICK OF IT...
...BUT I CAN'T GET RID OF IT.
SOR-RY.
I SHOULDN'T BE TELLING THIS TO A NOBODY LIKE YOU.

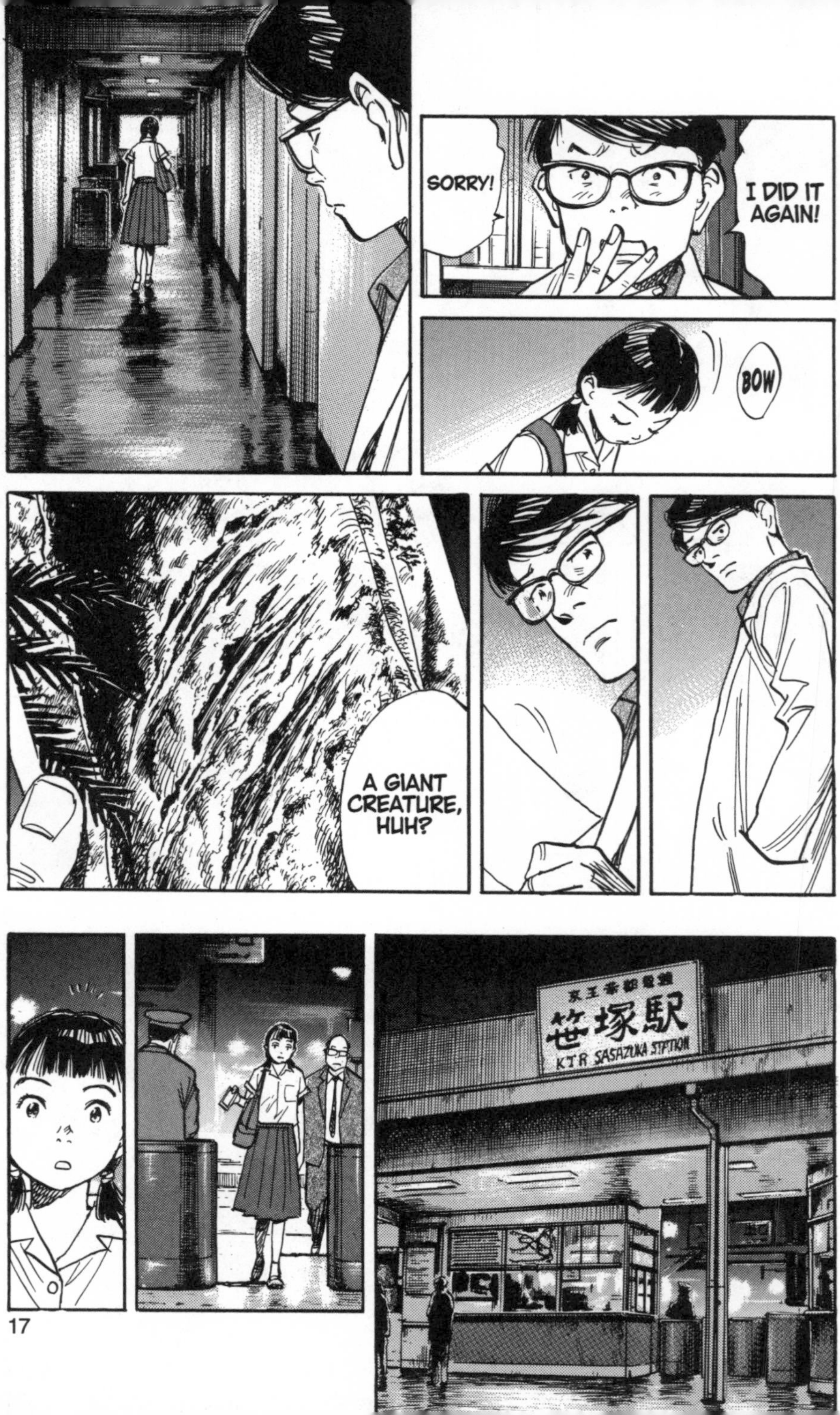
I DID IT AGAIN!
SORRY!
BOW
A GIANT CREATURE, HUH?
笹塚駅
KTR SASAZUKA STATION

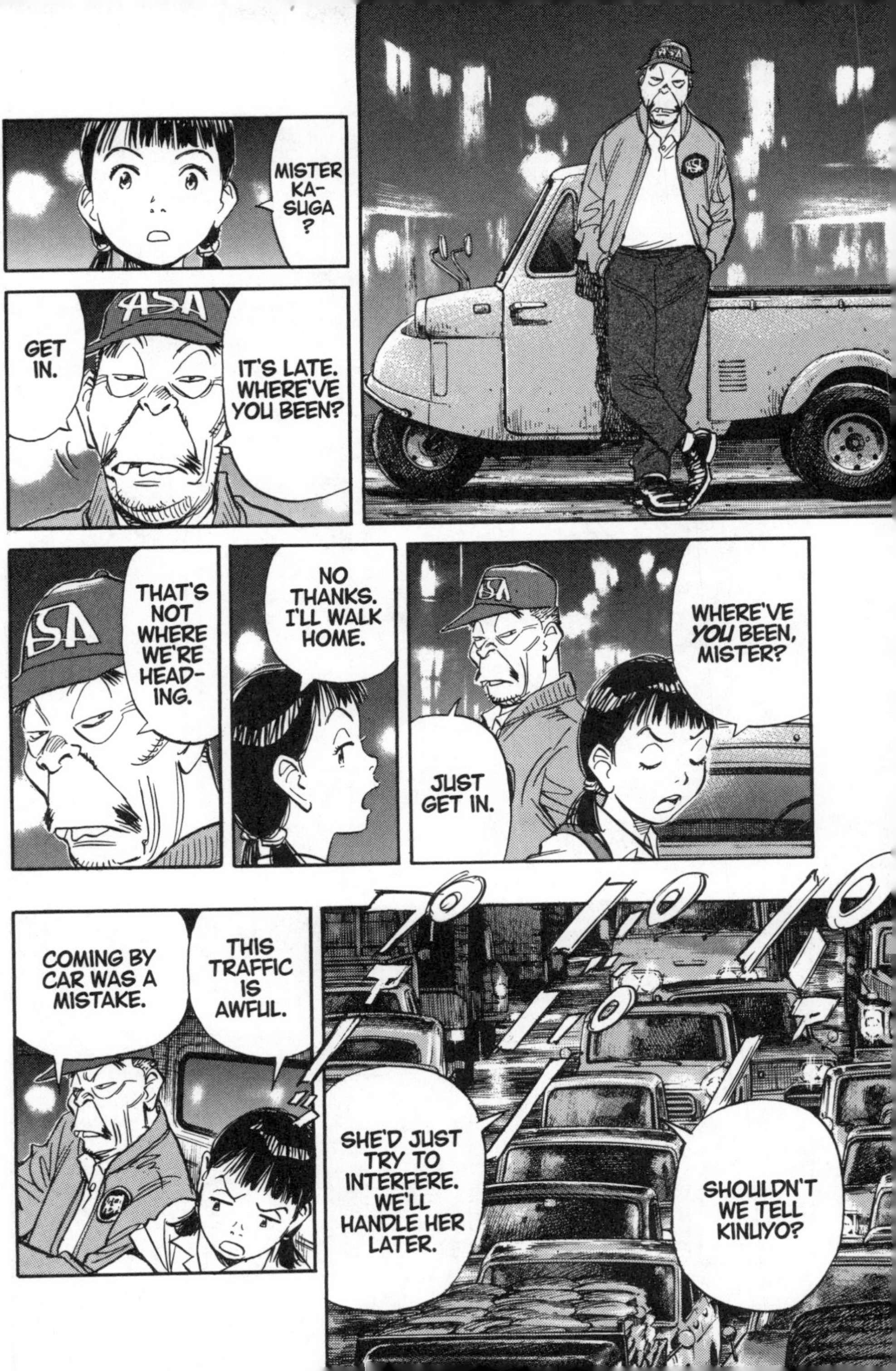
MISTER KA-SUGA?
IT'S LATE. WHERE'VE YOU BEEN?
GET IN.
WHERE'VE *YOU* BEEN, MISTER?
JUST GET IN.
NO THANKS. I'LL WALK HOME.
THAT'S NOT WHERE WE'RE HEAD-ING.
SHOULDN'T WE TELL KINUYO?
SHE'D JUST TRY TO INTERFERE. WE'LL HANDLE HER LATER.
THIS TRAFFIC IS AWFUL.
COMING BY CAR WAS A MISTAKE.

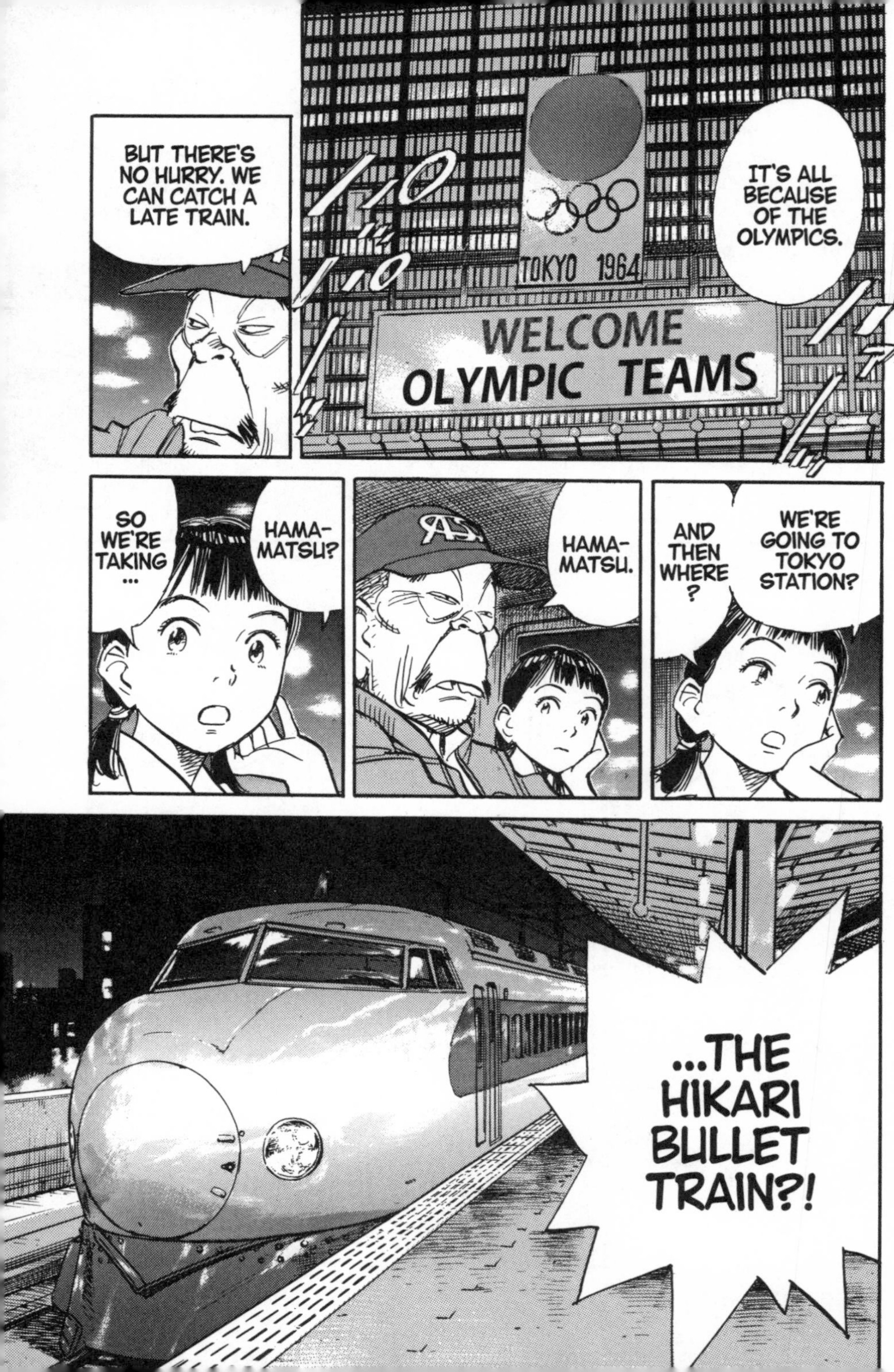
IT'S ALL BECAUSE OF THE OLYMPICS.
TOKYO 1964
WELCOME OLYMPIC TEAMS
BUT THERE'S NO HURRY. WE CAN CATCH A LATE TRAIN.
WE'RE GOING TO TOKYO STATION?
AND THEN WHERE?
HAMA-MATSU.
HAMA-MATSU?
SO WE'RE TAKING ...
...THE HIKARI BULLET TRAIN?!

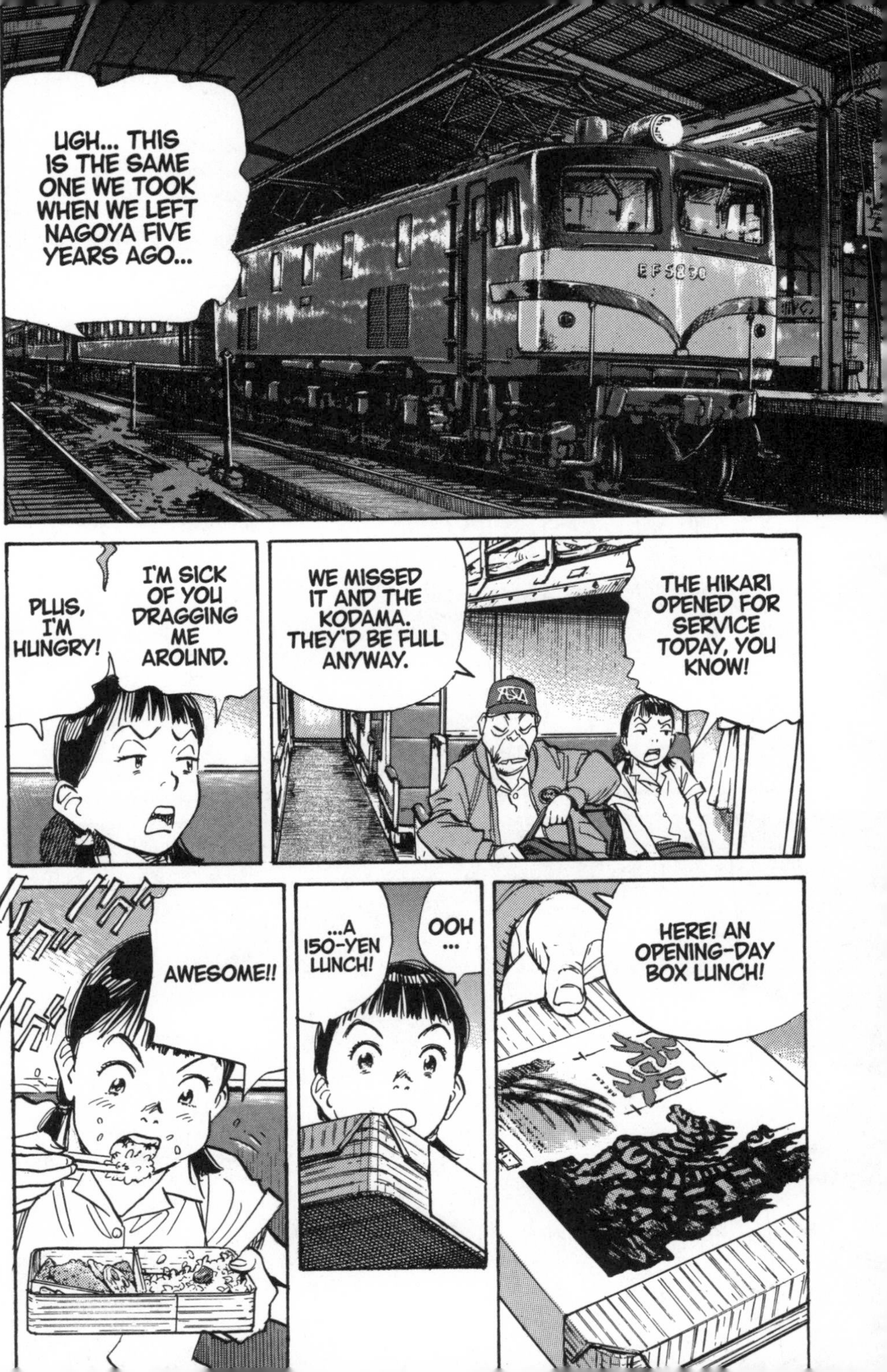
UGH... THIS IS THE SAME ONE WE TOOK WHEN WE LEFT NAGOYA FIVE YEARS AGO...
THE HIKARI OPENED FOR SERVICE TODAY, YOU KNOW!
WE MISSED IT AND THE KODAMA. THEY'D BE FULL ANYWAY.
I'M SICK OF YOU DRAGGING ME AROUND.
PLUS, I'M HUNGRY!
HERE! AN OPENING-DAY BOX LUNCH!
OOH ...
...A 150-YEN LUNCH!
AWESOME!!

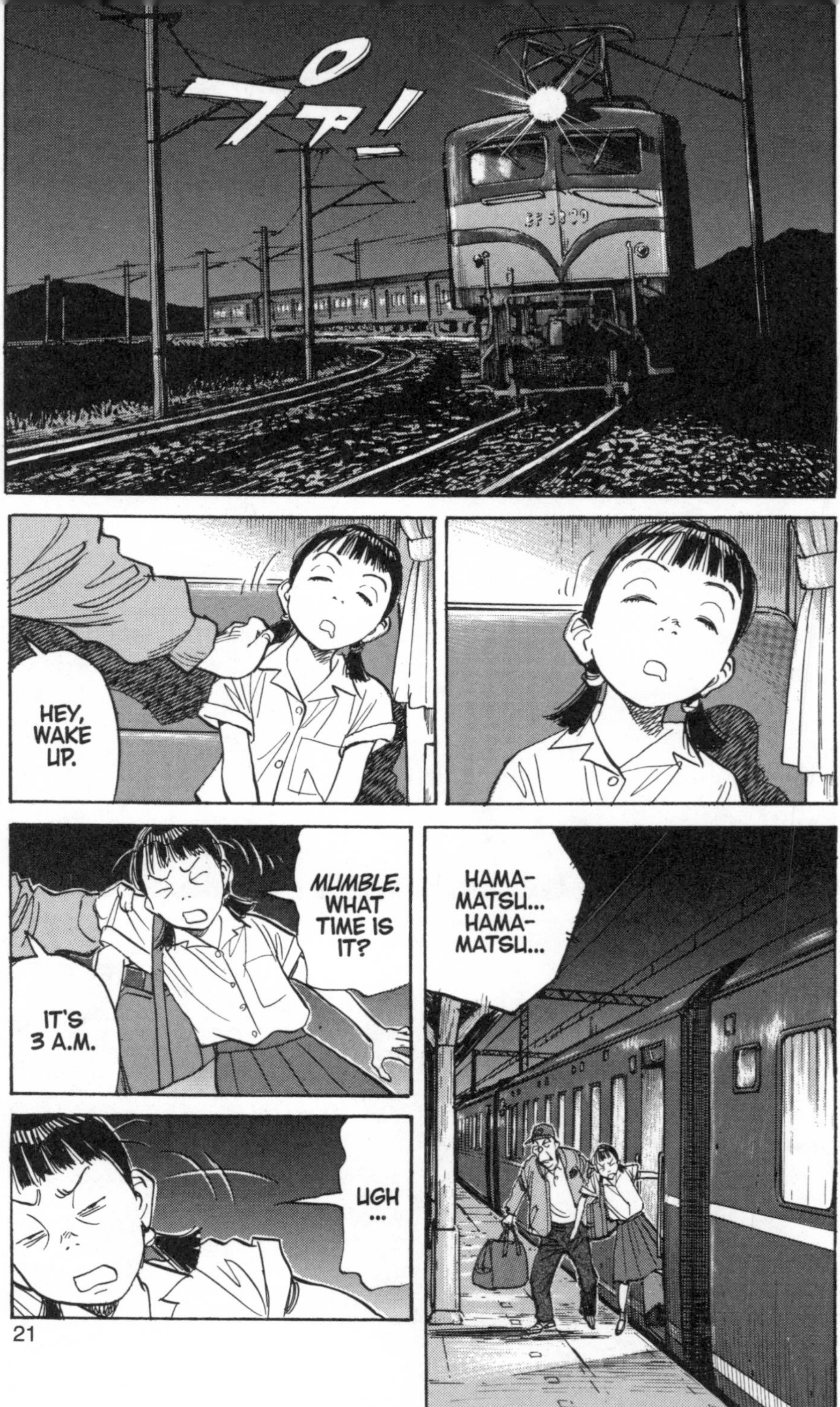
プァー!
HEY, WAKE UP.
HAMA-MATSU... HAMA-MATSU...
MUMBLE. WHAT TIME IS IT?
IT'S 3 A.M.
UGH ...

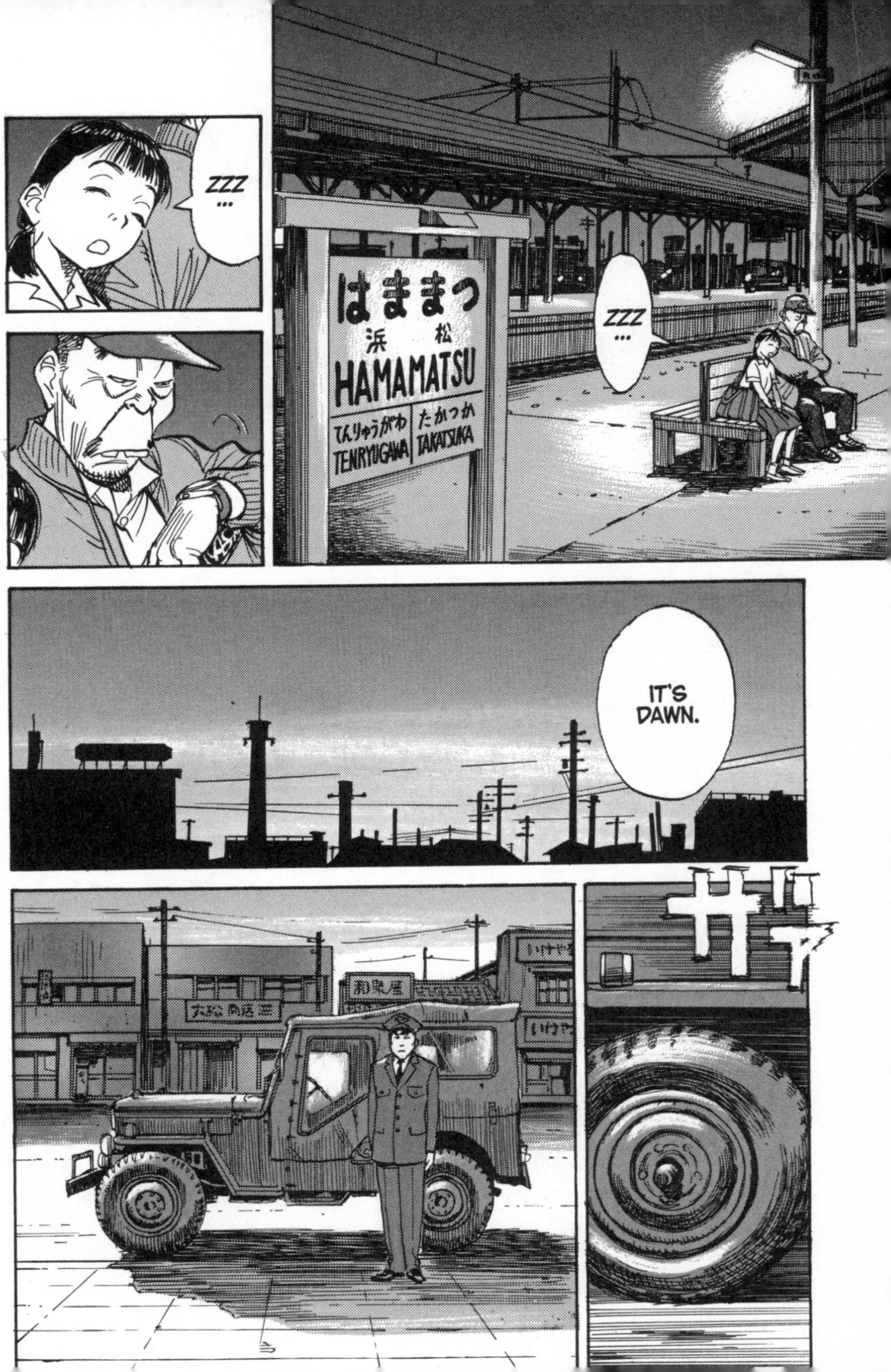
はままつ
浜松
HAMAMATSU
てんりゅうがわ TENRYUGAWA
たかつか TAKATSUKA
ZZZ ...
ZZZ ...
IT'S DAWN.

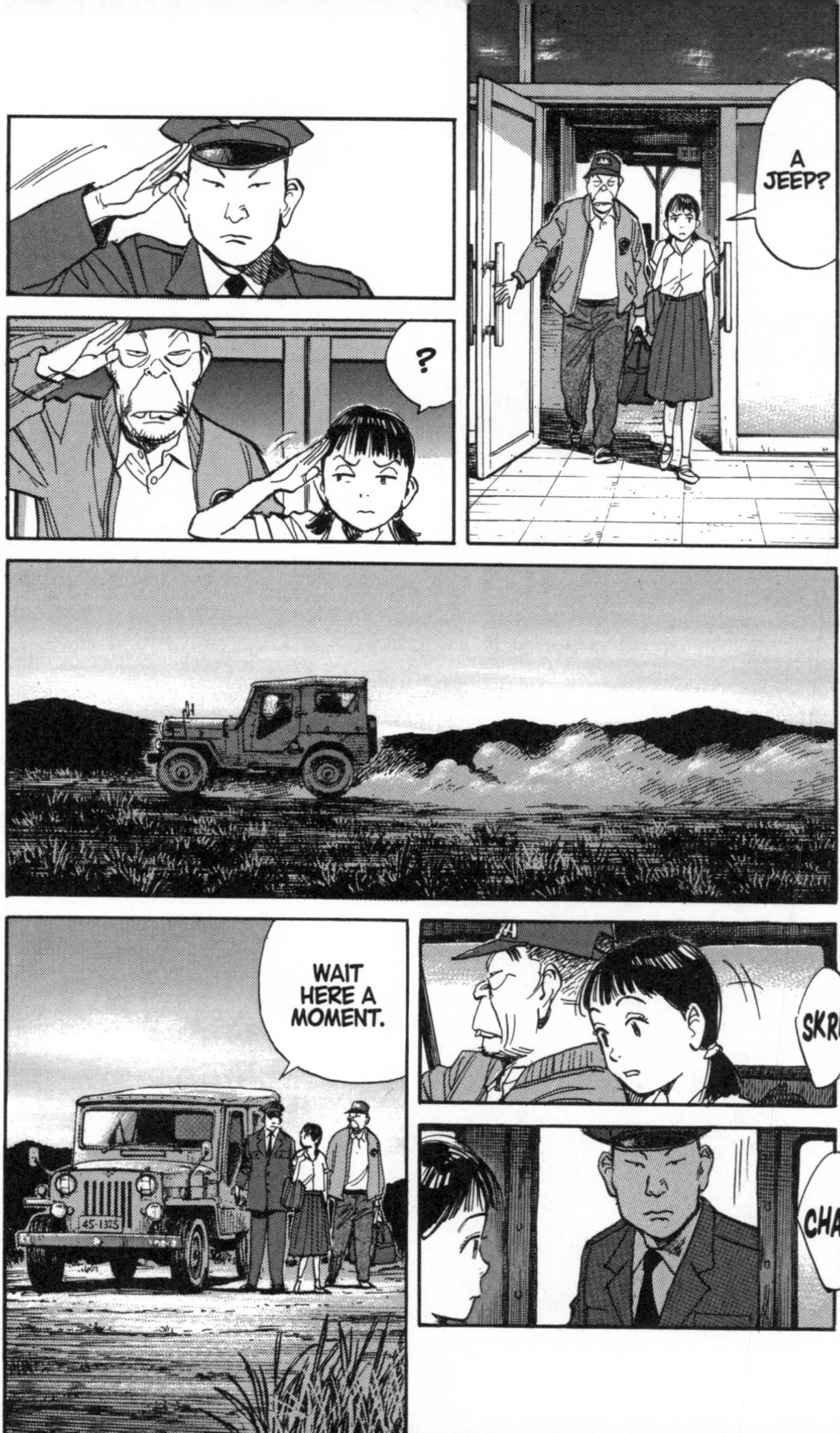
A JEEP?
?
WAIT HERE A MOMENT.
SKRIK
CHAK

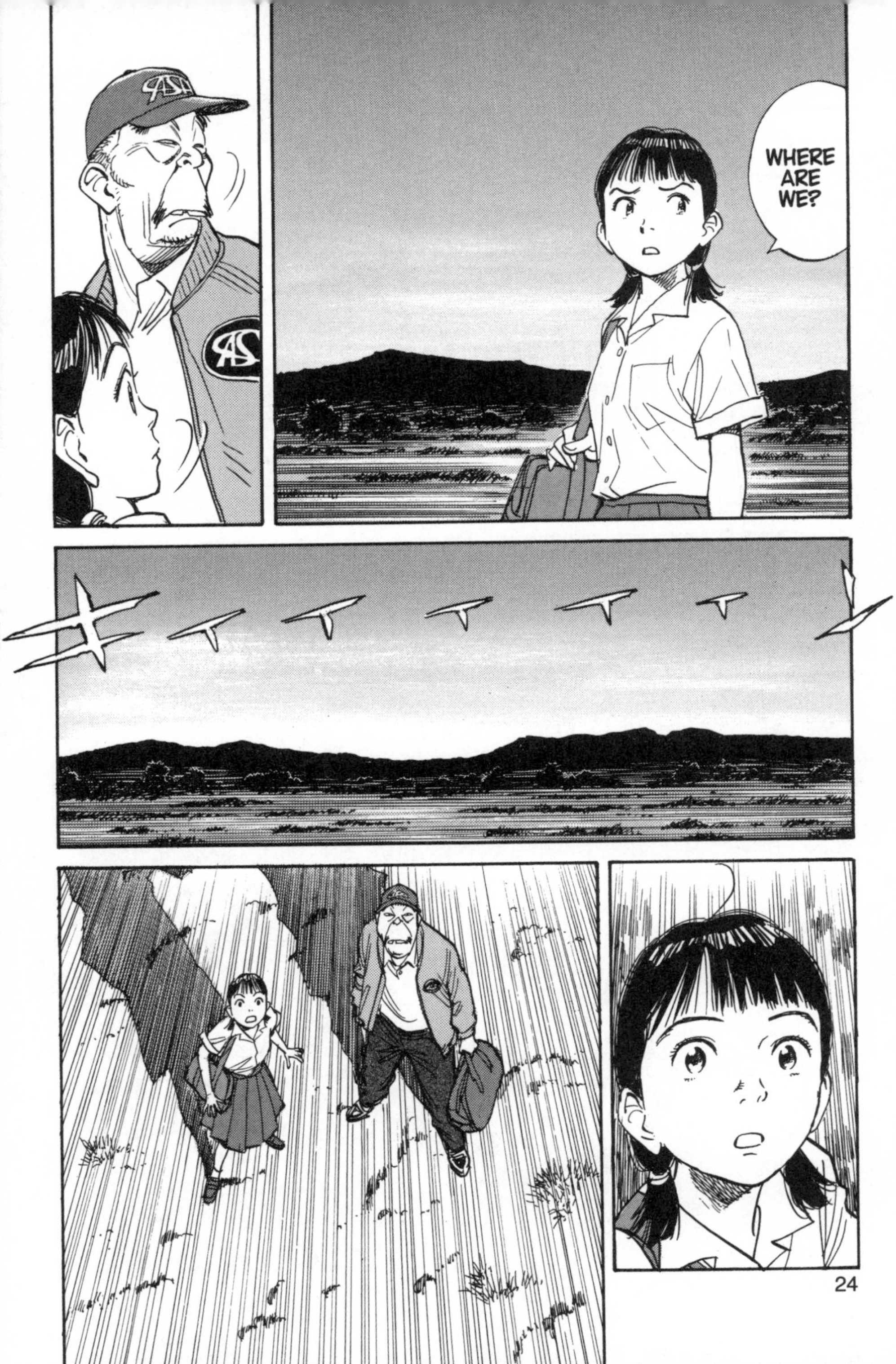
WHERE ARE WE?

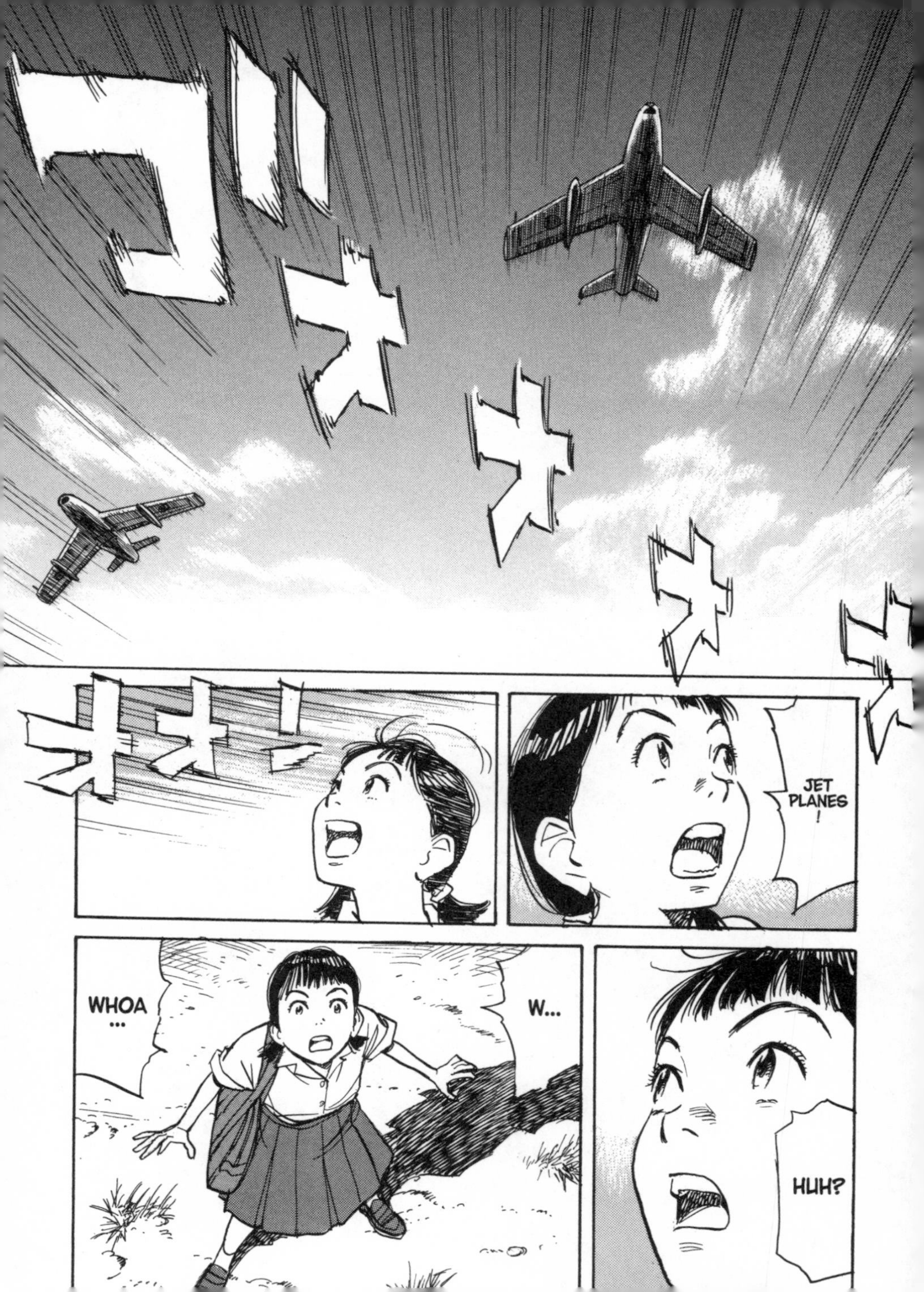
JET PLANES!
HUH?
W...
WHOA ...

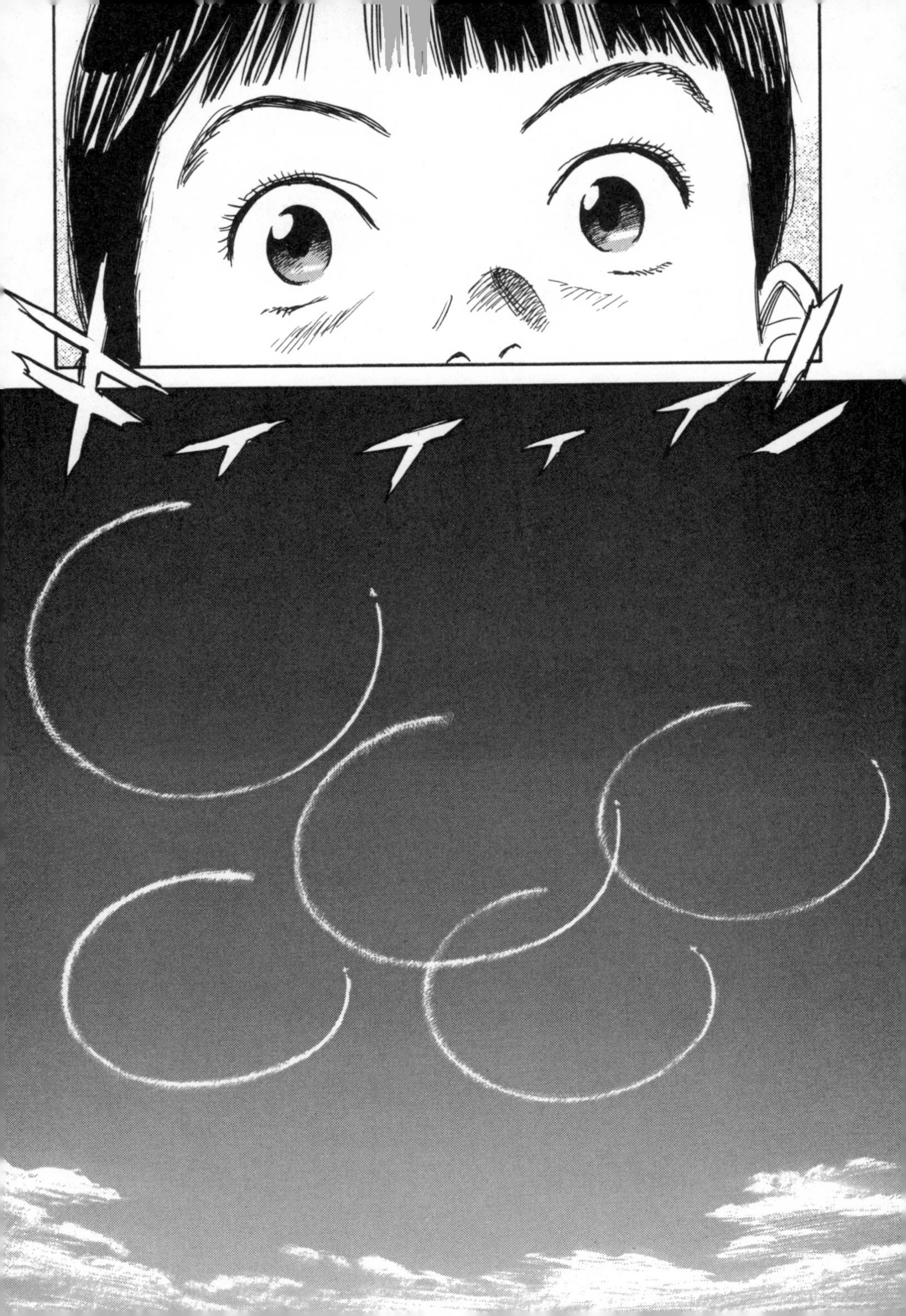
キィィィィン

Chapter 18 ● Five Rings

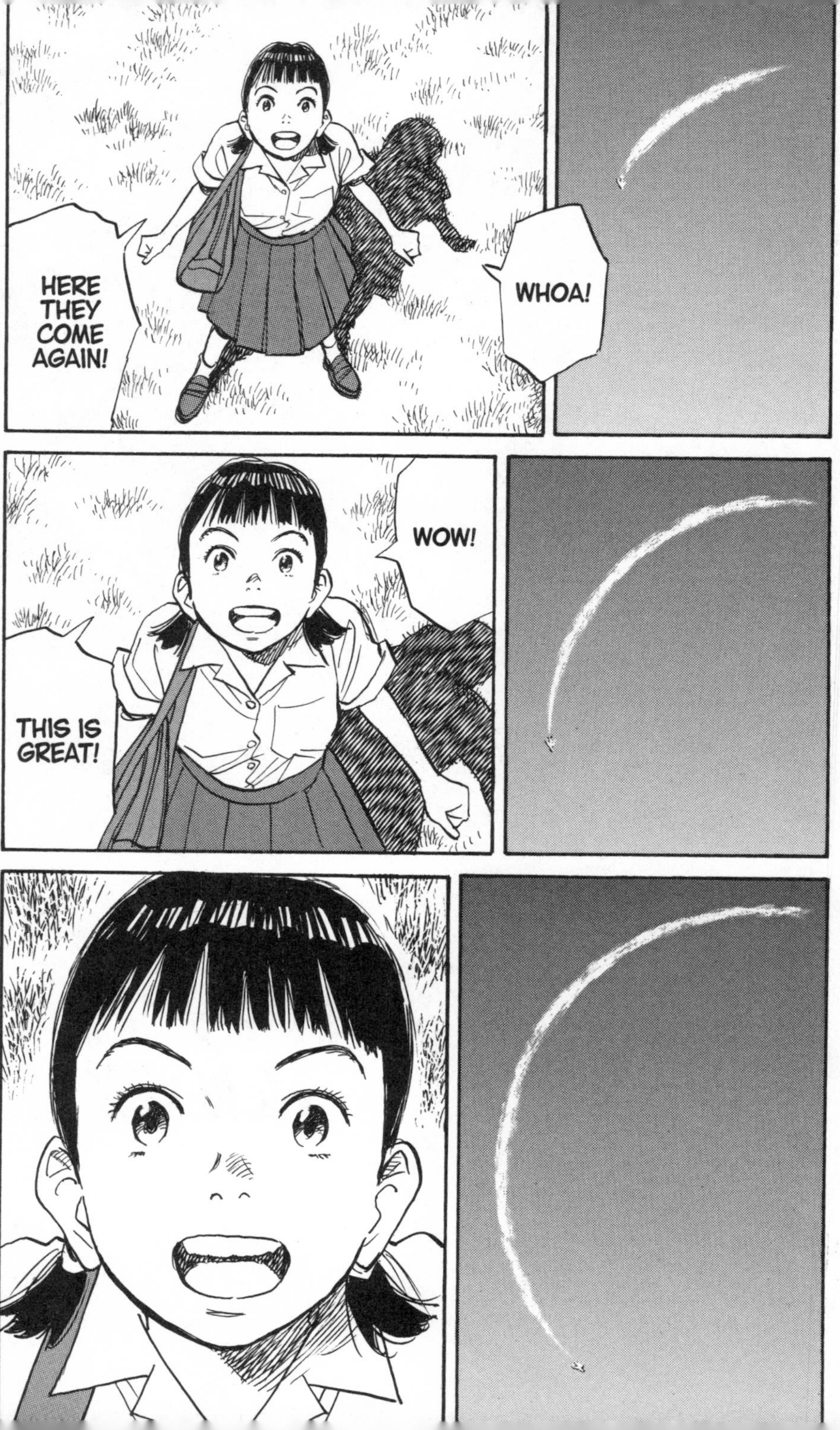
WHOA!
HERE THEY COME AGAIN!
WOW!
THIS IS GREAT!

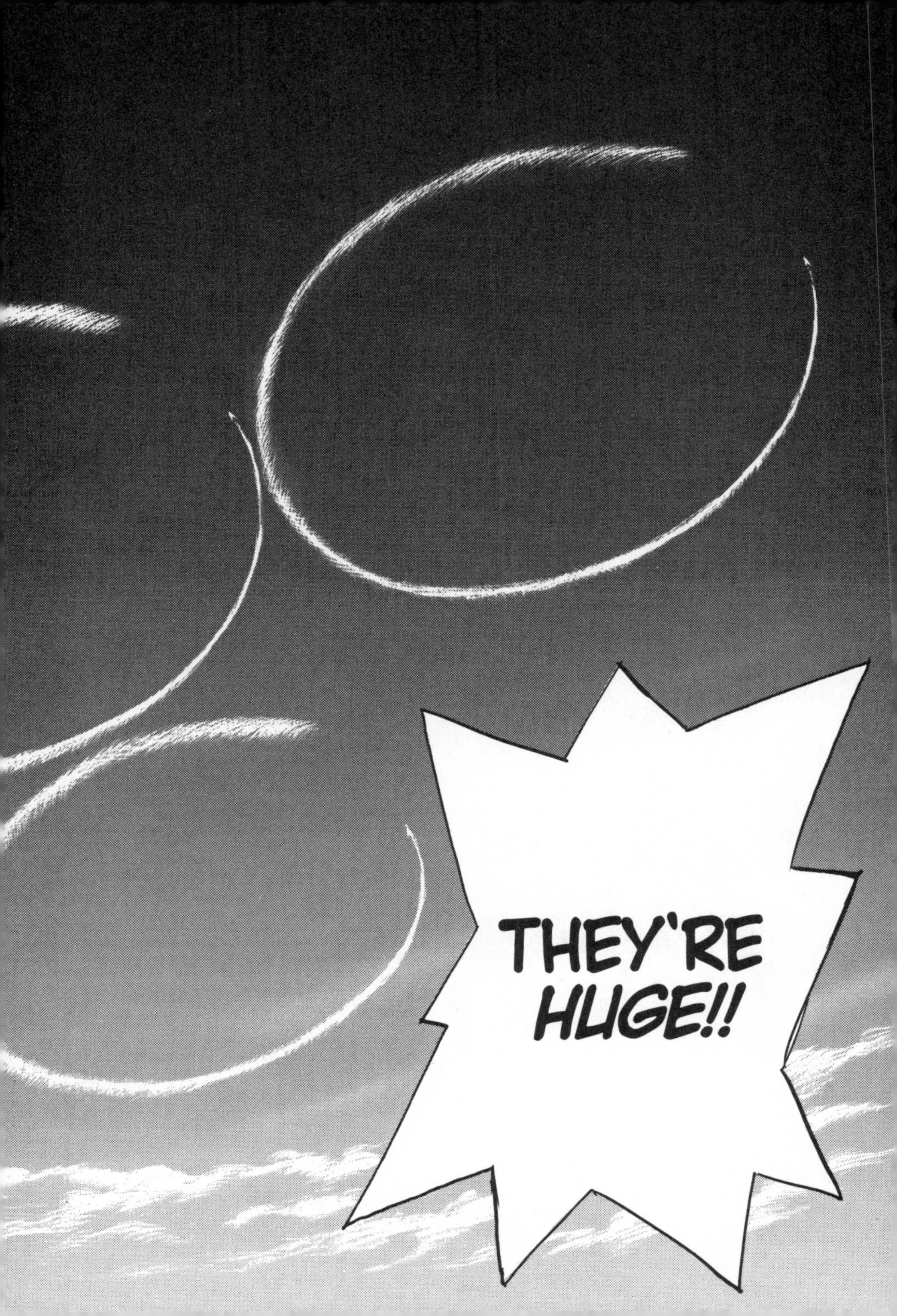
THEY'RE HUGE!!

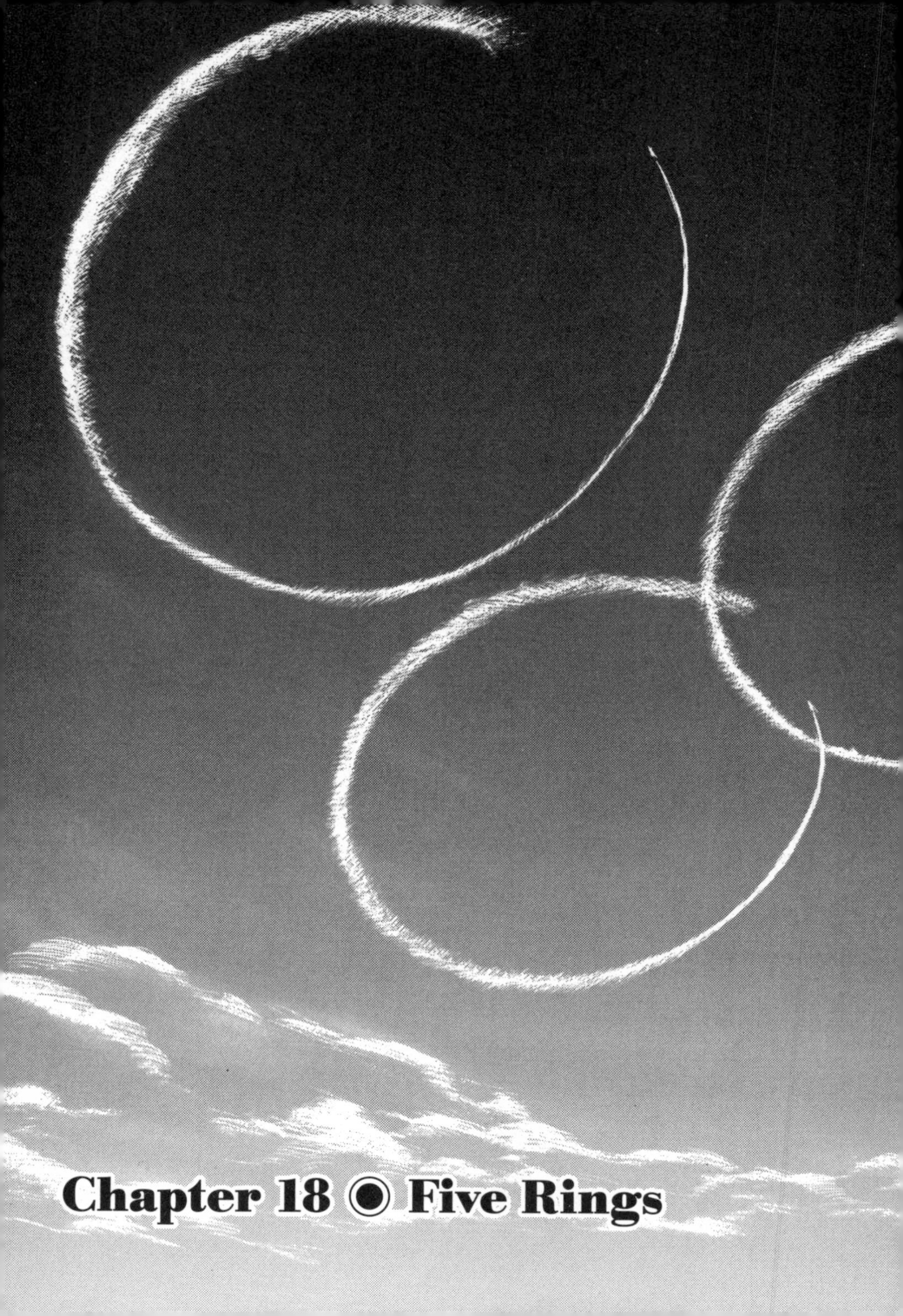

Chapter 18 ◉ Five Rings

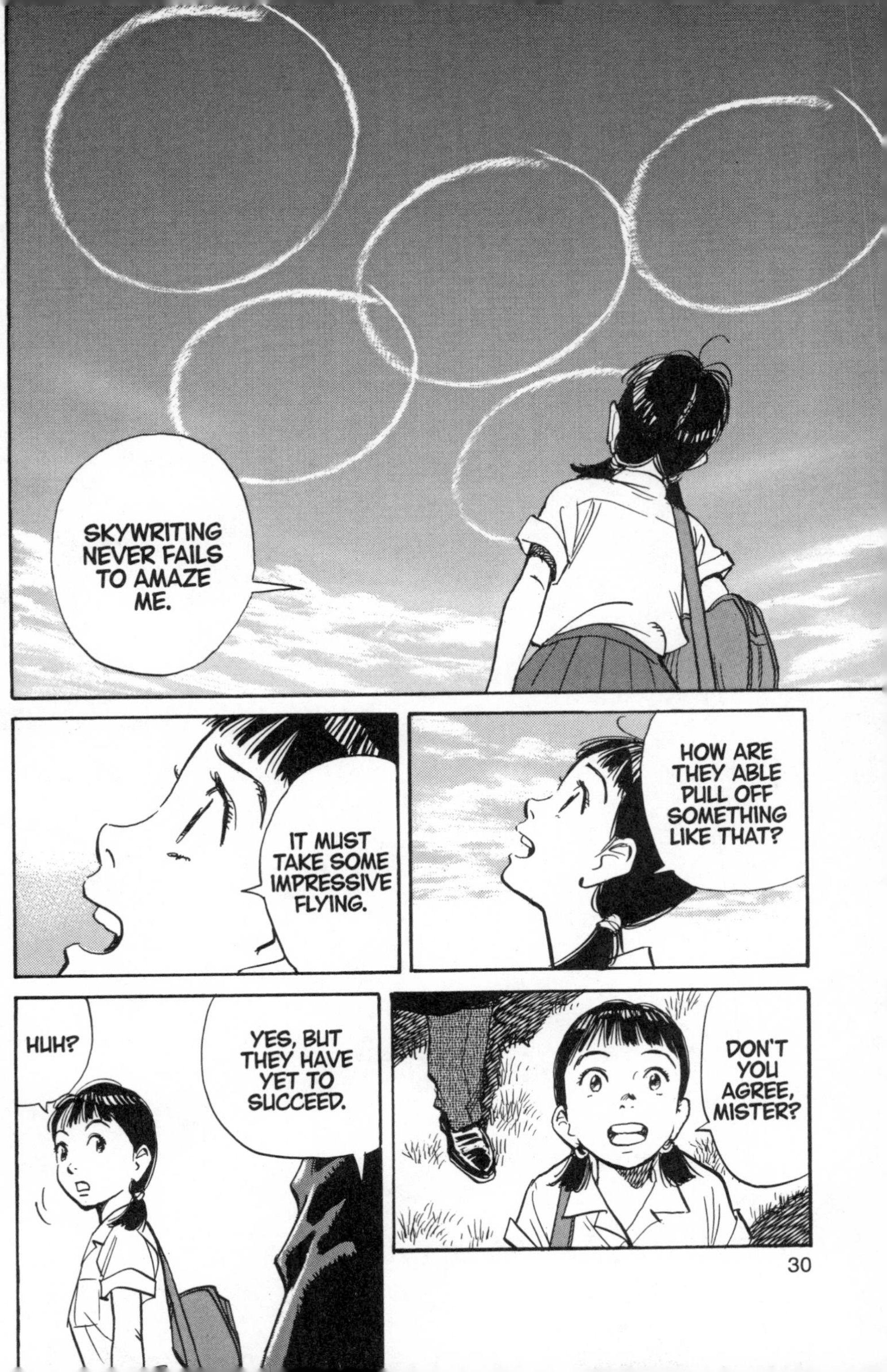
SKYWRITING NEVER FAILS TO AMAZE ME.
HOW ARE THEY ABLE PULL OFF SOMETHING LIKE THAT?
IT MUST TAKE SOME IMPRESSIVE FLYING.
DON'T YOU AGREE, MISTER?
YES, BUT THEY HAVE YET TO SUCCEED.
HUH?

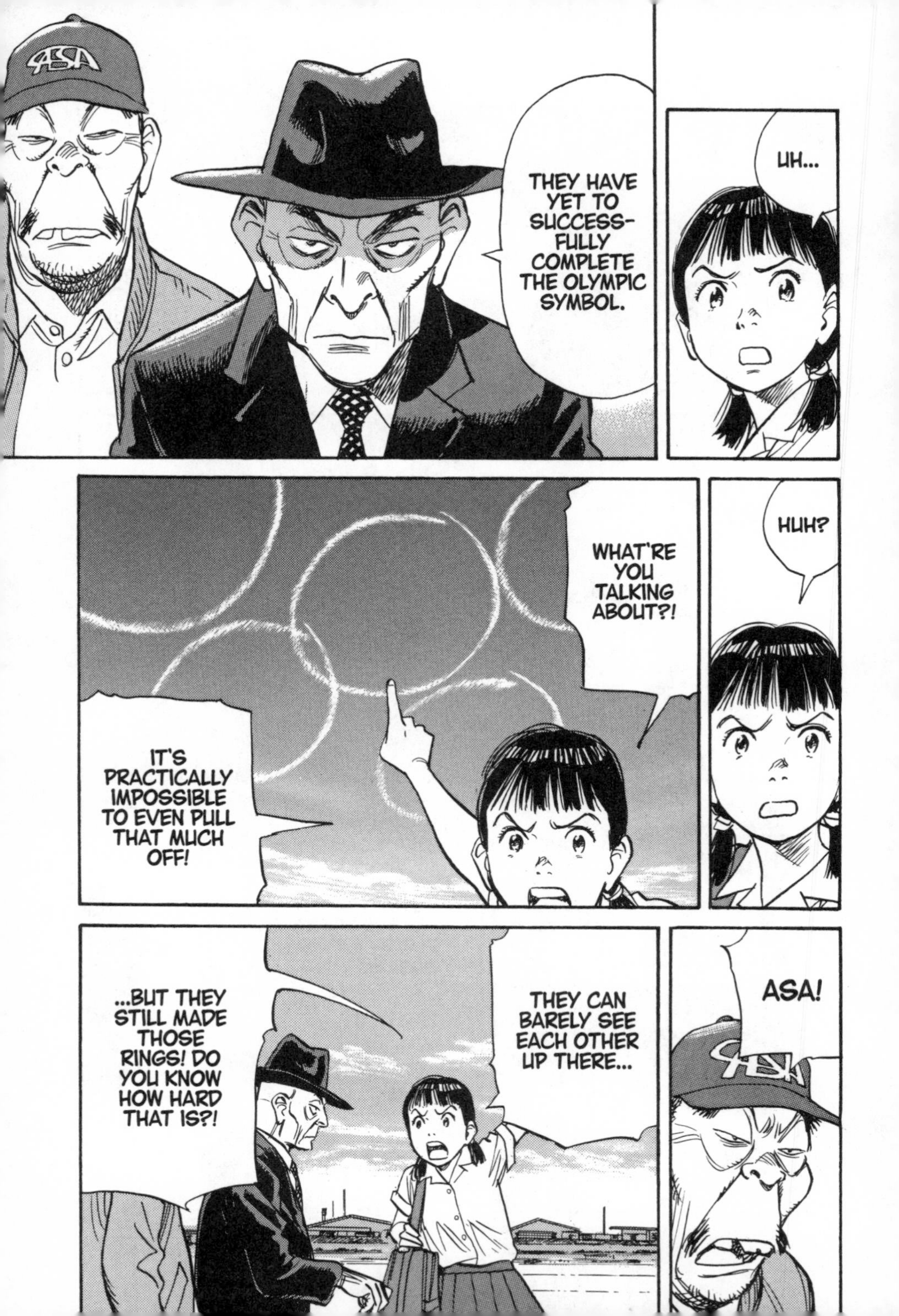
UH...
THEY HAVE YET TO SUCCESSFULLY COMPLETE THE OLYMPIC SYMBOL.
HUH?
WHAT'RE YOU TALKING ABOUT?!
IT'S PRACTICALLY IMPOSSIBLE TO EVEN PULL THAT MUCH OFF!
ASA!
THEY CAN BARELY SEE EACH OTHER UP THERE...
...BUT THEY STILL MADE THOSE RINGS! DO YOU KNOW HOW HARD THAT IS?!

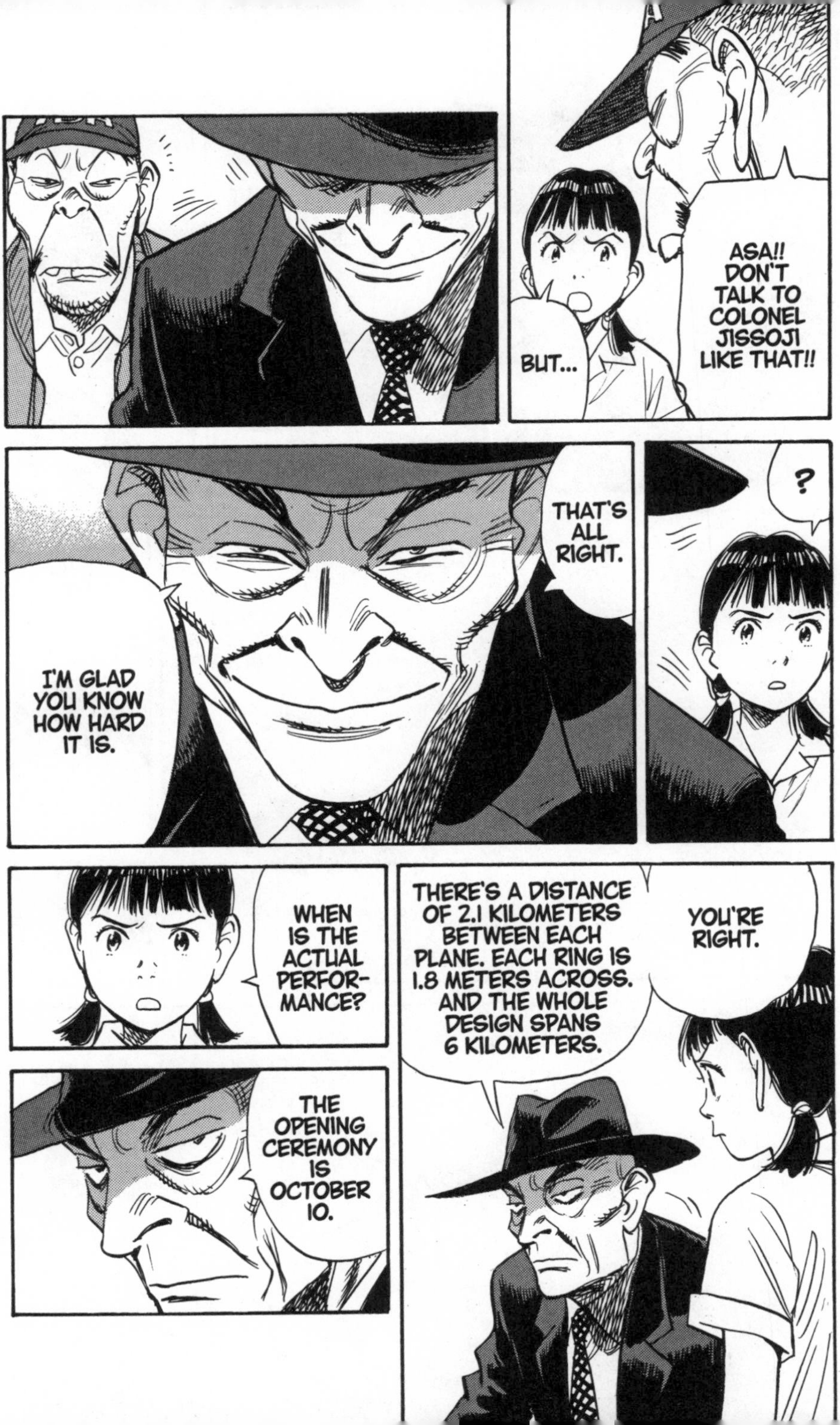
ASA!! DON'T TALK TO COLONEL JISSOJI LIKE THAT!!
BUT...
?
THAT'S ALL RIGHT.
I'M GLAD YOU KNOW HOW HARD IT IS.
YOU'RE RIGHT.
THERE'S A DISTANCE OF 2.1 KILOMETERS BETWEEN EACH PLANE. EACH RING IS 1.8 METERS ACROSS. AND THE WHOLE DESIGN SPANS 6 KILOMETERS.
WHEN IS THE ACTUAL PERFORMANCE?
THE OPENING CEREMONY IS OCTOBER 10.

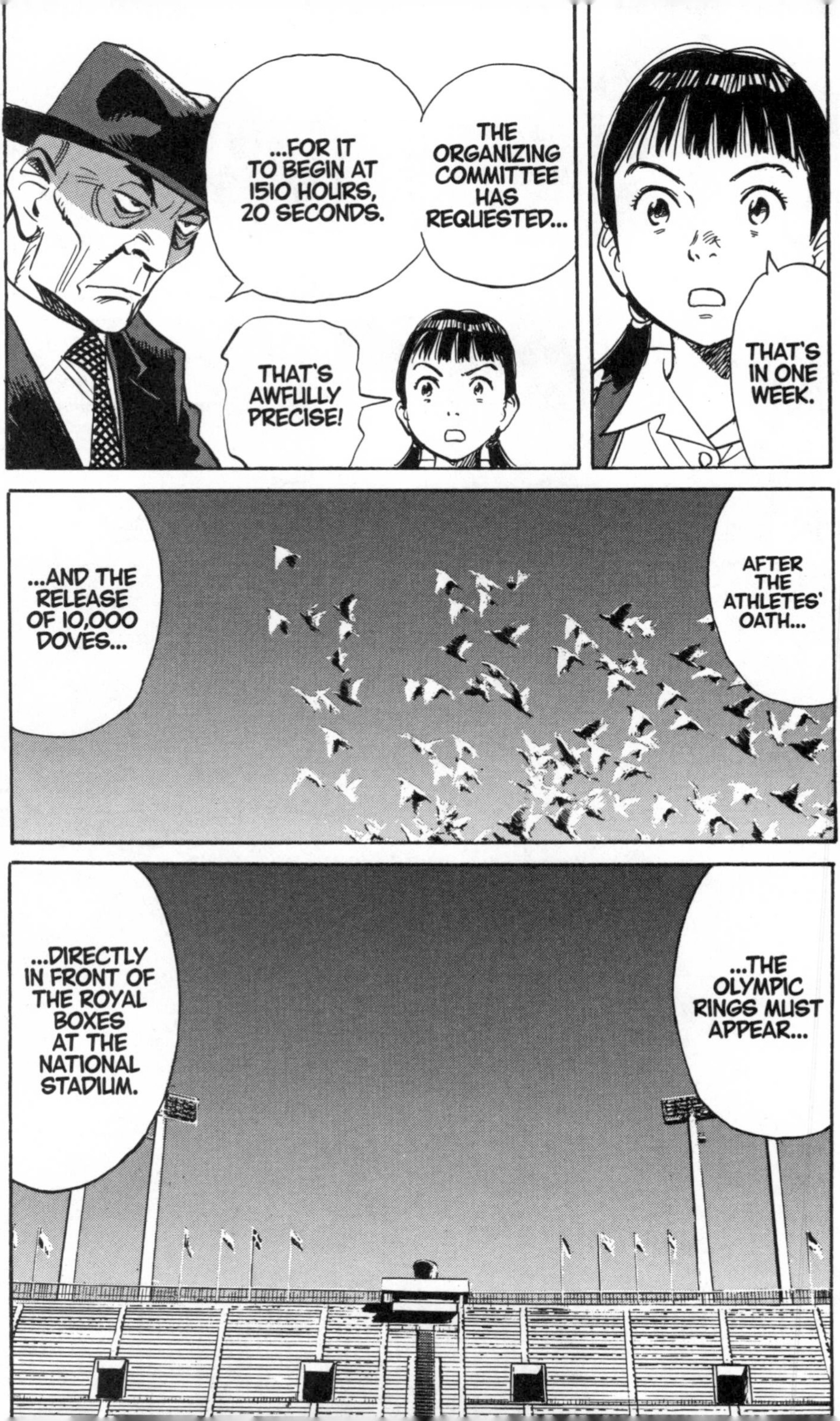
THAT'S IN ONE WEEK.
THE ORGANIZING COMMITTEE HAS REQUESTED...
...FOR IT TO BEGIN AT 1510 HOURS, 20 SECONDS.
THAT'S AWFULLY PRECISE!
AFTER THE ATHLETES' OATH...
...AND THE RELEASE OF 10,000 DOVES...
...THE OLYMPIC RINGS MUST APPEAR...
...DIRECTLY IN FRONT OF THE ROYAL BOXES AT THE NATIONAL STADIUM.

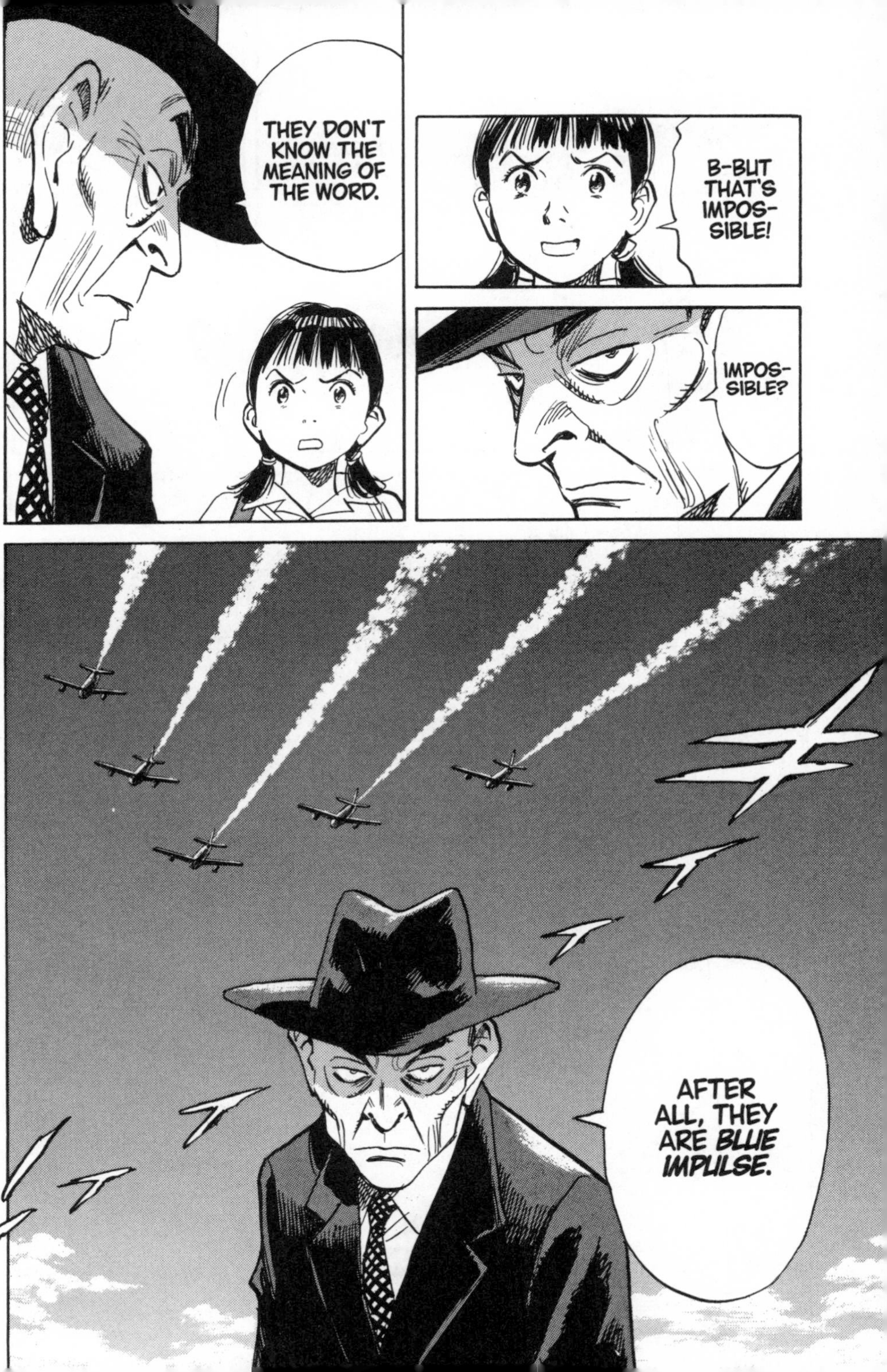
B-BUT THAT'S IMPOSSIBLE!
IMPOSSIBLE?
THEY DON'T KNOW THE MEANING OF THE WORD.
AFTER ALL, THEY ARE *BLUE IMPULSE*.

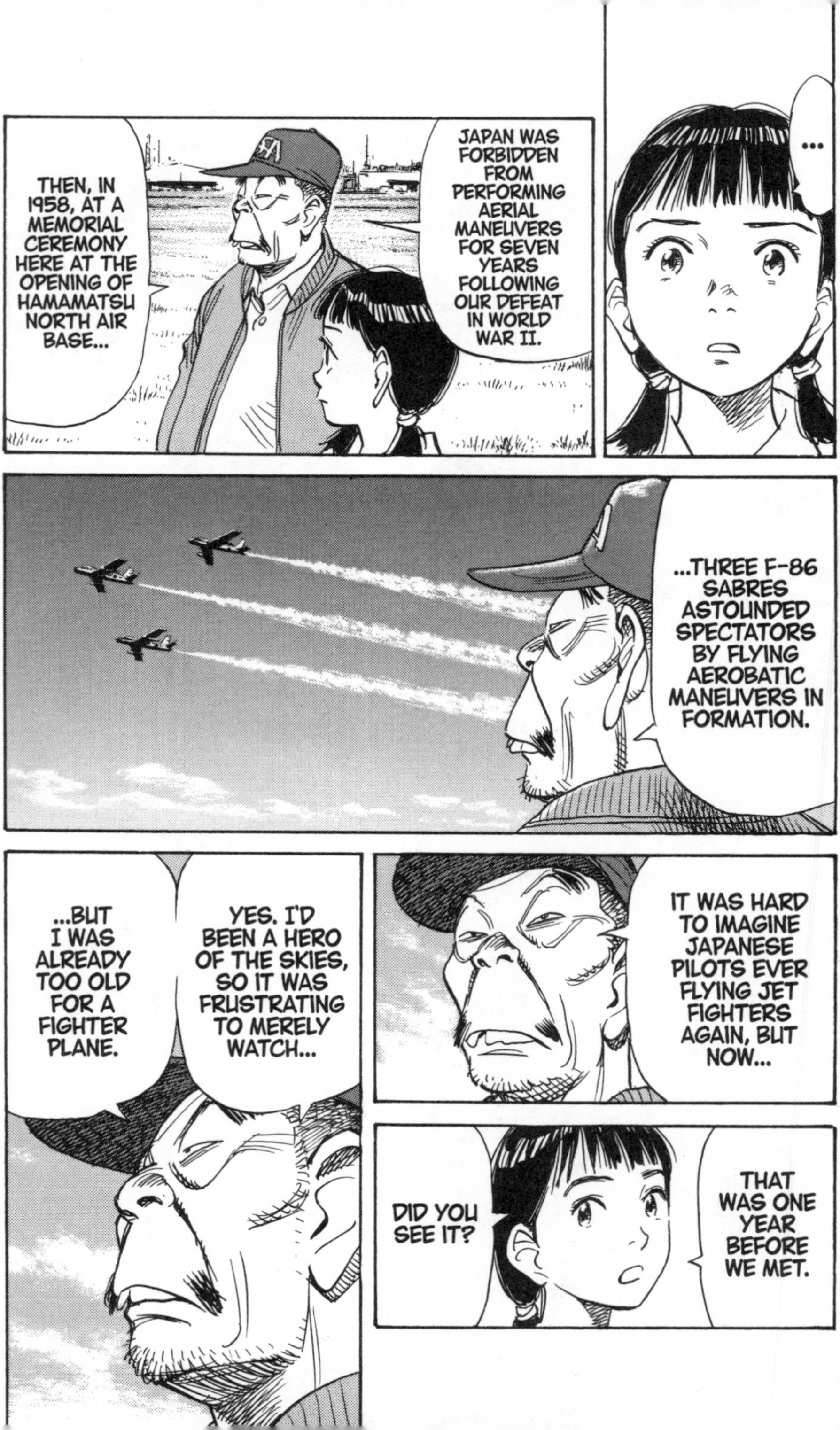
...
JAPAN WAS FORBIDDEN FROM PERFORMING AERIAL MANEUVERS FOR SEVEN YEARS FOLLOWING OUR DEFEAT IN WORLD WAR II.
THEN, IN 1958, AT A MEMORIAL CEREMONY HERE AT THE OPENING OF HAMAMATSU NORTH AIR BASE...
...THREE F-86 SABRES ASTOUNDED SPECTATORS BY FLYING AEROBATIC MANEUVERS IN FORMATION.
IT WAS HARD TO IMAGINE JAPANESE PILOTS EVER FLYING JET FIGHTERS AGAIN, BUT NOW...
THAT WAS ONE YEAR BEFORE WE MET.
DID YOU SEE IT?
YES. I'D BEEN A HERO OF THE SKIES, SO IT WAS FRUSTRATING TO MERELY WATCH...
...BUT I WAS ALREADY TOO OLD FOR A FIGHTER PLANE.

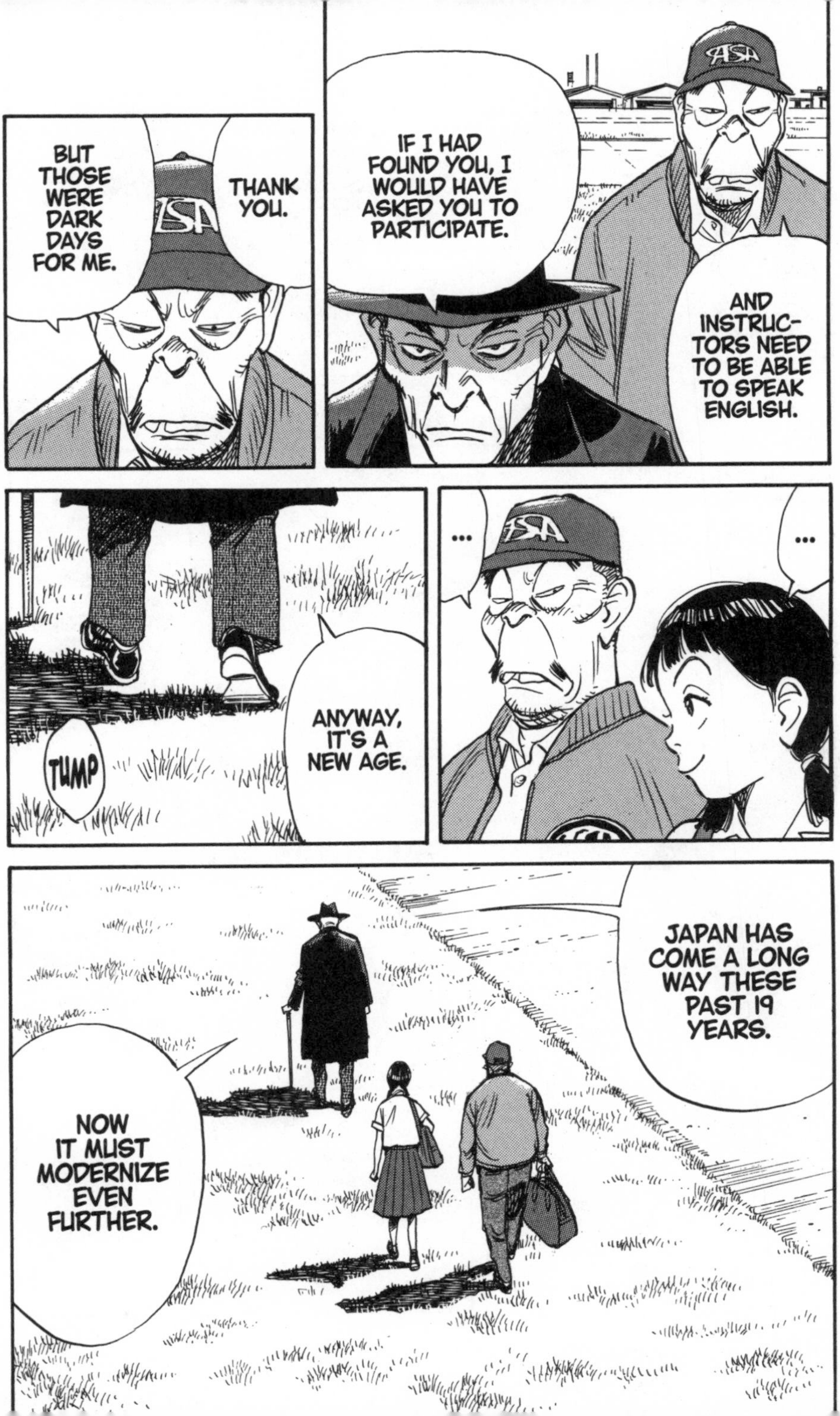
IF I HAD FOUND YOU, I WOULD HAVE ASKED YOU TO PARTICIPATE.
AND INSTRUCTORS NEED TO BE ABLE TO SPEAK ENGLISH.
THANK YOU.
BUT THOSE WERE DARK DAYS FOR ME.
...
...
ANYWAY, IT'S A NEW AGE.
TUMP
JAPAN HAS COME A LONG WAY THESE PAST 19 YEARS.
NOW IT MUST MODERNIZE EVEN FURTHER.

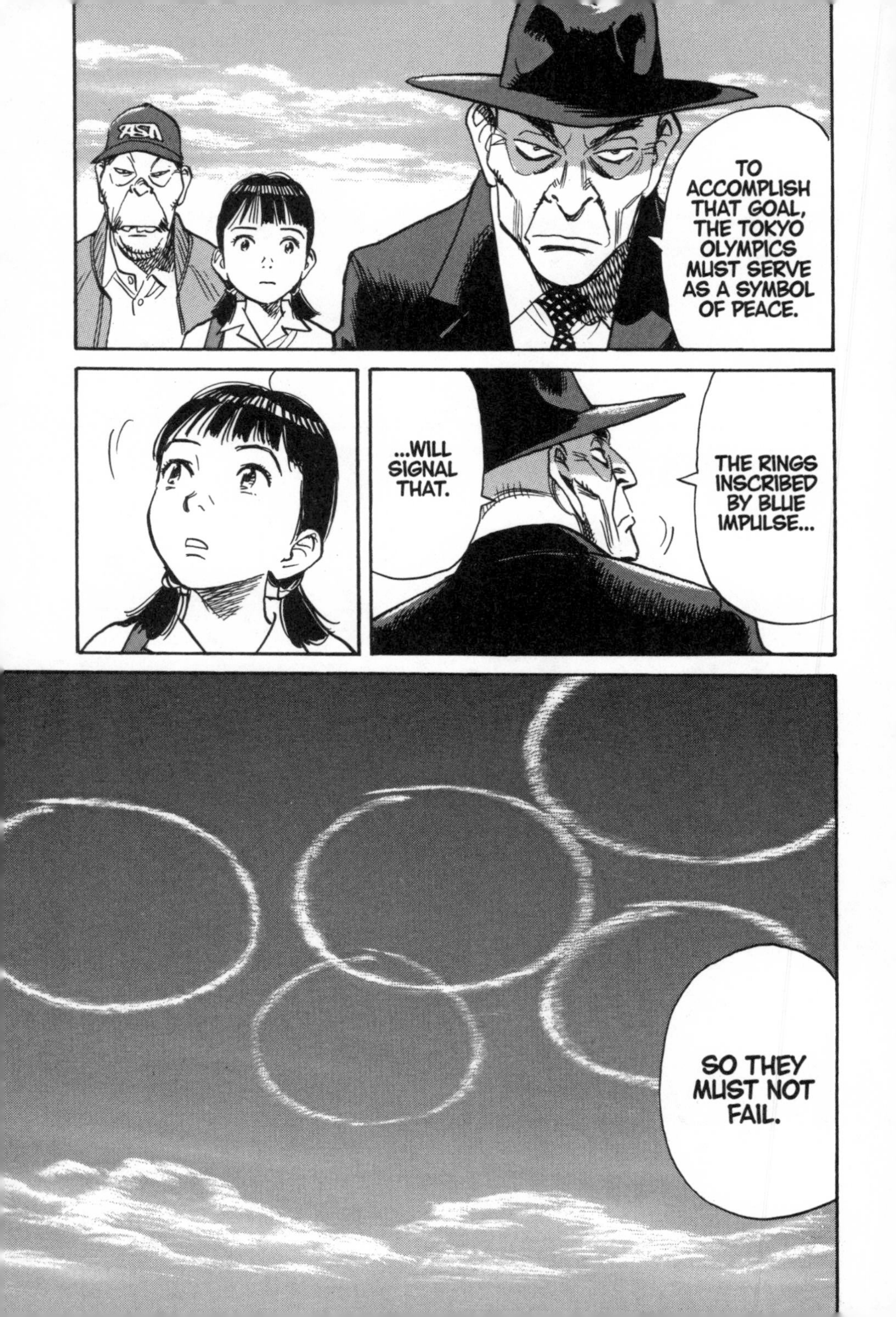
TO ACCOMPLISH THAT GOAL, THE TOKYO OLYMPICS MUST SERVE AS A SYMBOL OF PEACE.
THE RINGS INSCRIBED BY BLUE IMPULSE...
...WILL SIGNAL THAT.
SO THEY MUST NOT FAIL.

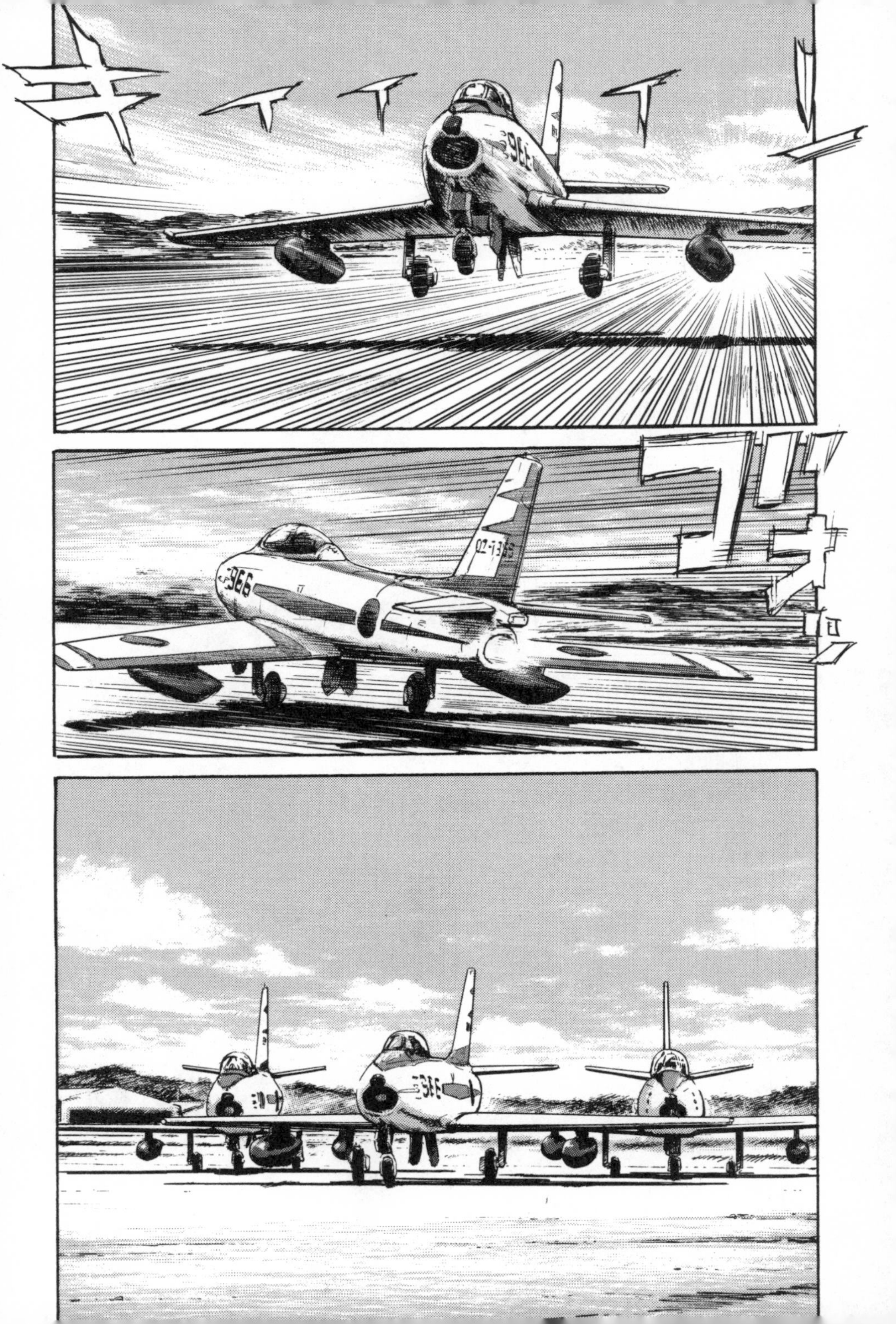
キイイイン
ゴォ

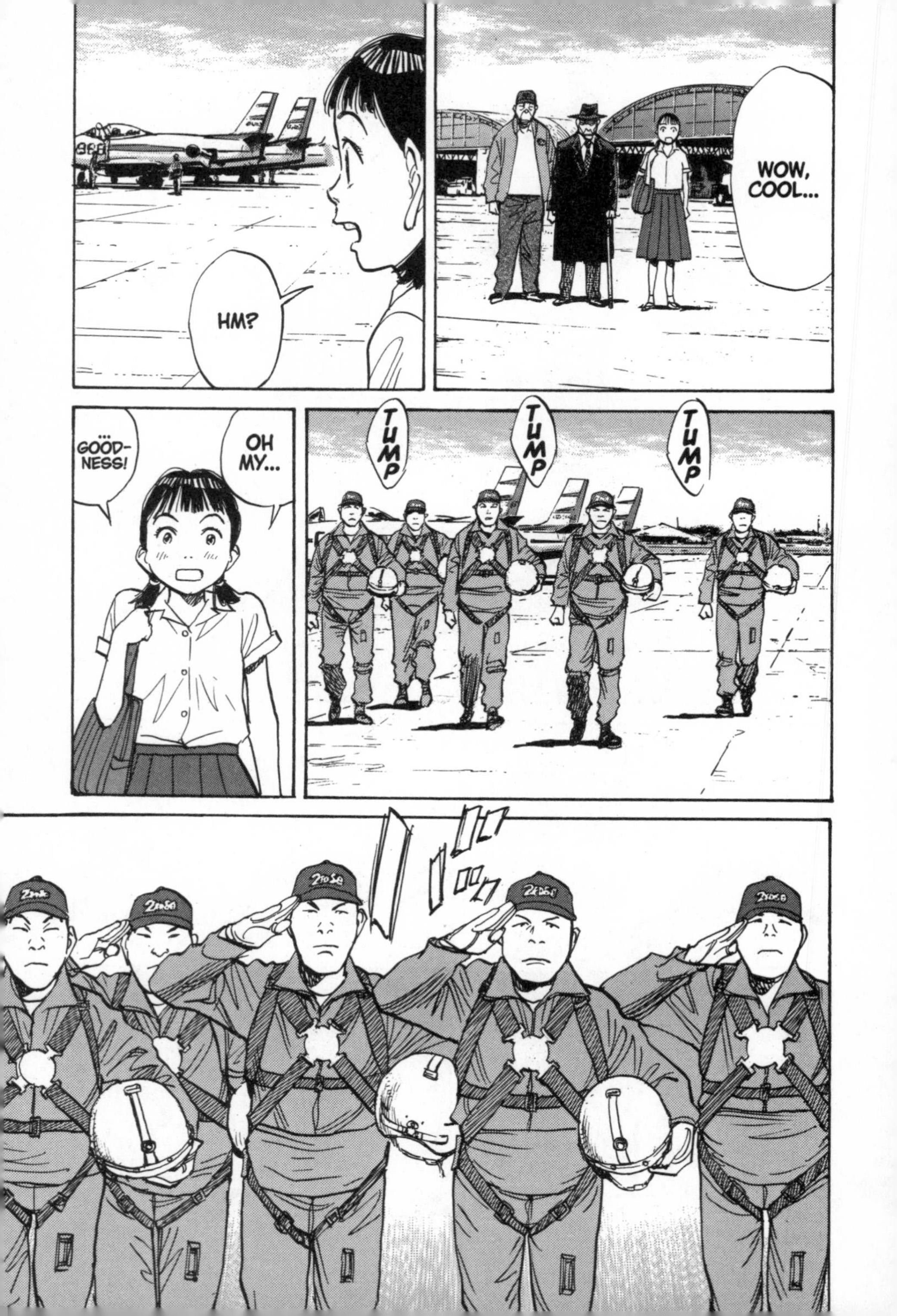
WOW, COOL...
HM?
TUMP
TUMP
TUMP
OH MY...
...GOODNESS!

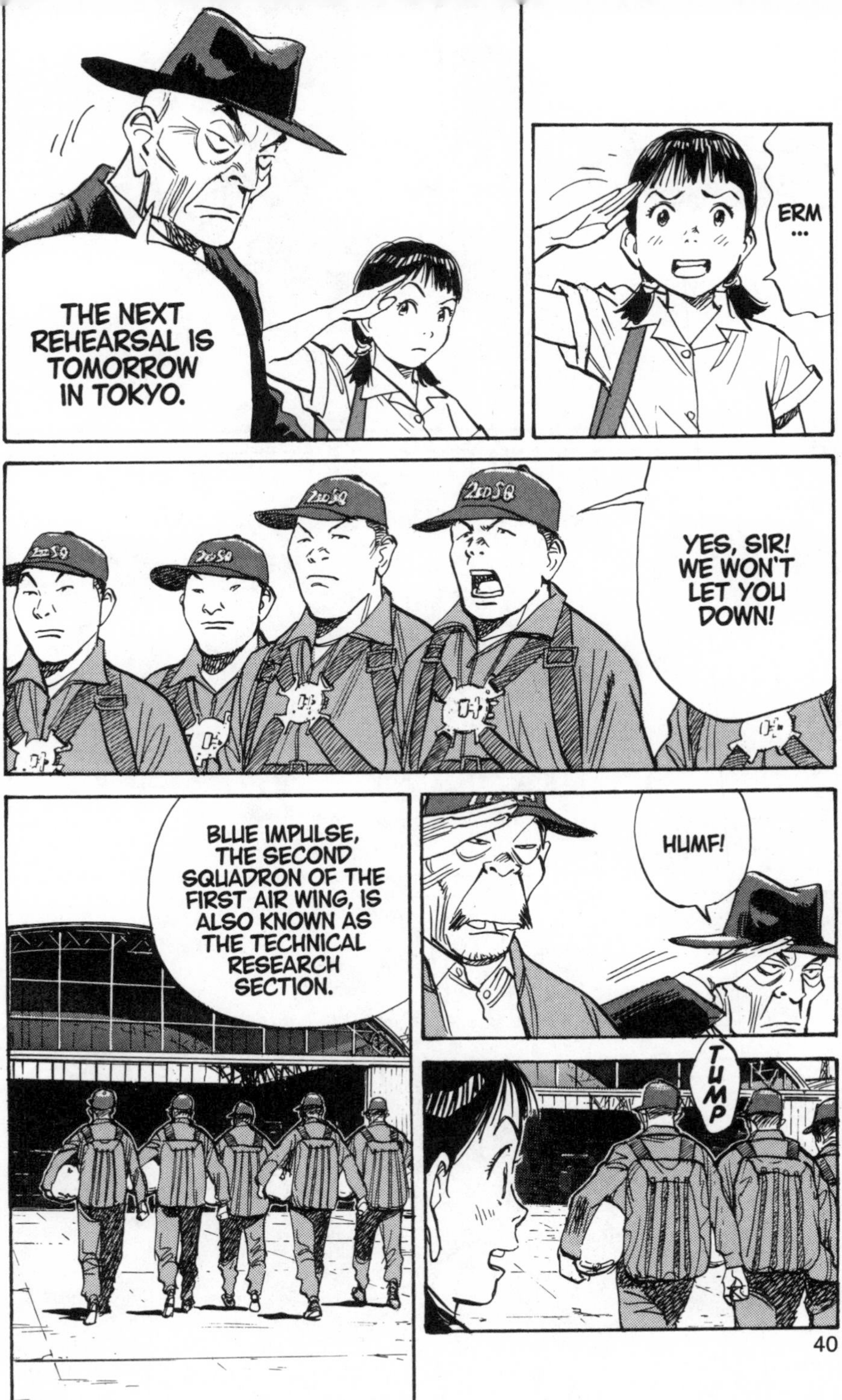

ERM ...
THE NEXT REHEARSAL IS TOMORROW IN TOKYO.
YES, SIR! WE WON'T LET YOU DOWN!
HUMF!
TUMP
BLUE IMPULSE, THE SECOND SQUADRON OF THE FIRST AIR WING, IS ALSO KNOWN AS THE TECHNICAL RESEARCH SECTION.

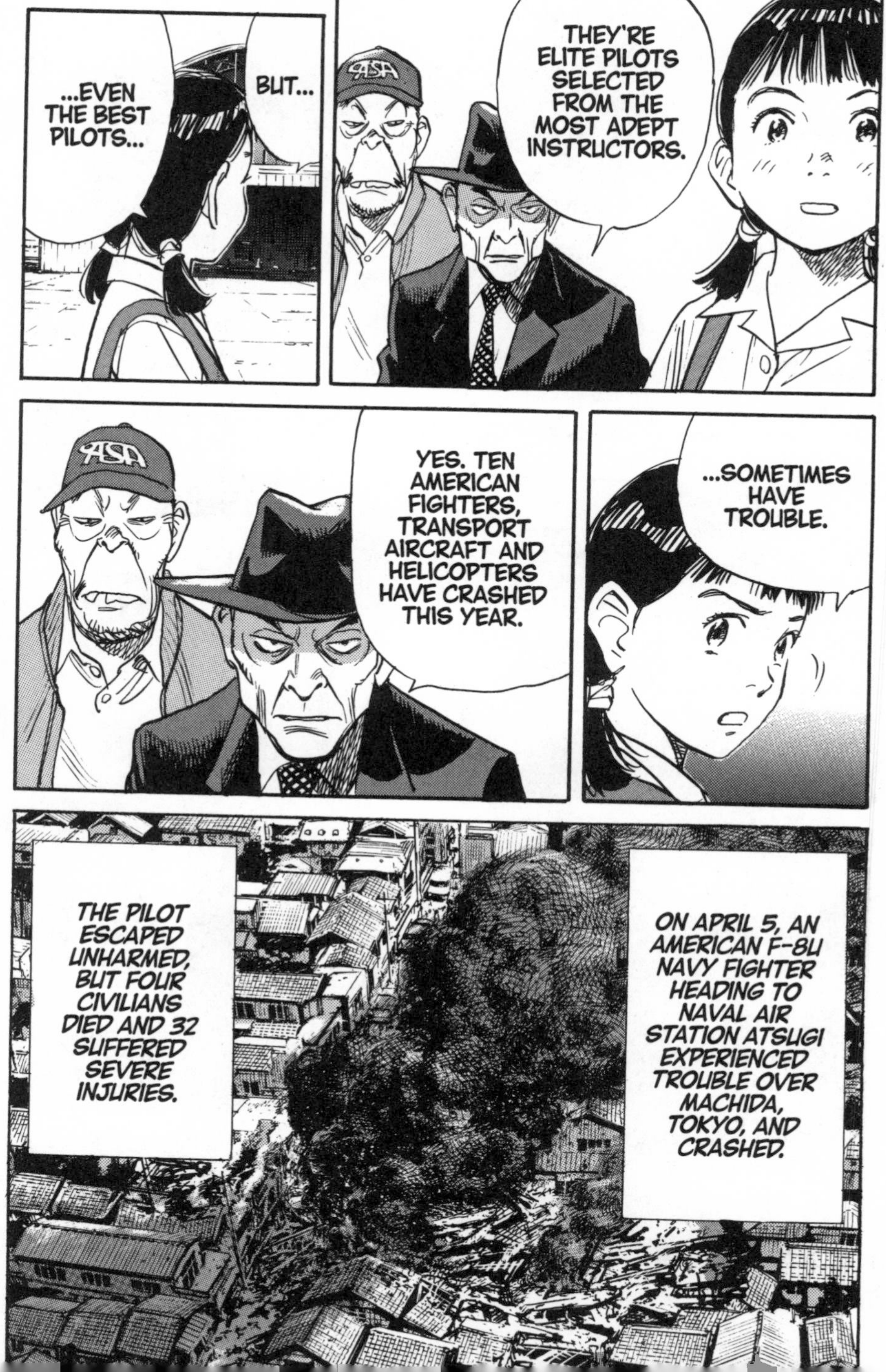
THEY'RE ELITE PILOTS SELECTED FROM THE MOST ADEPT INSTRUCTORS.
BUT...
...EVEN THE BEST PILOTS...
...SOMETIMES HAVE TROUBLE.
YES. TEN AMERICAN FIGHTERS, TRANSPORT AIRCRAFT AND HELICOPTERS HAVE CRASHED THIS YEAR.
ON APRIL 5, AN AMERICAN F-8U NAVY FIGHTER HEADING TO NAVAL AIR STATION ATSUGI EXPERIENCED TROUBLE OVER MACHIDA, TOKYO, AND CRASHED.
THE PILOT ESCAPED UNHARMED, BUT FOUR CIVILIANS DIED AND 32 SUFFERED SEVERE INJURIES.

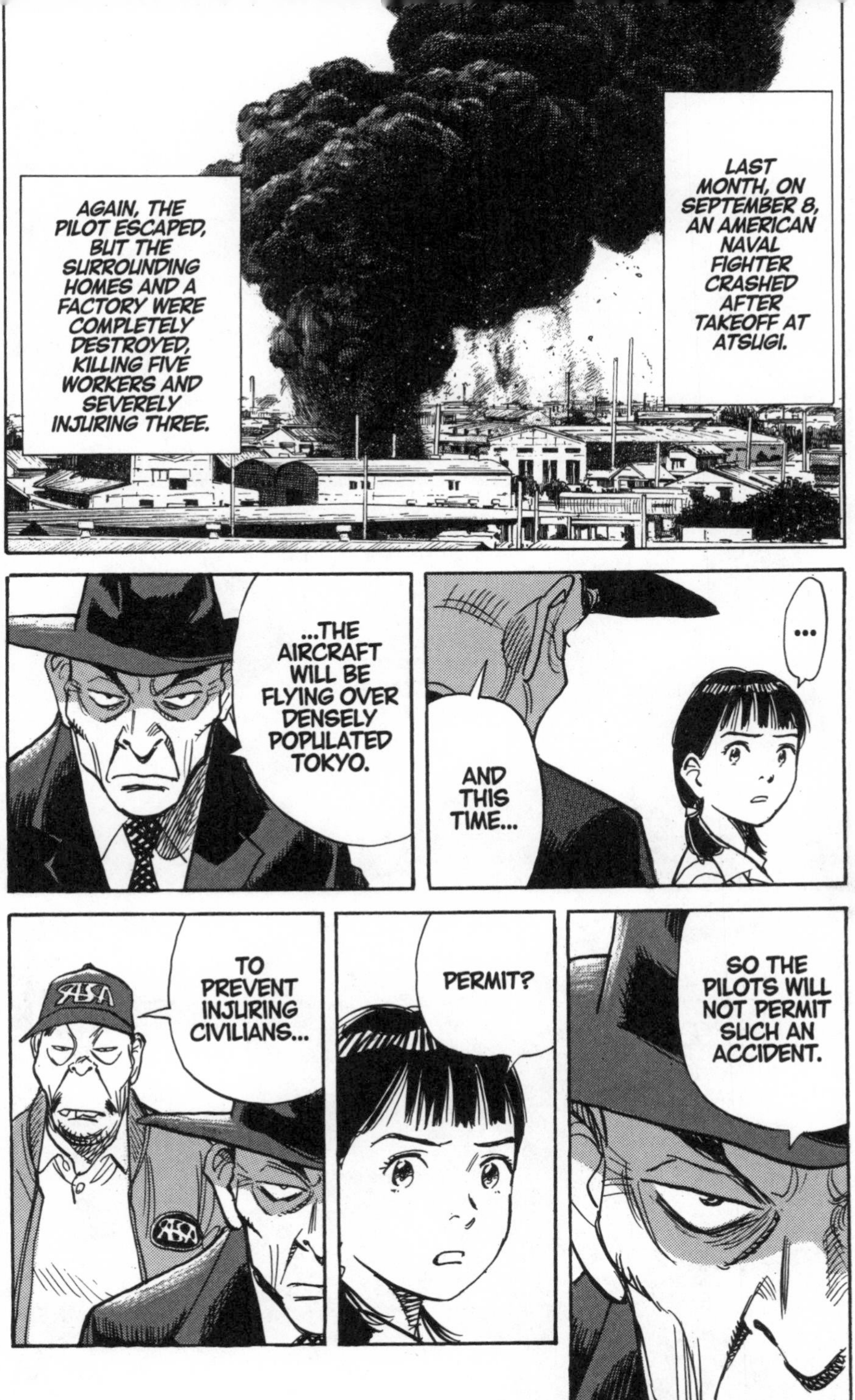
LAST MONTH, ON SEPTEMBER 8, AN AMERICAN NAVAL FIGHTER CRASHED AFTER TAKEOFF AT ATSUGI.
AGAIN, THE PILOT ESCAPED, BUT THE SURROUNDING HOMES AND A FACTORY WERE COMPLETELY DESTROYED, KILLING FIVE WORKERS AND SEVERELY INJURING THREE.
...
AND THIS TIME...
...THE AIRCRAFT WILL BE FLYING OVER DENSELY POPULATED TOKYO.
SO THE PILOTS WILL NOT PERMIT SUCH AN ACCIDENT.
PERMIT?
TO PREVENT INJURING CIVILIANS...

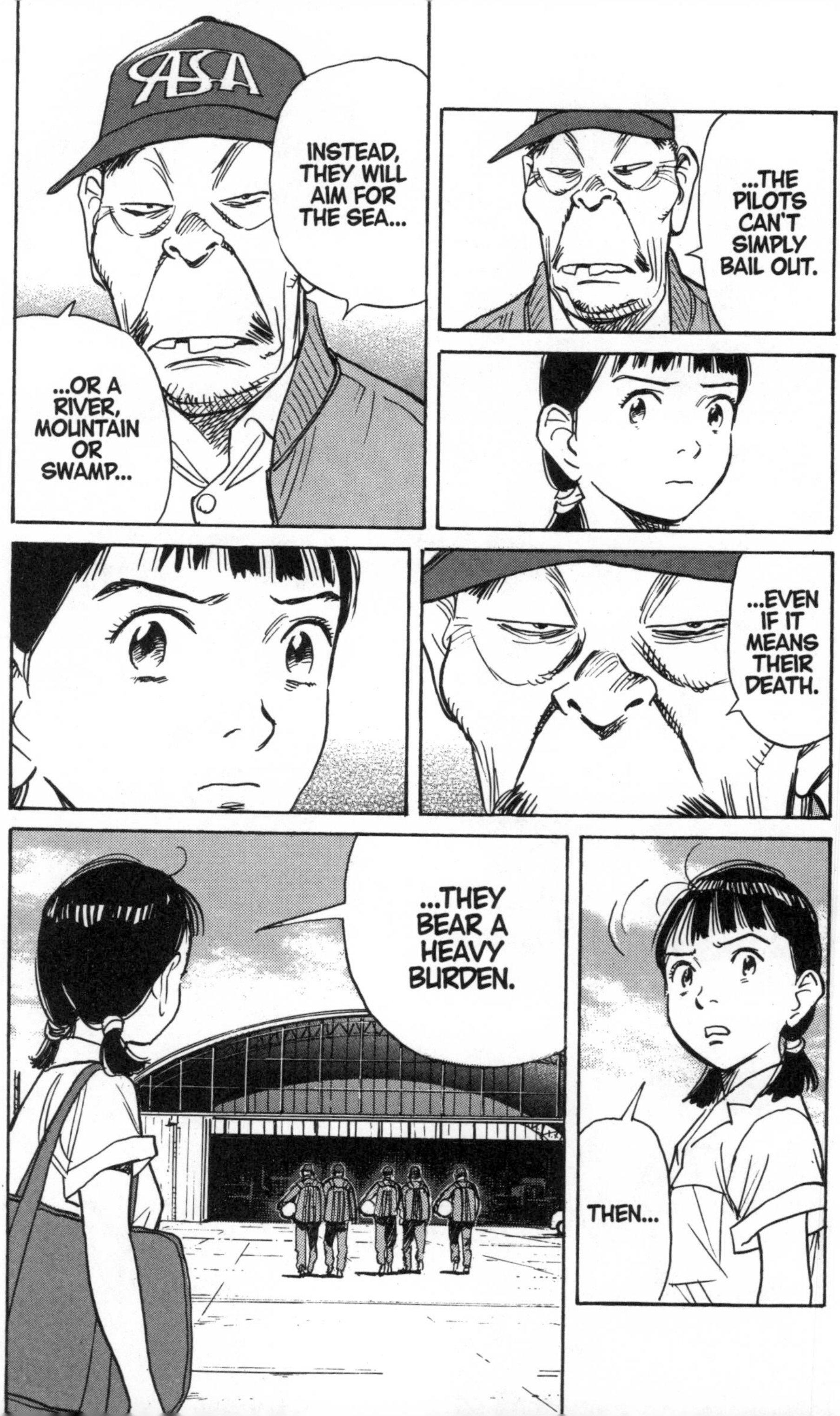
...THE PILOTS CAN'T SIMPLY BAIL OUT.
INSTEAD, THEY WILL AIM FOR THE SEA...
...OR A RIVER, MOUNTAIN OR SWAMP...
...EVEN IF IT MEANS THEIR DEATH.
THEN...
...THEY BEAR A HEAVY BURDEN.

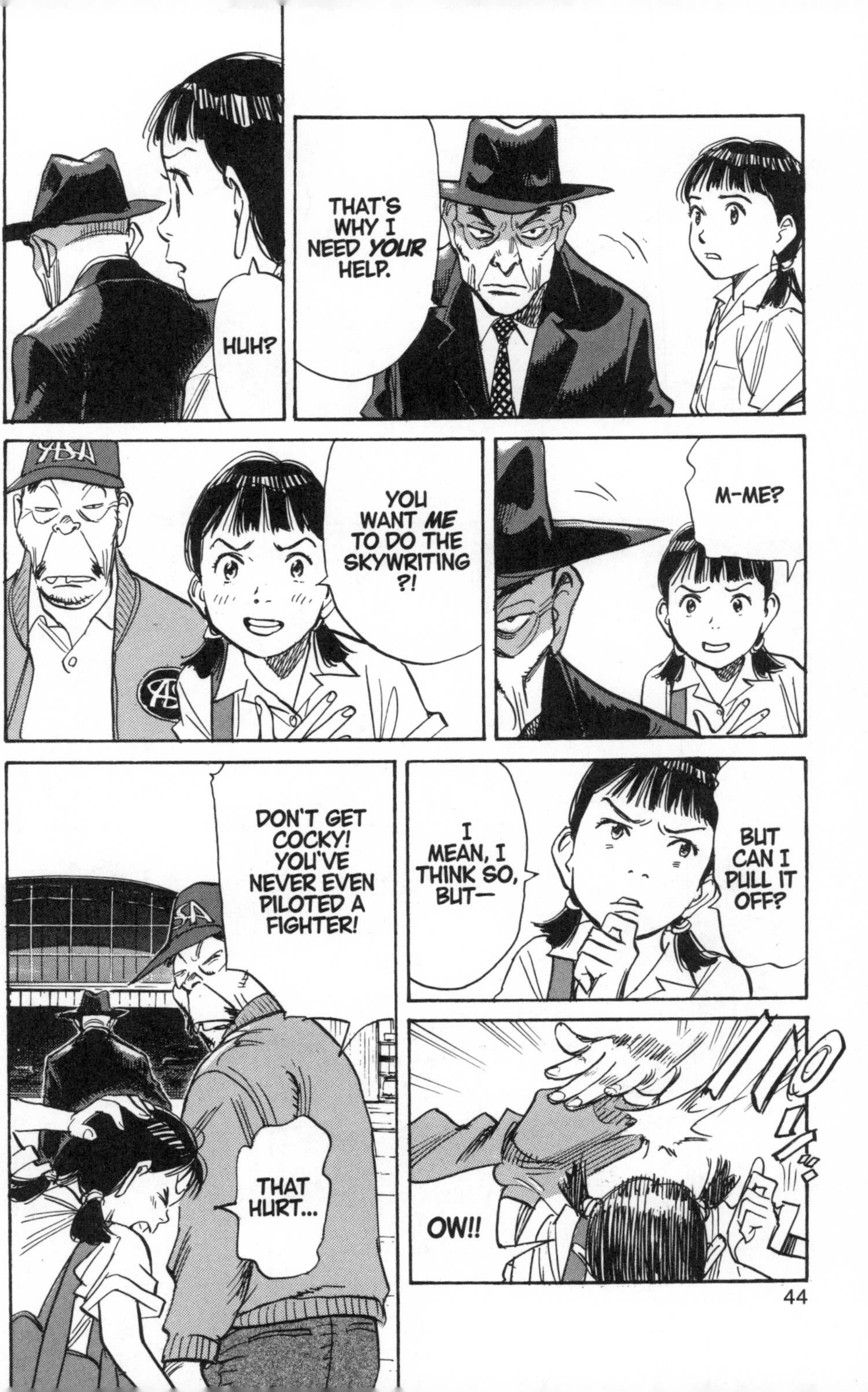
THAT'S WHY I NEED *YOUR* HELP.
HUH?
M-ME?
YOU WANT *ME* TO DO THE SKYWRITING?!
BUT CAN I PULL IT OFF?
I MEAN, I THINK SO, BUT—
OW!!
DON'T GET COCKY! YOU'VE NEVER EVEN PILOTED A FIGHTER!
THAT HURT...

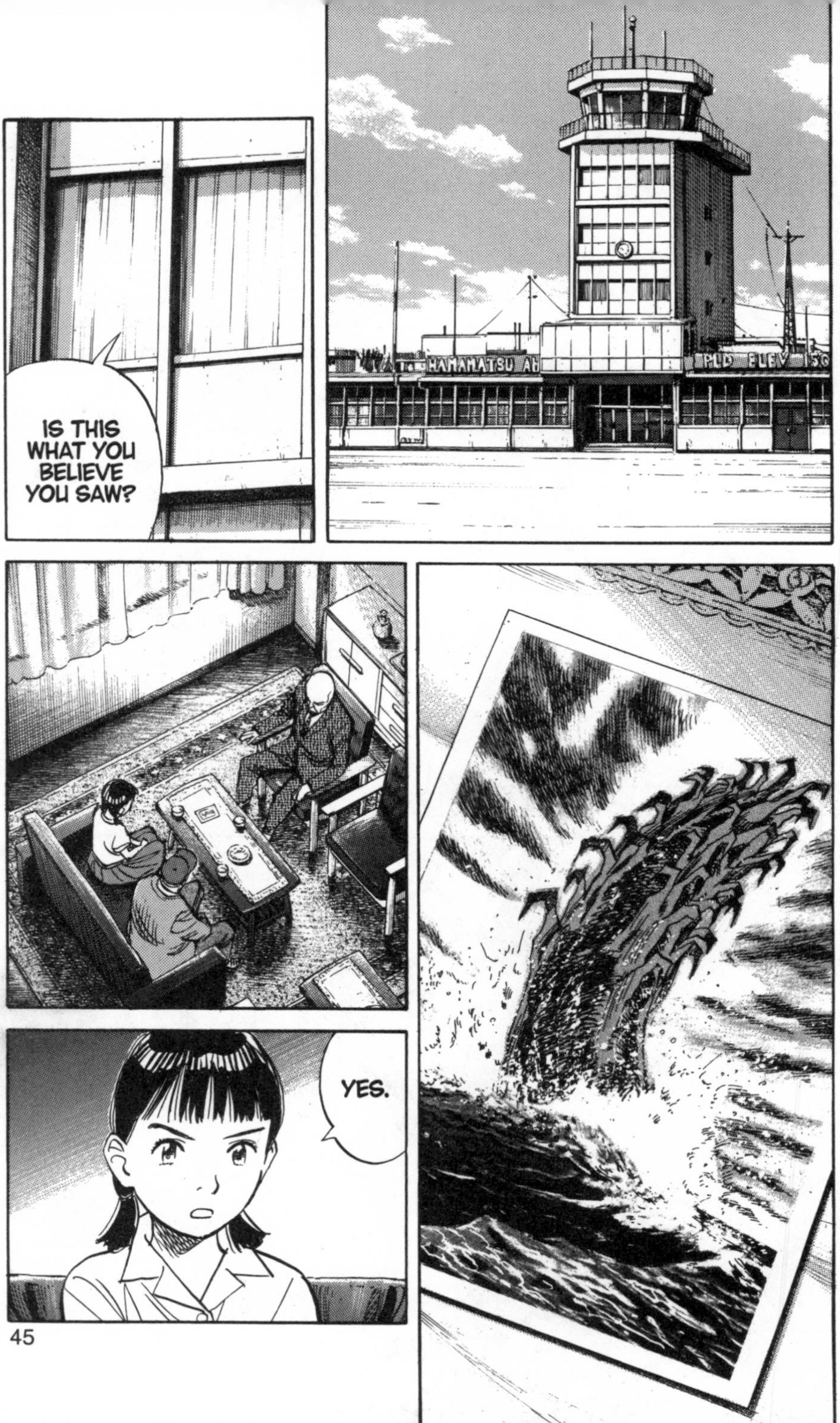
IS THIS WHAT YOU BELIEVE YOU SAW?
YES.

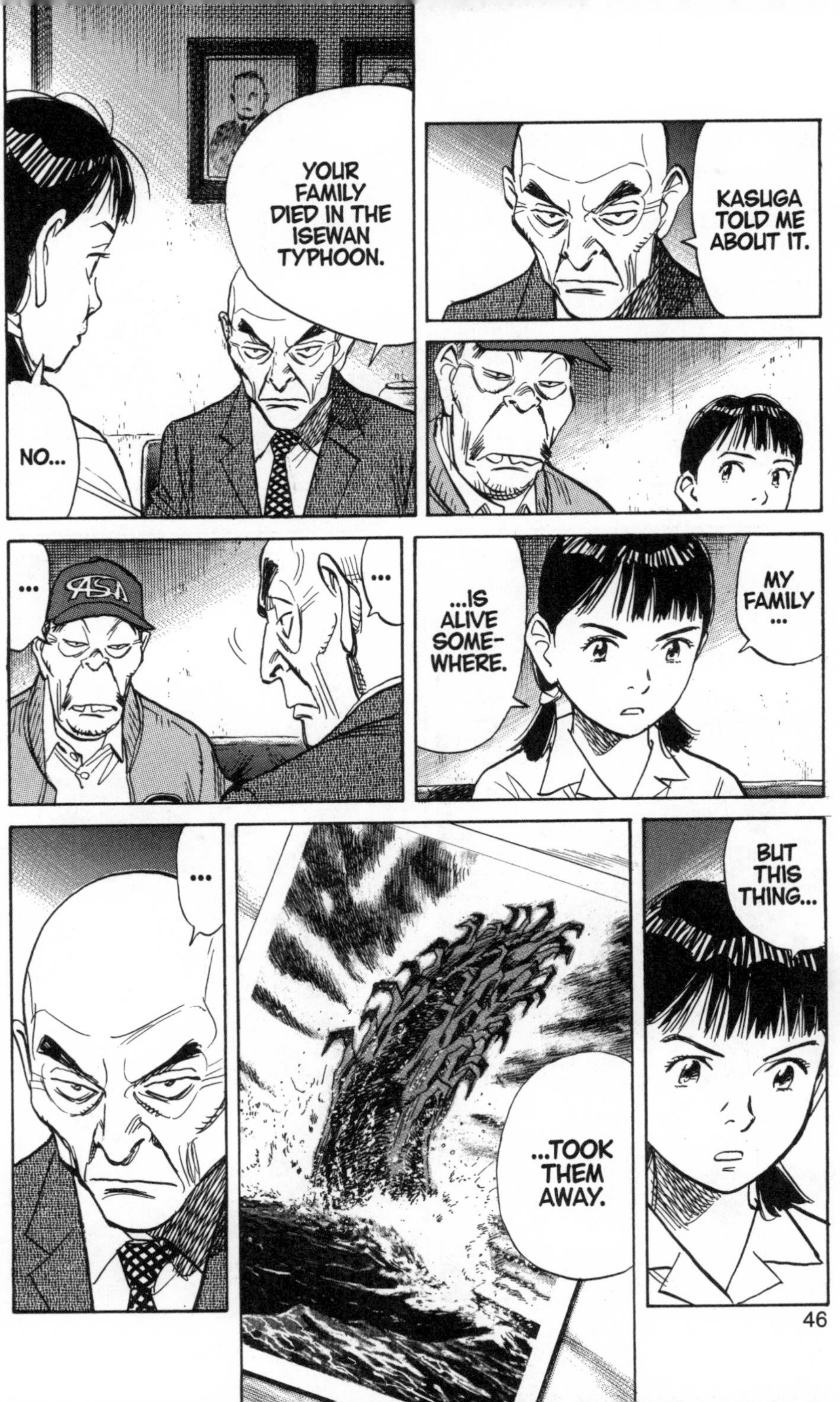
KASUGA TOLD ME ABOUT IT.
YOUR FAMILY DIED IN THE ISEWAN TYPHOON.
NO...
MY FAMILY...
...IS ALIVE SOMEWHERE.
...
...
BUT THIS THING...
...TOOK THEM AWAY.
...

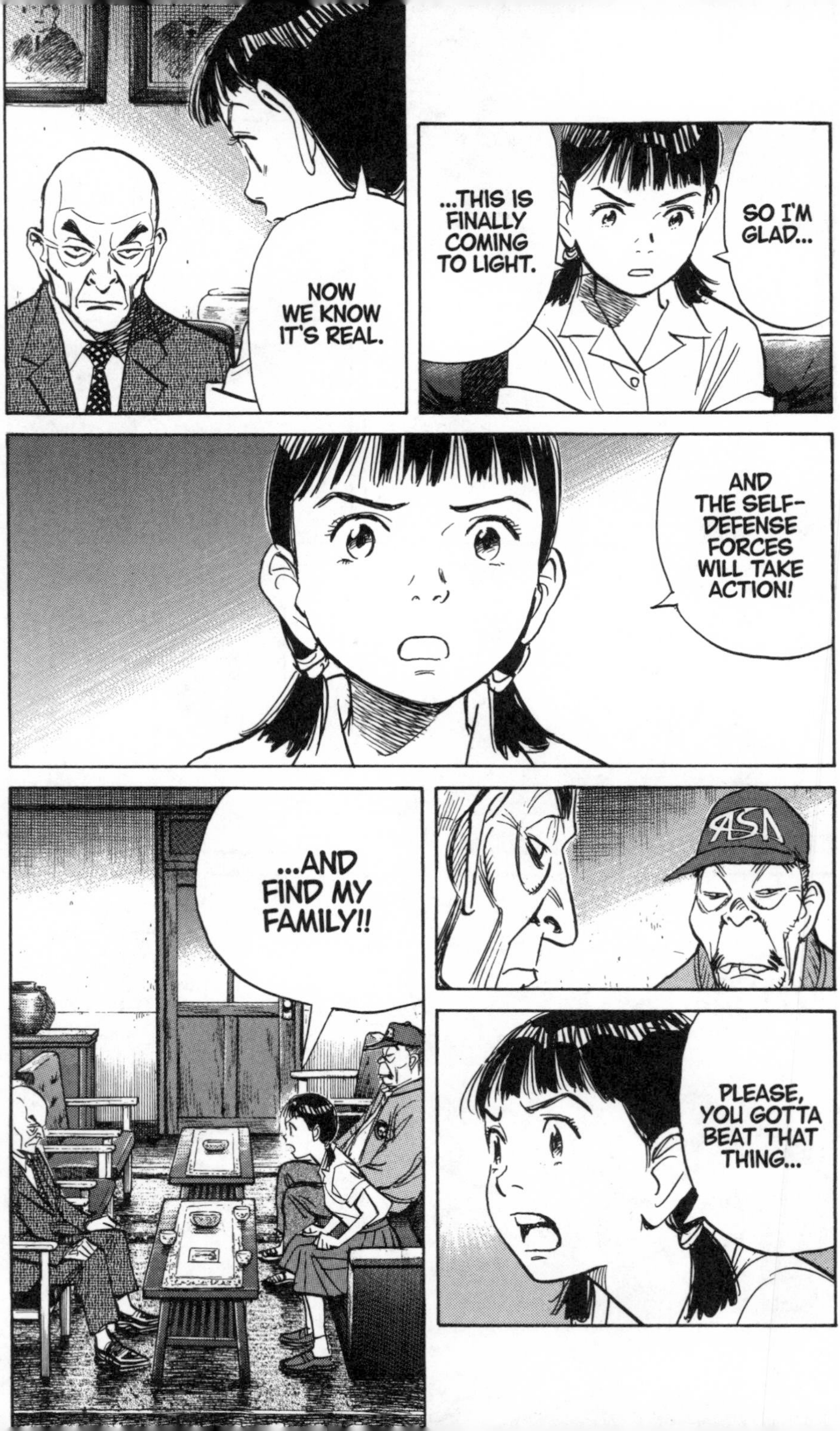
SO I'M GLAD...
...THIS IS FINALLY COMING TO LIGHT.
NOW WE KNOW IT'S REAL.
AND THE SELF-DEFENSE FORCES WILL TAKE ACTION!
PLEASE, YOU GOTTA BEAT THAT THING...
...AND FIND MY FAMILY!!

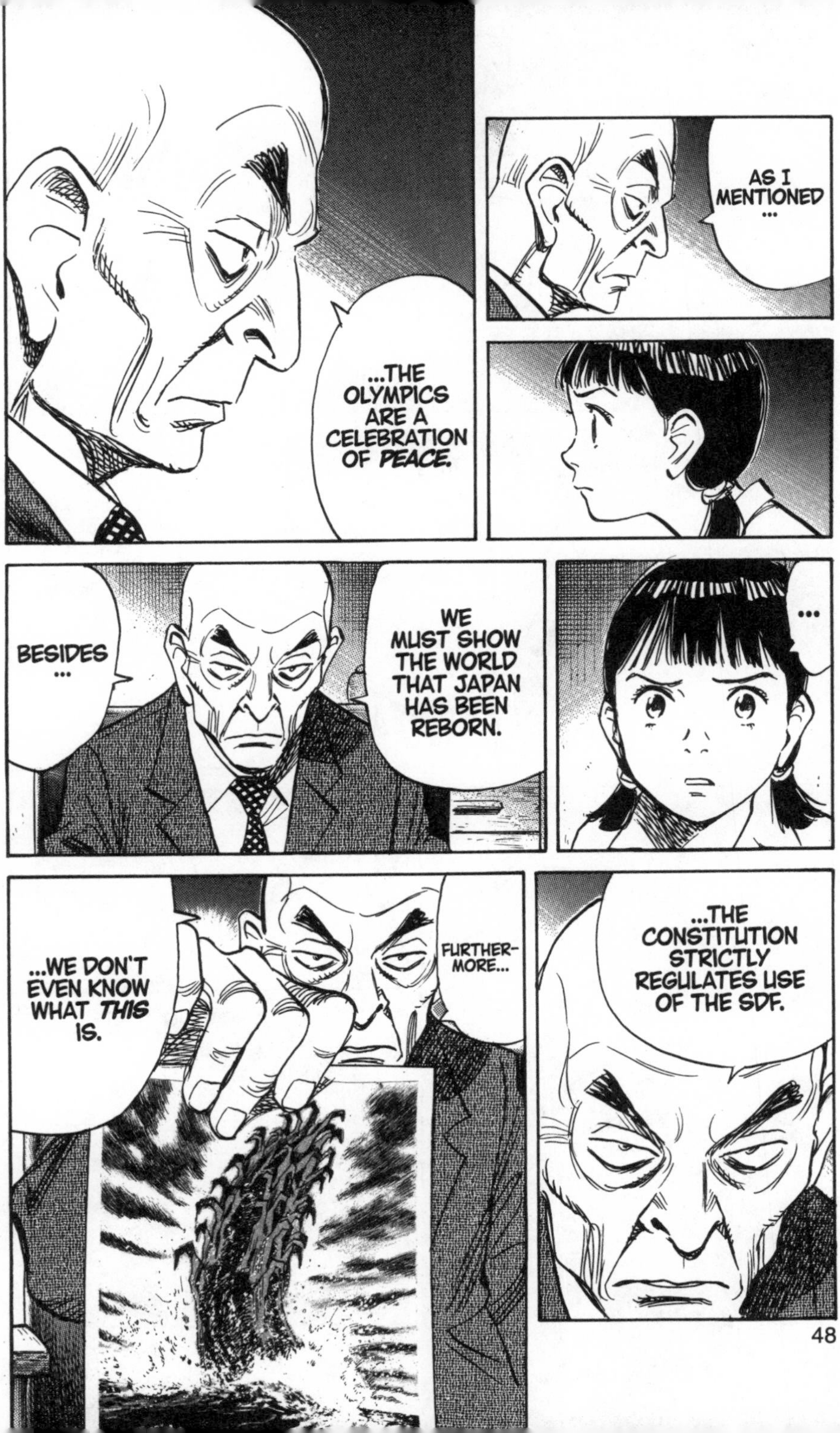
AS I MENTIONED ...
...THE OLYMPICS ARE A CELEBRATION OF *PEACE.*
...
WE MUST SHOW THE WORLD THAT JAPAN HAS BEEN REBORN.
BESIDES ...
...THE CONSTITUTION STRICTLY REGULATES USE OF THE SDF.
FURTHER-MORE...
...WE DON'T EVEN KNOW WHAT *THIS* IS.

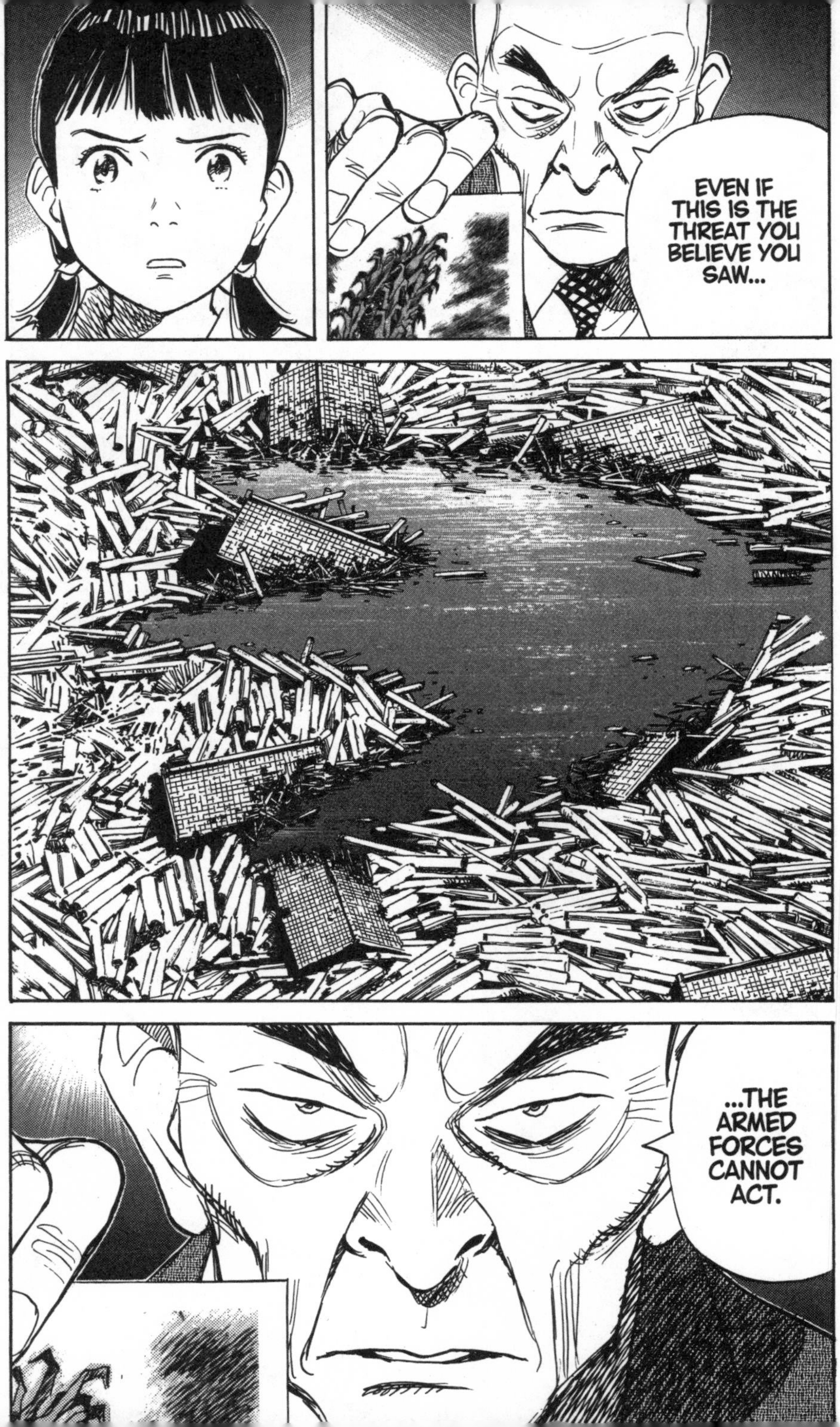
EVEN IF THIS IS THE THREAT YOU BELIEVE YOU SAW...
...THE ARMED FORCES CANNOT ACT.

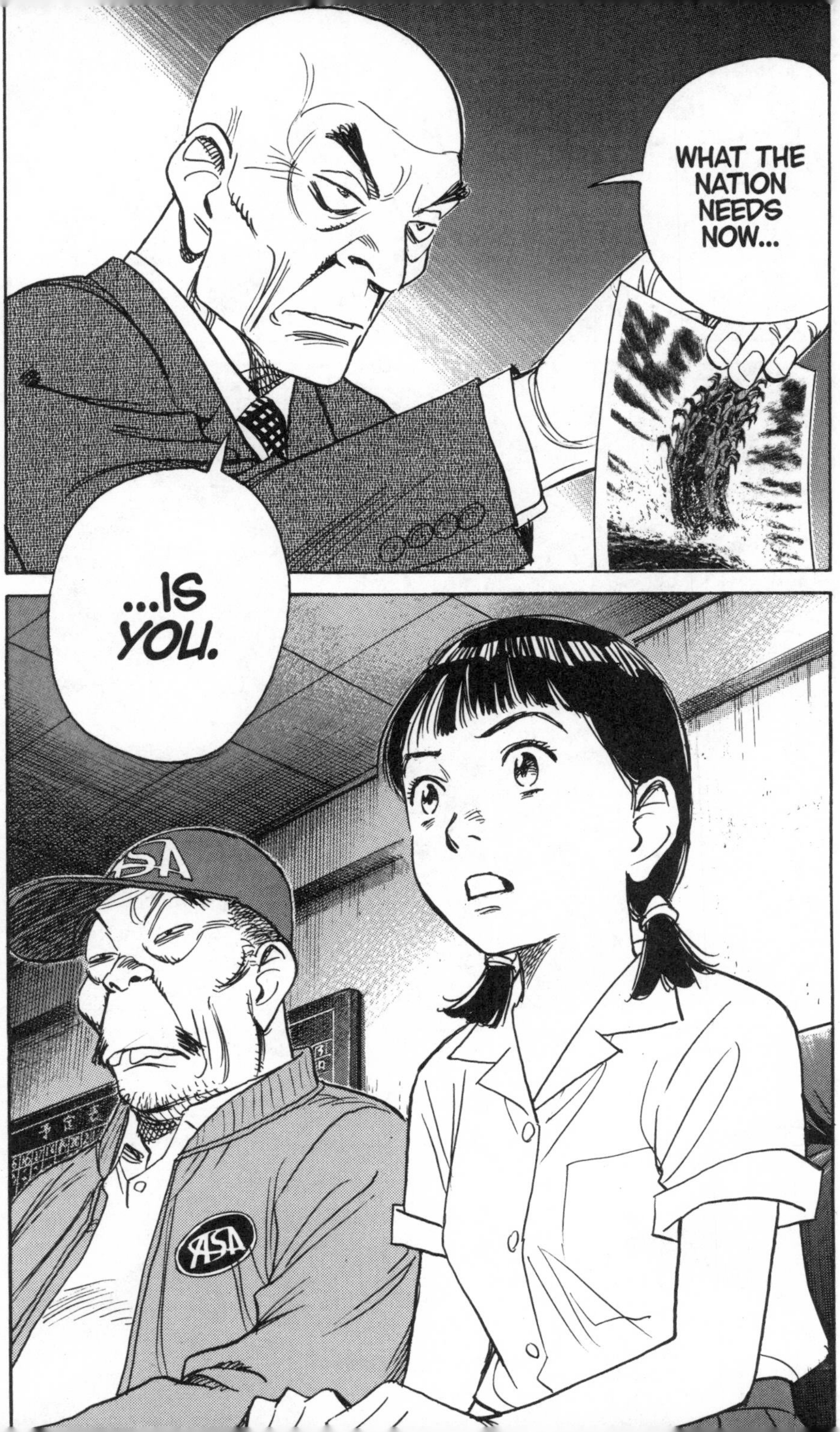
WHAT THE NATION NEEDS NOW...
...IS YOU.

ASADORA!

ASADORA!

Chapter 19 ● Things You Can't Say

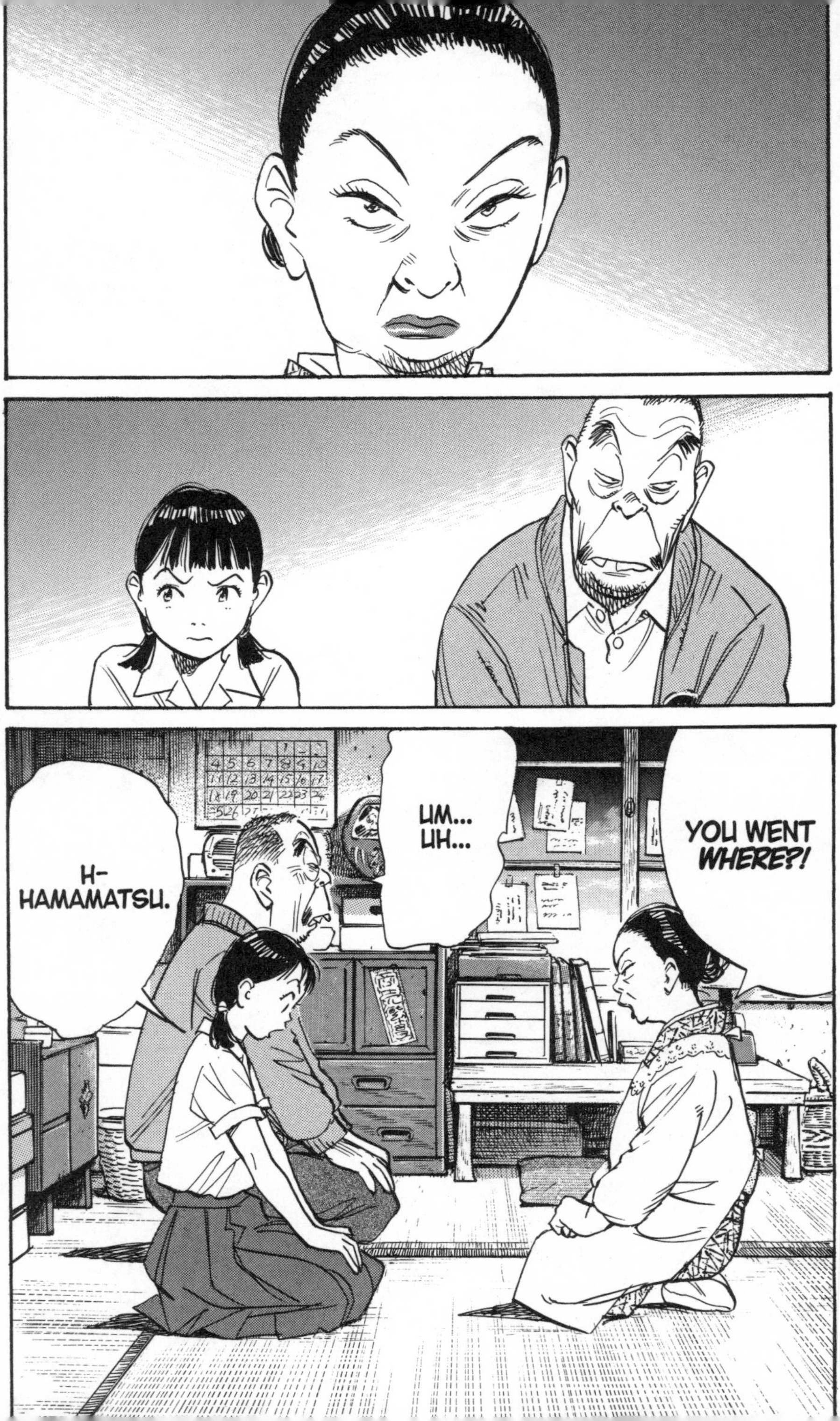
YOU WENT WHERE?!
UM... UH...
H- HAMAMATSU.

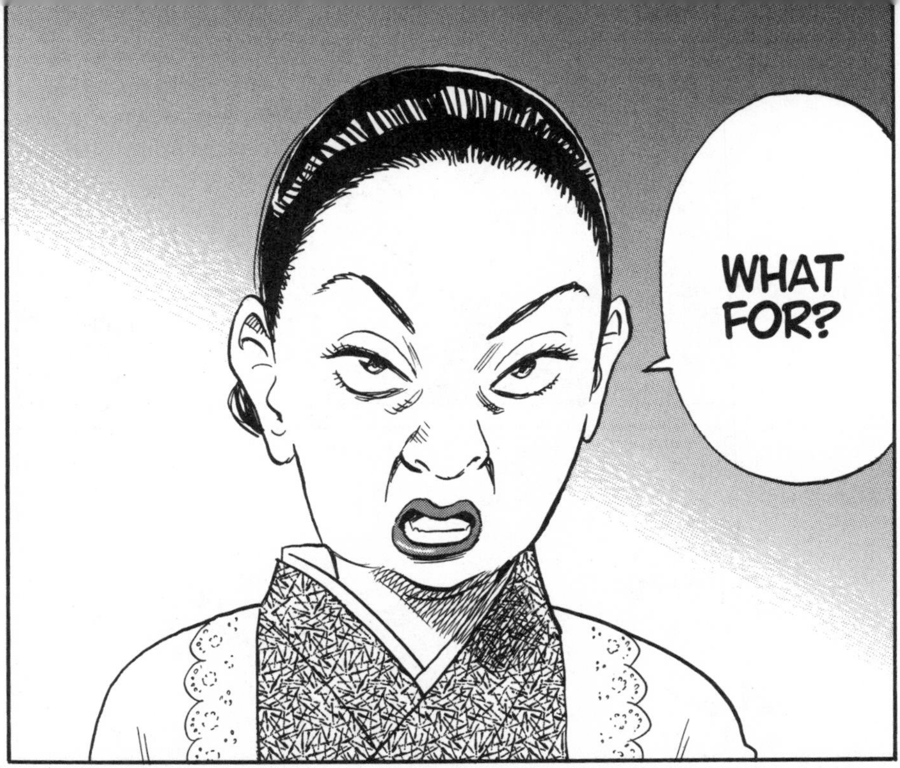
WHAT FOR?

Chapter 19 ◉ Things You Can't Say

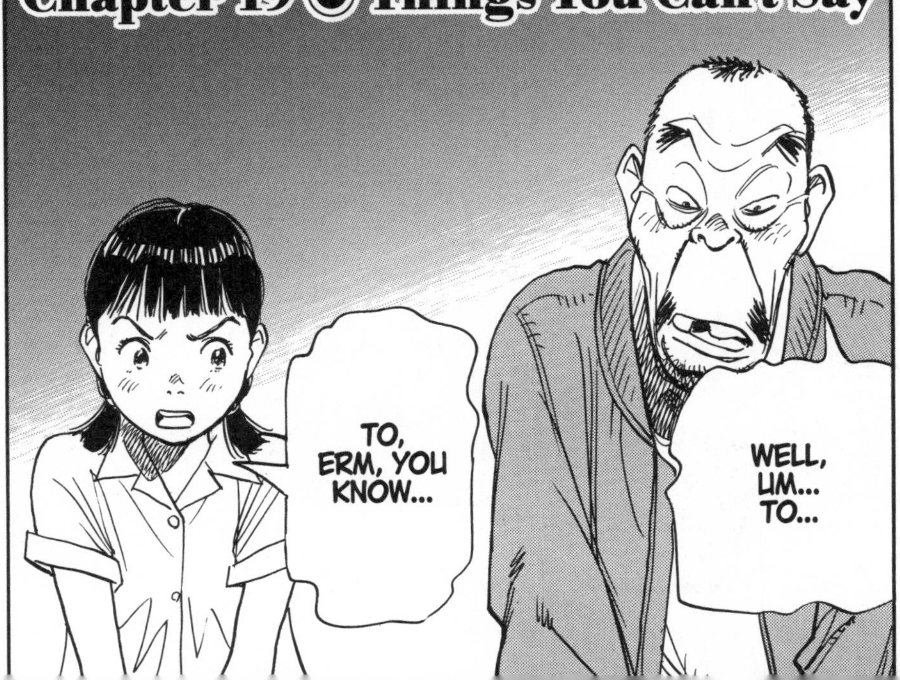
WELL, UM... TO...
TO, ERM, YOU KNOW...

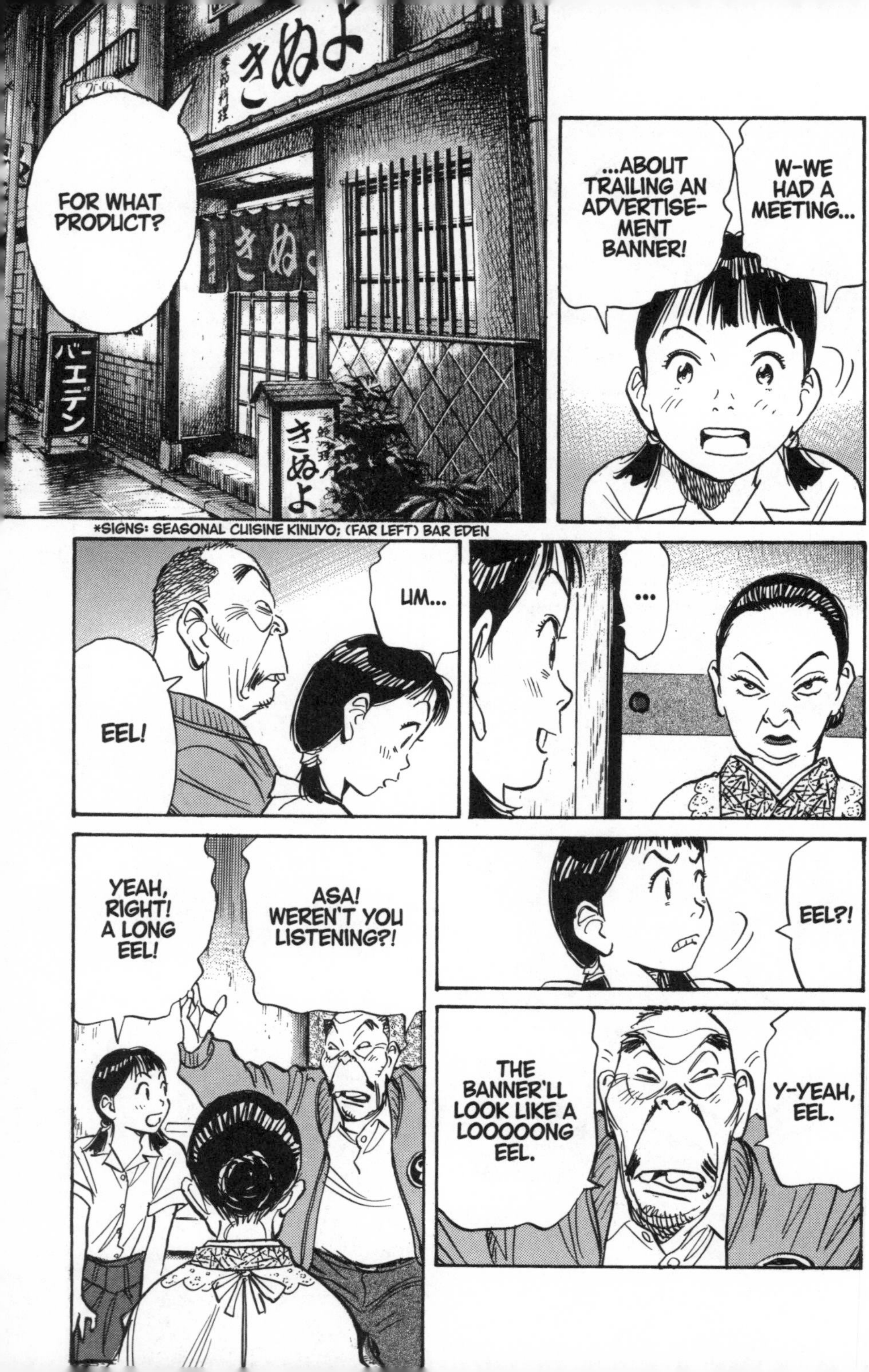
W-WE HAD A MEETING...
...ABOUT TRAILING AN ADVERTISEMENT BANNER!
FOR WHAT PRODUCT?
きぬよ
バーエデン
...
UM...
EEL!
EEL?!
Y-YEAH, EEL.
THE BANNER'LL LOOK LIKE A LOOOOONG EEL.
ASA! WEREN'T YOU LISTENING?!
YEAH, RIGHT! A LONG EEL!
*SIGNS: SEASONAL CUISINE KINUYO; (FAR LEFT) BAR EDEN

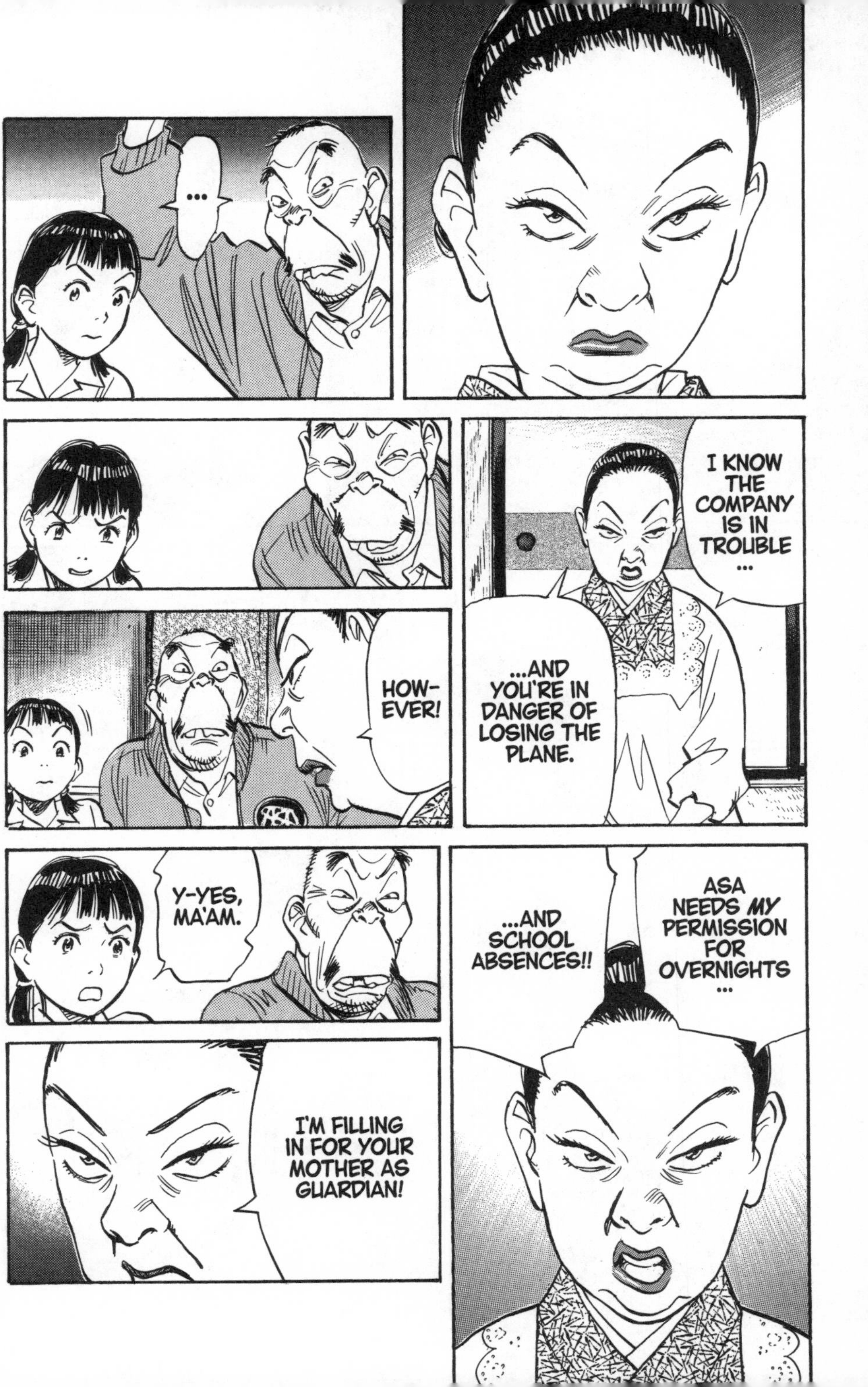
...
I KNOW THE COMPANY IS IN TROUBLE ...
...AND YOU'RE IN DANGER OF LOSING THE PLANE.
HOW-EVER!
ASA NEEDS *MY* PERMISSION FOR OVERNIGHTS ...
...AND SCHOOL ABSENCES!!
Y-YES, MA'AM.
I'M FILLING IN FOR YOUR MOTHER AS GUARDIAN!

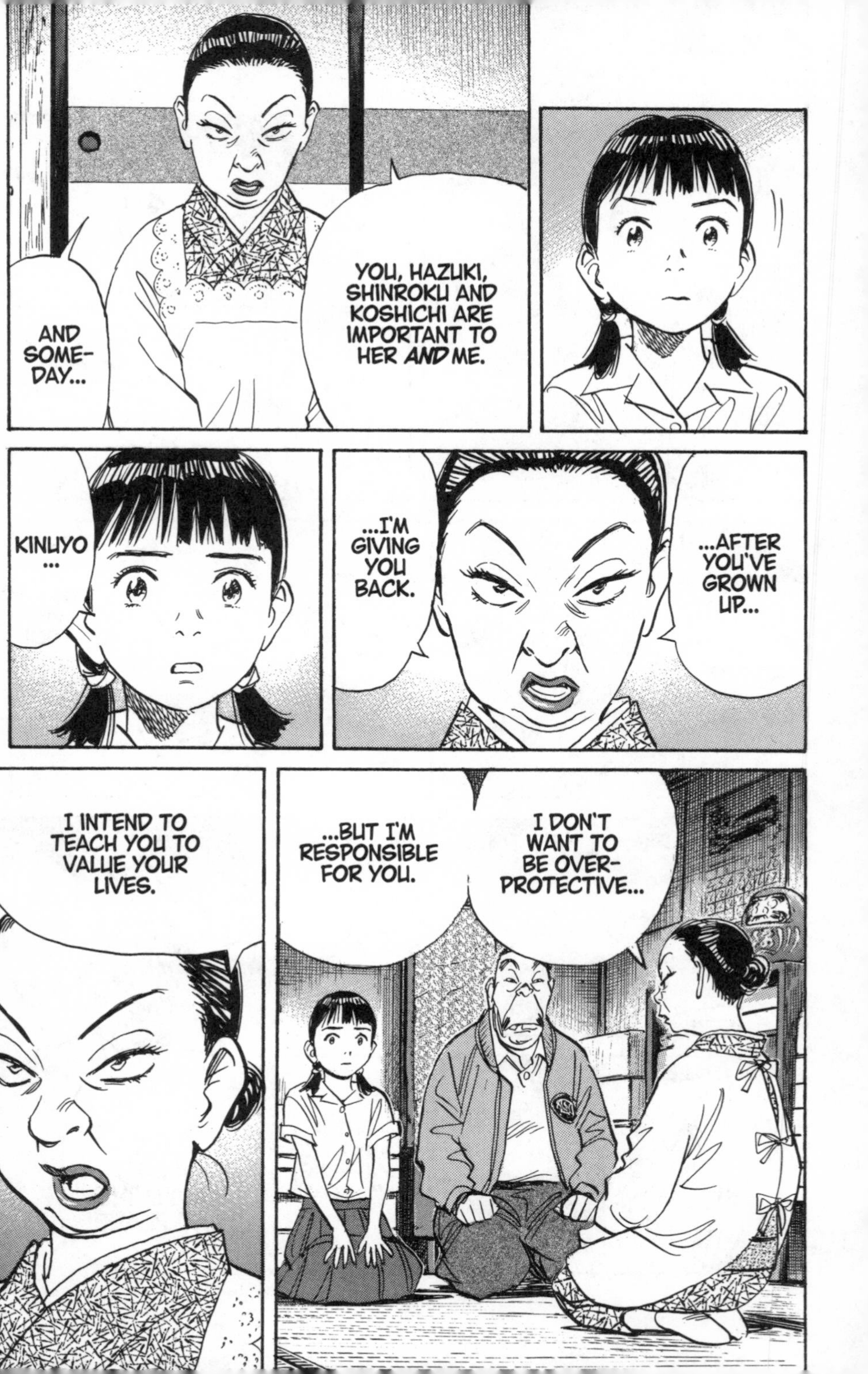
YOU, HAZUKI, SHINROKU AND KOSHICHI ARE IMPORTANT TO HER *AND* ME.
AND SOME-DAY...
...AFTER YOU'VE GROWN UP...
...I'M GIVING YOU BACK.
KINUYO...
I DON'T WANT TO BE OVER-PROTECTIVE...
...BUT I'M RESPONSIBLE FOR YOU.
I INTEND TO TEACH YOU TO VALUE YOUR LIVES.

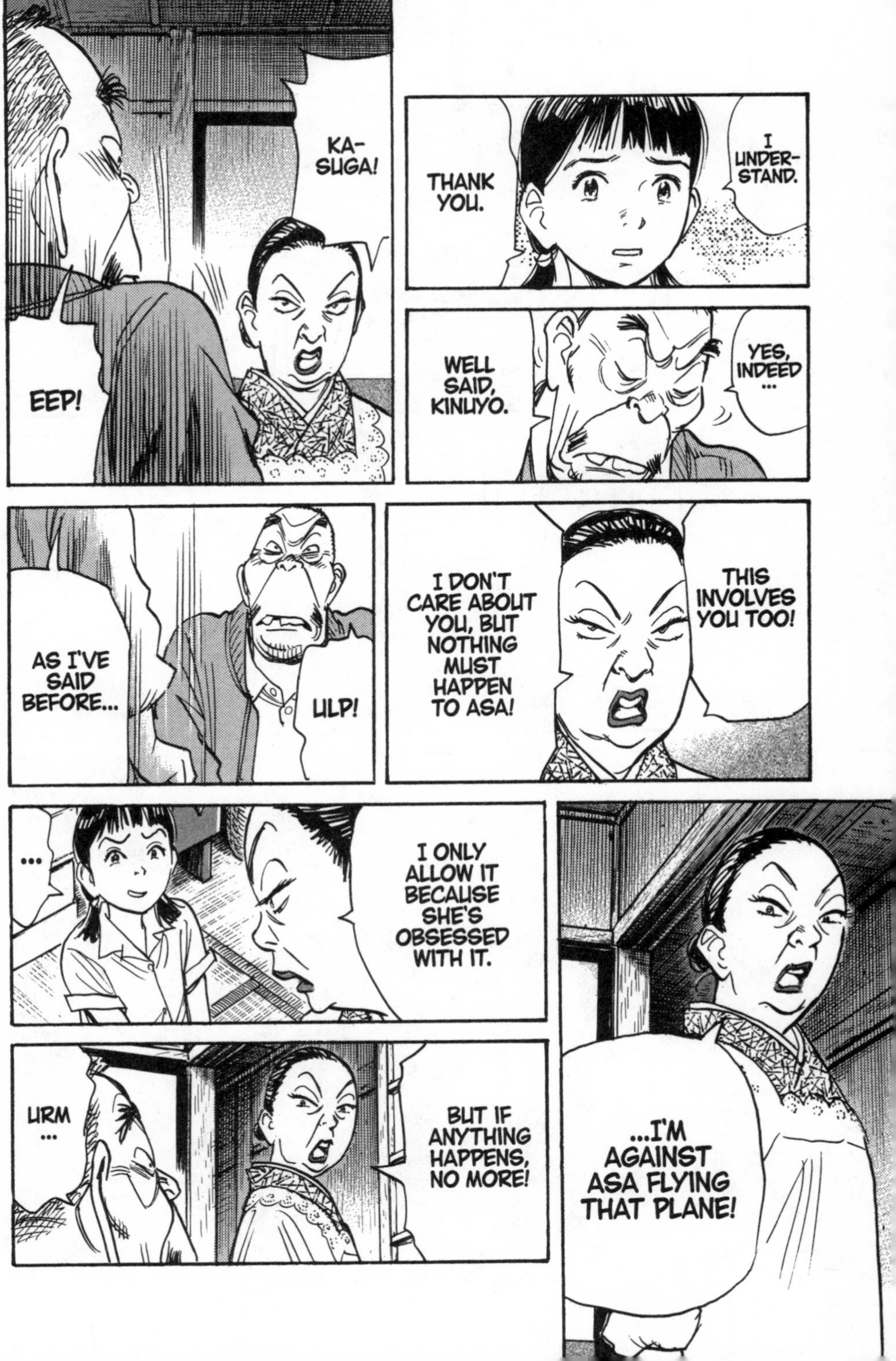
I UNDERSTAND.
THANK YOU.
YES, INDEED ...
WELL SAID, KINUYO.
KA-SUGA!
EEP!
THIS INVOLVES YOU TOO!
I DON'T CARE ABOUT YOU, BUT NOTHING MUST HAPPEN TO ASA!
ULP!
AS I'VE SAID BEFORE...
...I'M AGAINST ASA FLYING THAT PLANE!
I ONLY ALLOW IT BECAUSE SHE'S OBSESSED WITH IT.
...
BUT IF ANYTHING HAPPENS, NO MORE!
URM ...

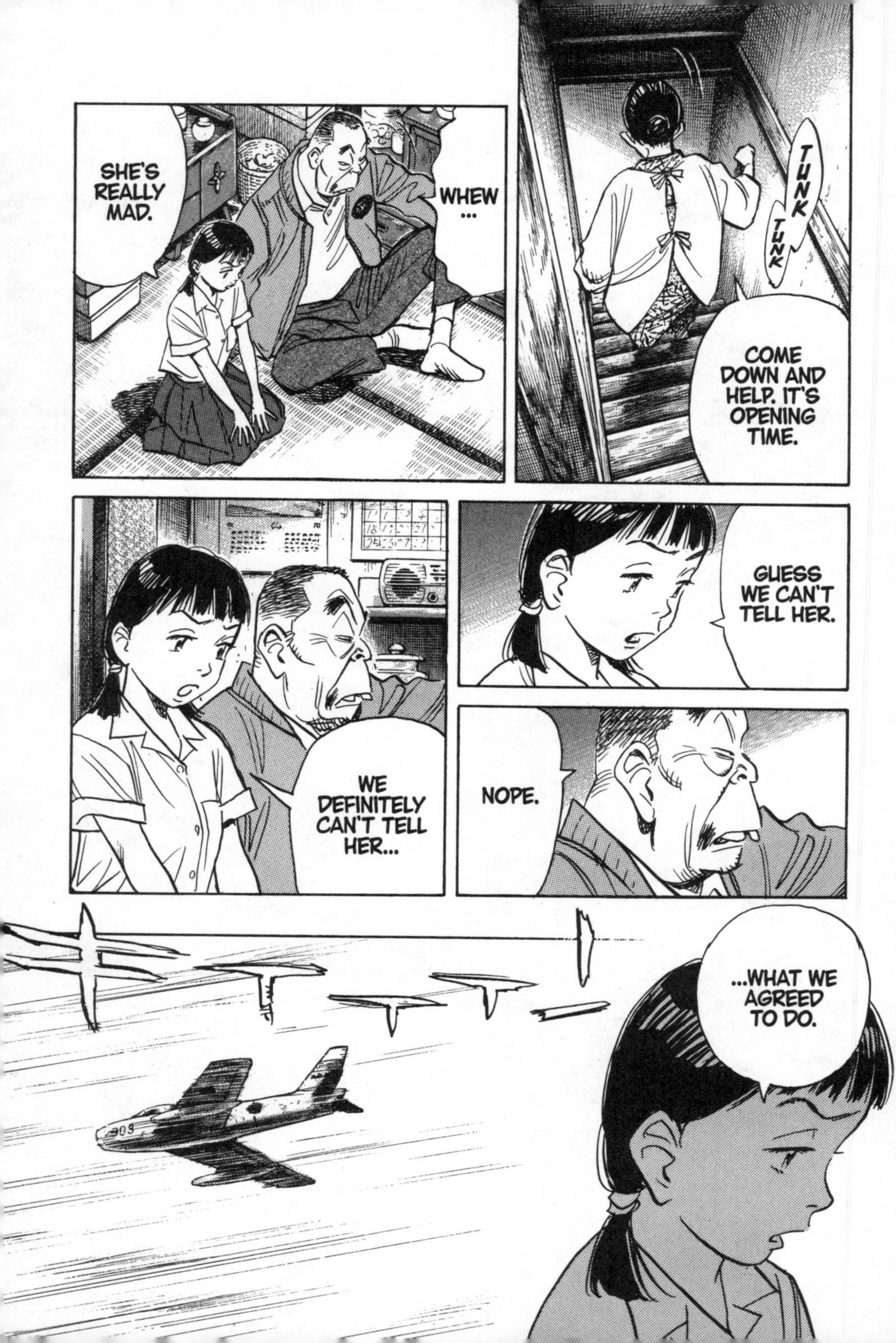
TUNK TUNK
COME DOWN AND HELP. IT'S OPENING TIME.
WHEW...
SHE'S REALLY MAD.
GUESS WE CAN'T TELL HER.
NOPE.
WE DEFINITELY CAN'T TELL HER...
...WHAT WE AGREED TO DO.

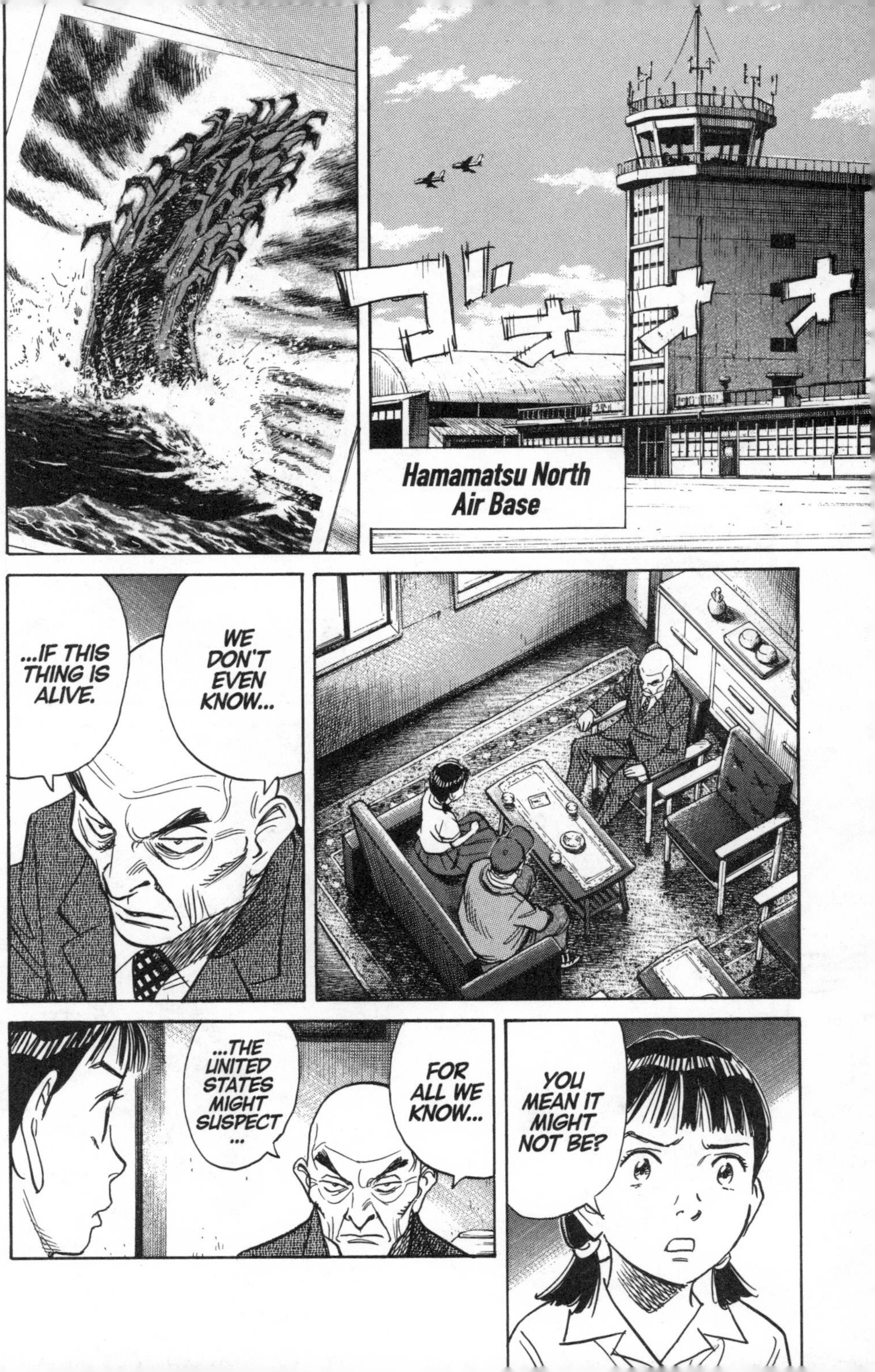
ゴォオオ
Hamamatsu North Air Base
WE DON'T EVEN KNOW...
...IF THIS THING IS ALIVE.
YOU MEAN IT MIGHT NOT BE?
FOR ALL WE KNOW...
...THE UNITED STATES MIGHT SUSPECT ...

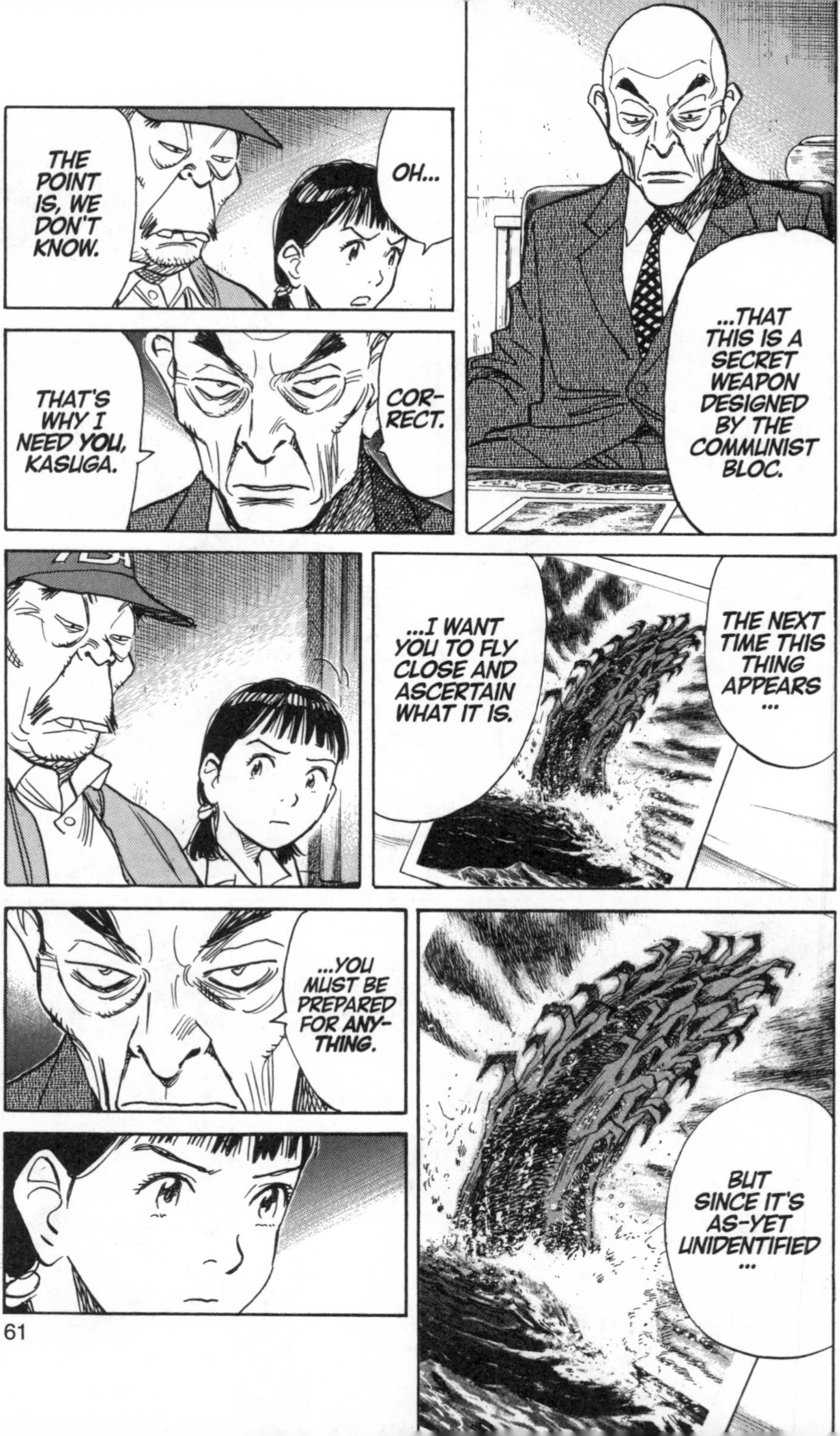
...THAT THIS IS A SECRET WEAPON DESIGNED BY THE COMMUNIST BLOC.
OH...
THE POINT IS, WE DON'T KNOW.
COR-RECT.
THAT'S WHY I NEED YOU, KASUGA.
THE NEXT TIME THIS THING APPEARS ...
...I WANT YOU TO FLY CLOSE AND ASCERTAIN WHAT IT IS.
BUT SINCE IT'S AS-YET UNIDENTIFIED ...
...YOU MUST BE PREPARED FOR ANY-THING.

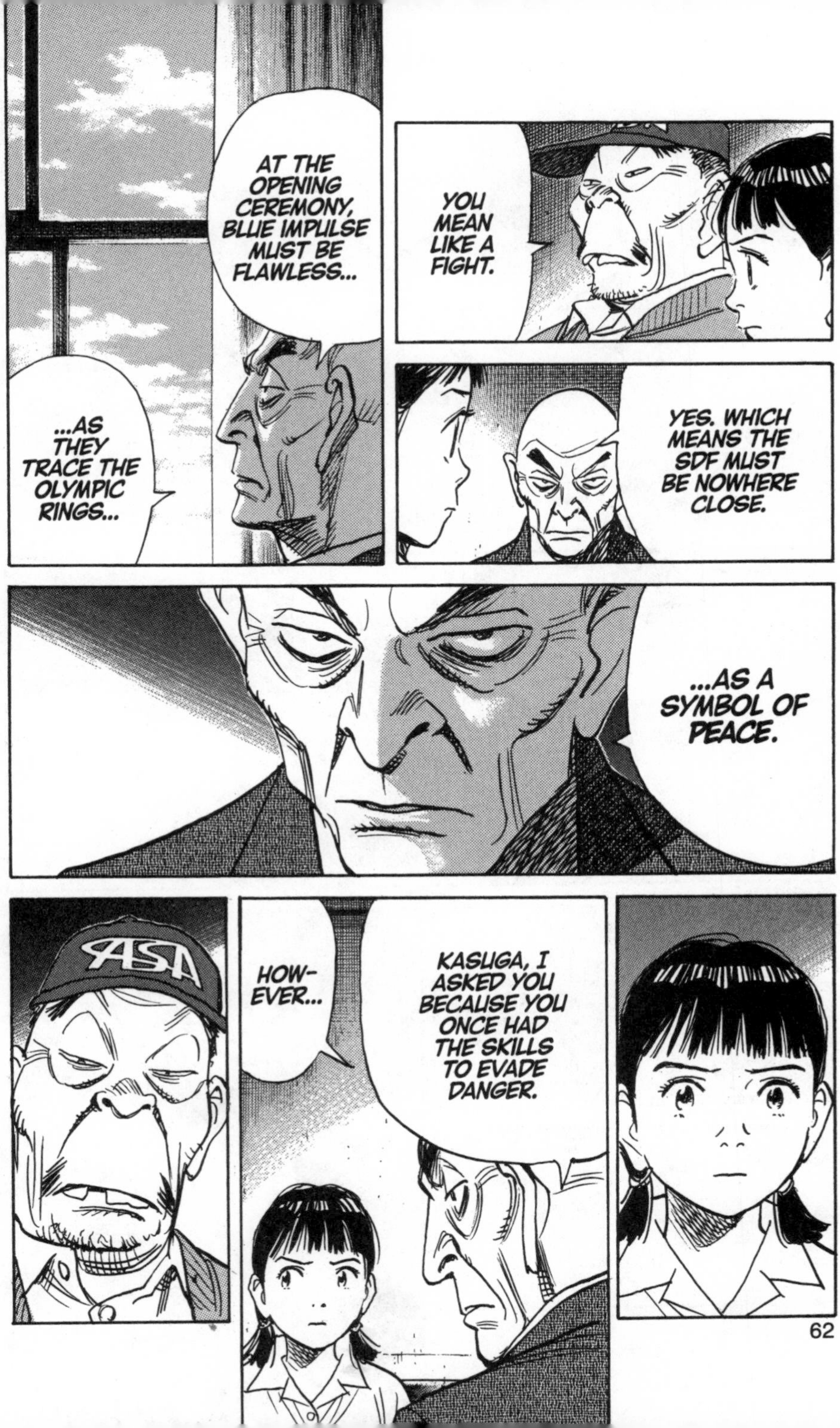
YOU MEAN LIKE A FIGHT.
YES. WHICH MEANS THE SDF MUST BE NOWHERE CLOSE.
AT THE OPENING CEREMONY, BLUE IMPULSE MUST BE FLAWLESS...
...AS THEY TRACE THE OLYMPIC RINGS...
...AS A SYMBOL OF PEACE.
KASUGA, I ASKED YOU BECAUSE YOU ONCE HAD THE SKILLS TO EVADE DANGER.
HOW-EVER...
ASA

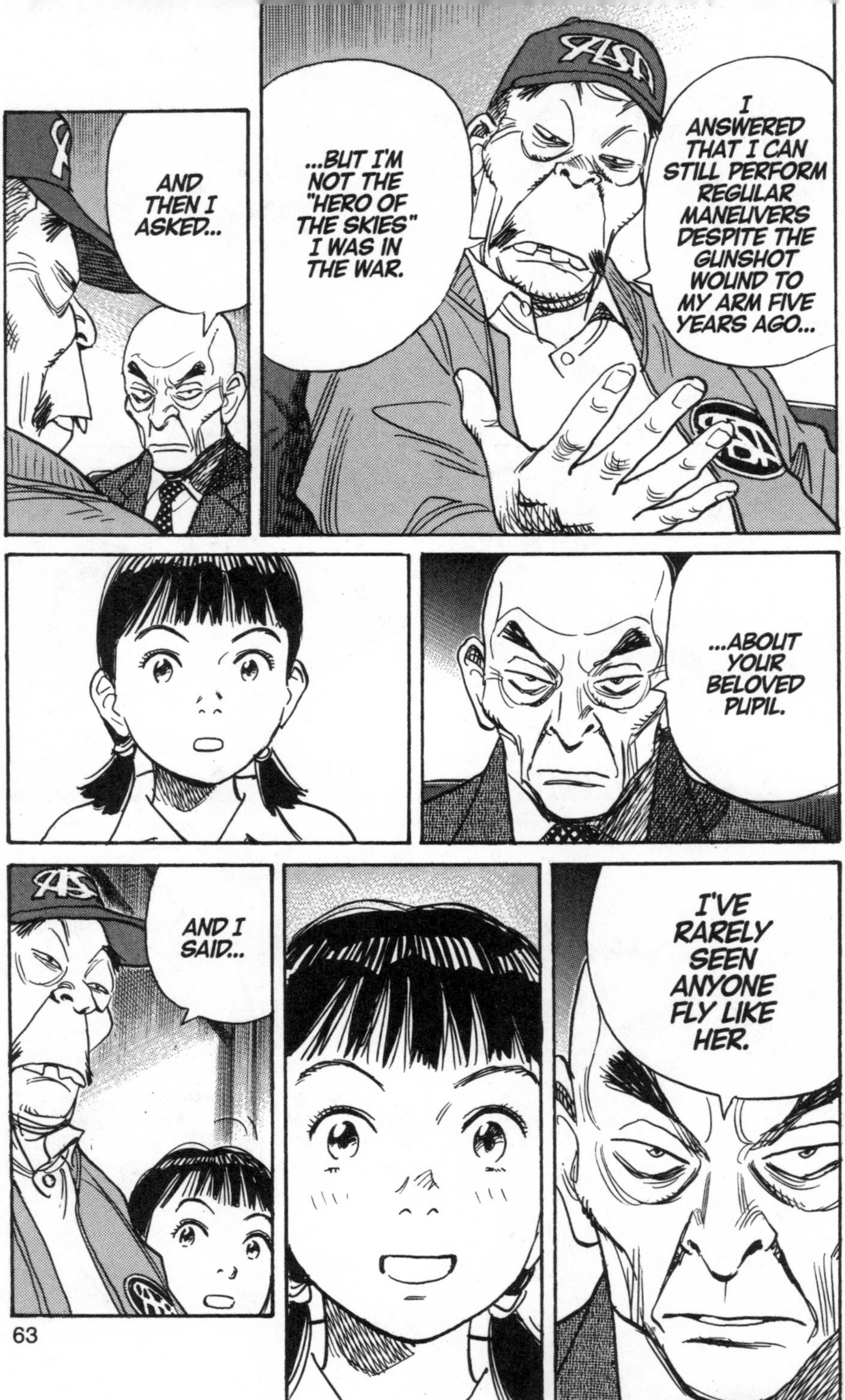
I ANSWERED THAT I CAN STILL PERFORM REGULAR MANEUVERS DESPITE THE GUNSHOT WOUND TO MY ARM FIVE YEARS AGO...
...BUT I'M NOT THE "HERO OF THE SKIES" I WAS IN THE WAR.
AND THEN I ASKED...
...ABOUT YOUR BELOVED PUPIL.
I'VE RARELY SEEN ANYONE FLY LIKE HER.
AND I SAID...

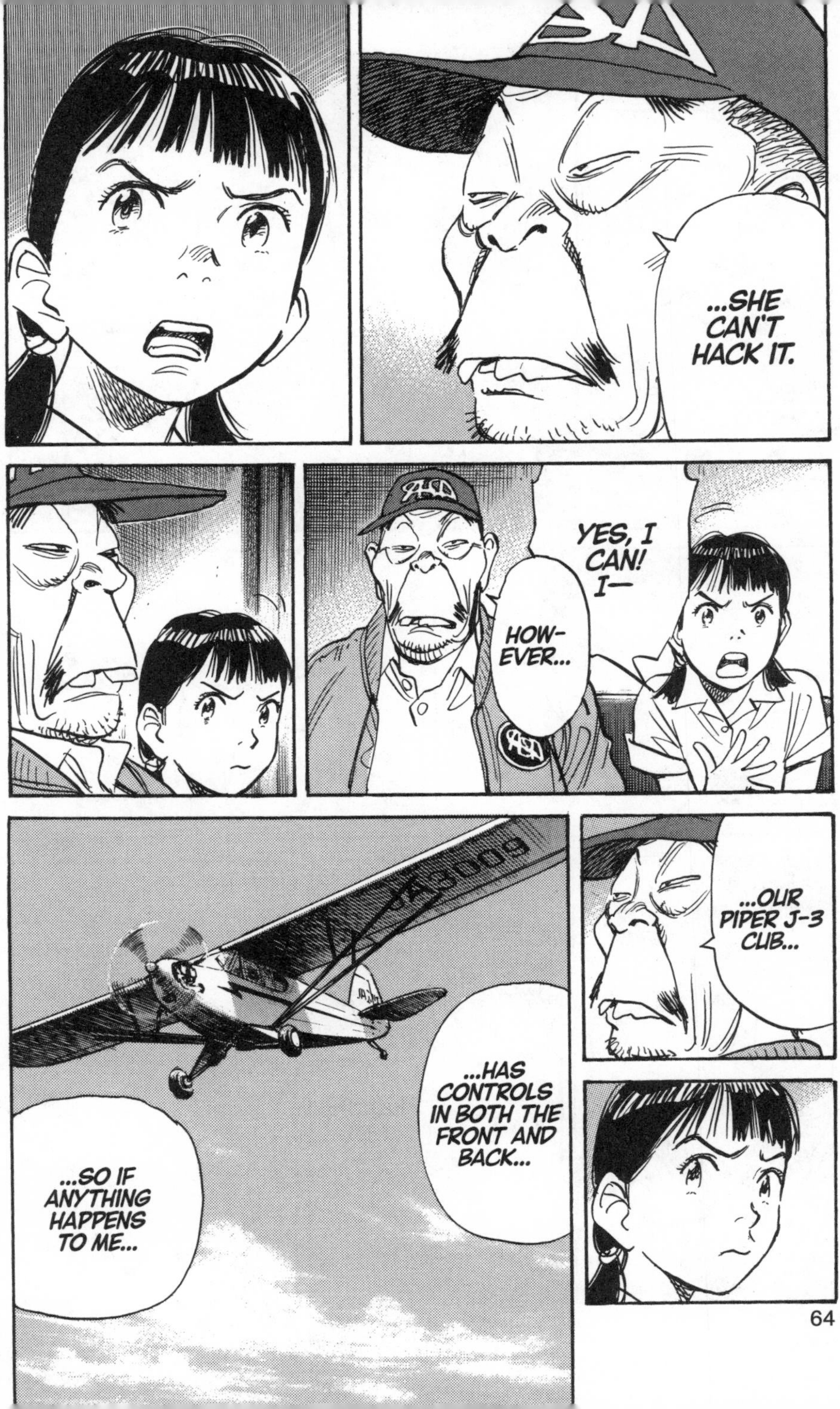
...SHE CAN'T HACK IT.
YES, I CAN! I—
HOW-EVER...
...OUR PIPER J-3 CUB...
...HAS CONTROLS IN BOTH THE FRONT AND BACK...
...SO IF ANYTHING HAPPENS TO ME...

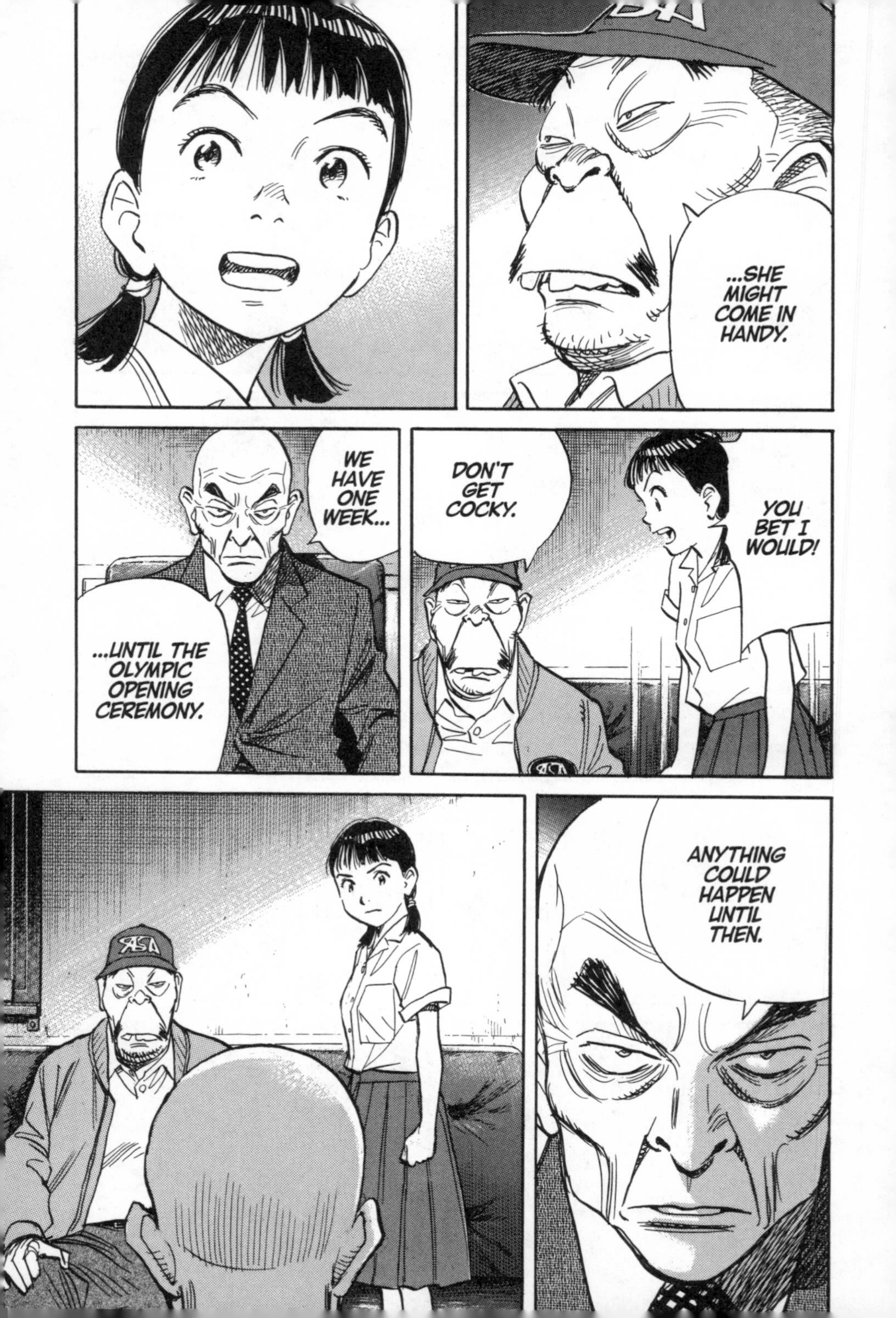
...SHE MIGHT COME IN HANDY.
DON'T GET COCKY.
YOU BET I WOULD!
WE HAVE ONE WEEK...
...UNTIL THE OLYMPIC OPENING CEREMONY.
ANYTHING COULD HAPPEN UNTIL THEN.

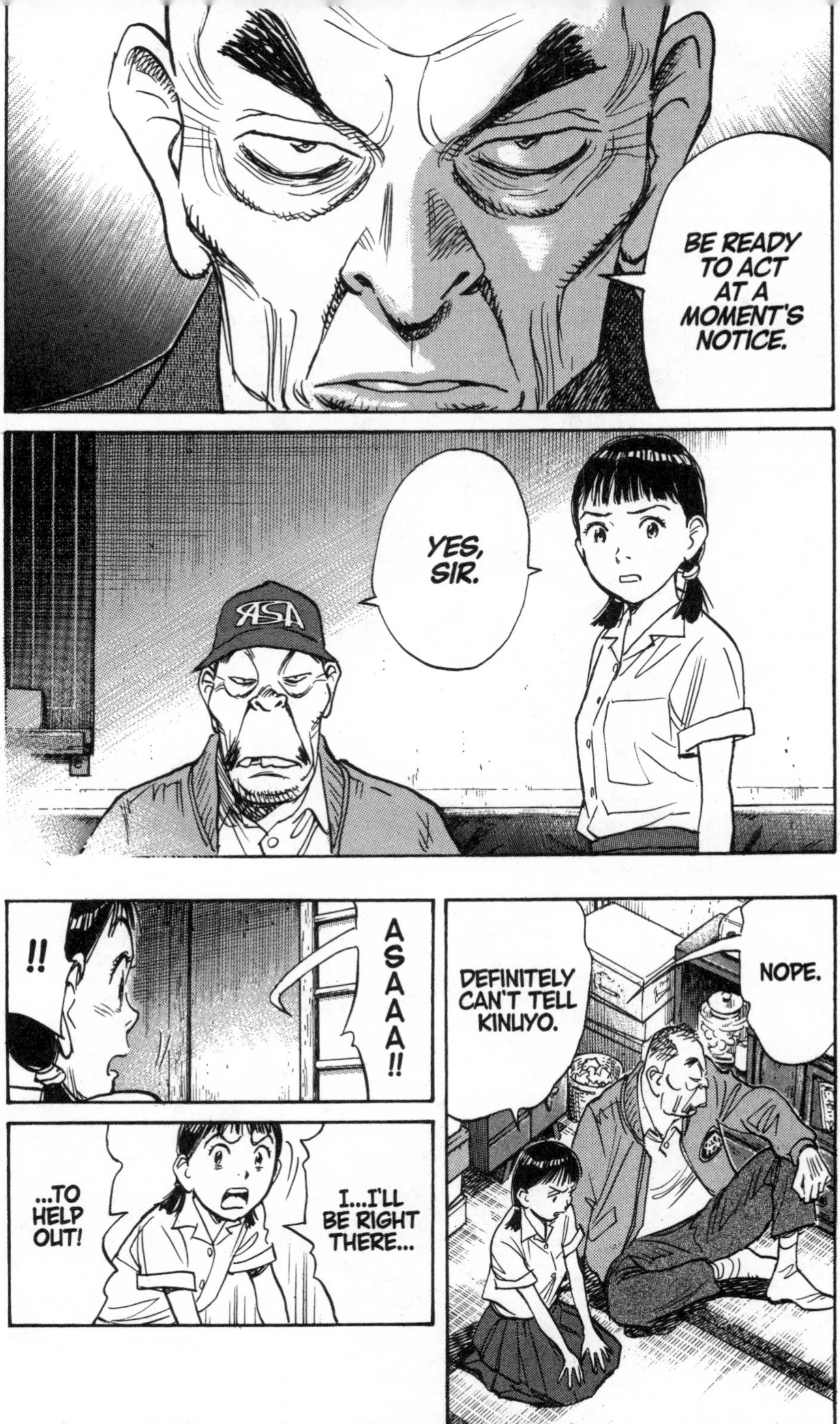
BE READY TO ACT AT A MOMENT'S NOTICE.
YES, SIR.
NOPE.
DEFINITELY CAN'T TELL KINUYO.
ASAAAA!!
!!
I...I'LL BE RIGHT THERE...
...TO HELP OUT!

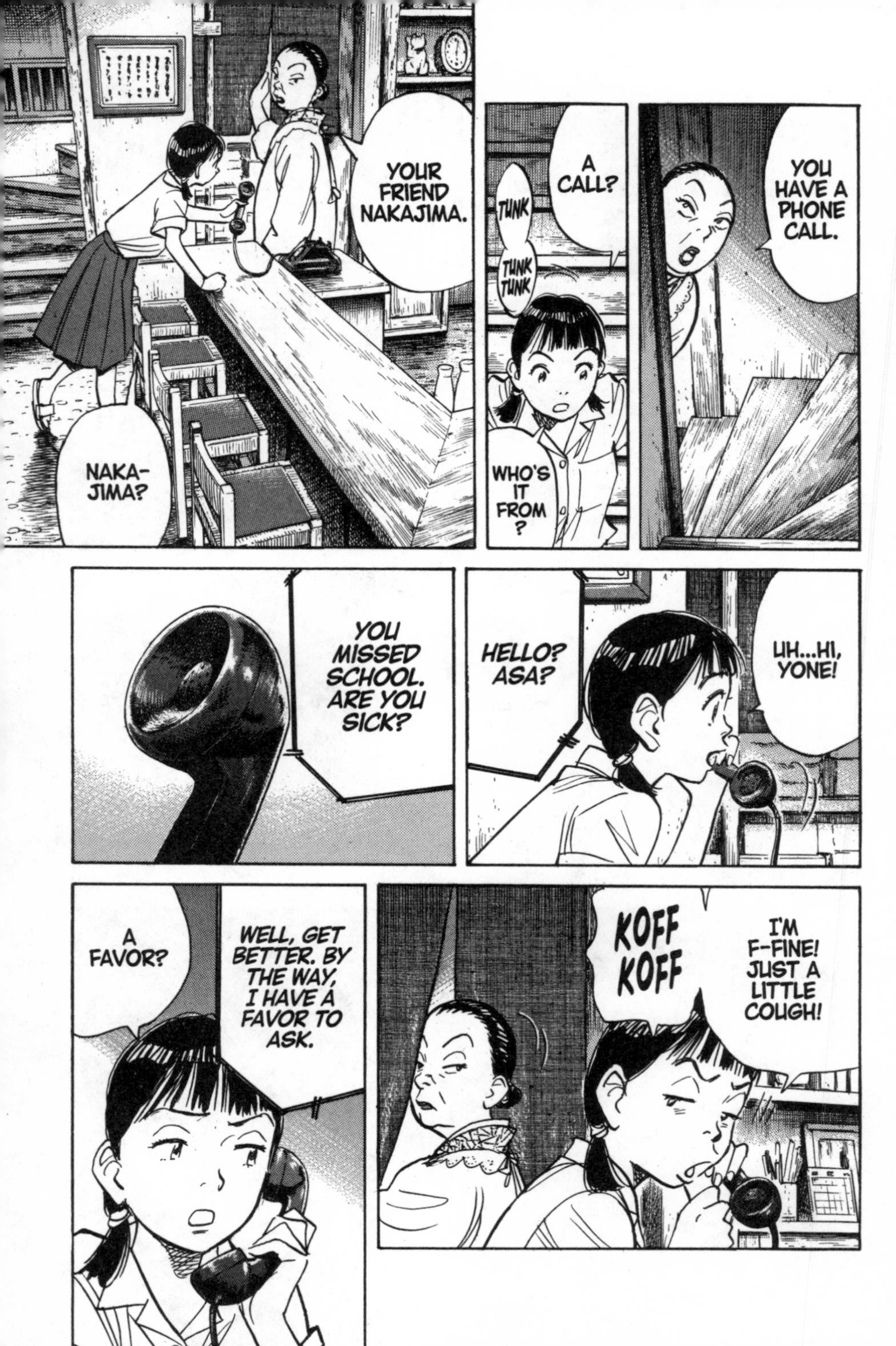
YOU HAVE A PHONE CALL.
A CALL?
TUNK
TUNK TUNK
WHO'S IT FROM?
YOUR FRIEND NAKAJIMA.
NAKA-JIMA?
HELLO? ASA?
UH...HI, YONE!
YOU MISSED SCHOOL. ARE YOU SICK?
KOFF KOFF
I'M F-FINE! JUST A LITTLE COUGH!
WELL, GET BETTER. BY THE WAY, I HAVE A FAVOR TO ASK.
A FAVOR?

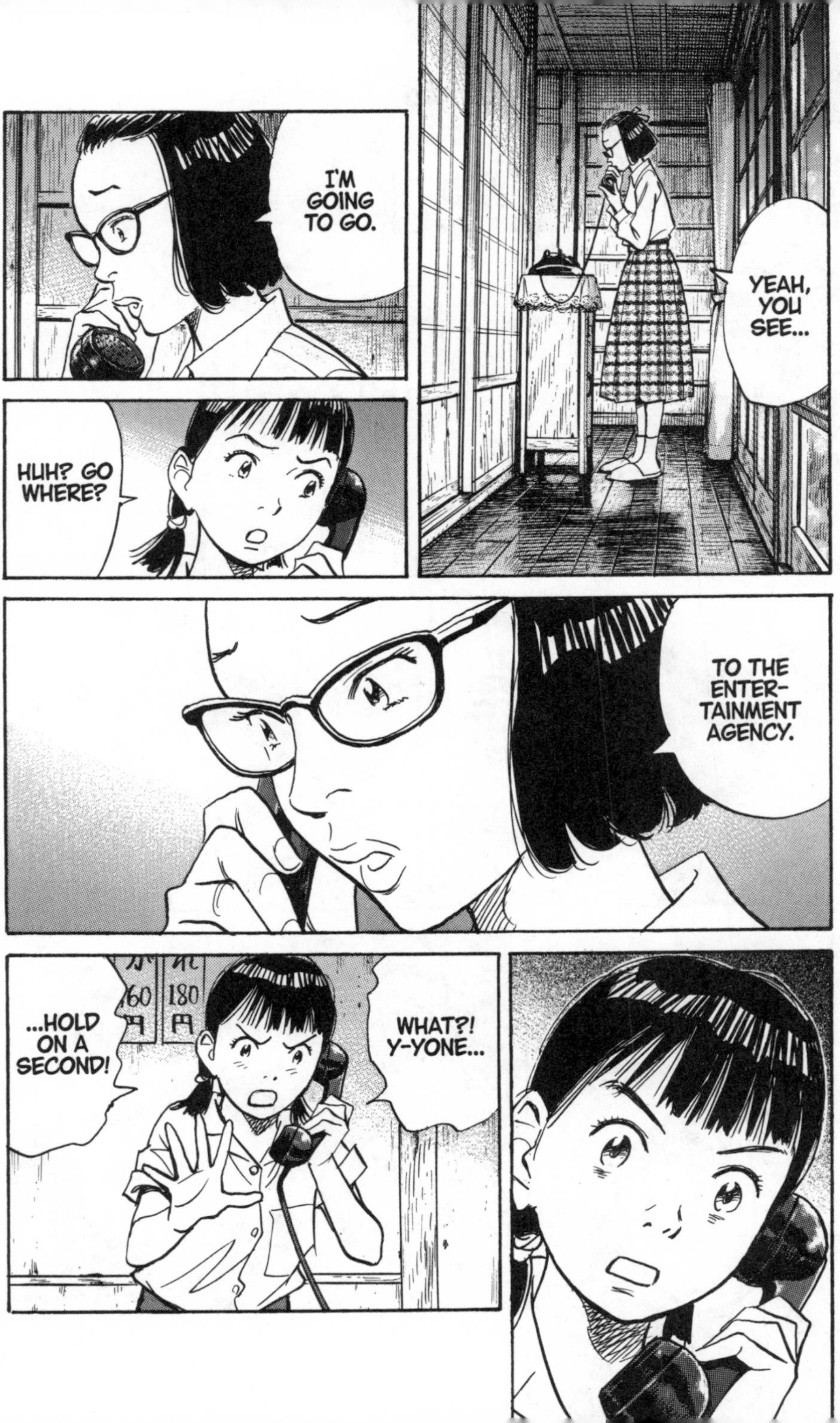
YEAH, YOU SEE...
I'M GOING TO GO.
HUH? GO WHERE?
TO THE ENTER-TAINMENT AGENCY.
WHAT?! Y-YONE...
...HOLD ON A SECOND!

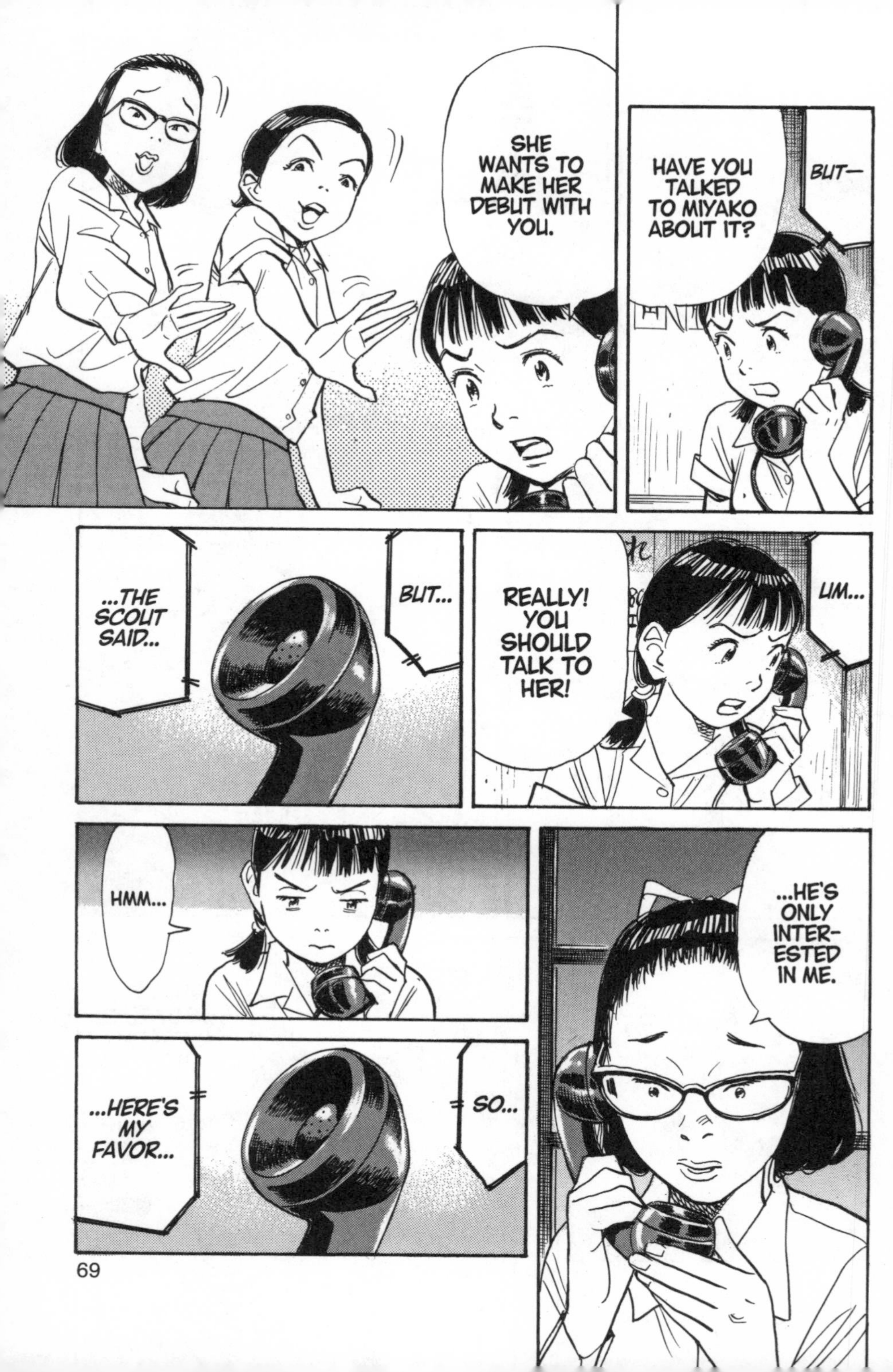
BUT—
HAVE YOU TALKED TO MIYAKO ABOUT IT?
SHE WANTS TO MAKE HER DEBUT WITH YOU.
UM...
REALLY! YOU SHOULD TALK TO HER!
BUT...
...THE SCOUT SAID...
...HE'S ONLY INTER-ESTED IN ME.
HMM...
SO...
...HERE'S MY FAVOR...

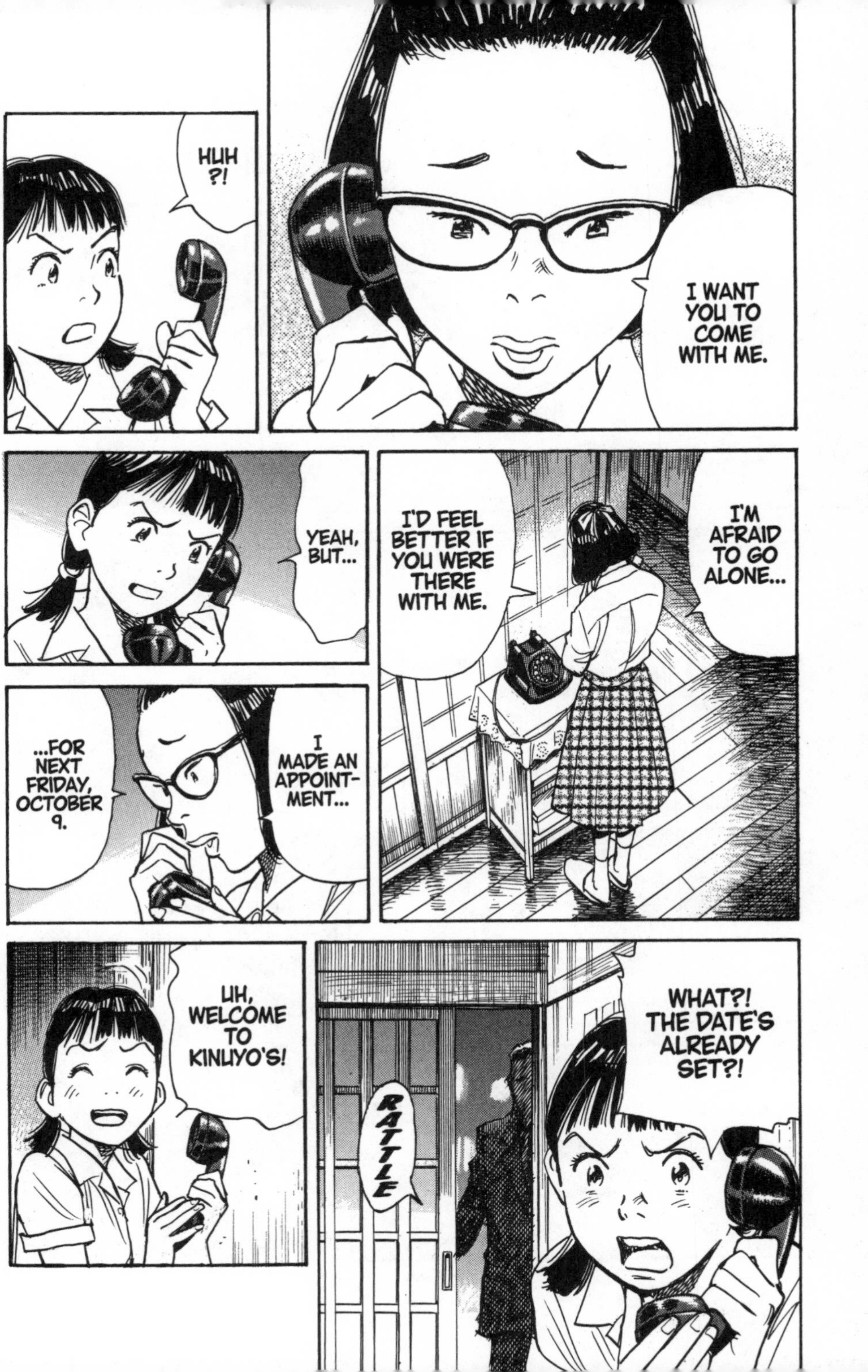
I WANT YOU TO COME WITH ME.
HUH ?!
I'M AFRAID TO GO ALONE...
I'D FEEL BETTER IF YOU WERE THERE WITH ME.
YEAH, BUT...
I MADE AN APPOINT-MENT...
...FOR NEXT FRIDAY, OCTOBER 9.
WHAT?! THE DATE'S ALREADY SET?!
RATTLE
UH, WELCOME TO KINUYO'S!

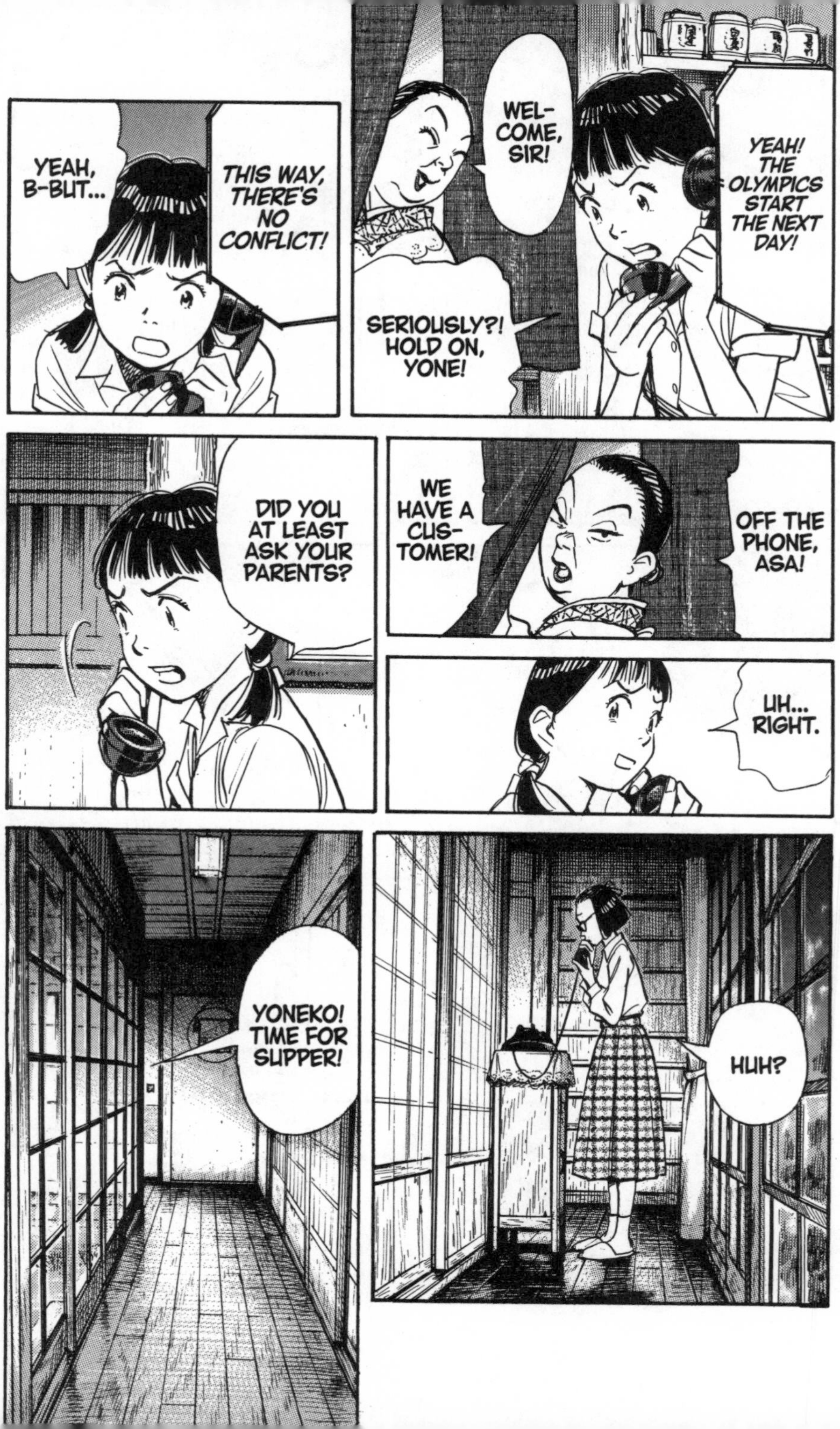
YEAH! THE OLYMPICS START THE NEXT DAY!
WEL-COME, SIR!
SERIOUSLY?! HOLD ON, YONE!
THIS WAY, THERE'S NO CONFLICT!
YEAH, B-BUT...
OFF THE PHONE, ASA!
WE HAVE A CUS-TOMER!
UH... RIGHT.
DID YOU AT LEAST ASK YOUR PARENTS?
HUH?
YONEKO! TIME FOR SUPPER!

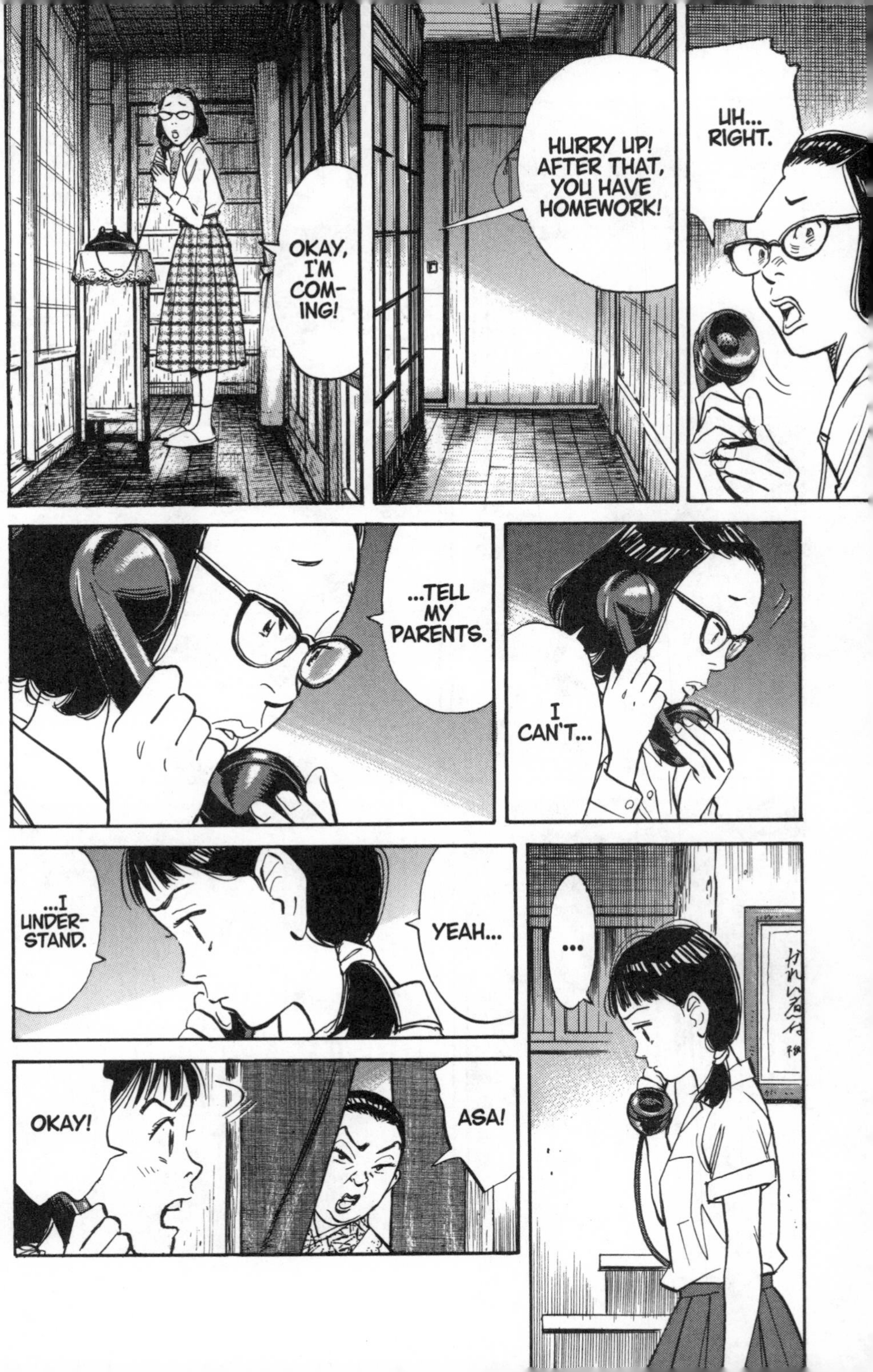
UH... RIGHT.
HURRY UP! AFTER THAT, YOU HAVE HOMEWORK!
OKAY, I'M COM-ING!
I CAN'T...
...TELL MY PARENTS.
...
YEAH...
...I UNDER-STAND.
ASA!
OKAY!

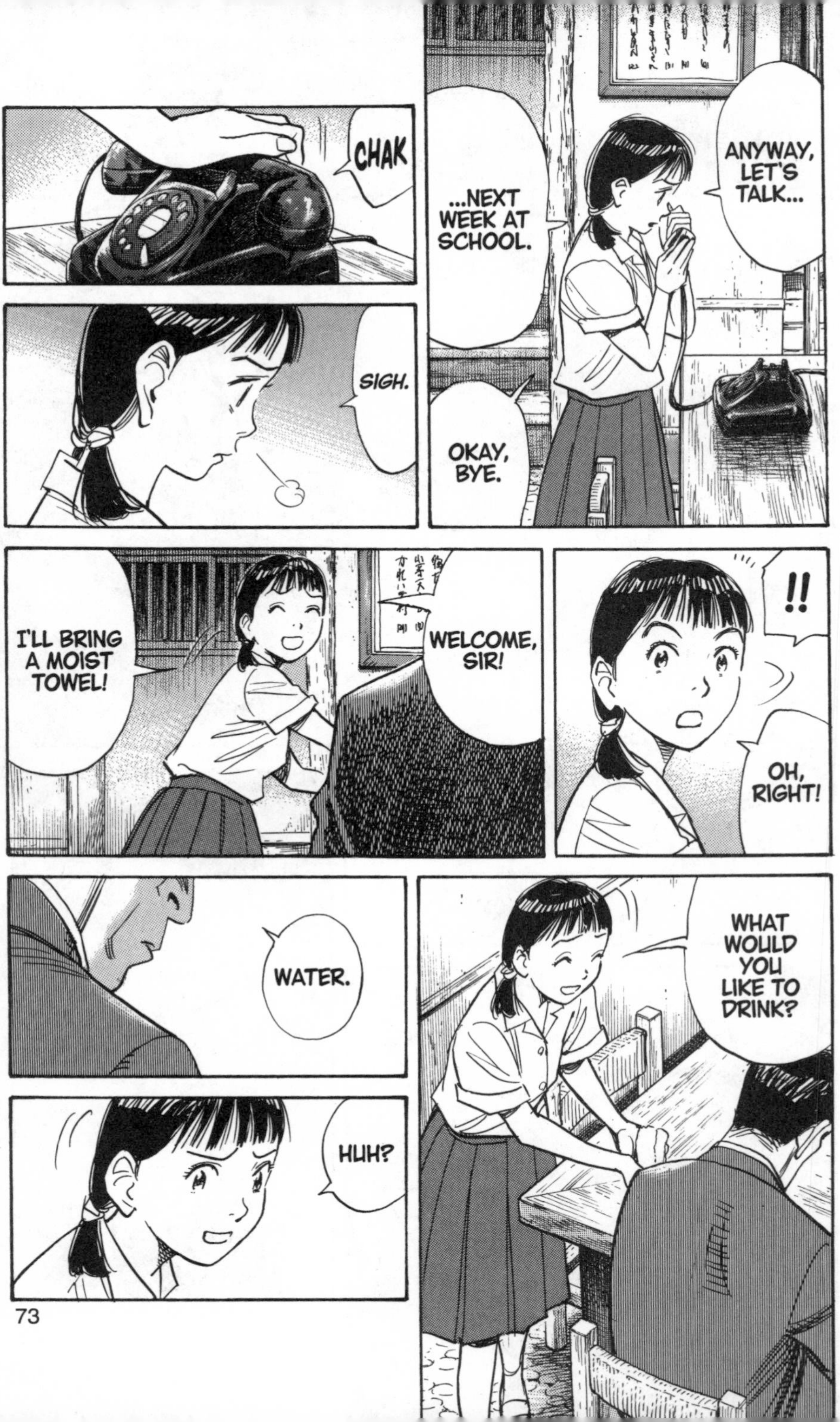
ANYWAY, LET'S TALK...
...NEXT WEEK AT SCHOOL.
OKAY, BYE.
CHAK
SIGH.
!!
OH, RIGHT!
WELCOME, SIR!
I'LL BRING A MOIST TOWEL!
WHAT WOULD YOU LIKE TO DRINK?
WATER.
HUH?

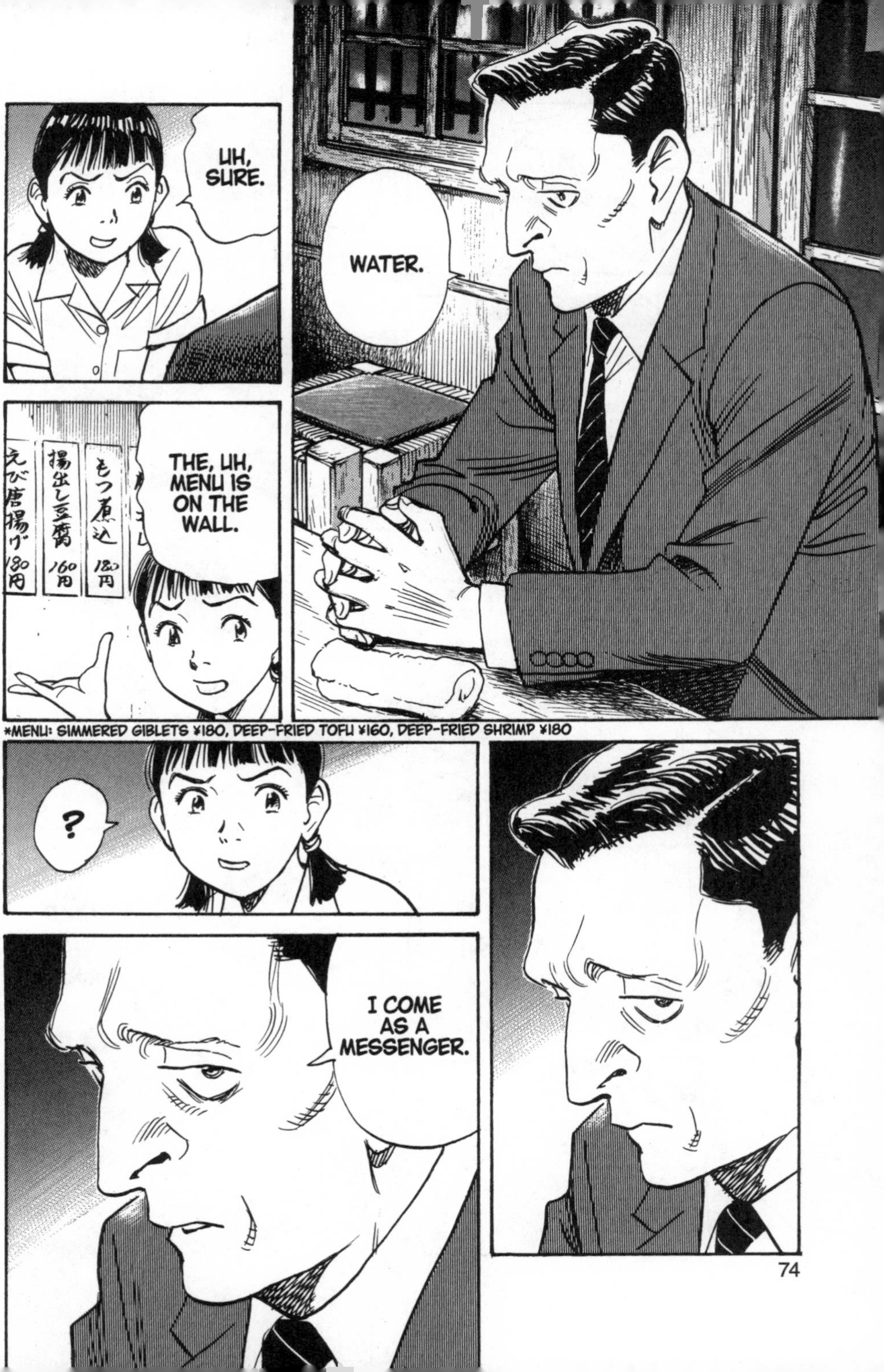
WATER.
UH, SURE.
THE, UH, MENU IS ON THE WALL.
もつ煮込 180円
揚出し豆腐 160円
えび唐揚げ 180円
*MENU: SIMMERED GIBLETS ¥180, DEEP-FRIED TOFU ¥160, DEEP-FRIED SHRIMP ¥180
?
I COME AS A MESSENGER.

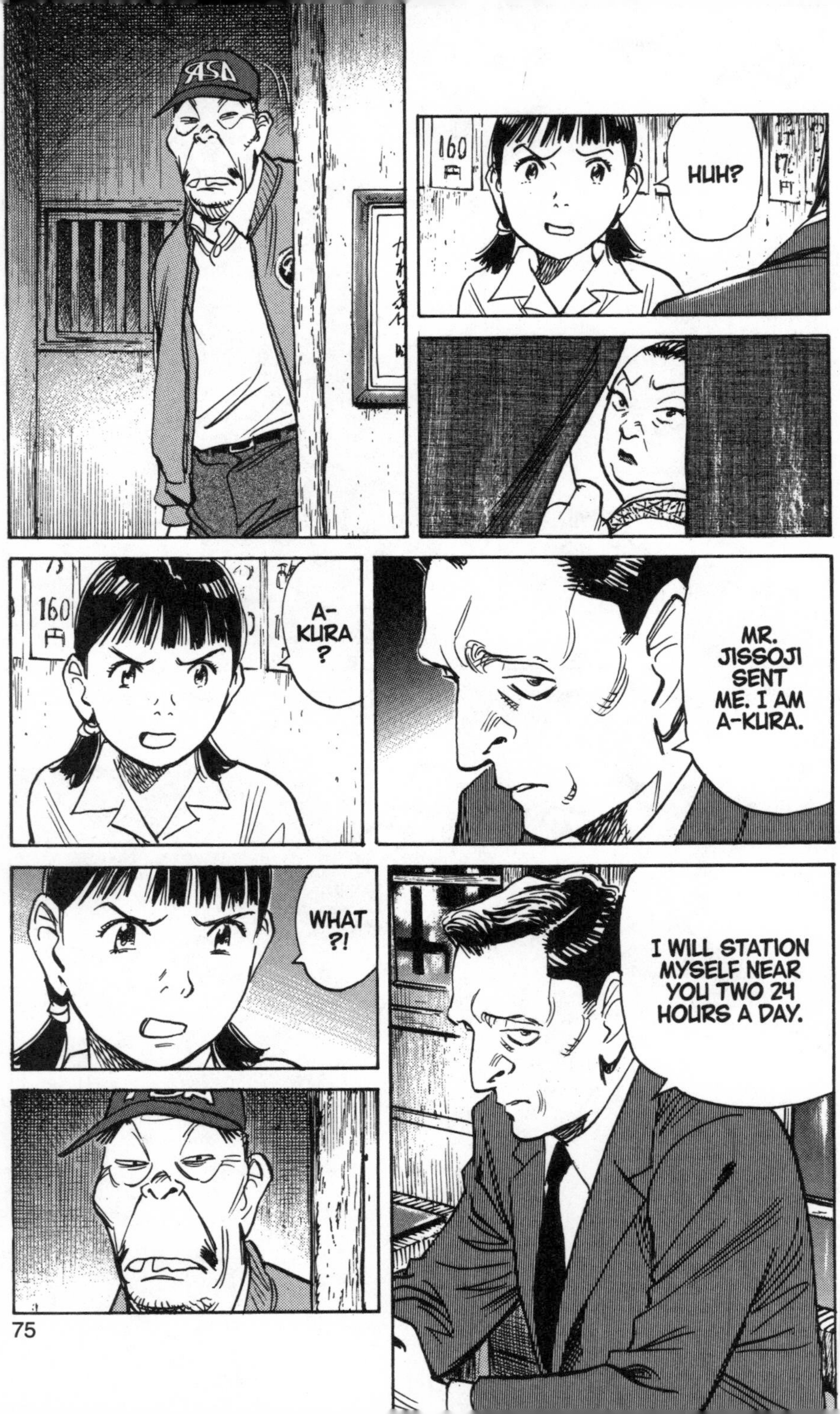
HUH?
MR. JISSOJI SENT ME. I AM A-KURA.
A-KURA?
I WILL STATION MYSELF NEAR YOU TWO 24 HOURS A DAY.
WHAT?!

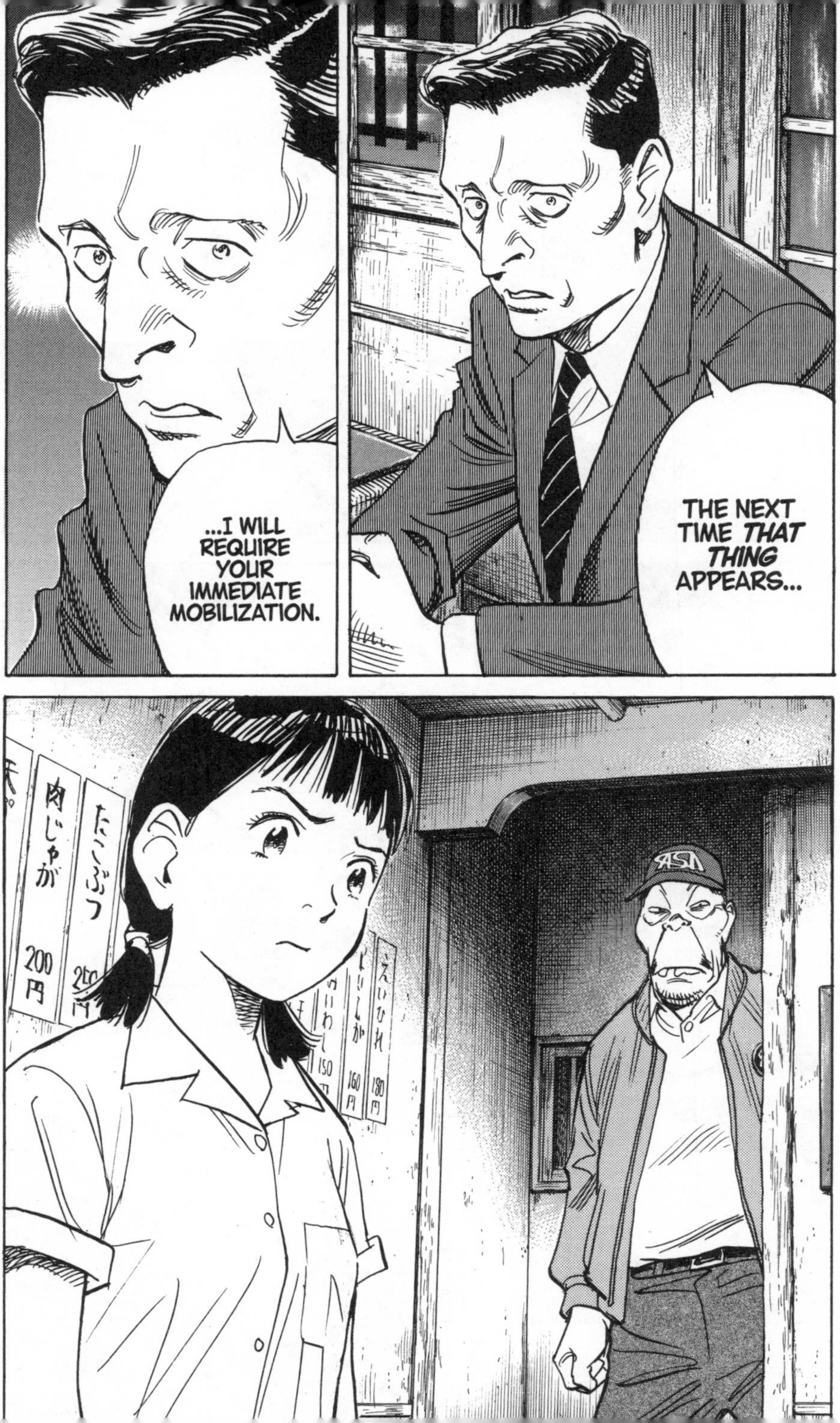
THE NEXT TIME *THAT THING* APPEARS...
...I WILL REQUIRE YOUR IMMEDIATE MOBILIZATION.
たこぶつ
肉じゃが
200円

Chapter 20 ● The Search Begins

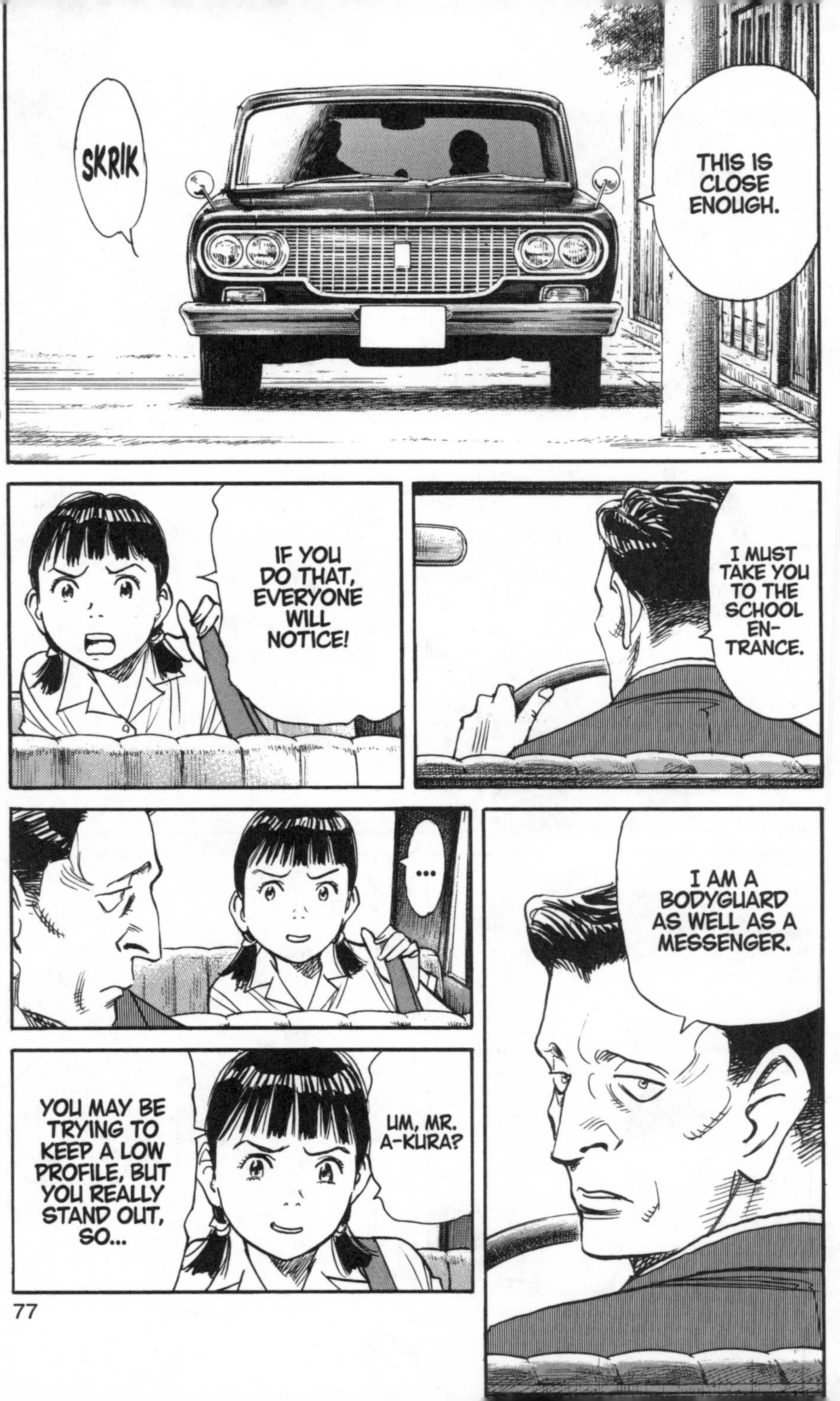
THIS IS CLOSE ENOUGH.
SKRIK
I MUST TAKE YOU TO THE SCHOOL EN-TRANCE.
IF YOU DO THAT, EVERYONE WILL NOTICE!
I AM A BODYGUARD AS WELL AS A MESSENGER.
...
UM, MR. A-KURA?
YOU MAY BE TRYING TO KEEP A LOW PROFILE, BUT YOU REALLY STAND OUT, SO...

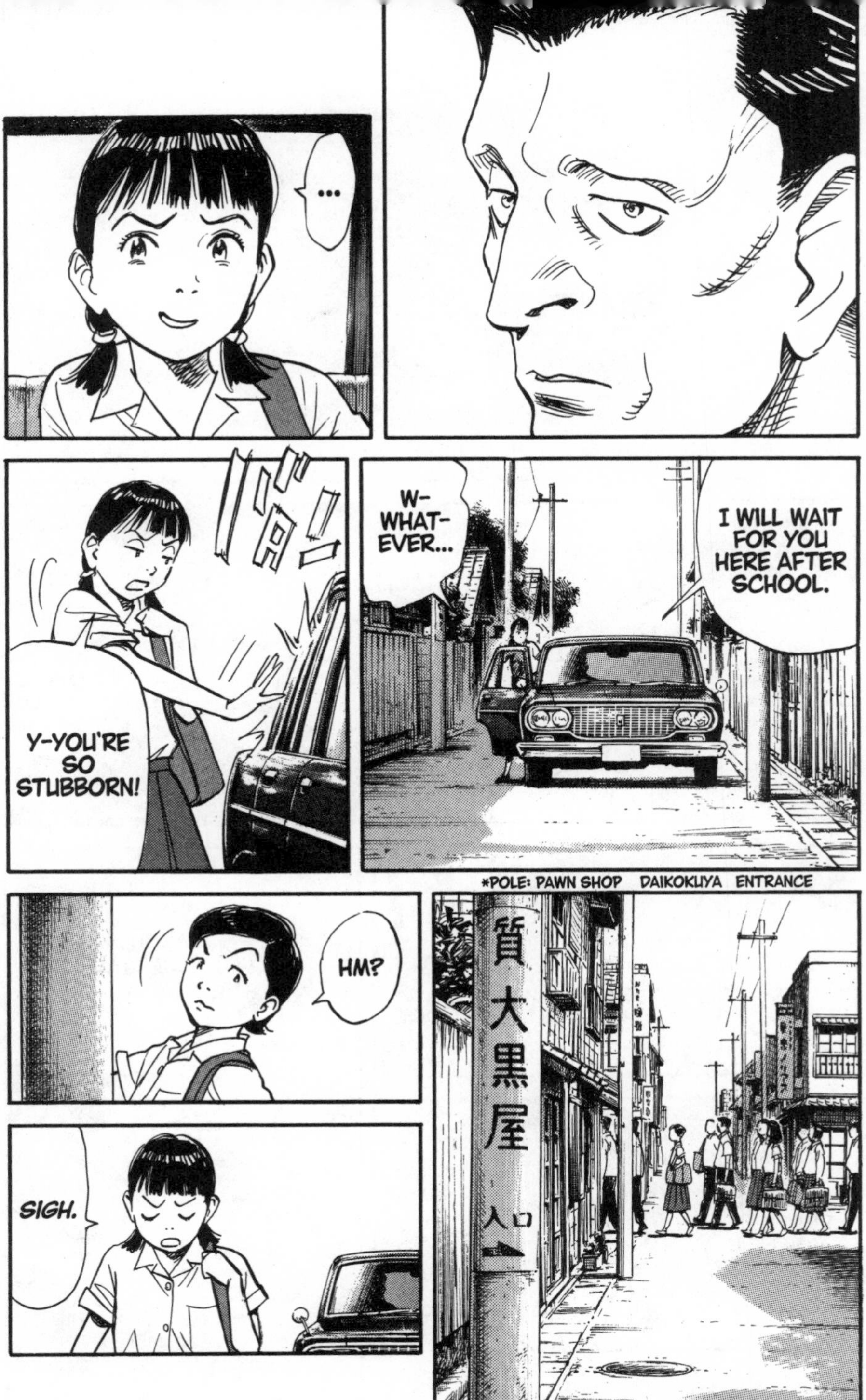
...
I WILL WAIT FOR YOU HERE AFTER SCHOOL.
W-WHATEVER...
Y-YOU'RE SO STUBBORN!
*POLE: PAWN SHOP DAIKOKUYA ENTRANCE
質大黒屋
入口
HM?
SIGH.

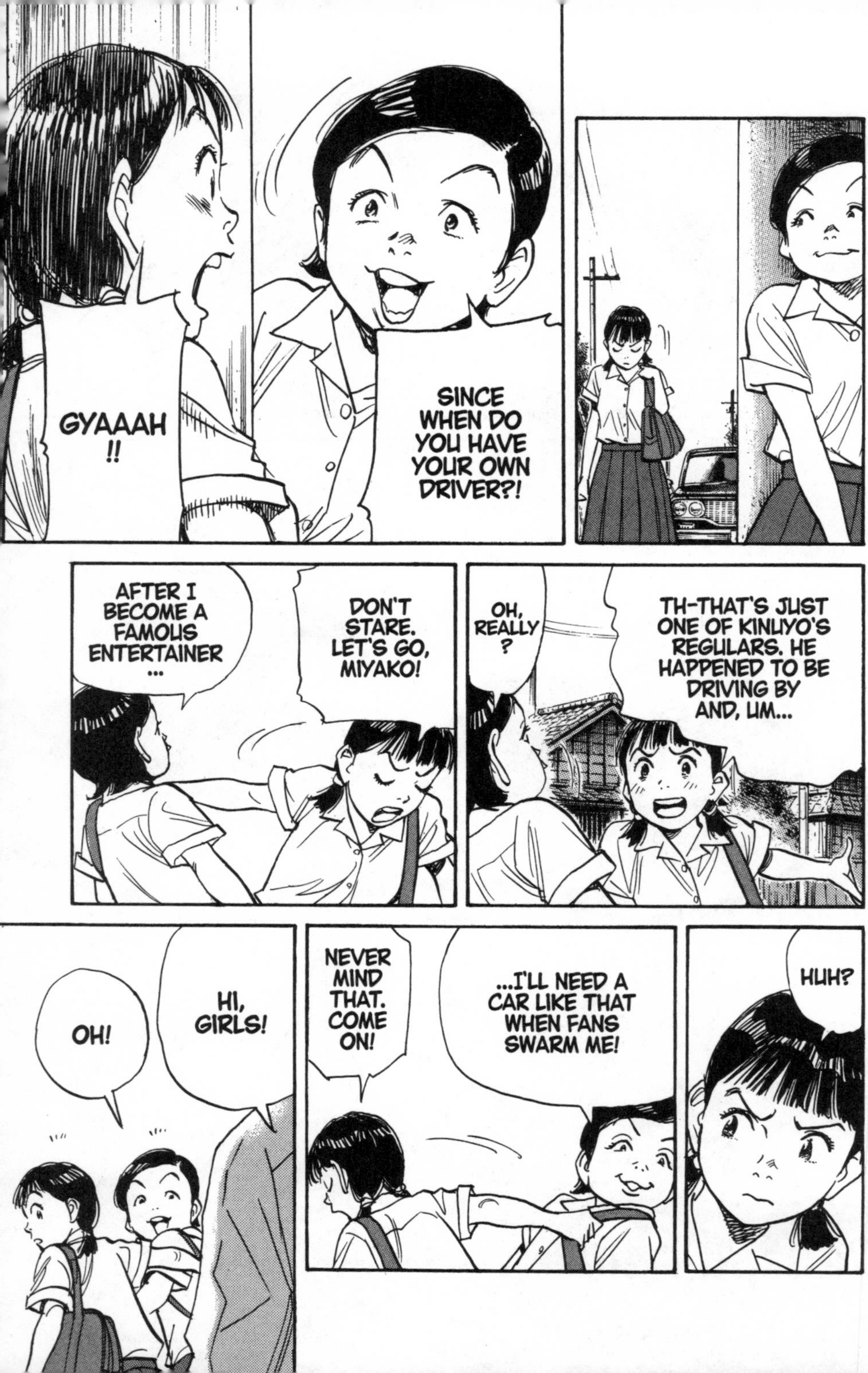
SINCE WHEN DO YOU HAVE YOUR OWN DRIVER?!
GYAAAH!!
TH-THAT'S JUST ONE OF KINUYO'S REGULARS. HE HAPPENED TO BE DRIVING BY AND, UM...
OH, REALLY?
DON'T STARE. LET'S GO, MIYAKO!
AFTER I BECOME A FAMOUS ENTERTAINER...
HUH?
...I'LL NEED A CAR LIKE THAT WHEN FANS SWARM ME!
NEVER MIND THAT. COME ON!
HI, GIRLS!
OH!

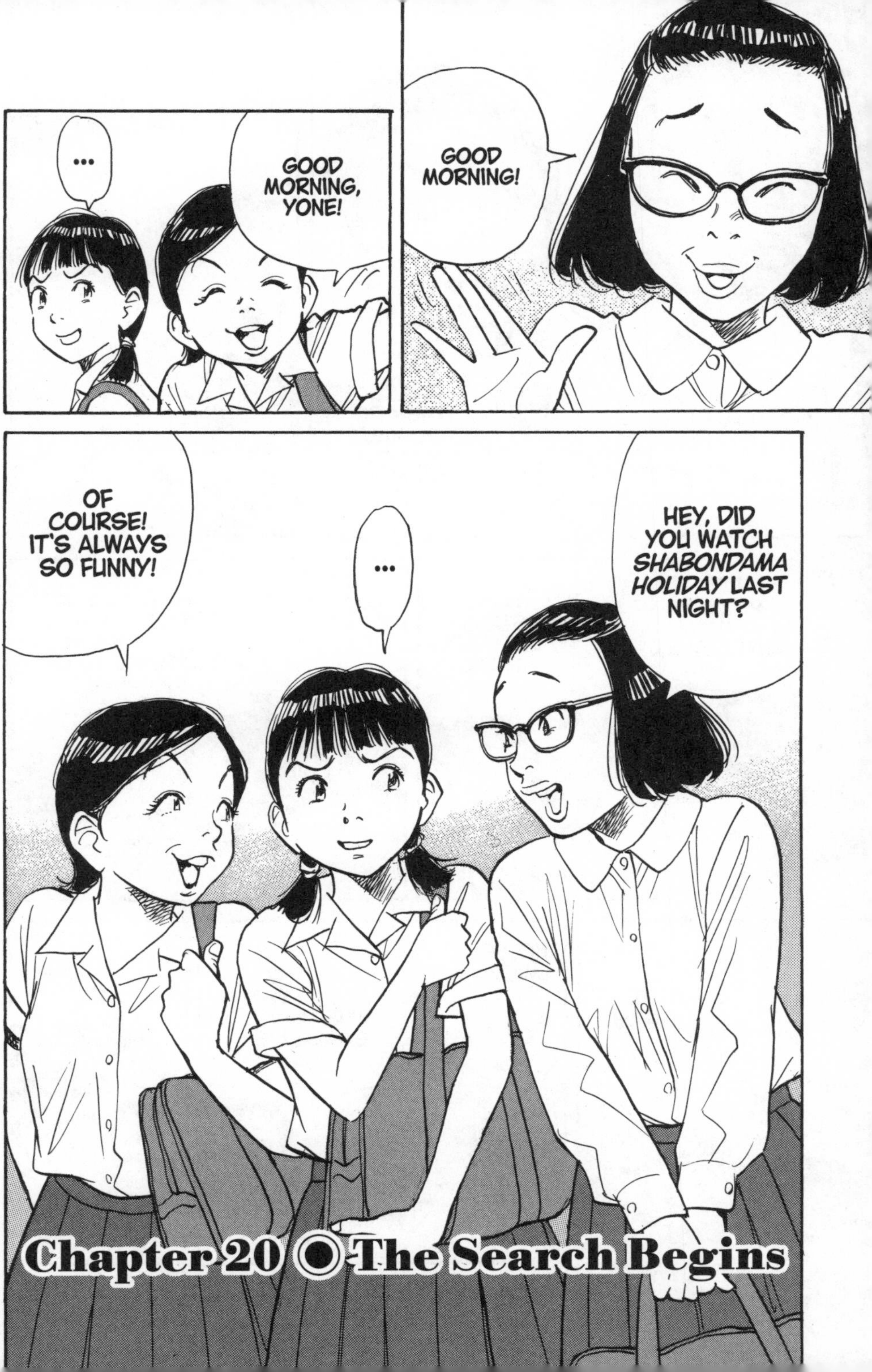
GOOD MORNING!
GOOD MORNING, YONE!
...
HEY, DID YOU WATCH *SHABONDAMA HOLIDAY* LAST NIGHT?
...
OF COURSE! IT'S ALWAYS SO FUNNY!
Chapter 20 ● The Search Begins

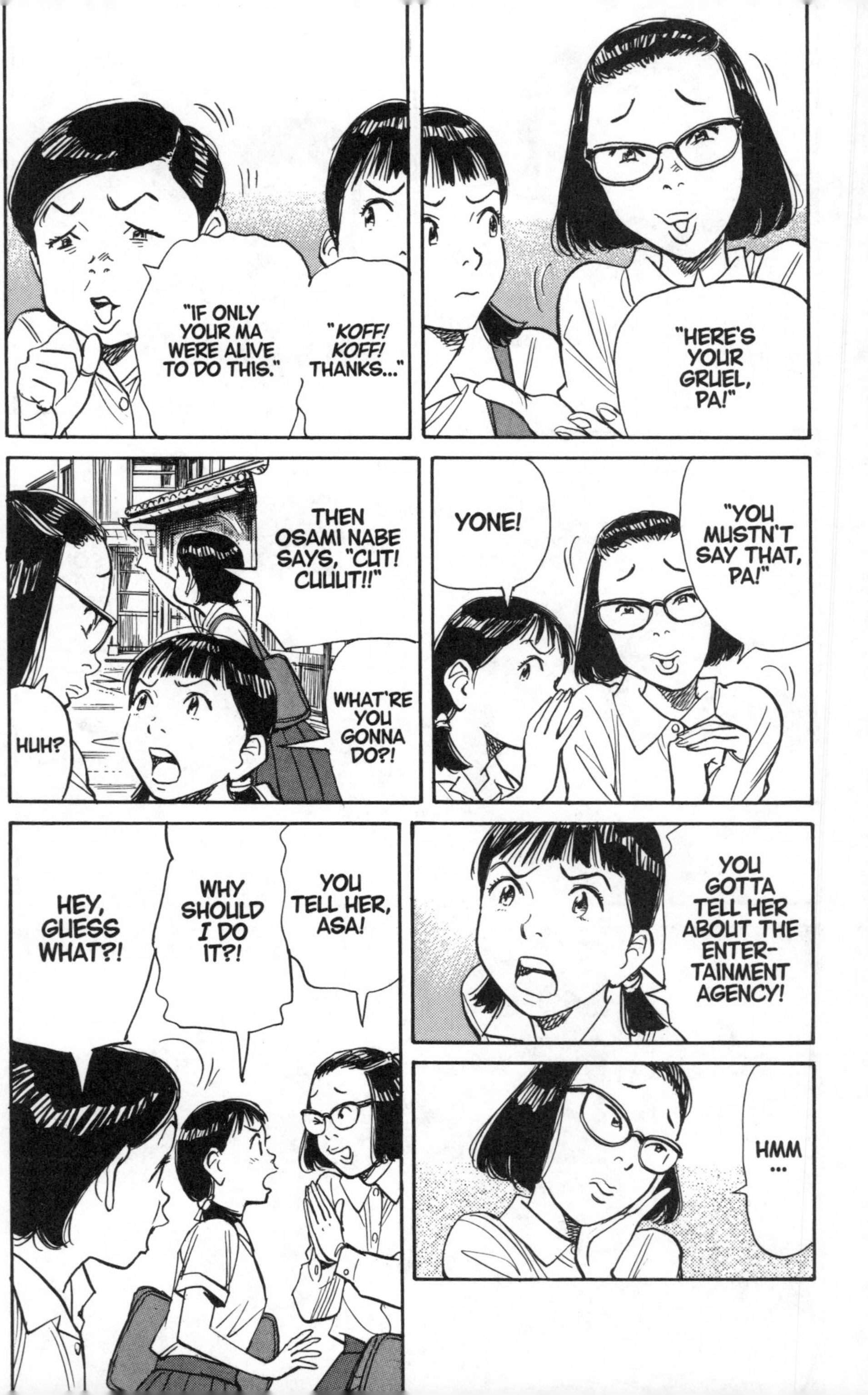
"HERE'S YOUR GRUEL, PA!"
"KOFF! KOFF! THANKS..."
"IF ONLY YOUR MA WERE ALIVE TO DO THIS."
"YOU MUSTN'T SAY THAT, PA!"
YONE!
THEN OSAMI NABE SAYS, "CUT! CUUUT!!"
WHAT'RE YOU GONNA DO?!
HUH?
YOU GOTTA TELL HER ABOUT THE ENTER-TAINMENT AGENCY!
HMM ...
YOU TELL HER, ASA!
WHY SHOULD I DO IT?!
HEY, GUESS WHAT?!

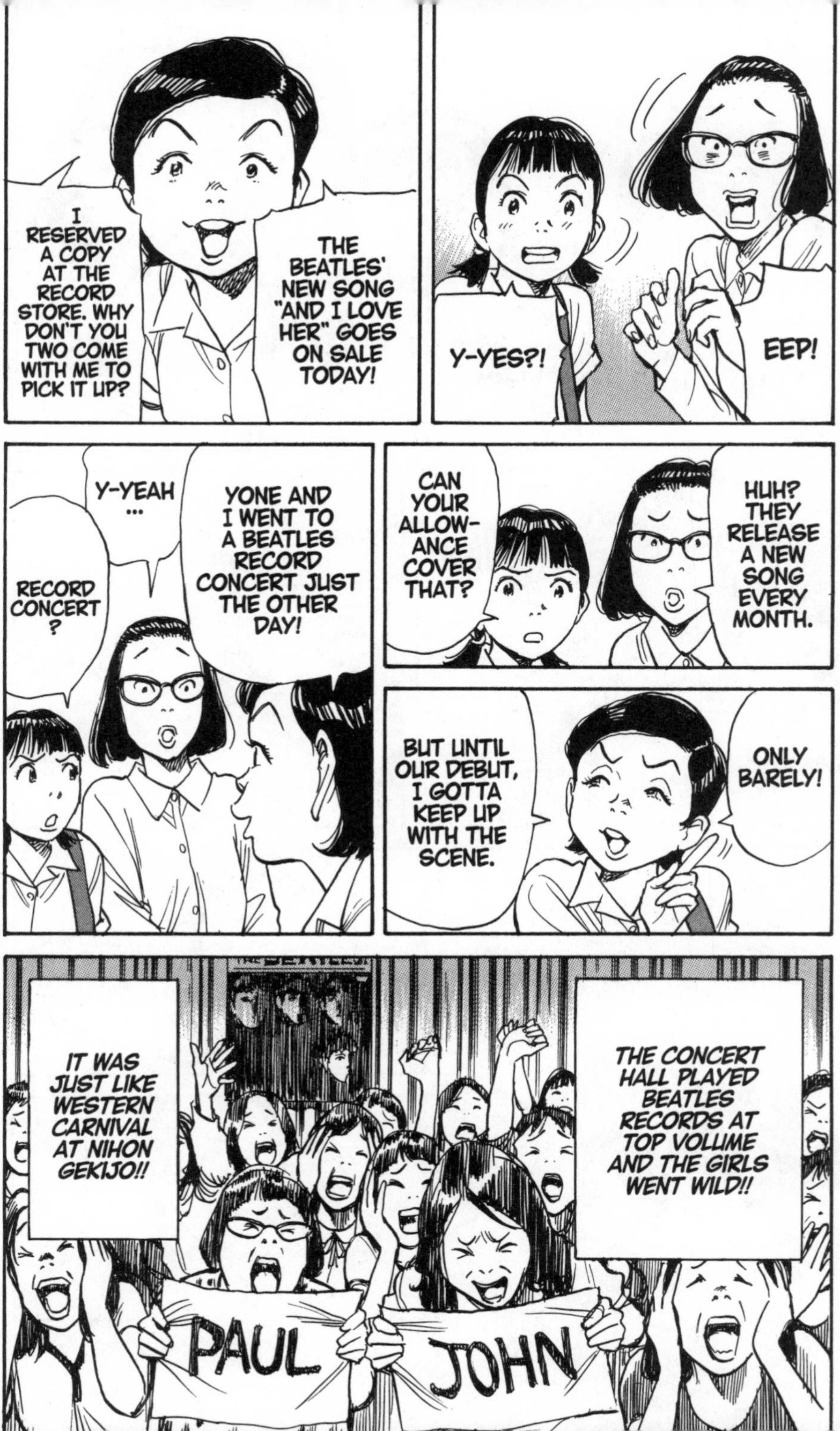
EEP!
Y-YES?!
THE BEATLES' NEW SONG "AND I LOVE HER" GOES ON SALE TODAY!
I RESERVED A COPY AT THE RECORD STORE. WHY DON'T YOU TWO COME WITH ME TO PICK IT UP?
HUH? THEY RELEASE A NEW SONG EVERY MONTH.
CAN YOUR ALLOWANCE COVER THAT?
ONLY BARELY!
BUT UNTIL OUR DEBUT, I GOTTA KEEP UP WITH THE SCENE.
YONE AND I WENT TO A BEATLES RECORD CONCERT JUST THE OTHER DAY!
Y-YEAH ...
RECORD CONCERT ?
THE CONCERT HALL PLAYED BEATLES RECORDS AT TOP VOLUME AND THE GIRLS WENT WILD!!
IT WAS JUST LIKE WESTERN CARNIVAL AT NIHON GEKIJO!!
JOHN
PAUL

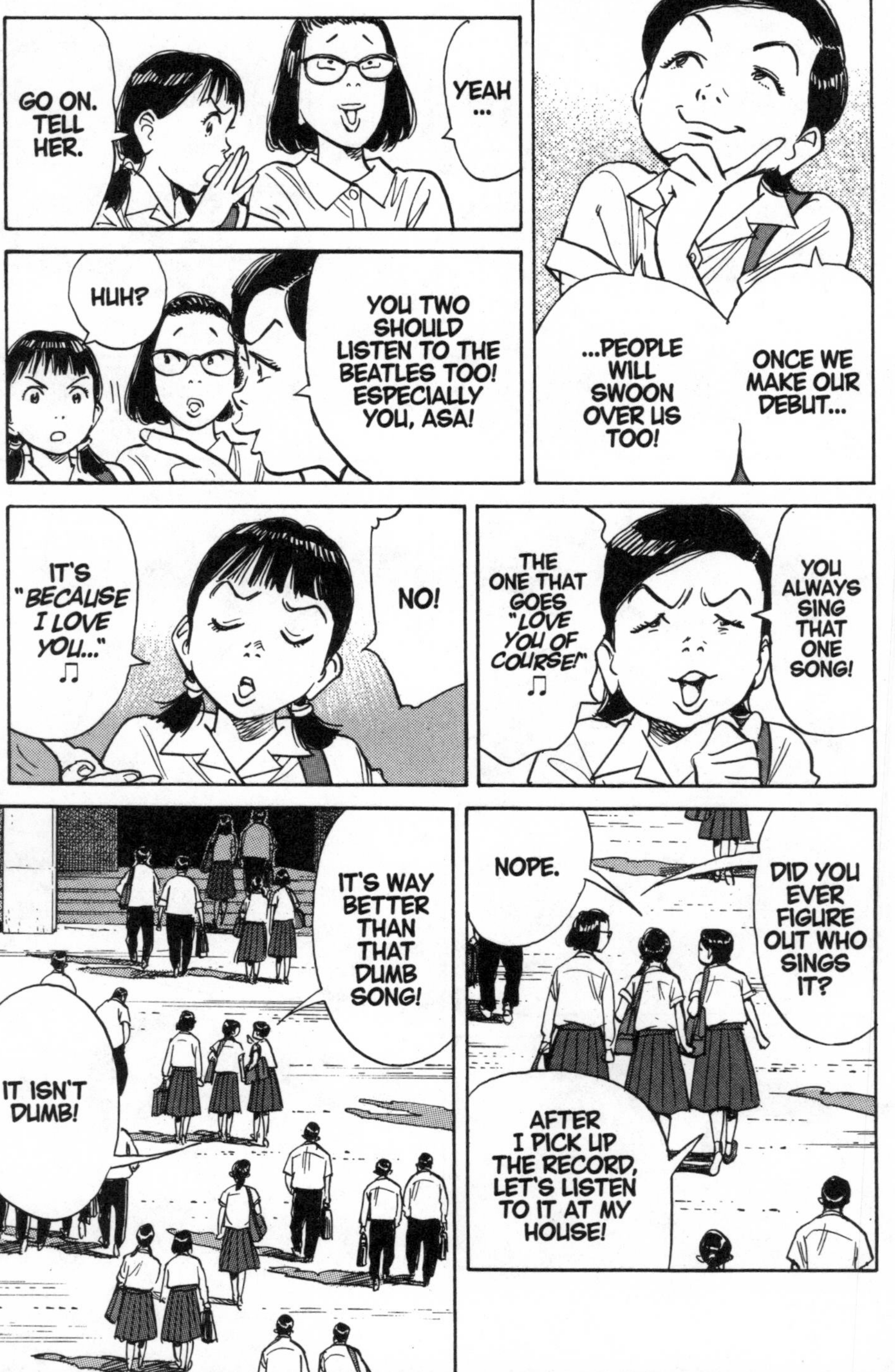
ONCE WE MAKE OUR DEBUT...
...PEOPLE WILL SWOON OVER US TOO!
YEAH ...
GO ON. TELL HER.
YOU TWO SHOULD LISTEN TO THE BEATLES TOO! ESPECIALLY YOU, ASA!
HUH?
YOU ALWAYS SING THAT ONE SONG!
THE ONE THAT GOES "*LOVE YOU OF COURSE!*" ♫
NO!
IT'S "*BECAUSE I LOVE YOU...*" ♫
DID YOU EVER FIGURE OUT WHO SINGS IT?
NOPE.
AFTER I PICK UP THE RECORD, LET'S LISTEN TO IT AT MY HOUSE!
IT'S WAY BETTER THAN THAT DUMB SONG!
IT ISN'T DUMB!

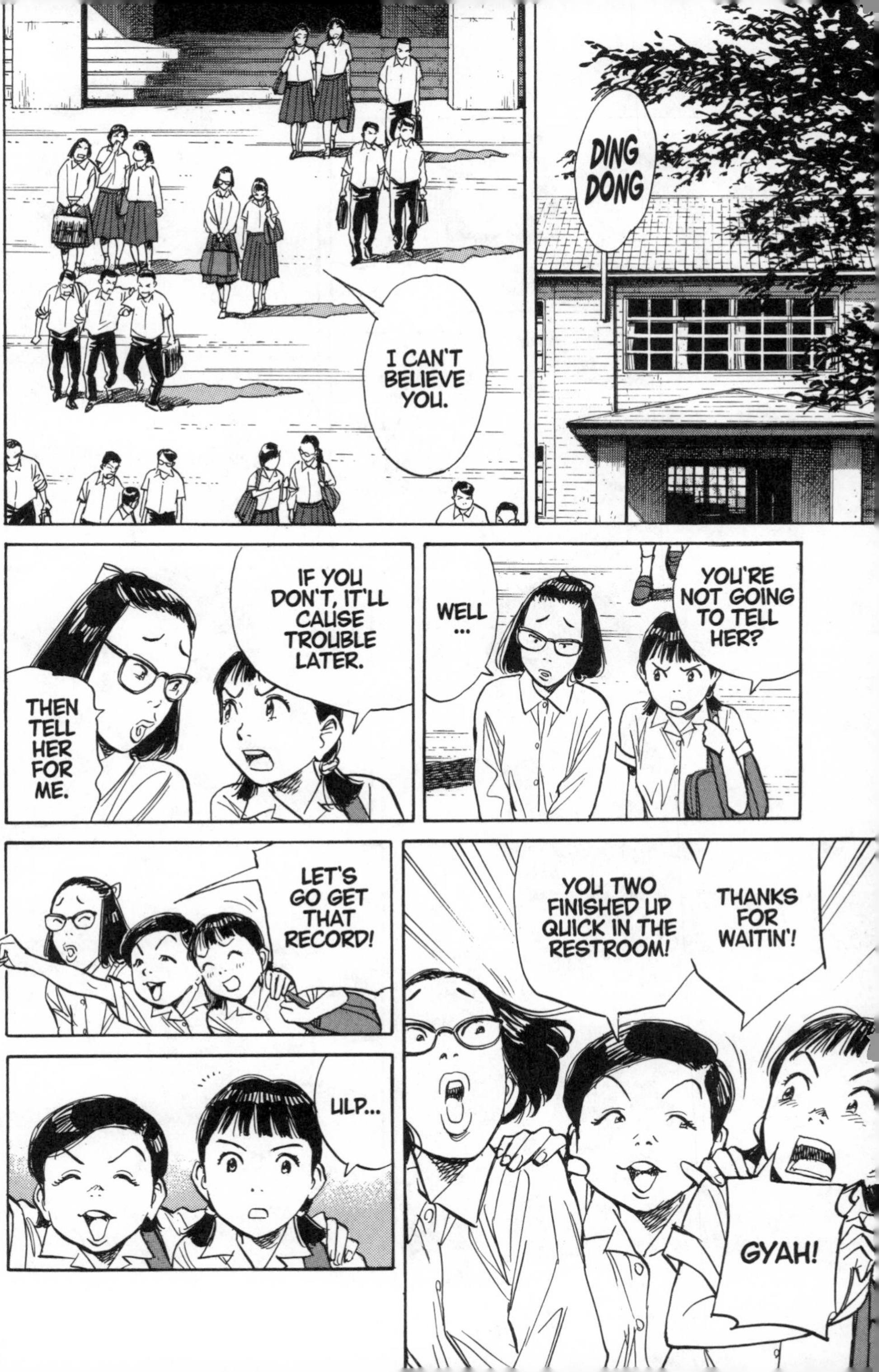
DING DONG
I CAN'T BELIEVE YOU.
YOU'RE NOT GOING TO TELL HER?
WELL ...
IF YOU DON'T, IT'LL CAUSE TROUBLE LATER.
THEN TELL HER FOR ME.
THANKS FOR WAITIN'!
YOU TWO FINISHED UP QUICK IN THE RESTROOM!
GYAH!
LET'S GO GET THAT RECORD!
ULP...

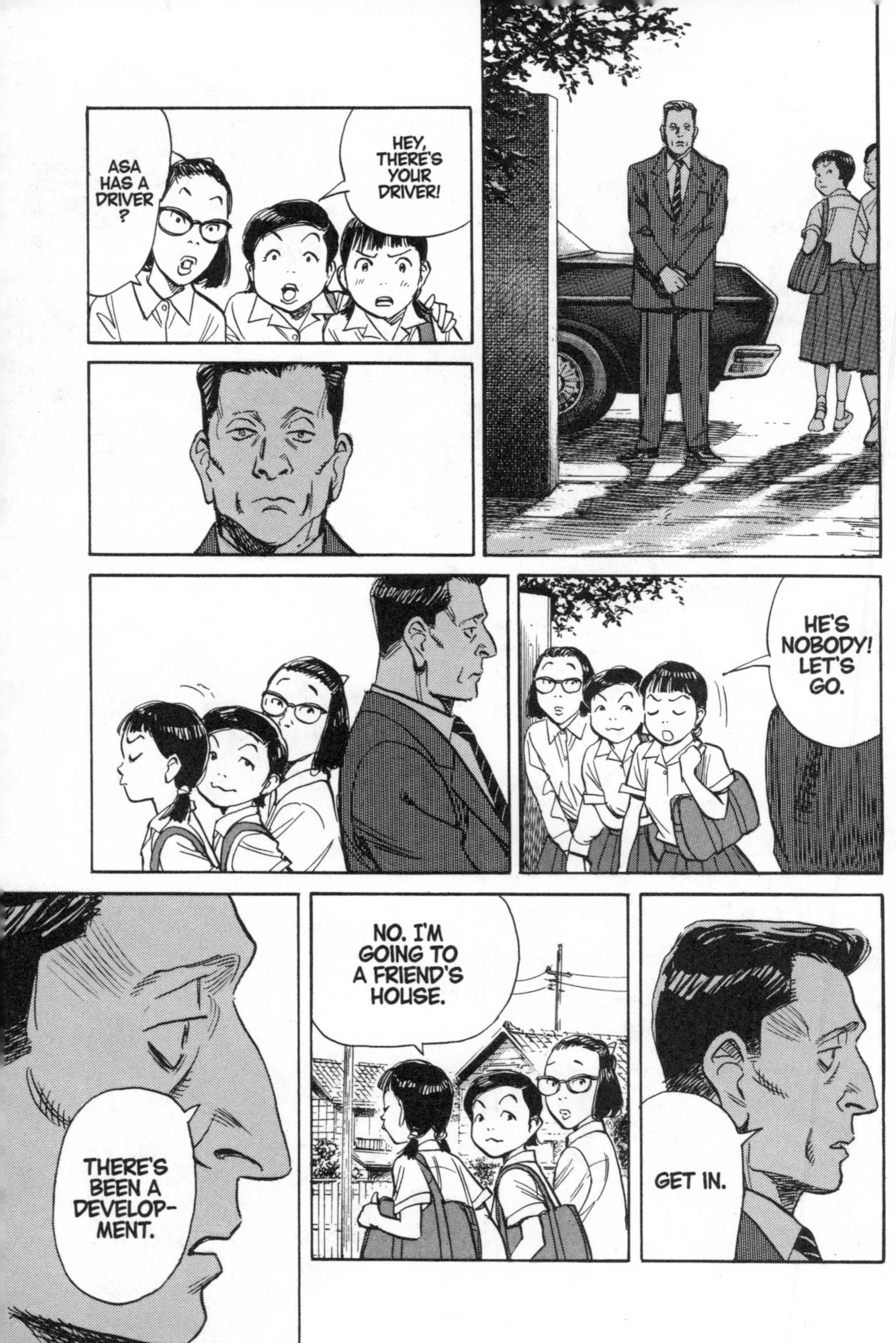
HEY, THERE'S YOUR DRIVER!
ASA HAS A DRIVER?
HE'S NOBODY! LET'S GO.
GET IN.
NO. I'M GOING TO A FRIEND'S HOUSE.
THERE'S BEEN A DEVELOPMENT.

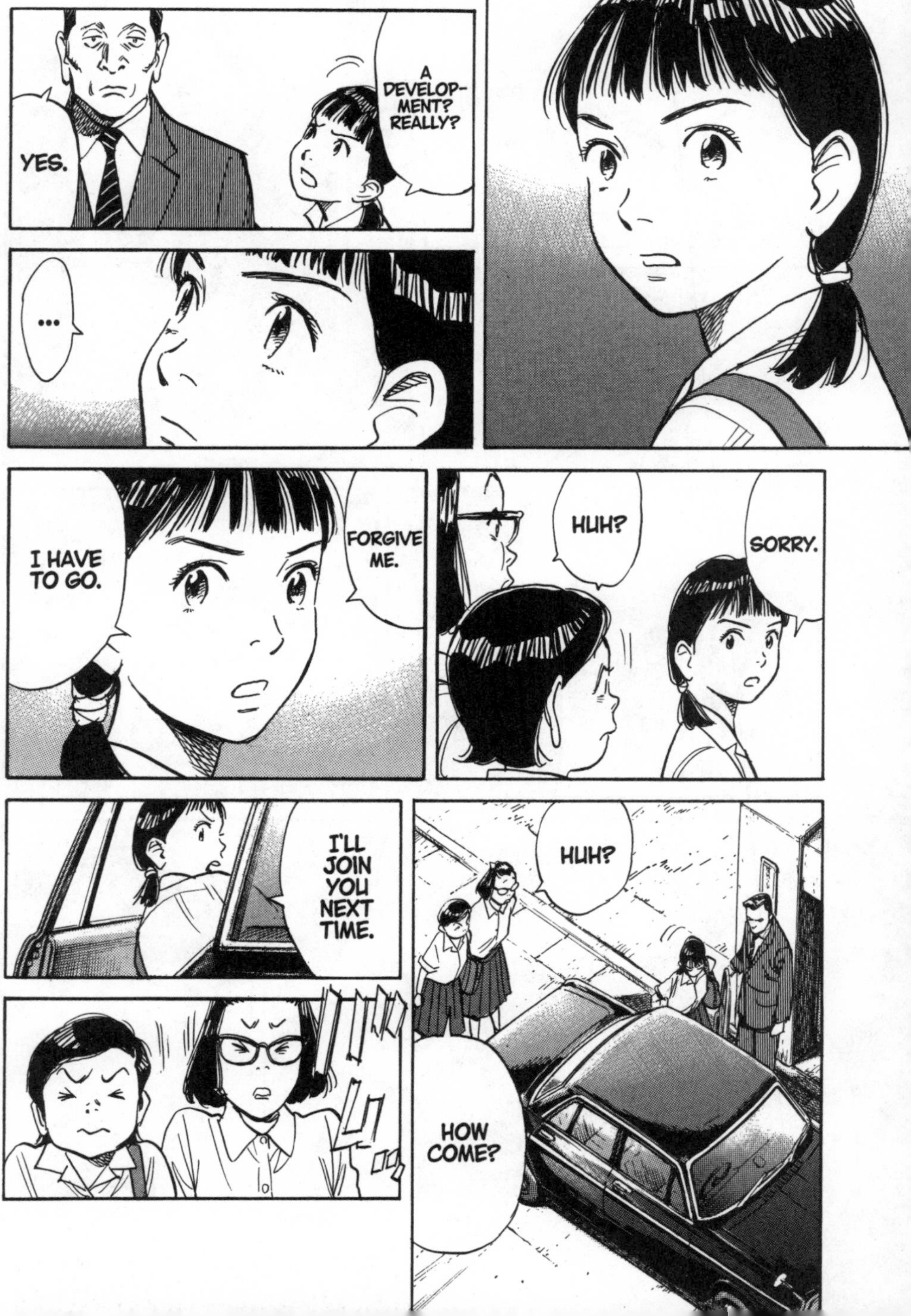
A DEVELOPMENT? REALLY?
YES.
...
SORRY.
HUH?
FORGIVE ME.
I HAVE TO GO.
HUH?
HOW COME?
I'LL JOIN YOU NEXT TIME.

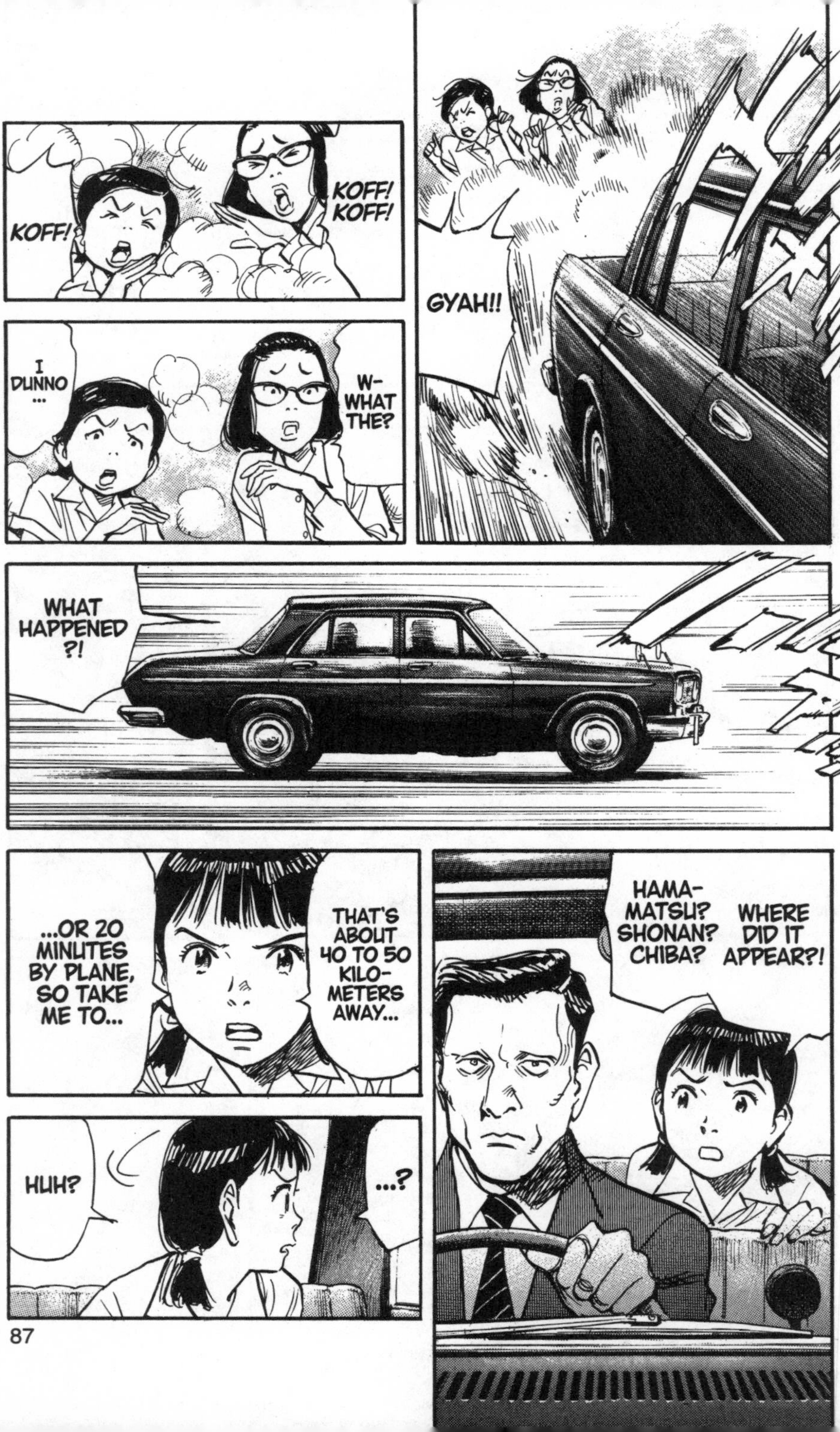
GYAH!!
KOFF! KOFF!
KOFF!
W-WHAT THE?
I DUNNO...
WHAT HAPPENED?!
WHERE DID IT APPEAR?!
HAMA-MATSU? SHONAN? CHIBA?
THAT'S ABOUT 40 TO 50 KILO-METERS AWAY...
...OR 20 MINUTES BY PLANE, SO TAKE ME TO...
...?
HUH?

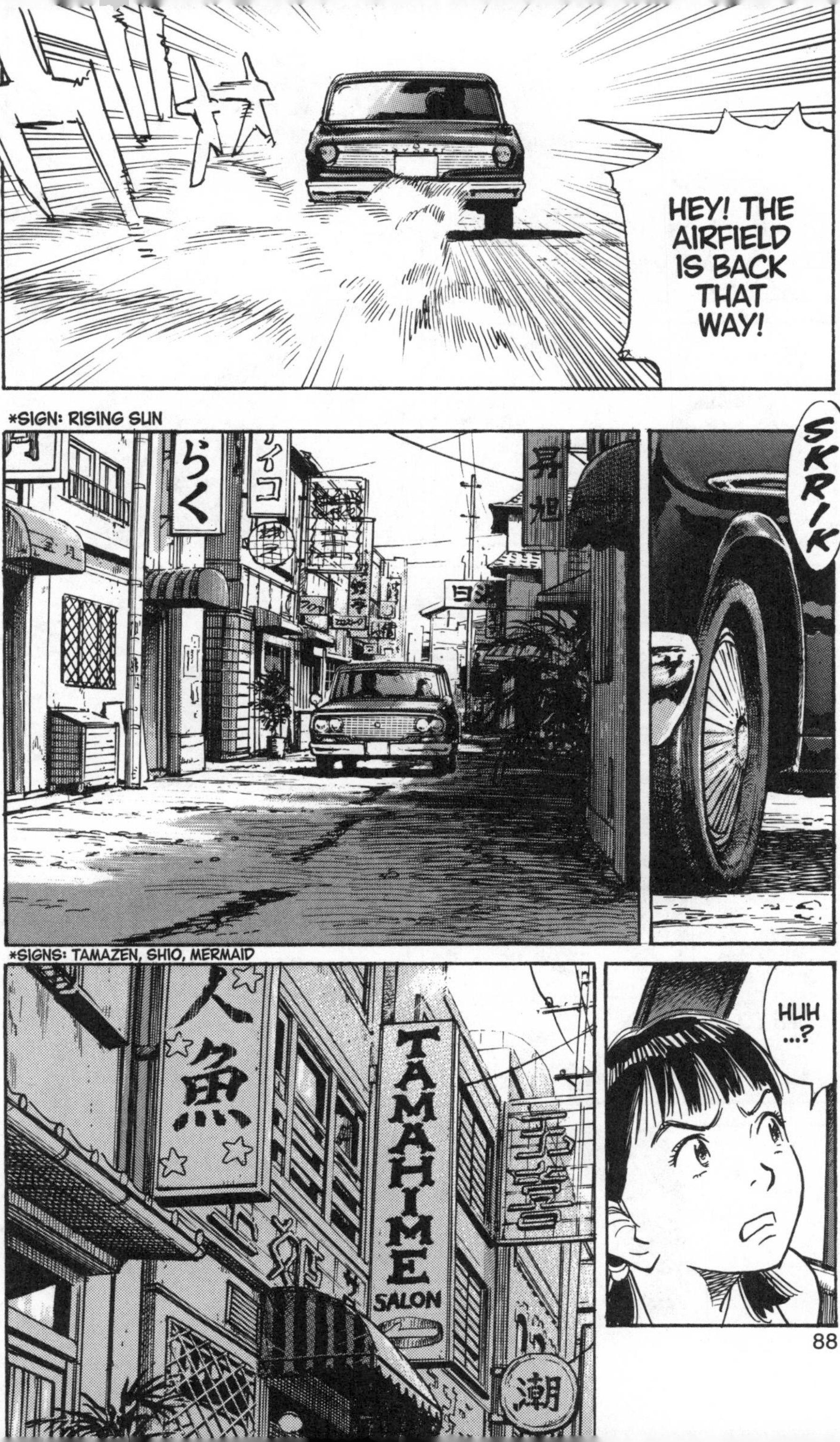
HEY! THE AIRFIELD IS BACK THAT WAY!
SKRIK
*SIGN: RISING SUN
HUH ...?
*SIGNS: TAMAZEN, SHIO, MERMAID
TAMAHIME SALON

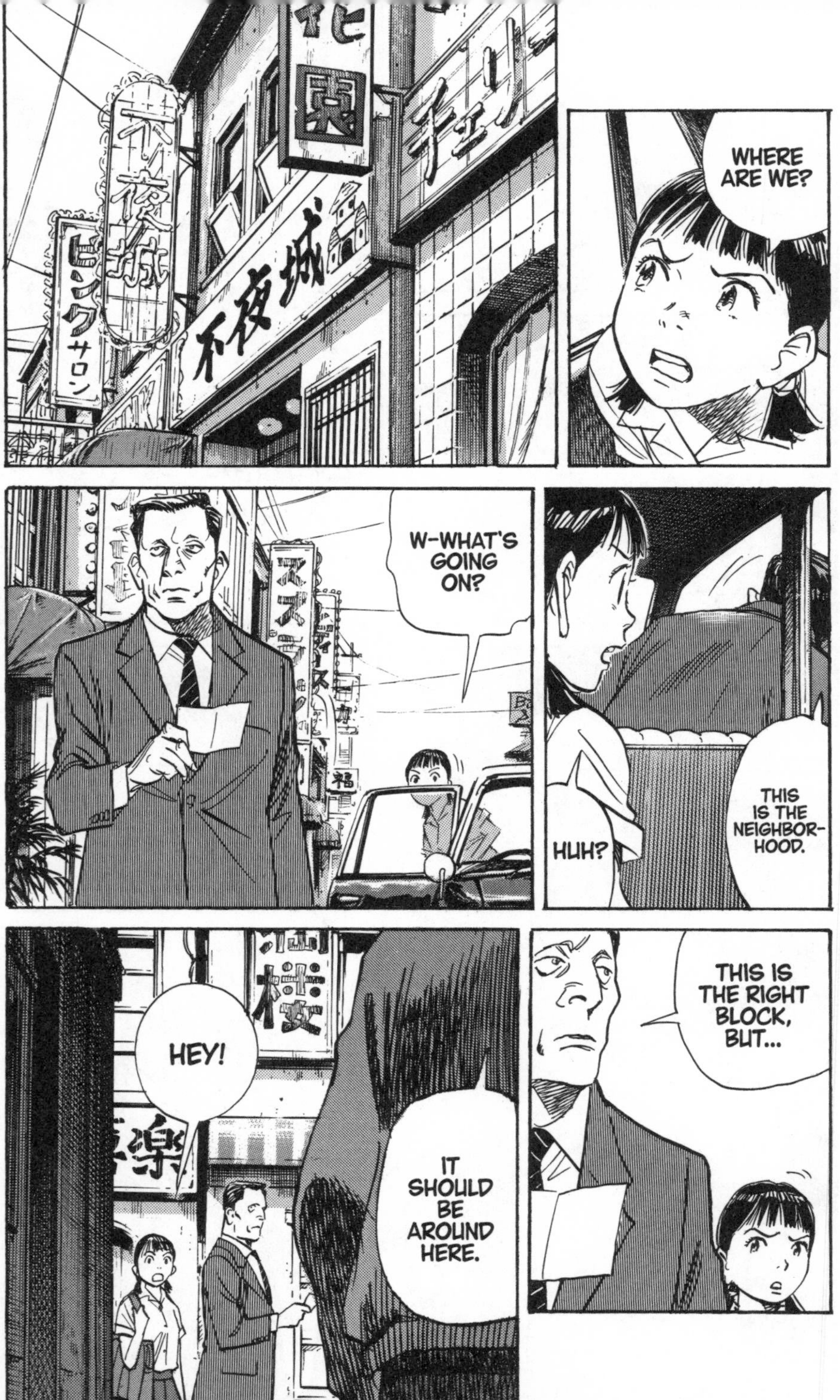
WHERE ARE WE?
チェリー
不夜城
ピンクサロン
THIS IS THE NEIGHBOR-HOOD.
HUH?
W-WHAT'S GOING ON?
THIS IS THE RIGHT BLOCK, BUT...
IT SHOULD BE AROUND HERE.
HEY!

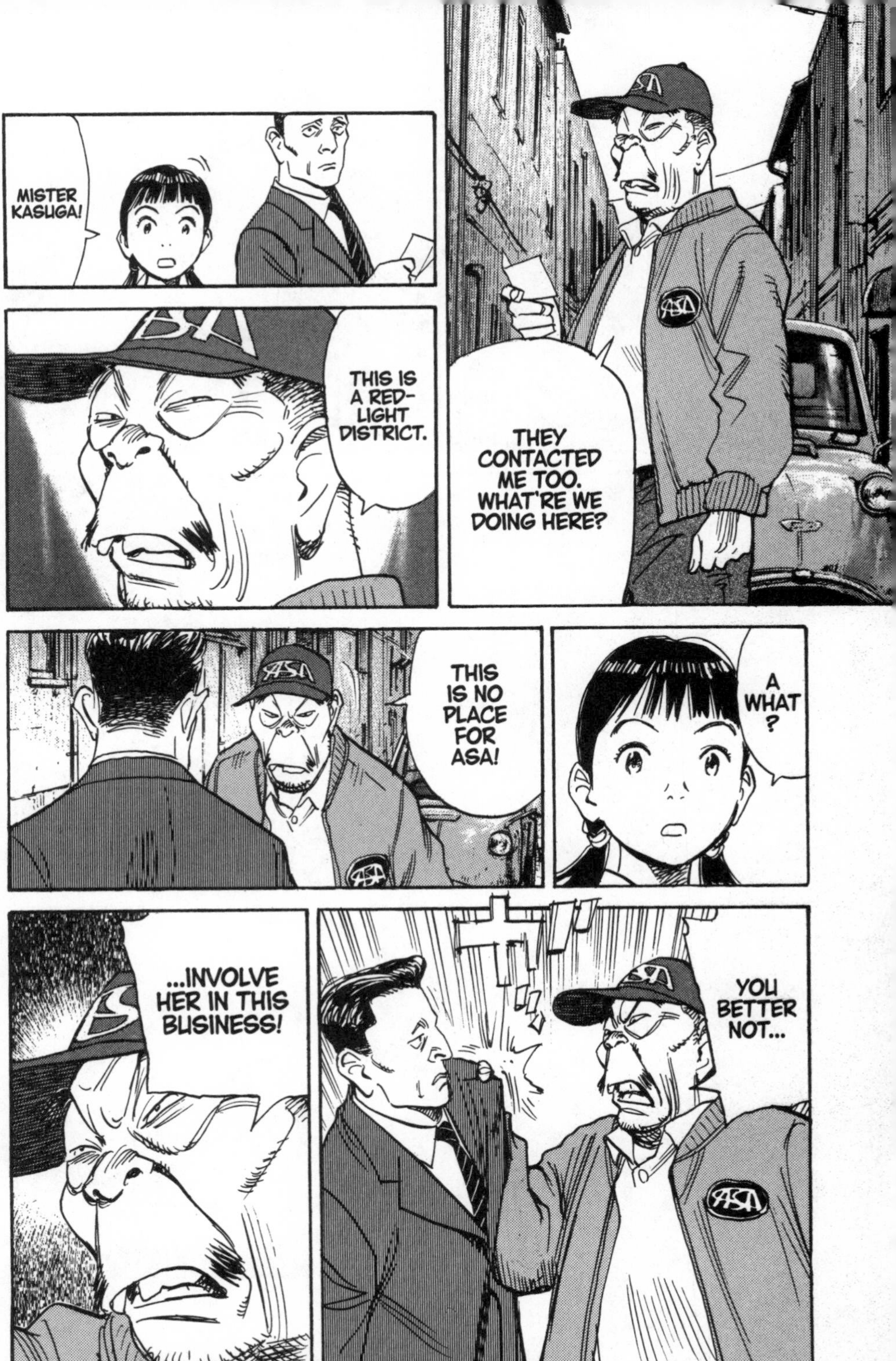
THEY CONTACTED ME TOO. WHAT'RE WE DOING HERE?
MISTER KASUGA!
THIS IS A RED-LIGHT DISTRICT.
A WHAT?
THIS IS NO PLACE FOR ASA!
YOU BETTER NOT...
...INVOLVE HER IN THIS BUSINESS!

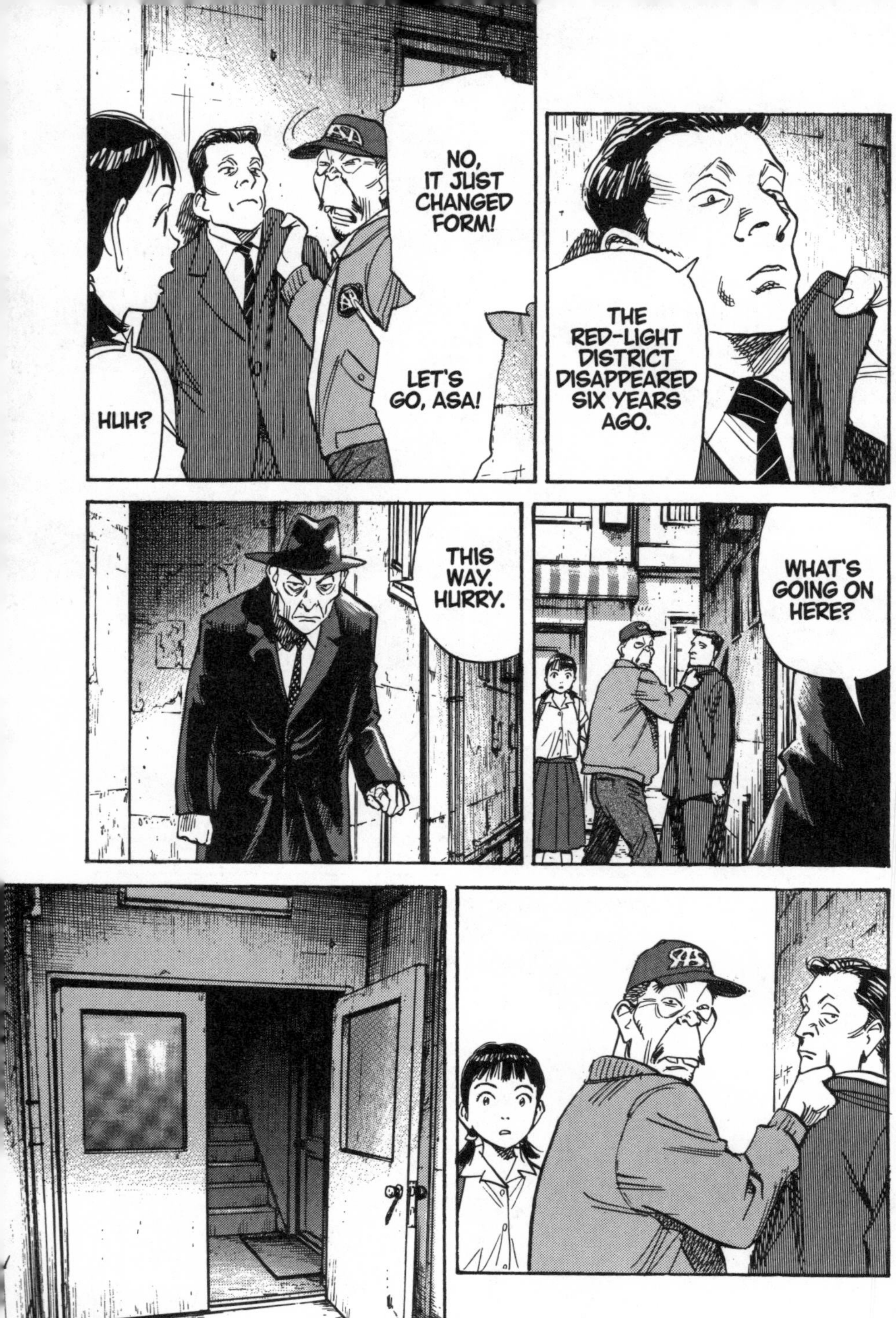
THE RED-LIGHT DISTRICT DISAPPEARED SIX YEARS AGO.
NO, IT JUST CHANGED FORM!
LET'S GO, ASA!
HUH?
WHAT'S GOING ON HERE?
THIS WAY. HURRY.

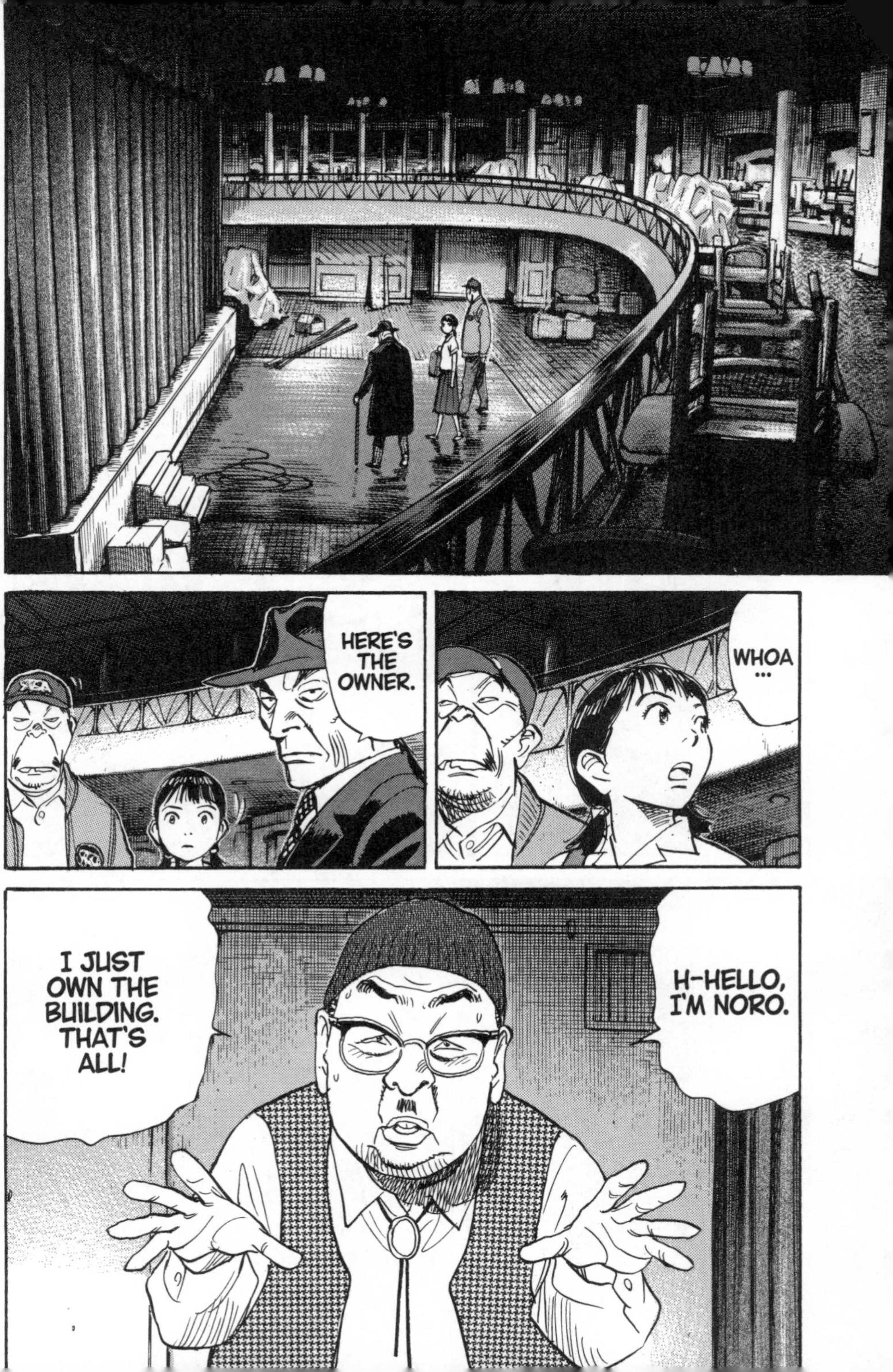
WHOA ...
HERE'S THE OWNER.
H-HELLO, I'M NORO.
I JUST OWN THE BUILDING. THAT'S ALL!

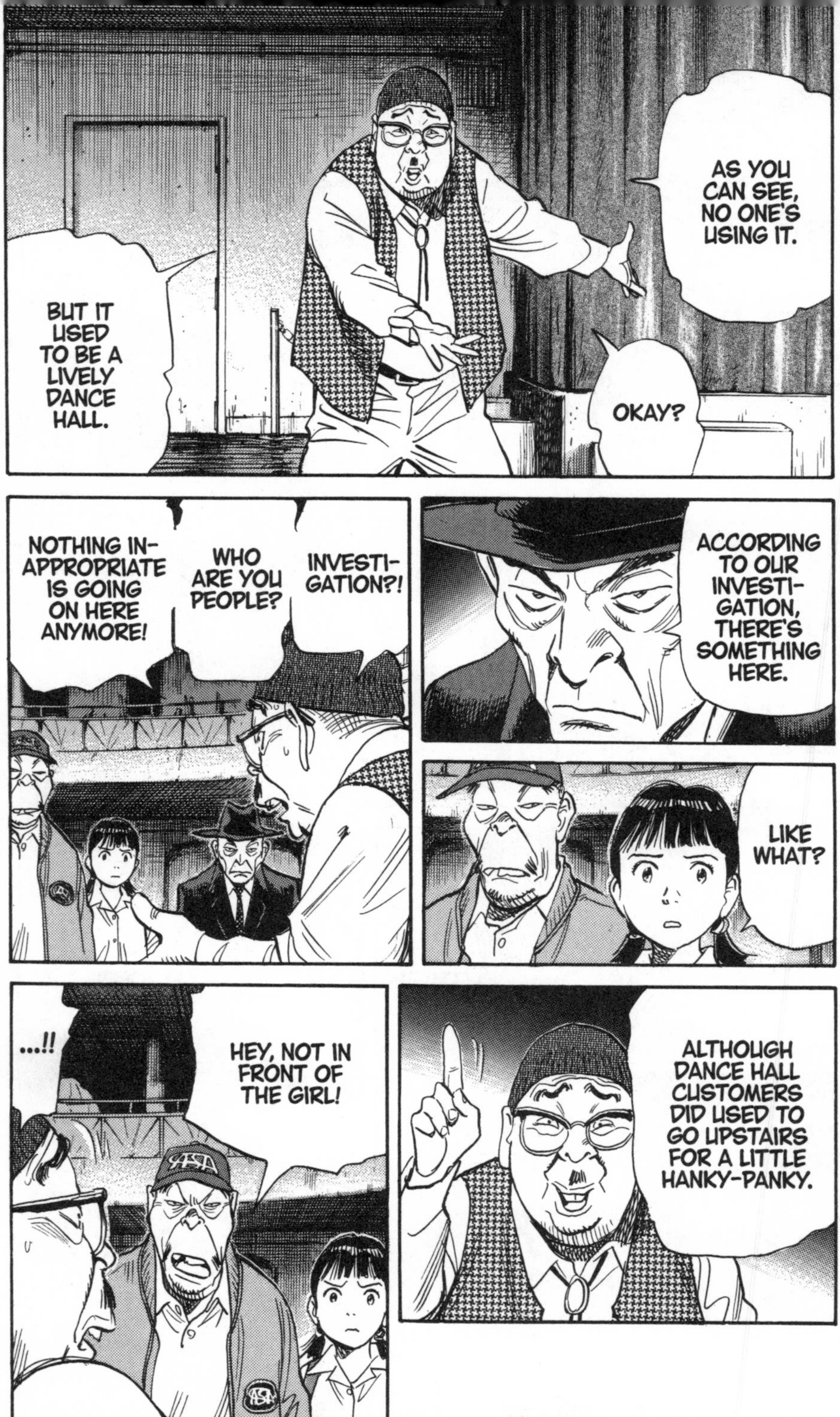
AS YOU CAN SEE, NO ONE'S USING IT.
OKAY?
BUT IT USED TO BE A LIVELY DANCE HALL.
ACCORDING TO OUR INVESTIGATION, THERE'S SOMETHING HERE.
LIKE WHAT?
INVESTIGATION?!
WHO ARE YOU PEOPLE?
NOTHING INAPPROPRIATE IS GOING ON HERE ANYMORE!
ALTHOUGH DANCE HALL CUSTOMERS DID USED TO GO UPSTAIRS FOR A LITTLE HANKY-PANKY.
HEY, NOT IN FRONT OF THE GIRL!
...!!

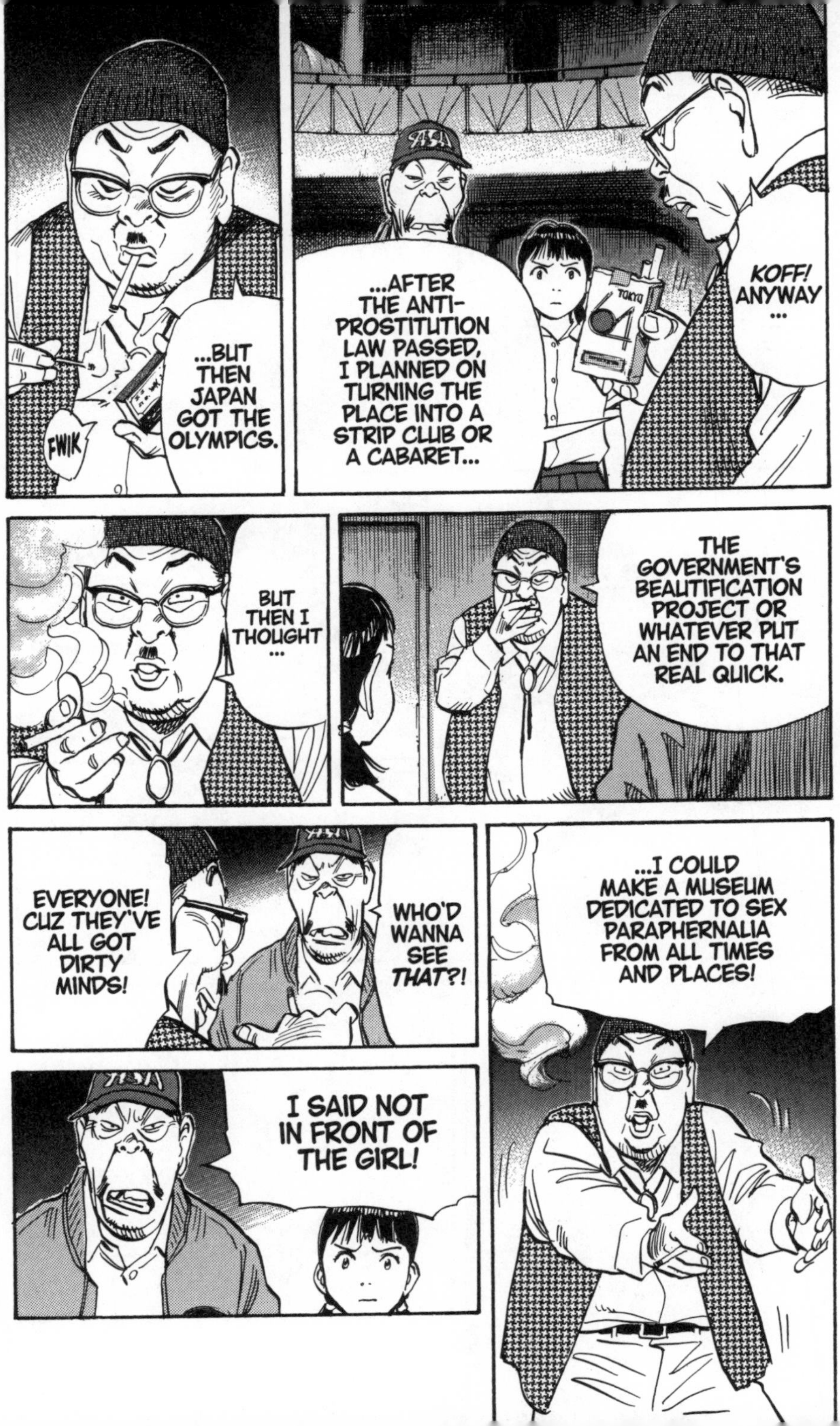
KOFF! ANYWAY ...
...AFTER THE ANTI-PROSTITUTION LAW PASSED, I PLANNED ON TURNING THE PLACE INTO A STRIP CLUB OR A CABARET...
...BUT THEN JAPAN GOT THE OLYMPICS.
FWIK
THE GOVERNMENT'S BEAUTIFICATION PROJECT OR WHATEVER PUT AN END TO THAT REAL QUICK.
BUT THEN I THOUGHT ...
...I COULD MAKE A MUSEUM DEDICATED TO SEX PARAPHERNALIA FROM ALL TIMES AND PLACES!
WHO'D WANNA SEE *THAT*?!
EVERYONE! CUZ THEY'VE ALL GOT DIRTY MINDS!
I SAID NOT IN FRONT OF THE GIRL!

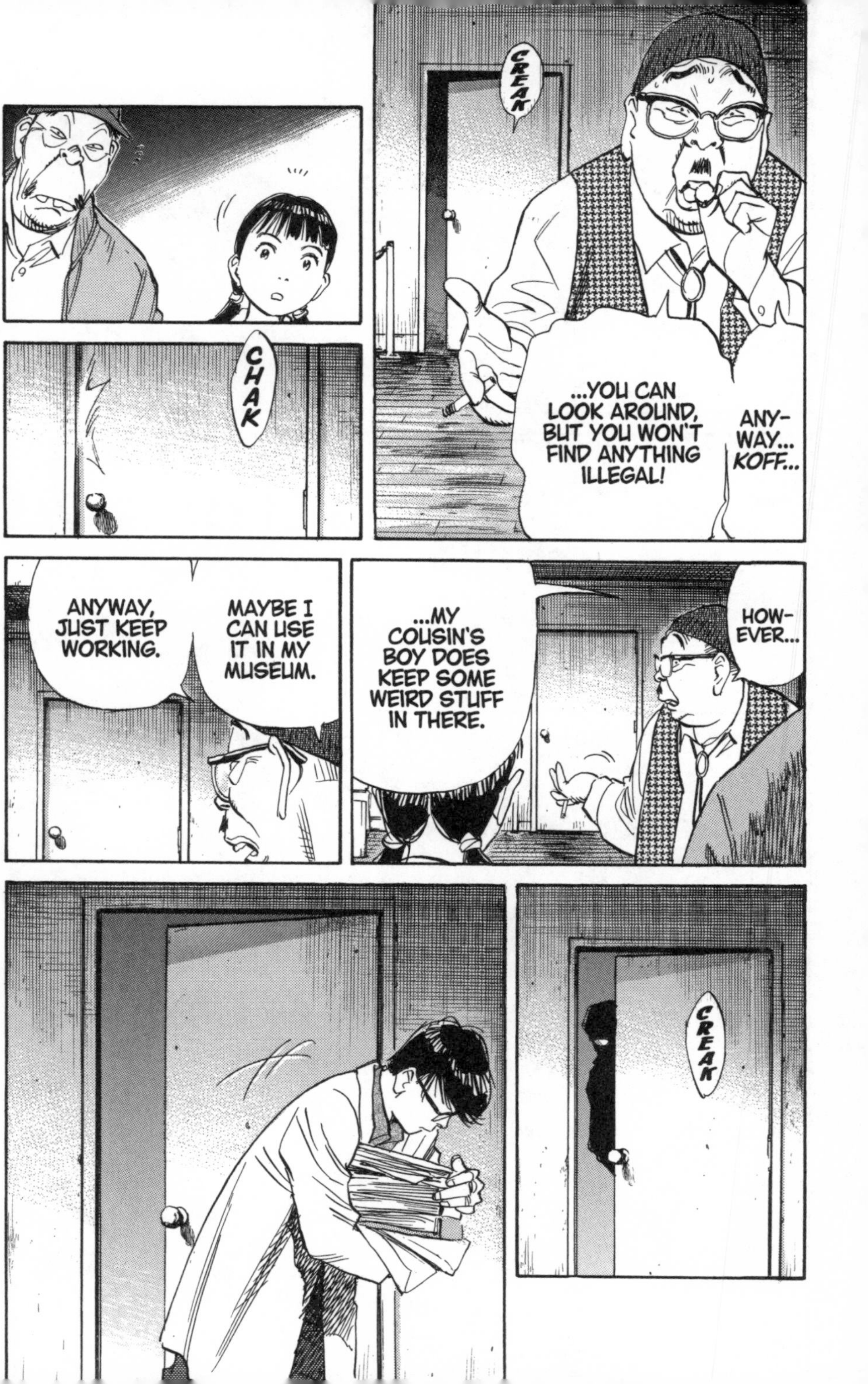
CREAK
ANY-WAY... KOFF...
...YOU CAN LOOK AROUND, BUT YOU WON'T FIND ANYTHING ILLEGAL!
CHAK
HOW-EVER...
...MY COUSIN'S BOY DOES KEEP SOME WEIRD STUFF IN THERE.
MAYBE I CAN USE IT IN MY MUSEUM.
ANYWAY, JUST KEEP WORKING.
CREAK

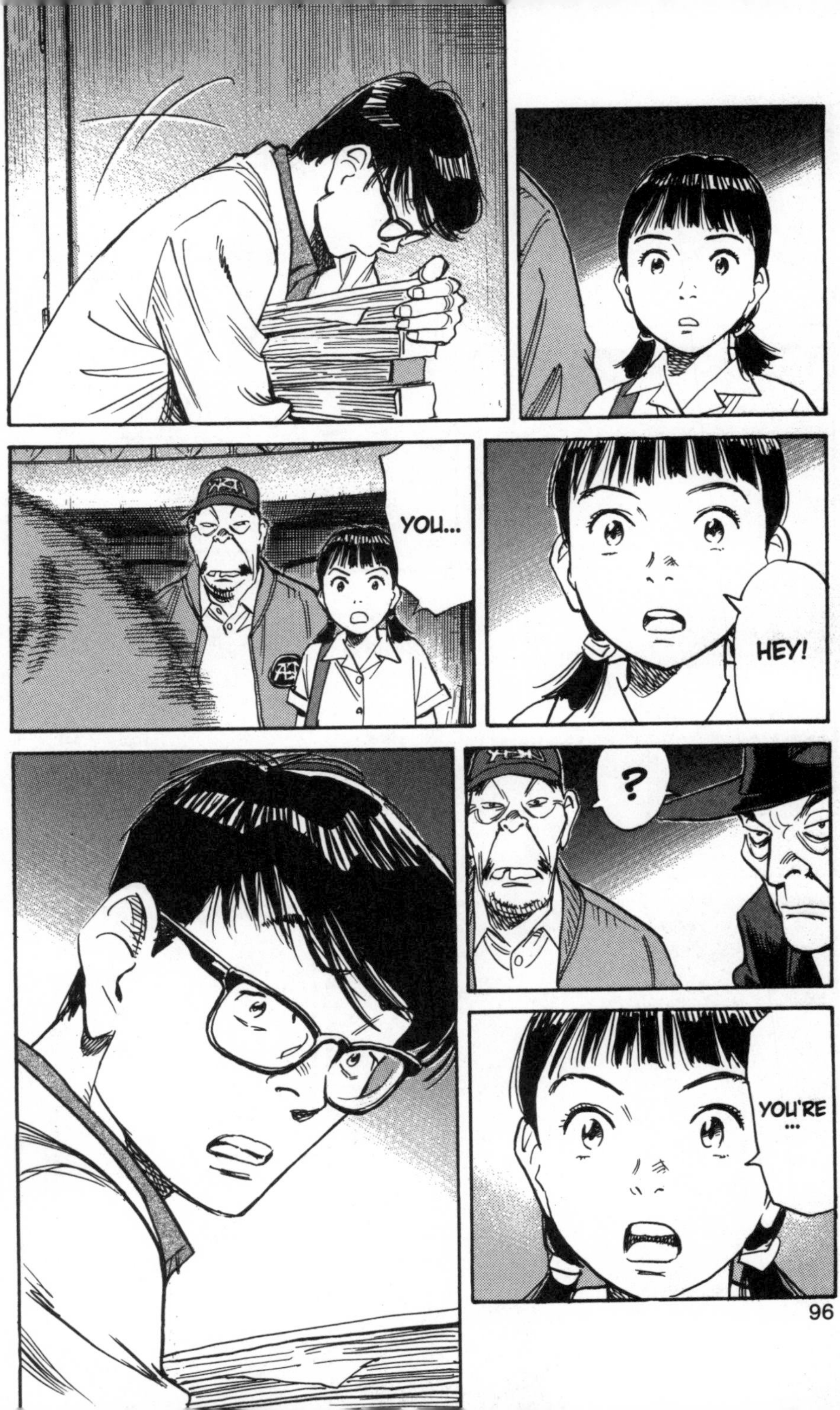
HEY!
YOU...
?
YOU'RE
...

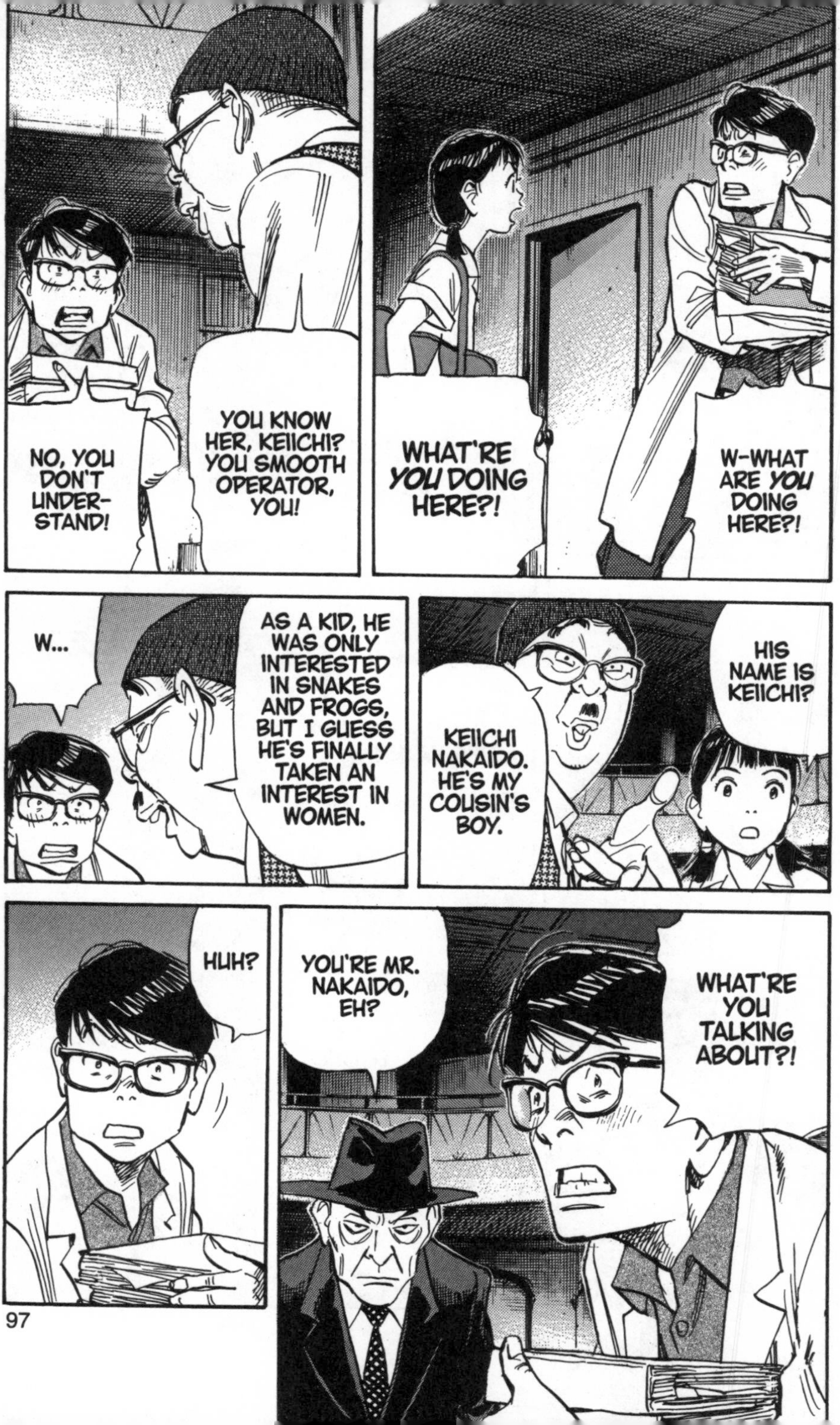
W-WHAT ARE YOU DOING HERE?!
WHAT'RE YOU DOING HERE?!
YOU KNOW HER, KEIICHI? YOU SMOOTH OPERATOR, YOU!
NO, YOU DON'T UNDER-STAND!
HIS NAME IS KEIICHI?
KEIICHI NAKAIDO. HE'S MY COUSIN'S BOY.
AS A KID, HE WAS ONLY INTERESTED IN SNAKES AND FROGS, BUT I GUESS HE'S FINALLY TAKEN AN INTEREST IN WOMEN.
W...
WHAT'RE YOU TALKING ABOUT?!
YOU'RE MR. NAKAIDO, EH?
HUH?

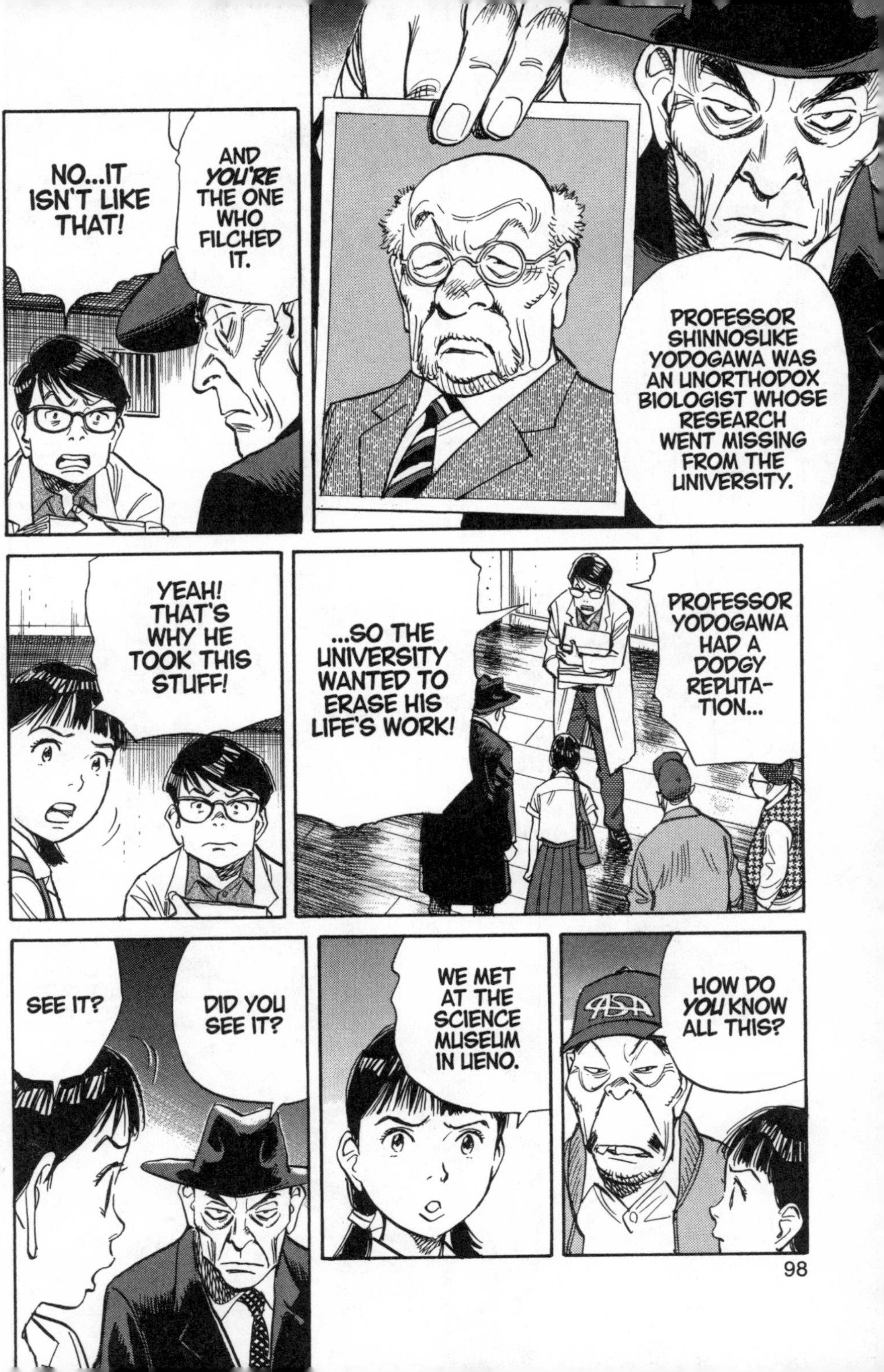
PROFESSOR SHINNOSUKE YODOGAWA WAS AN UNORTHODOX BIOLOGIST WHOSE RESEARCH WENT MISSING FROM THE UNIVERSITY.
AND *YOU'RE* THE ONE WHO FILCHED IT.
NO...IT ISN'T LIKE THAT!
PROFESSOR YODOGAWA HAD A DODGY REPUTA-TION...
...SO THE UNIVERSITY WANTED TO ERASE HIS LIFE'S WORK!
YEAH! THAT'S WHY HE TOOK THIS STUFF!
HOW DO *YOU* KNOW ALL THIS?
WE MET AT THE SCIENCE MUSEUM IN UENO.
DID YOU SEE IT?
SEE IT?

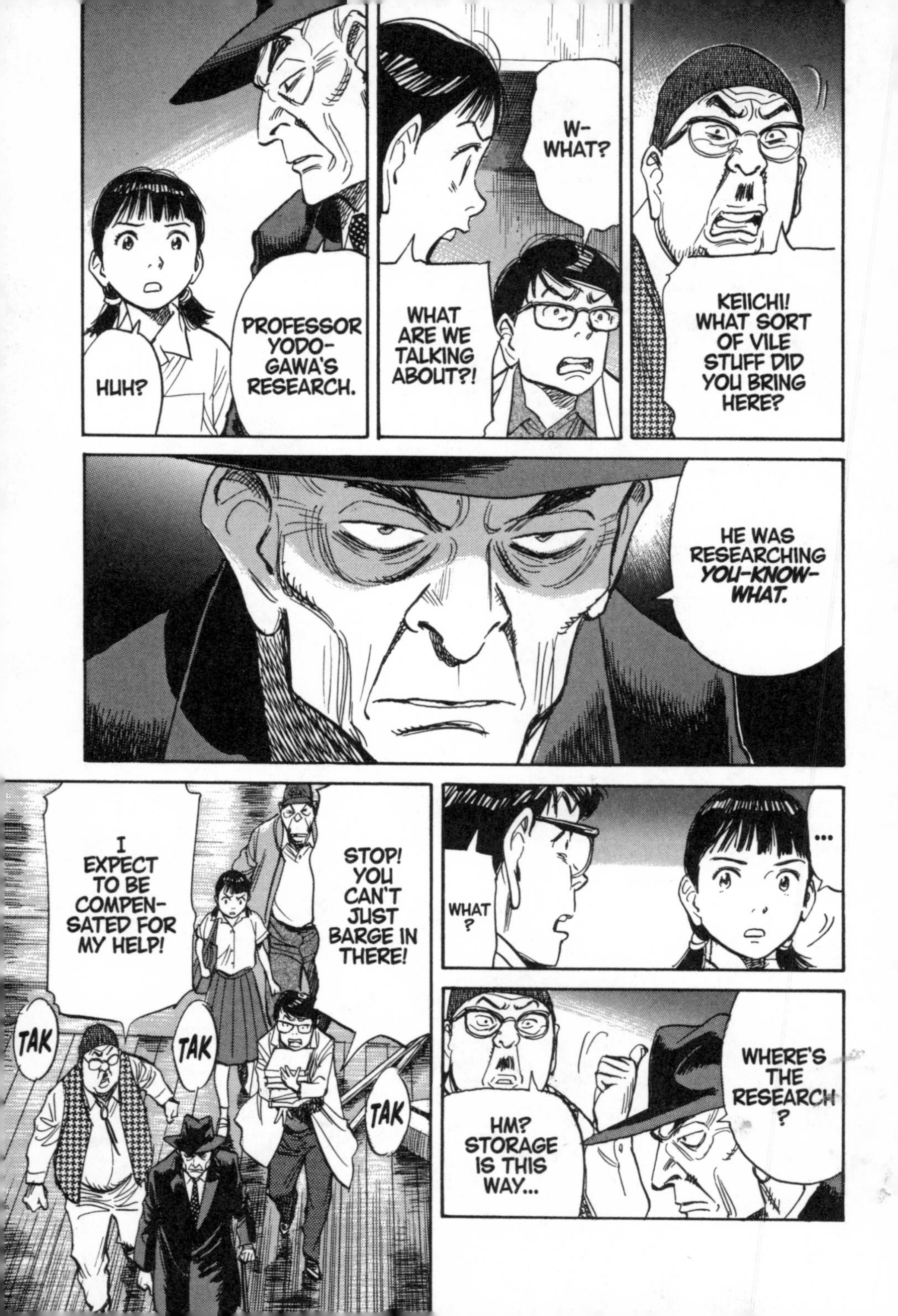
KEIICHI! WHAT SORT OF VILE STUFF DID YOU BRING HERE?
W- WHAT?
WHAT ARE WE TALKING ABOUT?!
PROFESSOR YODO-GAWA'S RESEARCH.
HUH?
HE WAS RESEARCHING *YOU-KNOW-WHAT.*
...
WHAT?
WHERE'S THE RESEARCH?
HM? STORAGE IS THIS WAY...
STOP! YOU CAN'T JUST BARGE IN THERE!
I EXPECT TO BE COMPEN-SATED FOR MY HELP!
TAK
TAK
TAK

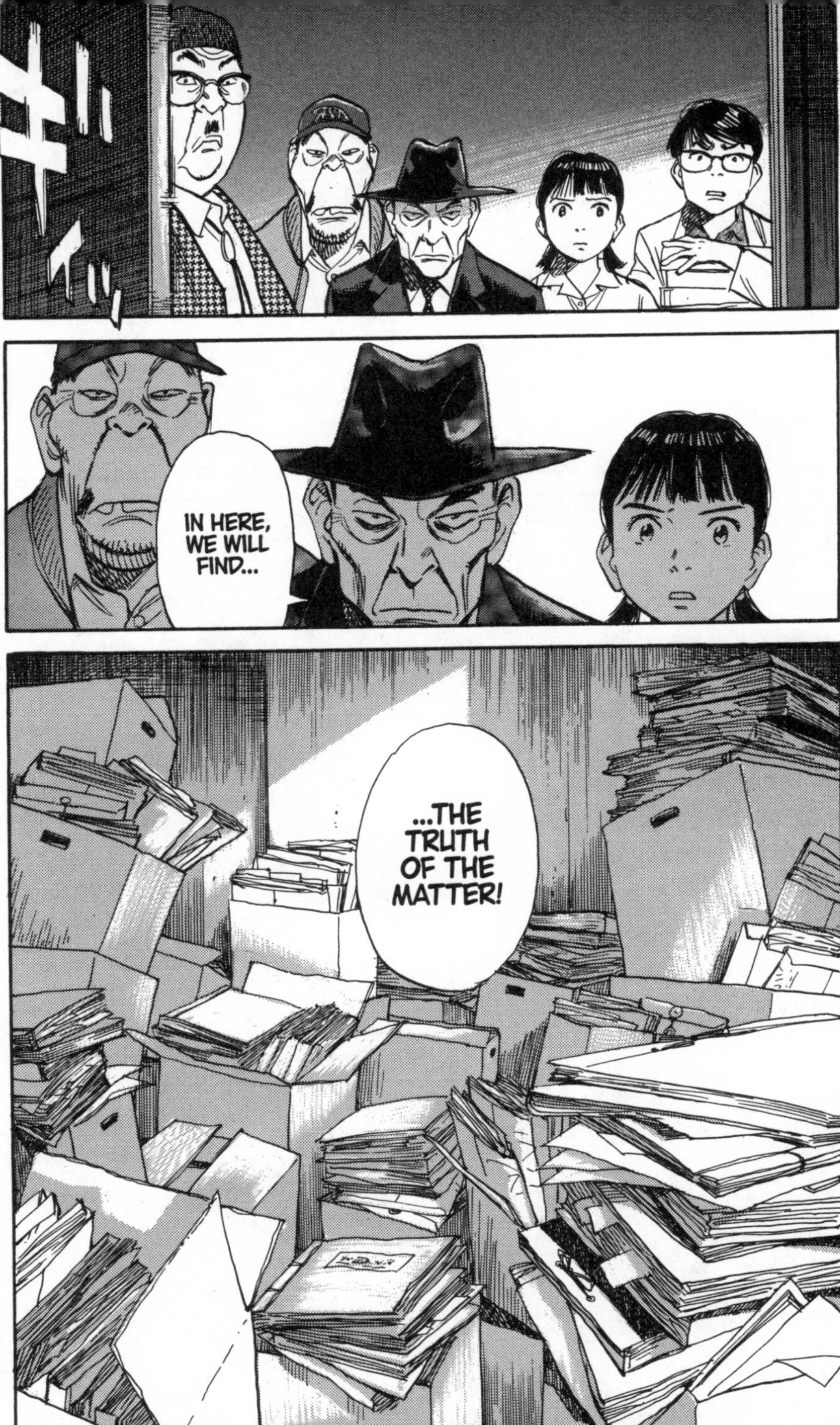
IN HERE, WE WILL FIND...
...THE TRUTH OF THE MATTER!

ASADORA!

ASADORA!

Chapter 21 ◉ Letters

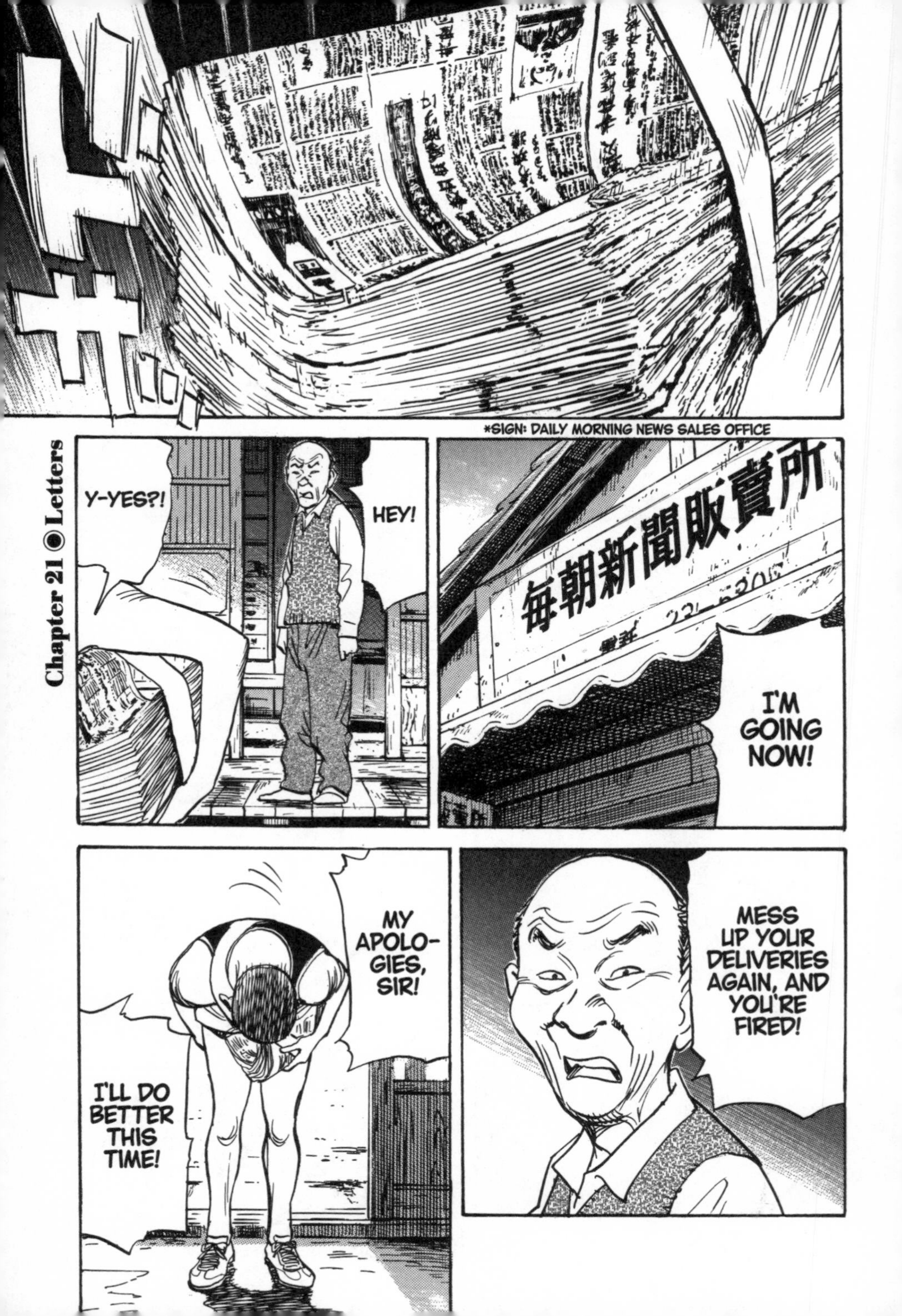
*SIGN: DAILY MORNING NEWS SALES OFFICE
毎朝新聞販賣所
I'M GOING NOW!
HEY!
Y-YES?!
MESS UP YOUR DELIVERIES AGAIN, AND YOU'RE FIRED!
MY APOLOGIES, SIR!
I'LL DO BETTER THIS TIME!

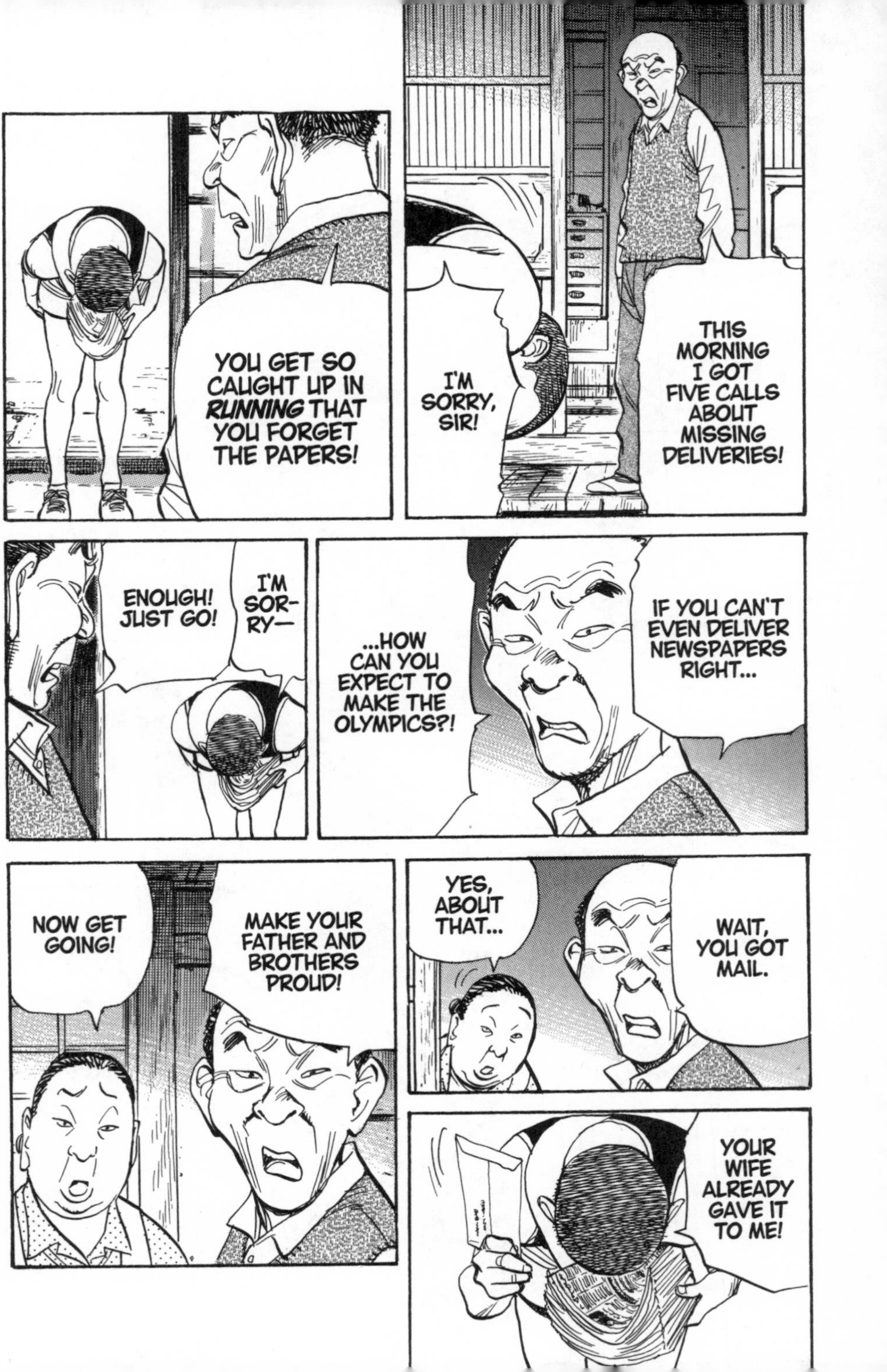
THIS MORNING I GOT FIVE CALLS ABOUT MISSING DELIVERIES!
I'M SORRY, SIR!
YOU GET SO CAUGHT UP IN *RUNNING* THAT YOU FORGET THE PAPERS!
IF YOU CAN'T EVEN DELIVER NEWSPAPERS RIGHT...
...HOW CAN YOU EXPECT TO MAKE THE OLYMPICS?!
I'M SORRY—
ENOUGH! JUST GO!
WAIT, YOU GOT MAIL.
YES, ABOUT THAT...
YOUR WIFE ALREADY GAVE IT TO ME!
MAKE YOUR FATHER AND BROTHERS PROUD!
NOW GET GOING!

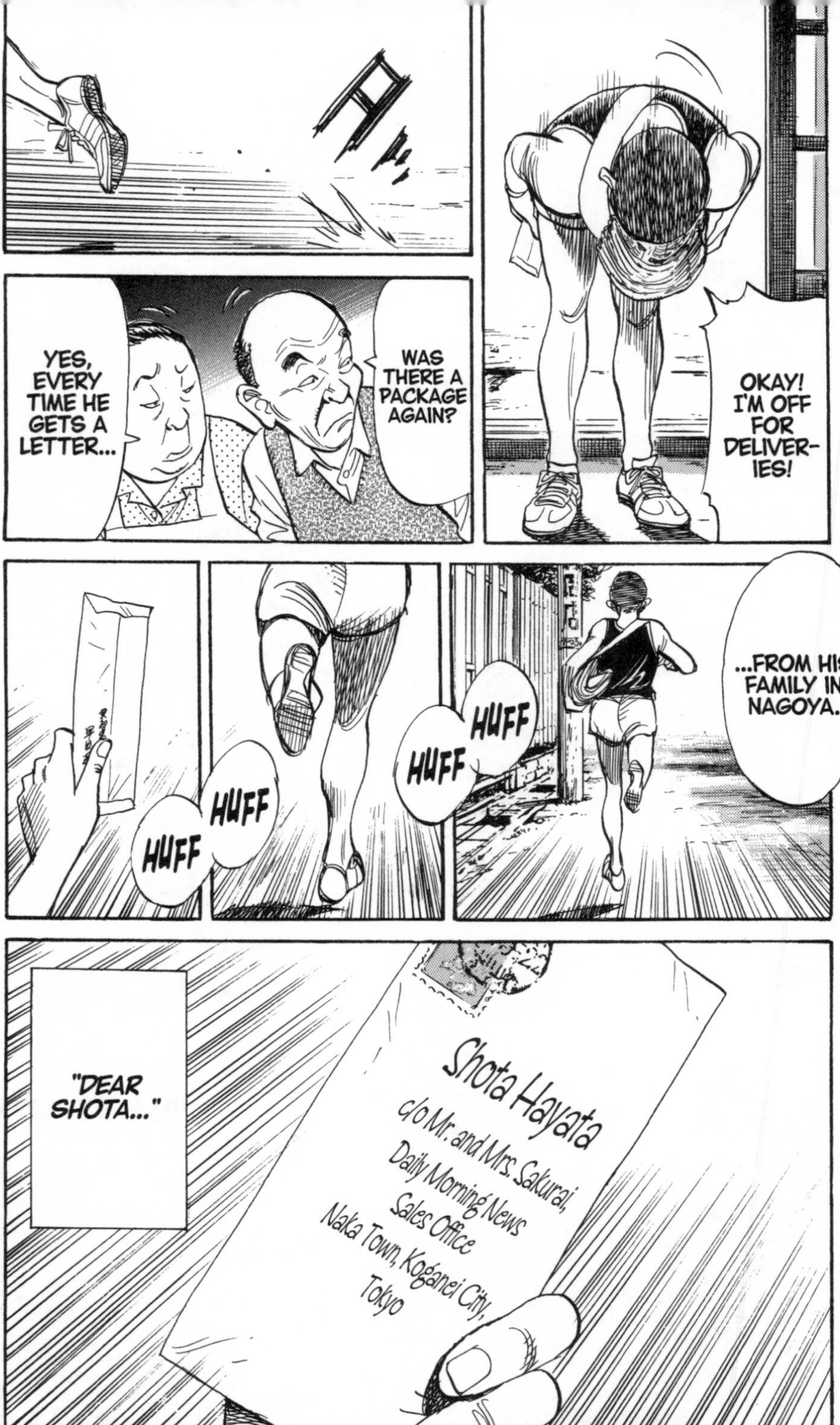
OKAY! I'M OFF FOR DELIVER-IES!
WAS THERE A PACKAGE AGAIN?
YES, EVERY TIME HE GETS A LETTER...
...FROM HIS FAMILY IN NAGOYA.
HUFF
HUFF
HUFF
HUFF
"DEAR SHOTA..."
Shota Hayata
c/o Mr. and Mrs. Sakurai,
Daily Morning News
Sales Office
Naka Town, Koganei City,
Tokyo

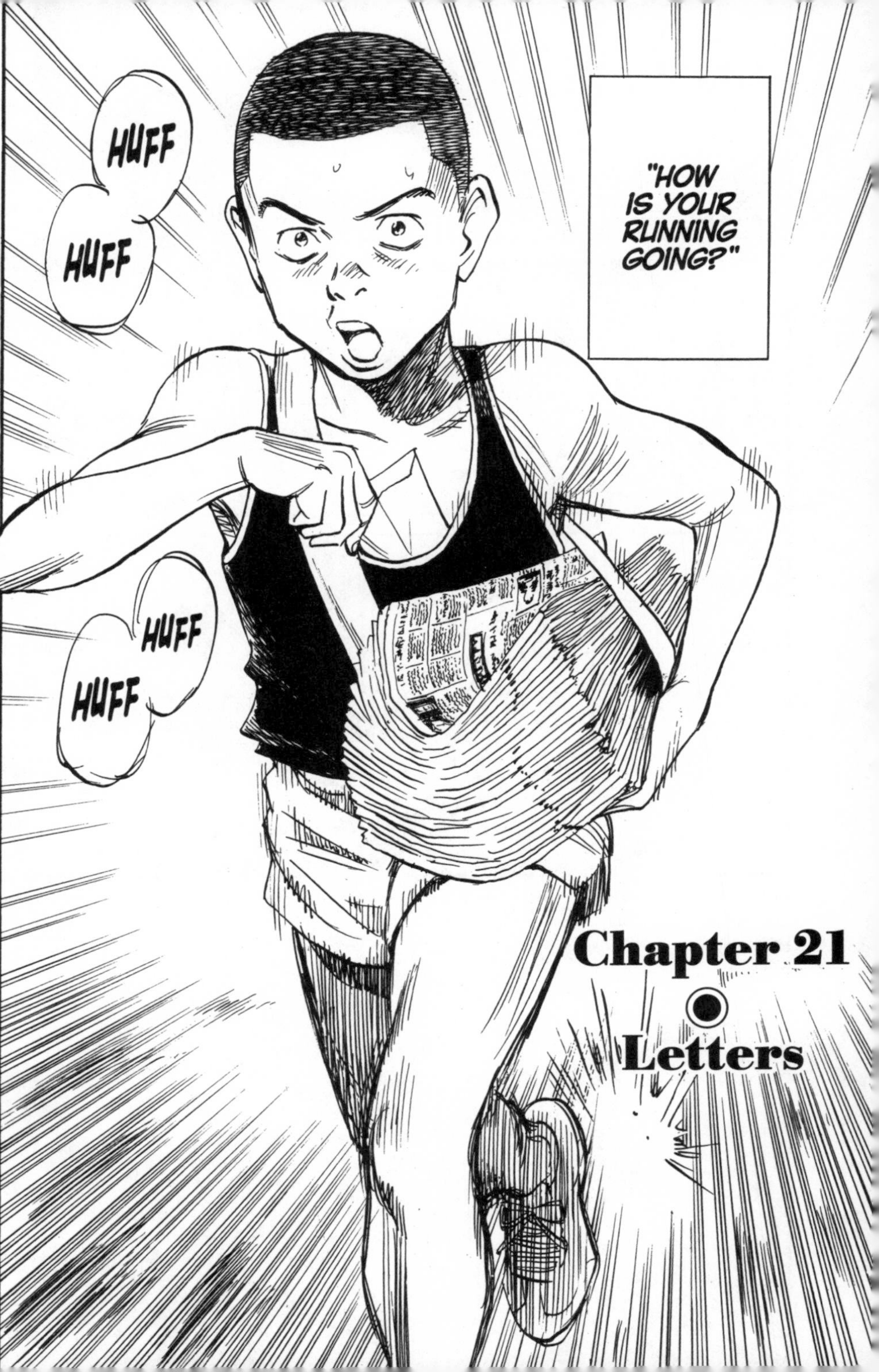
"HOW IS YOUR RUNNING GOING?"
HUFF
HUFF
HUFF
HUFF
Chapter 21
Letters

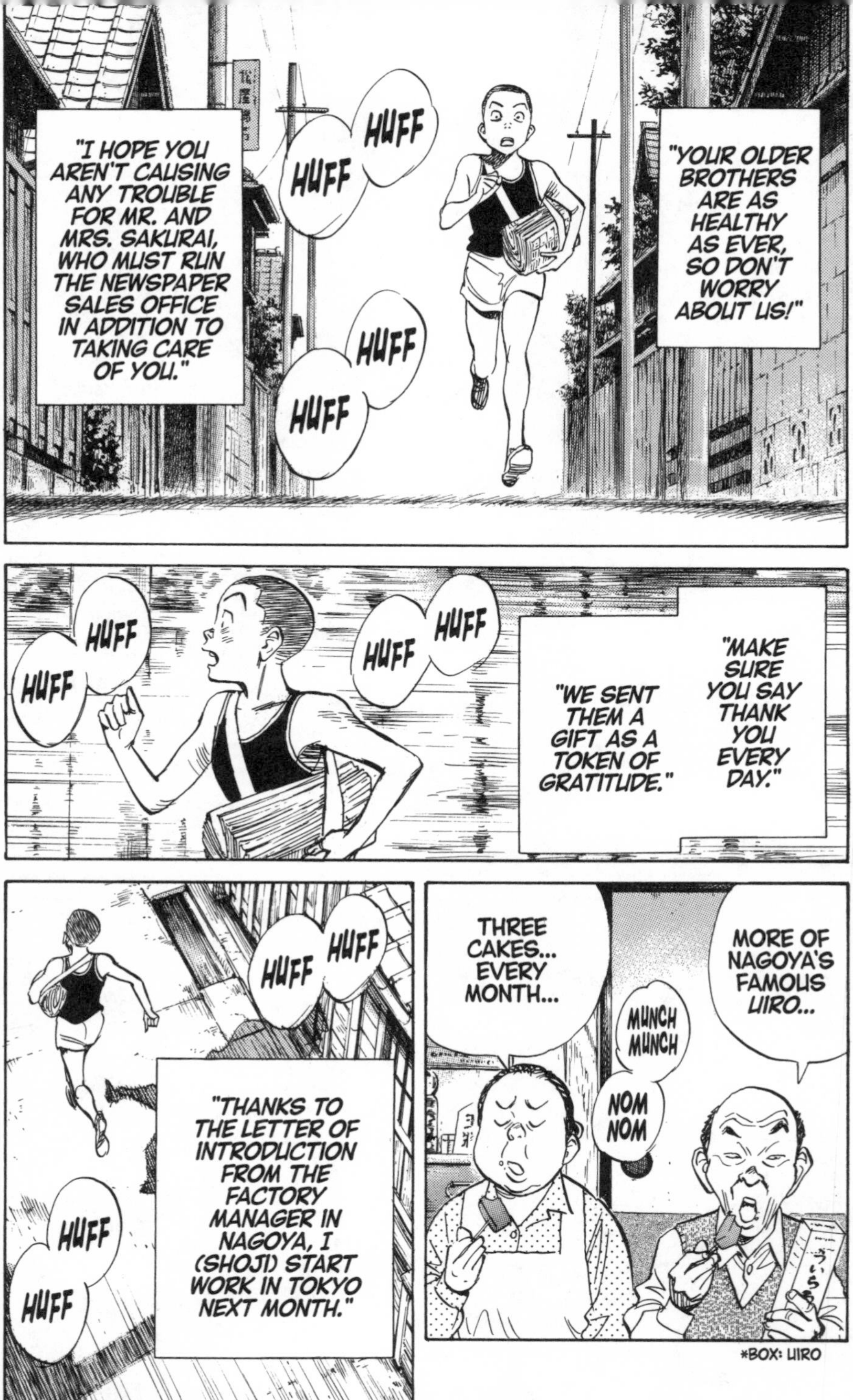
"YOUR OLDER BROTHERS ARE AS HEALTHY AS EVER, SO DON'T WORRY ABOUT US!"
HUFF
HUFF
HUFF
HUFF
"I HOPE YOU AREN'T CAUSING ANY TROUBLE FOR MR. AND MRS. SAKURAI, WHO MUST RUN THE NEWSPAPER SALES OFFICE IN ADDITION TO TAKING CARE OF YOU."
"MAKE SURE YOU SAY THANK YOU EVERY DAY."
"WE SENT THEM A GIFT AS A TOKEN OF GRATITUDE."
HUFF
HUFF
HUFF
HUFF
MORE OF NAGOYA'S FAMOUS UIRO...
THREE CAKES... EVERY MONTH...
MUNCH MUNCH
NOM NOM
HUFF
HUFF
"THANKS TO THE LETTER OF INTRODUCTION FROM THE FACTORY MANAGER IN NAGOYA, I (SHOJI) START WORK IN TOKYO NEXT MONTH."
HUFF
HUFF
*BOX: UIRO

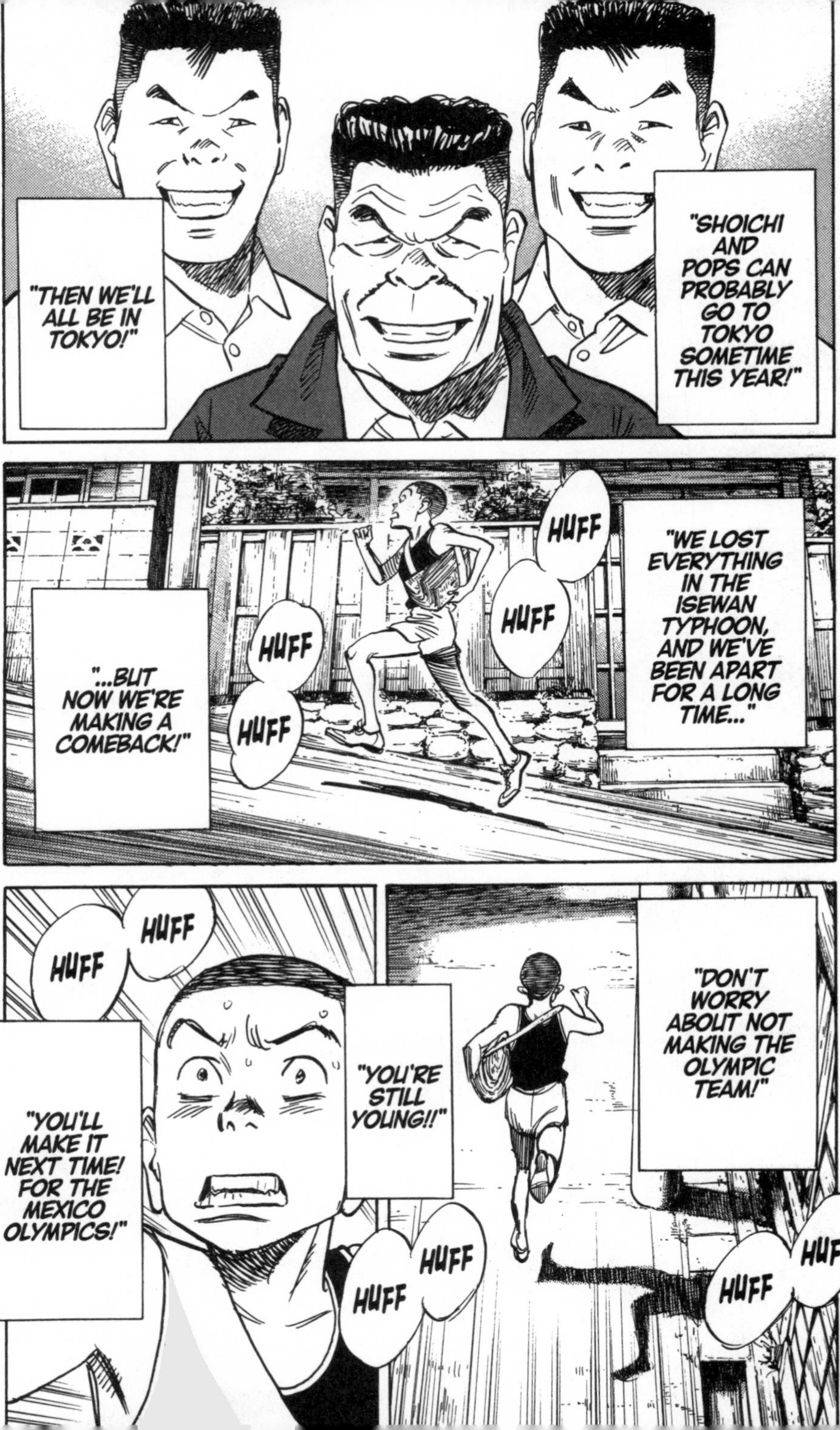
"SHOICHI AND POPS CAN PROBABLY GO TO TOKYO SOMETIME THIS YEAR!"
"THEN WE'LL ALL BE IN TOKYO!"
"WE LOST EVERYTHING IN THE ISEWAN TYPHOON, AND WE'VE BEEN APART FOR A LONG TIME..."
HUFF
HUFF
"...BUT NOW WE'RE MAKING A COMEBACK!"
HUFF
HUFF
"DON'T WORRY ABOUT NOT MAKING THE OLYMPIC TEAM!"
HUFF
HUFF
HUFF
HUFF
"YOU'RE STILL YOUNG!!"
"YOU'LL MAKE IT NEXT TIME! FOR THE MEXICO OLYMPICS!"
HUFF
HUFF

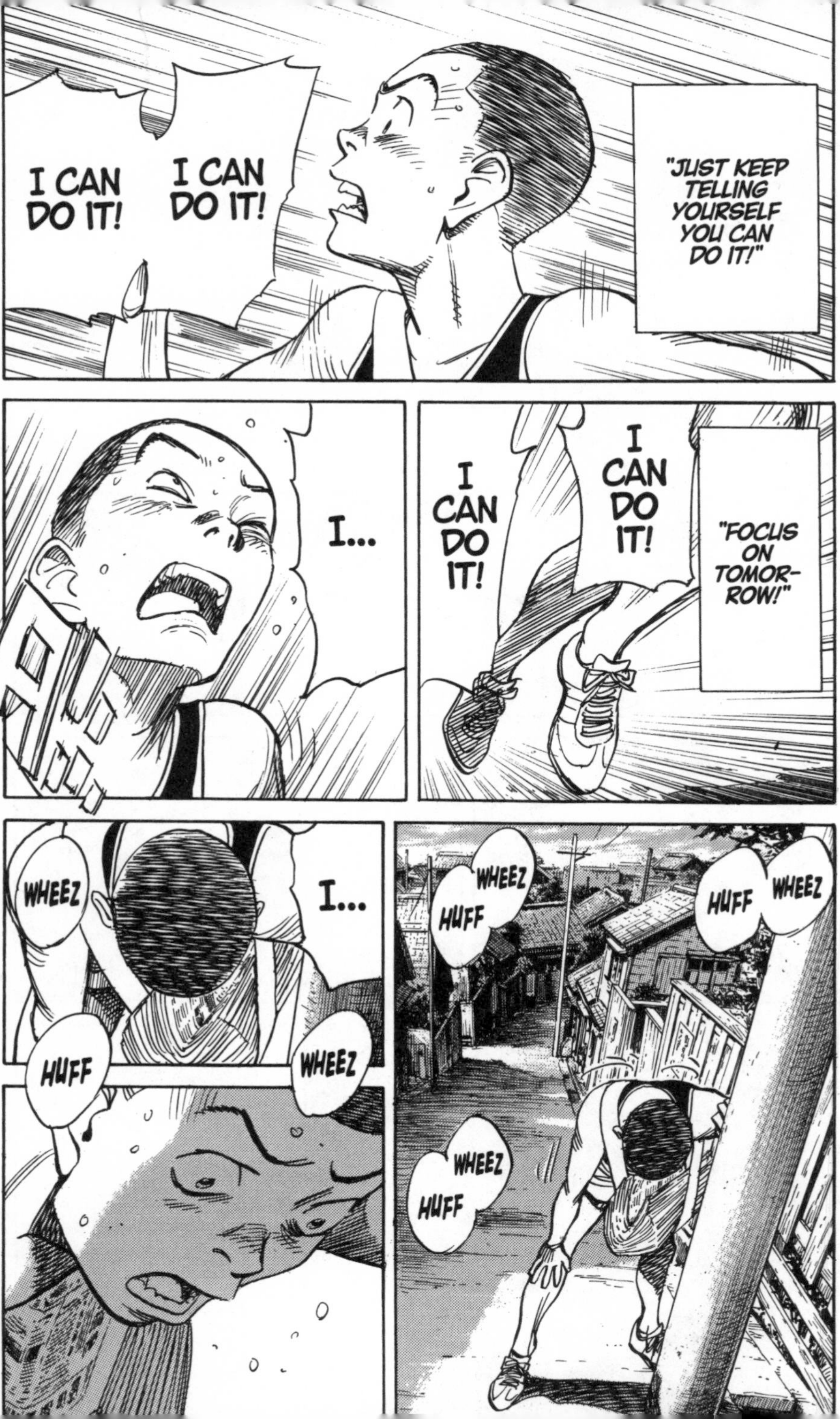
"JUST KEEP TELLING YOURSELF YOU CAN DO IT!"
I CAN DO IT!
I CAN DO IT!
"FOCUS ON TOMOR-ROW!"
I CAN DO IT!
I CAN DO IT!
I...
WHEEZ
HUFF
WHEEZ
HUFF
WHEEZ
HUFF
I...
WHEEZ
WHEEZ
HUFF

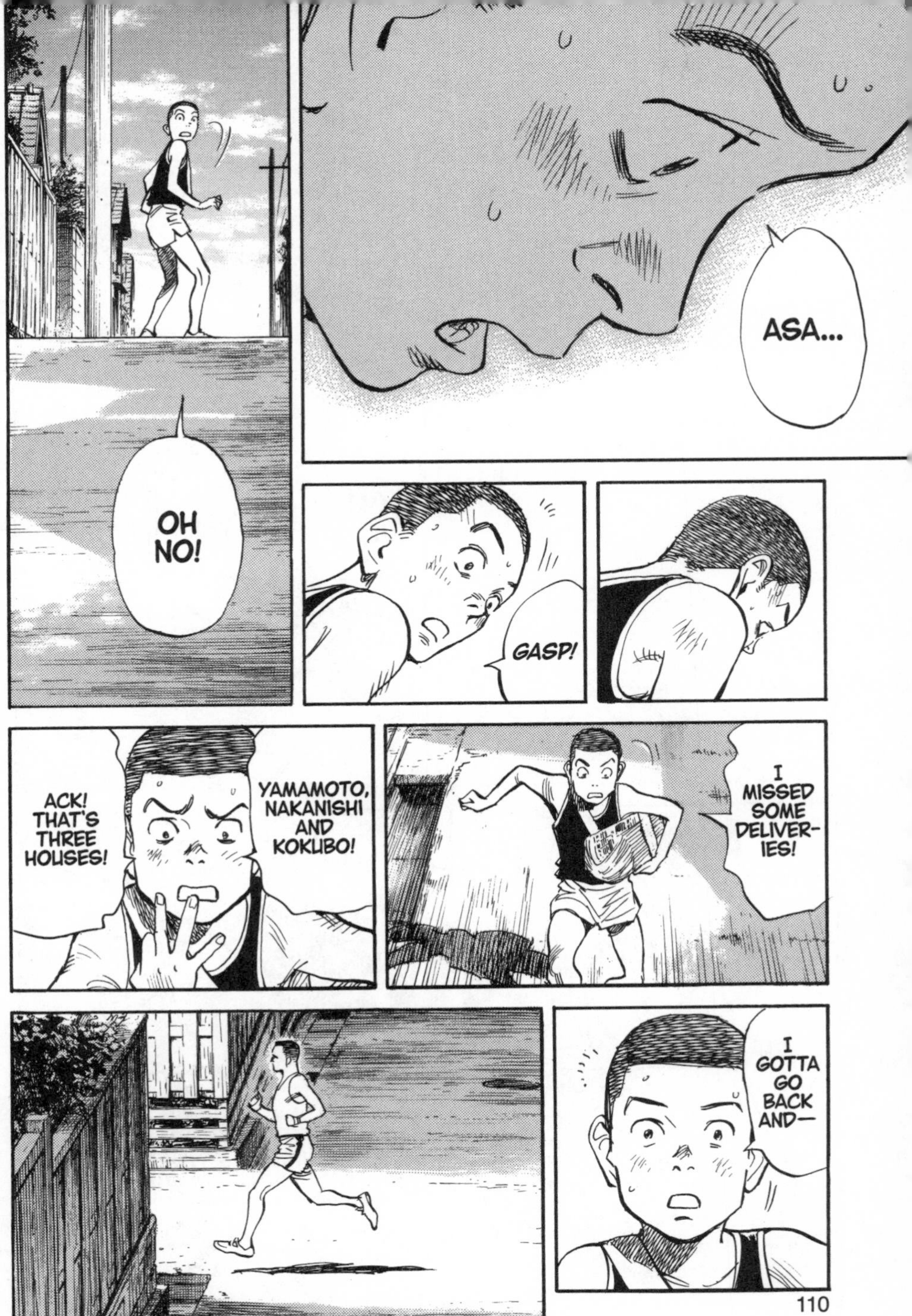
ASA...
GASP!
OH NO!
I MISSED SOME DELIVER-IES!
YAMAMOTO, NAKANISHI AND KOKUBO!
ACK! THAT'S THREE HOUSES!
I GOTTA GO BACK AND—

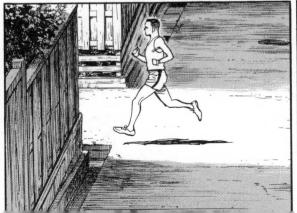

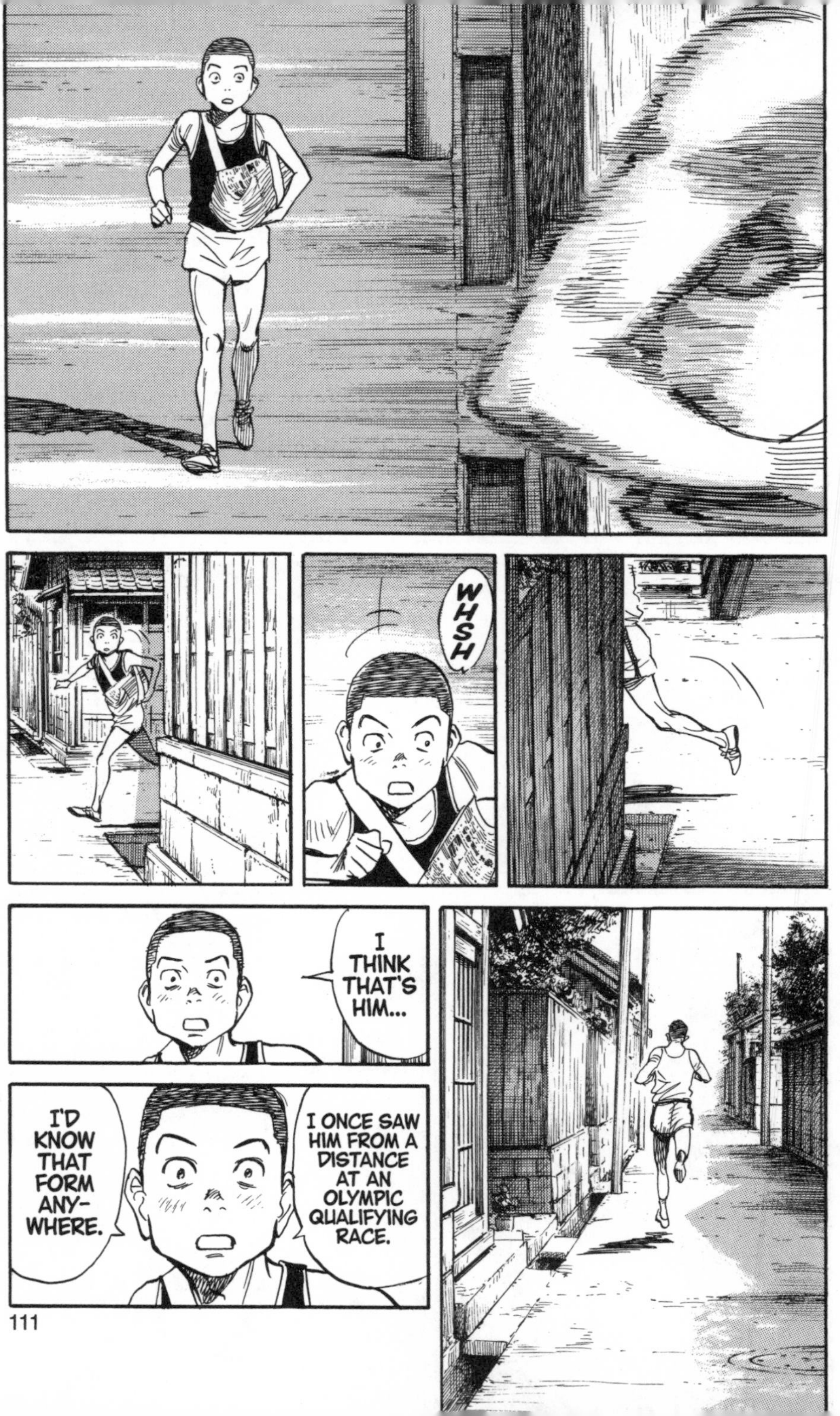
WHSH
I THINK THAT'S HIM...
I ONCE SAW HIM FROM A DISTANCE AT AN OLYMPIC QUALIFYING RACE.
I'D KNOW THAT FORM ANY-WHERE.

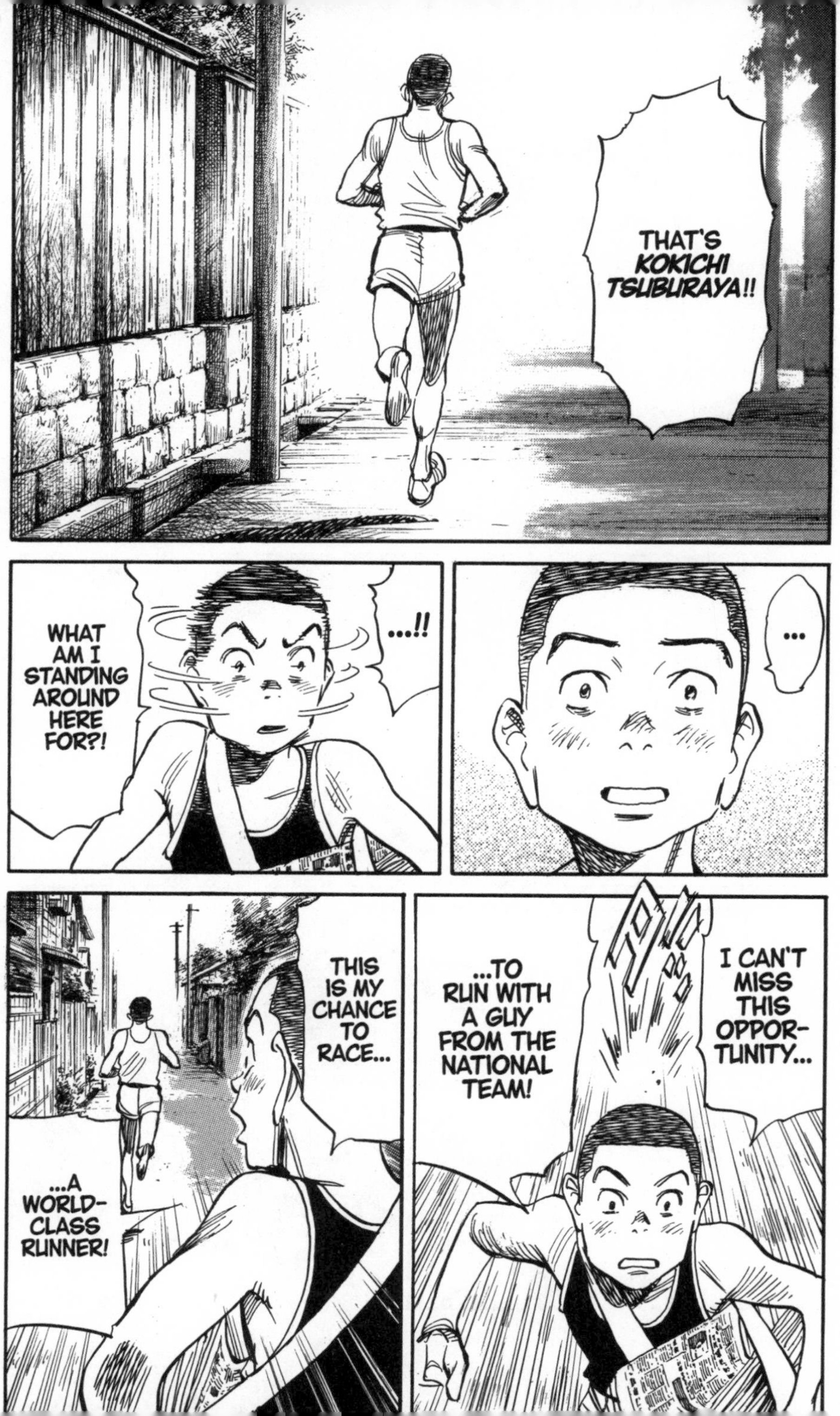
THAT'S KOKICHI TSUBURAYA!!
...
...!!
WHAT AM I STANDING AROUND HERE FOR?!
I CAN'T MISS THIS OPPOR-TUNITY...
...TO RUN WITH A GUY FROM THE NATIONAL TEAM!
THIS IS MY CHANCE TO RACE...
...A WORLD-CLASS RUNNER!

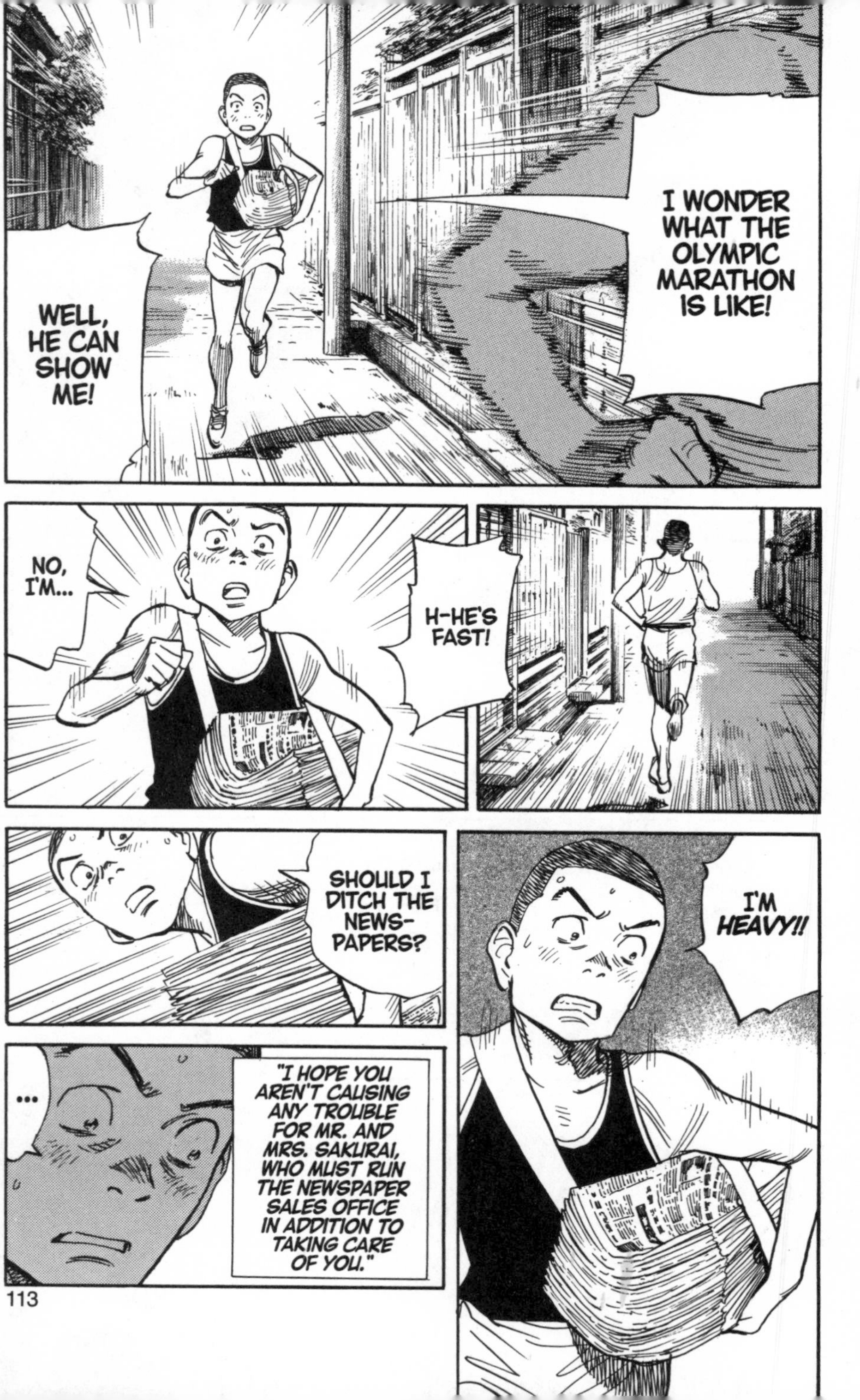

I WONDER WHAT THE OLYMPIC MARATHON IS LIKE!
WELL, HE CAN SHOW ME!
H-HE'S FAST!
NO, I'M...
I'M *HEAVY!!*
SHOULD I DITCH THE NEWS-PAPERS?
"I HOPE YOU AREN'T CAUSING ANY TROUBLE FOR MR. AND MRS. SAKURAI, WHO MUST RUN THE NEWSPAPER SALES OFFICE IN ADDITION TO TAKING CARE OF YOU."
...

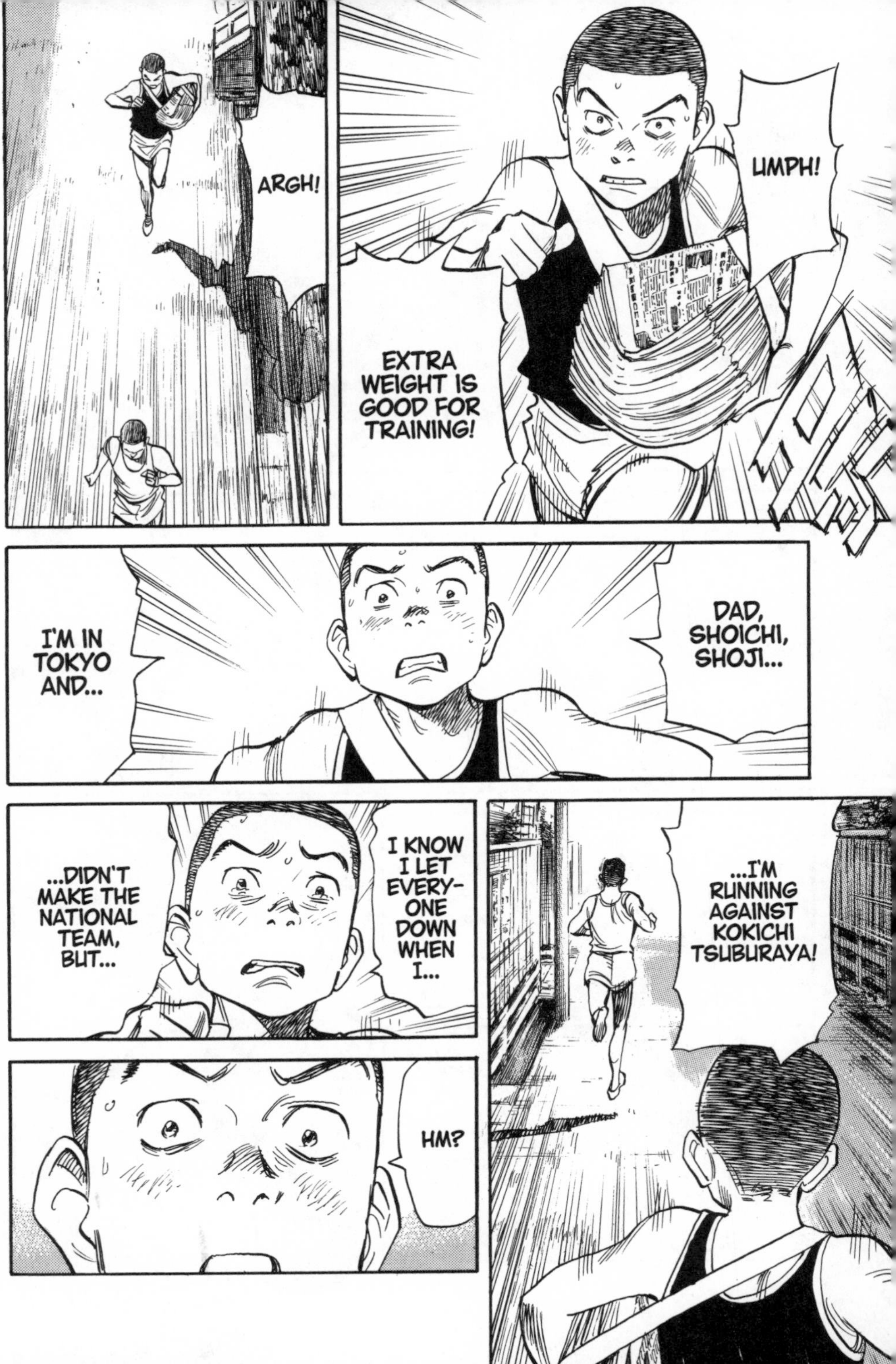
UMPH!
EXTRA WEIGHT IS GOOD FOR TRAINING!
ARGH!
DAD, SHOICHI, SHOJI...
I'M IN TOKYO AND...
...I'M RUNNING AGAINST KOKICHI TSUBURAYA!
I KNOW I LET EVERY-ONE DOWN WHEN I...
...DIDN'T MAKE THE NATIONAL TEAM, BUT...
HM?

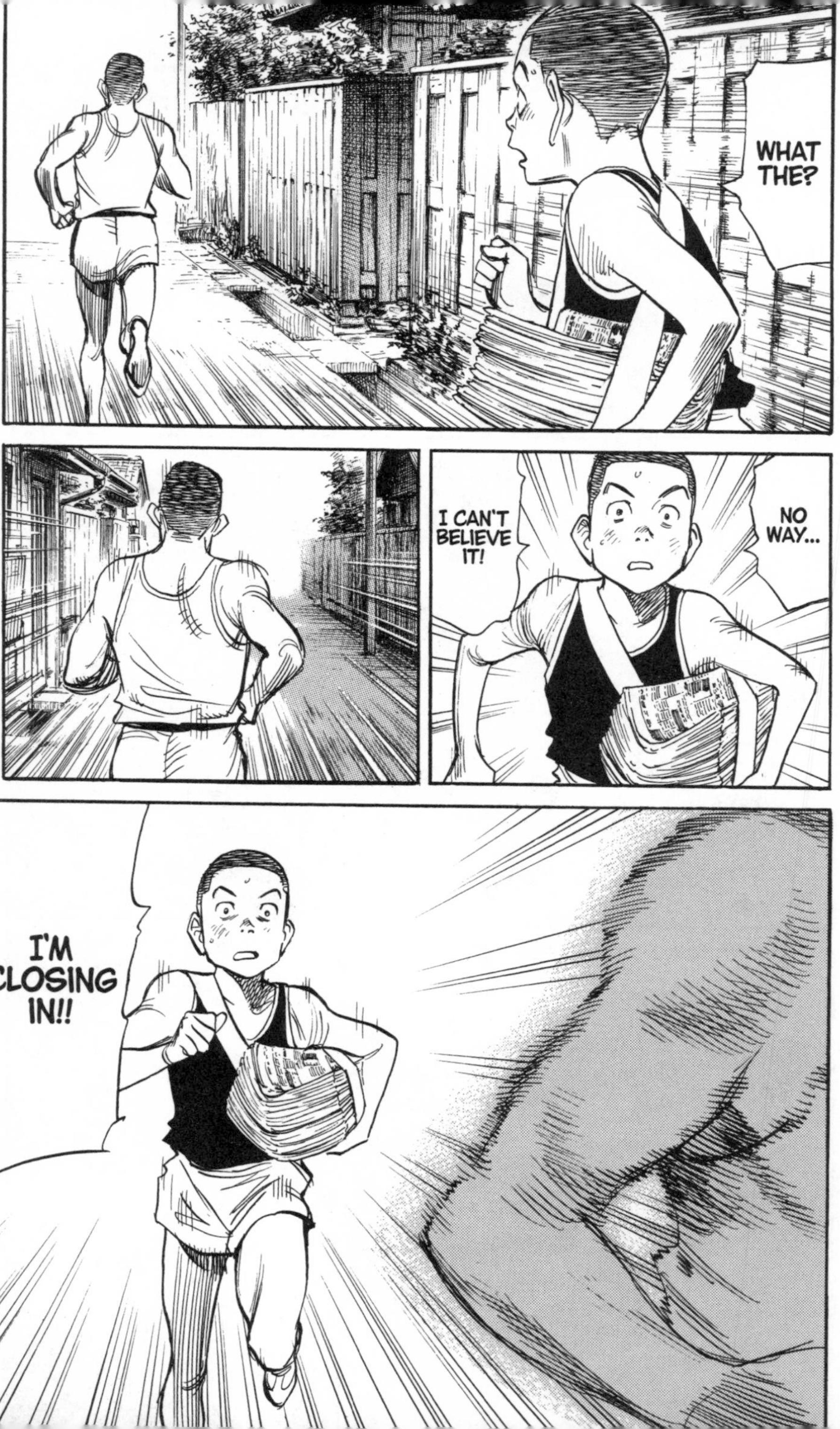
WHAT THE?
NO WAY...
I CAN'T BELIEVE IT!
I'M CLOSING IN!!

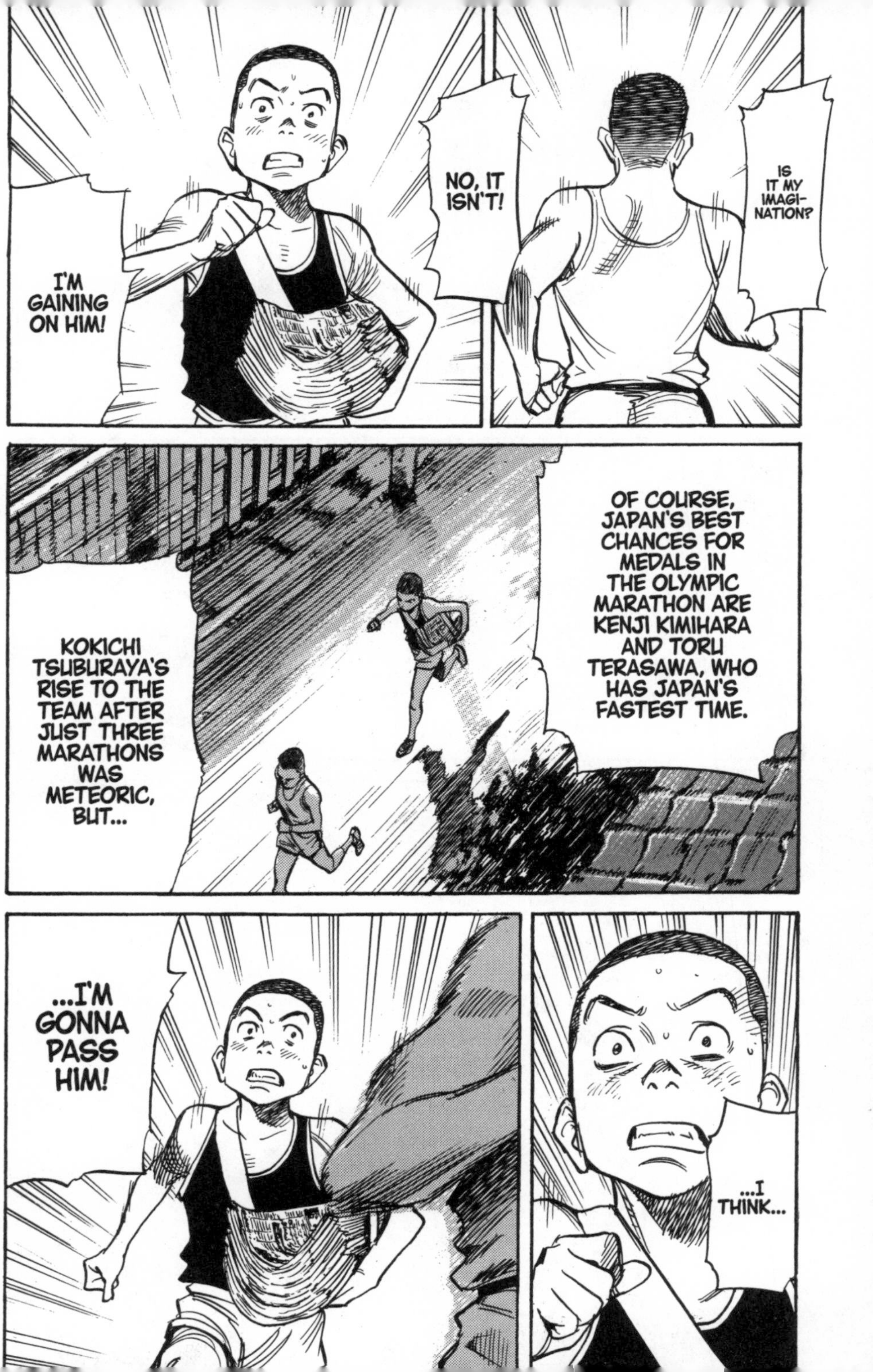
IS IT MY IMAGINATION?
NO, IT ISN'T!
I'M GAINING ON HIM!
OF COURSE, JAPAN'S BEST CHANCES FOR MEDALS IN THE OLYMPIC MARATHON ARE KENJI KIMIHARA AND TORU TERASAWA, WHO HAS JAPAN'S FASTEST TIME.
KOKICHI TSUBURAYA'S RISE TO THE TEAM AFTER JUST THREE MARATHONS WAS METEORIC, BUT...
...I THINK...
...I'M GONNA PASS HIM!

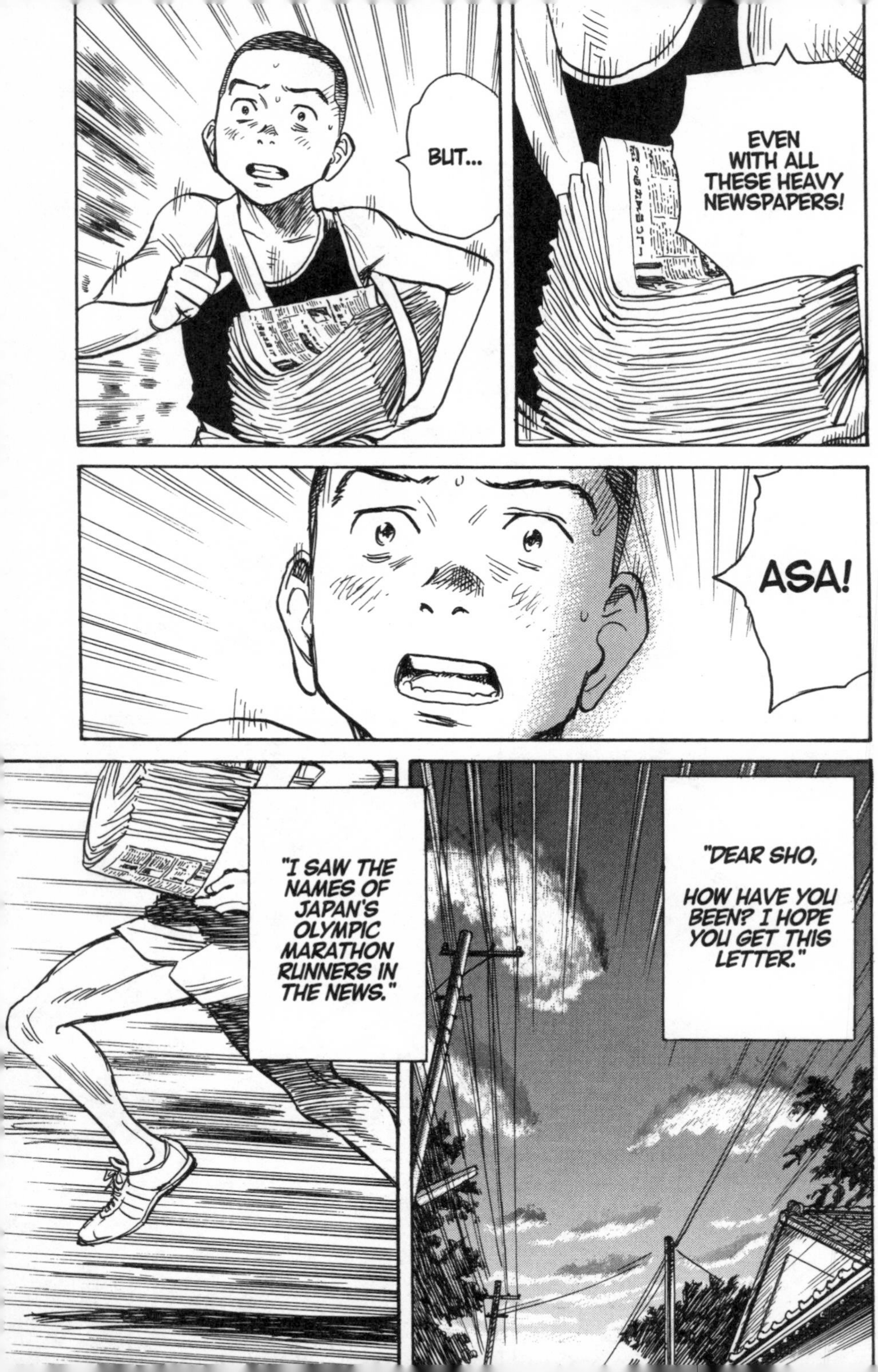
EVEN WITH ALL THESE HEAVY NEWSPAPERS!
BUT...
ASA!
"DEAR SHO,
HOW HAVE YOU BEEN? I HOPE YOU GET THIS LETTER."
"I SAW THE NAMES OF JAPAN'S OLYMPIC MARATHON RUNNERS IN THE NEWS."

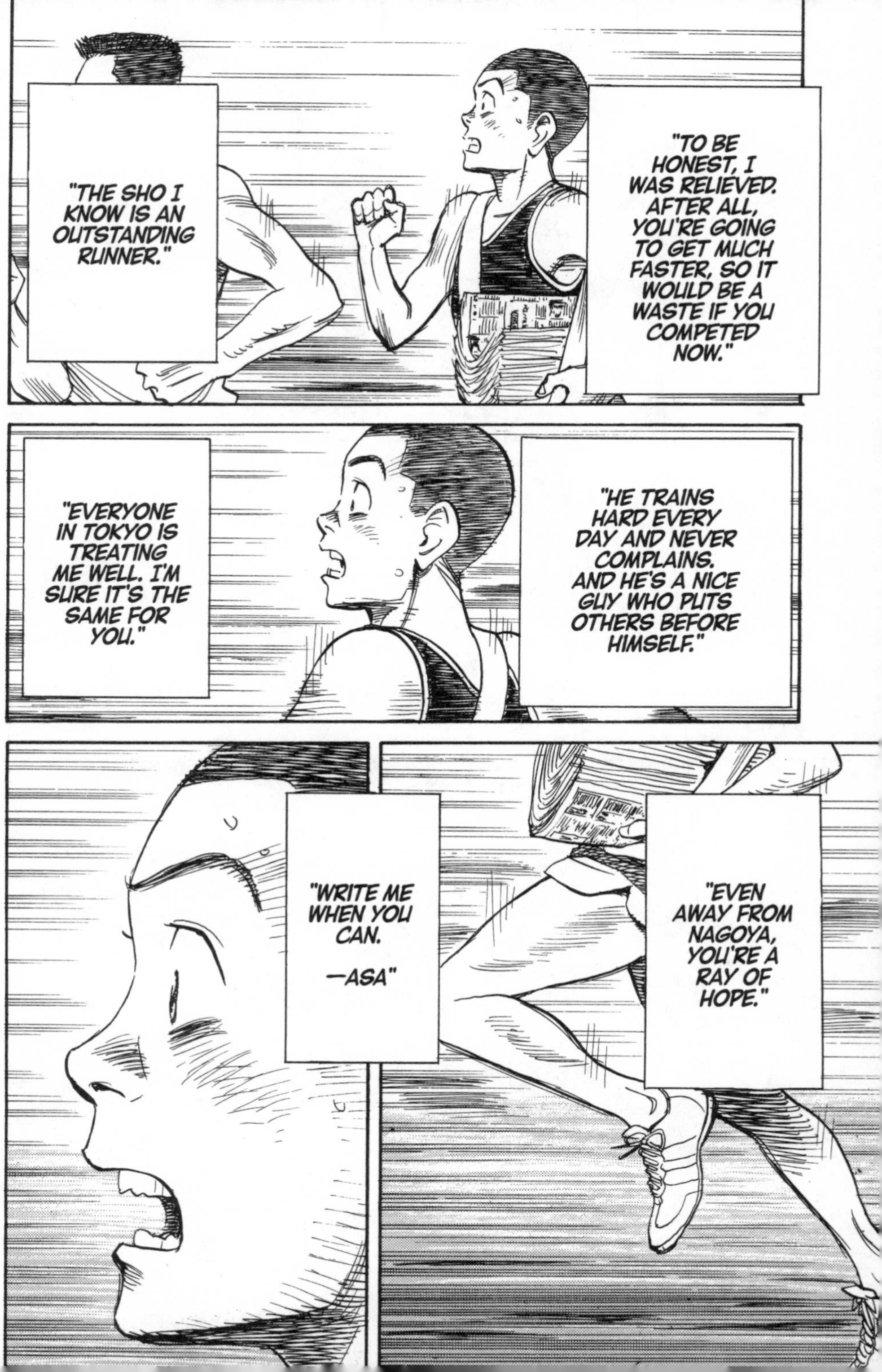
"TO BE HONEST, I WAS RELIEVED. AFTER ALL, YOU'RE GOING TO GET MUCH FASTER, SO IT WOULD BE A WASTE IF YOU COMPETED NOW."
"THE SHO I KNOW IS AN OUTSTANDING RUNNER."
"HE TRAINS HARD EVERY DAY AND NEVER COMPLAINS. AND HE'S A NICE GUY WHO PUTS OTHERS BEFORE HIMSELF."
"EVERYONE IN TOKYO IS TREATING ME WELL. I'M SURE IT'S THE SAME FOR YOU."
"EVEN AWAY FROM NAGOYA, YOU'RE A RAY OF HOPE."
"WRITE ME WHEN YOU CAN.
—ASA"

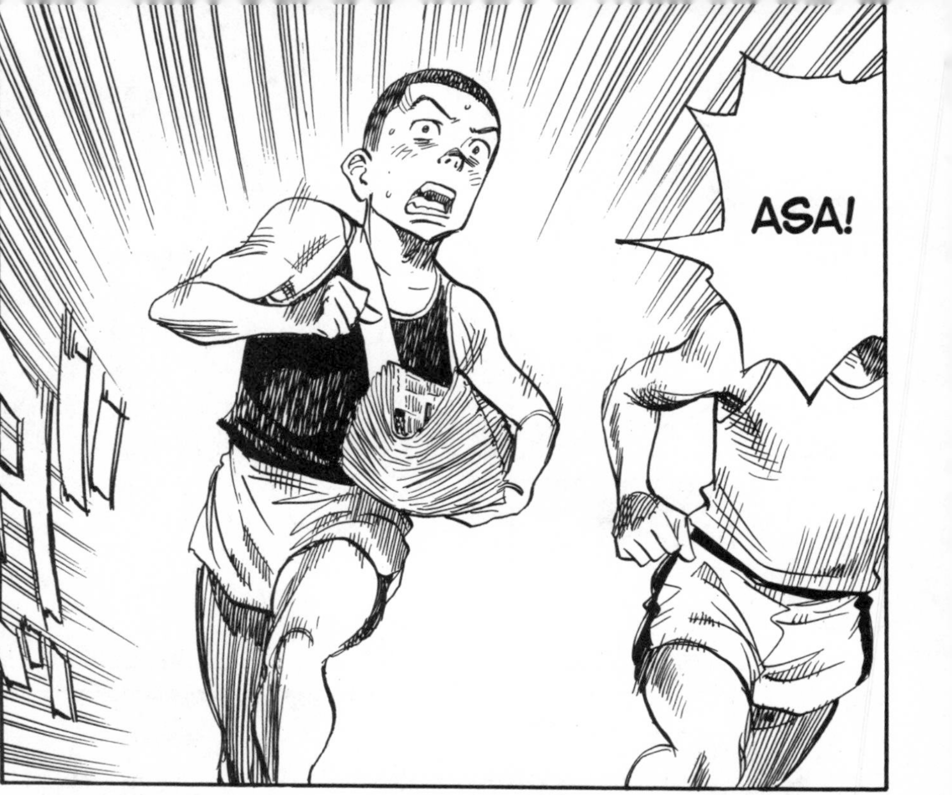
ASA!

*SIGNS: PINK SPOT SALON, EL DORADO, BLACK ROSE

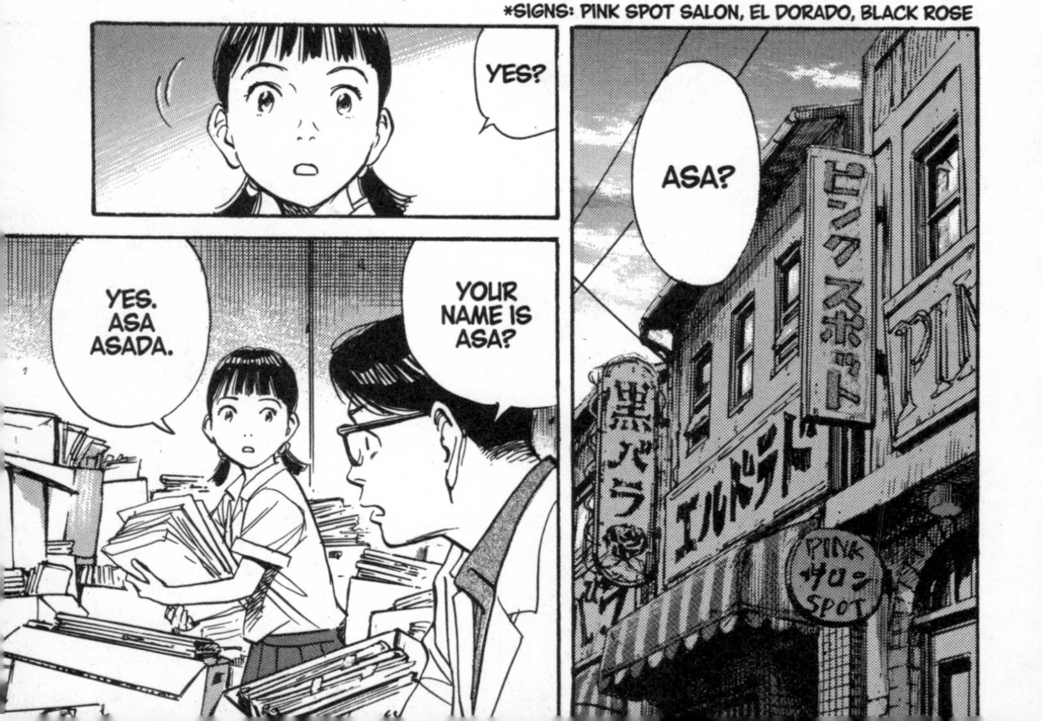
ASA?
ピンクスポット
エルドラド
黒バラ
PINK サロン SPOT
YES?
YOUR NAME IS ASA?
YES. ASA ASADA.

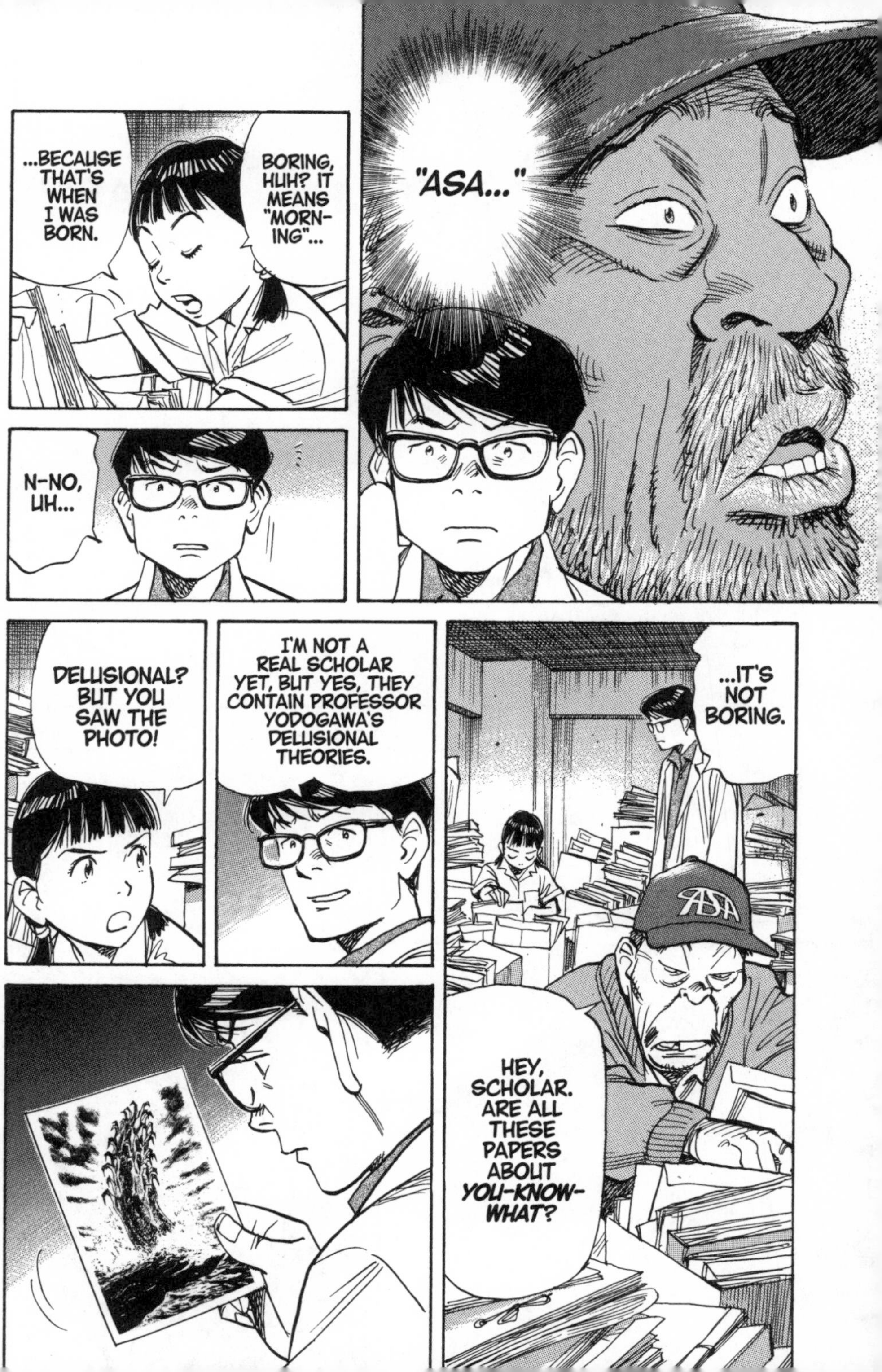
"ASA..."
BORING, HUH? IT MEANS "MORNING"...
...BECAUSE THAT'S WHEN I WAS BORN.
N-NO, UH...
...IT'S NOT BORING.
HEY, SCHOLAR. ARE ALL THESE PAPERS ABOUT *YOU-KNOW-WHAT*?
I'M NOT A REAL SCHOLAR YET, BUT YES, THEY CONTAIN PROFESSOR YODOGAWA'S DELUSIONAL THEORIES.
DELUSIONAL? BUT YOU SAW THE PHOTO!
ASA

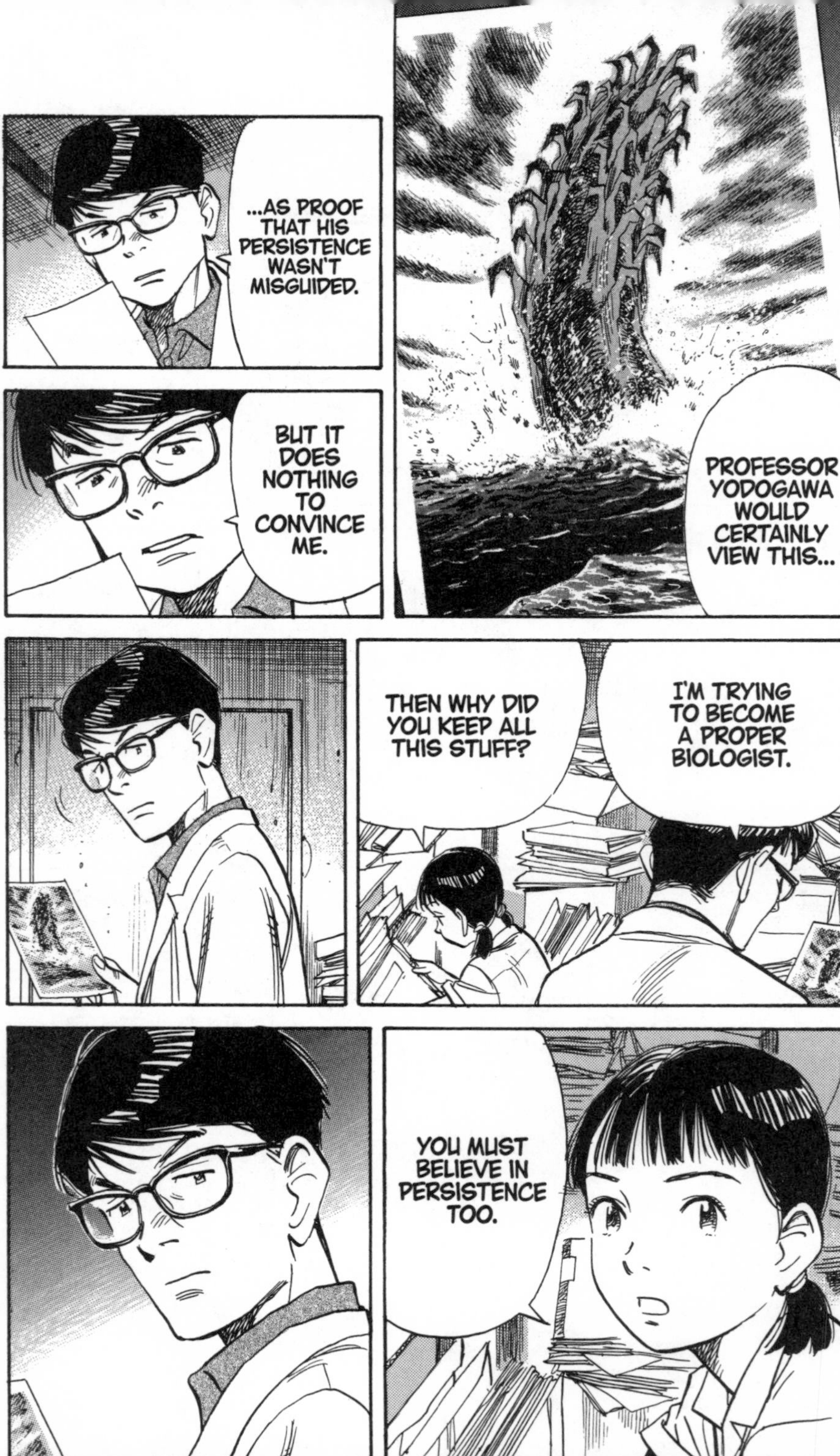
PROFESSOR YODOGAWA WOULD CERTAINLY VIEW THIS...
...AS PROOF THAT HIS PERSISTENCE WASN'T MISGUIDED.
BUT IT DOES NOTHING TO CONVINCE ME.
I'M TRYING TO BECOME A PROPER BIOLOGIST.
THEN WHY DID YOU KEEP ALL THIS STUFF?
YOU MUST BELIEVE IN PERSISTENCE TOO.

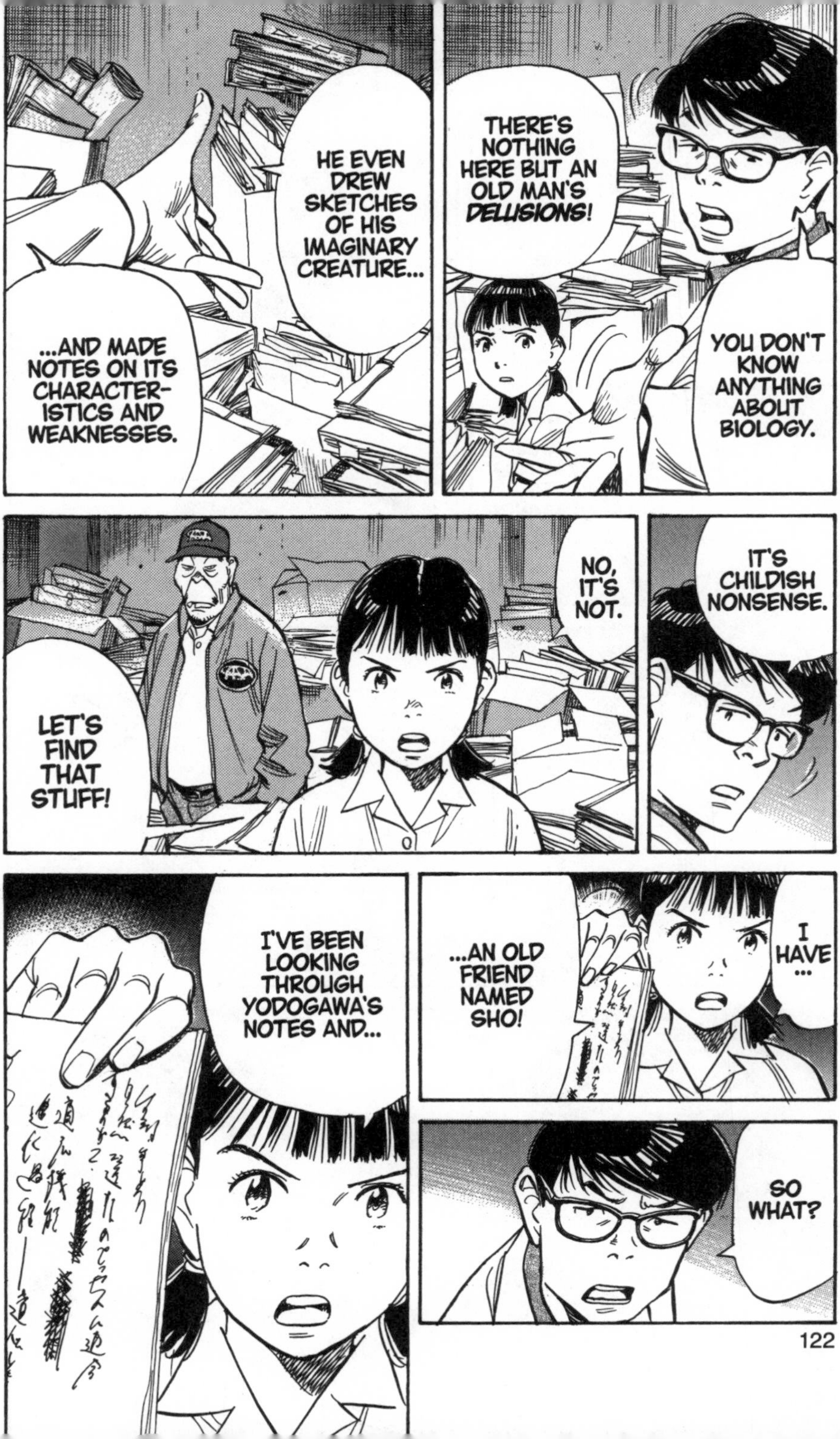
THERE'S NOTHING HERE BUT AN OLD MAN'S ***DELLUSIONS***!
YOU DON'T KNOW ANYTHING ABOUT BIOLOGY.
HE EVEN DREW SKETCHES OF HIS IMAGINARY CREATURE...
...AND MADE NOTES ON ITS CHARACTER-ISTICS AND WEAKNESSES.
IT'S CHILDISH NONSENSE.
NO, IT'S NOT.
LET'S FIND THAT STUFF!
I HAVE...
...AN OLD FRIEND NAMED SHO!
SO WHAT?
I'VE BEEN LOOKING THROUGH YODOGAWA'S NOTES AND...

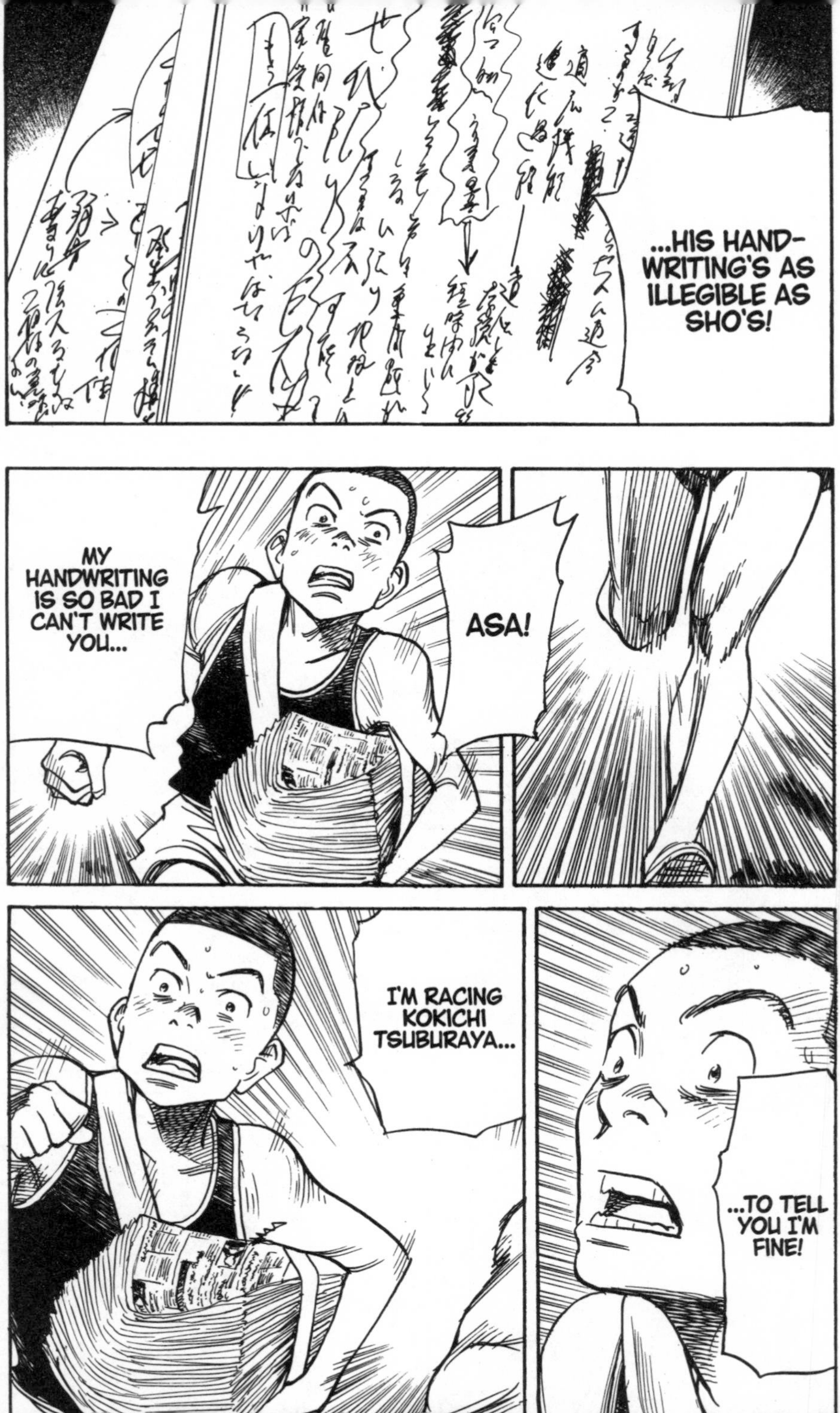
...HIS HAND-WRITING'S AS ILLEGIBLE AS SHO'S!
ASA!
MY HANDWRITING IS SO BAD I CAN'T WRITE YOU...
I'M RACING KOKICHI TSUBURAYA...
...TO TELL YOU I'M FINE!

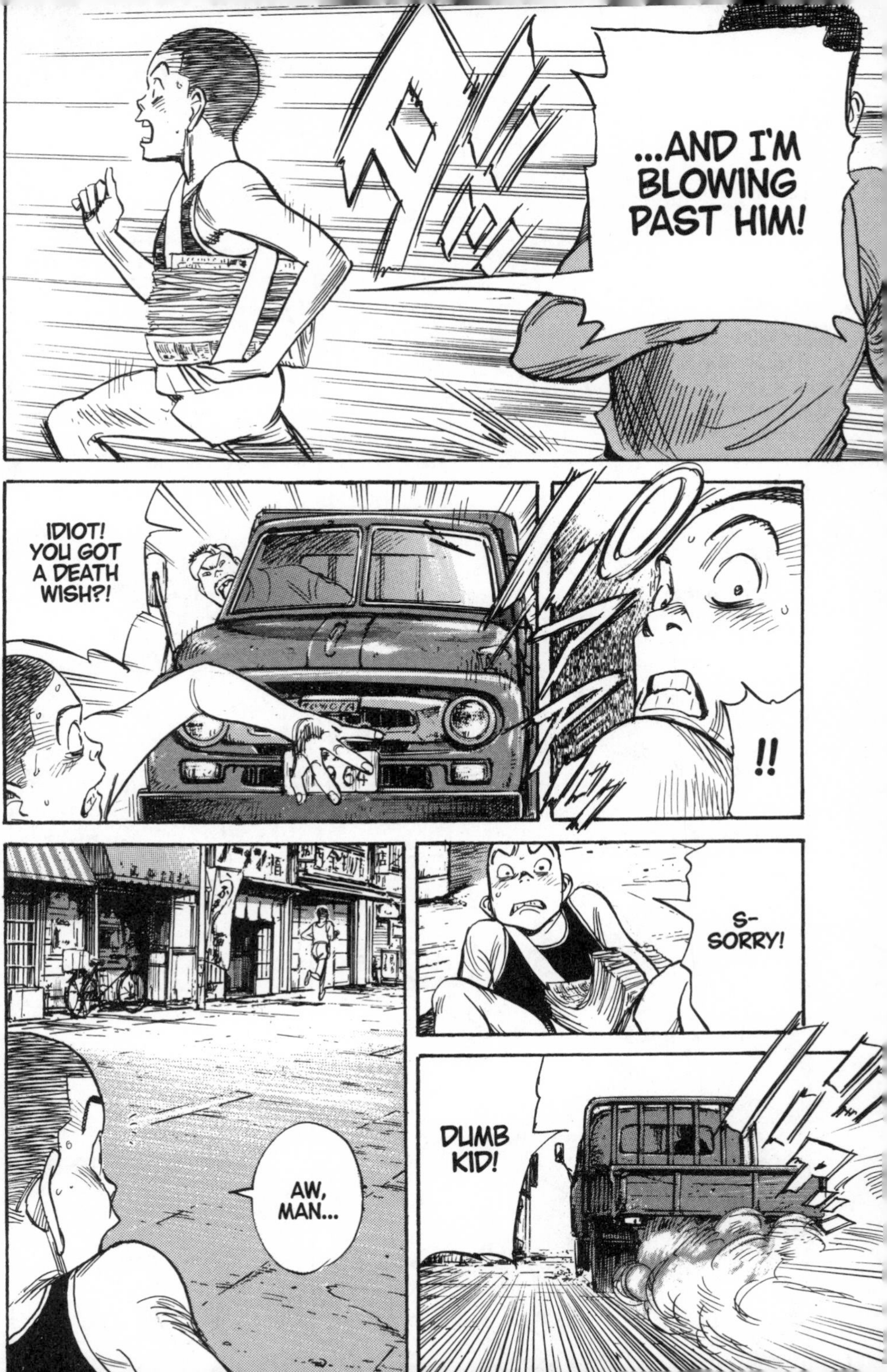
...AND I'M BLOWING PAST HIM!
!!
IDIOT! YOU GOT A DEATH WISH?!
S-SORRY!
DUMB KID!
AW, MAN...

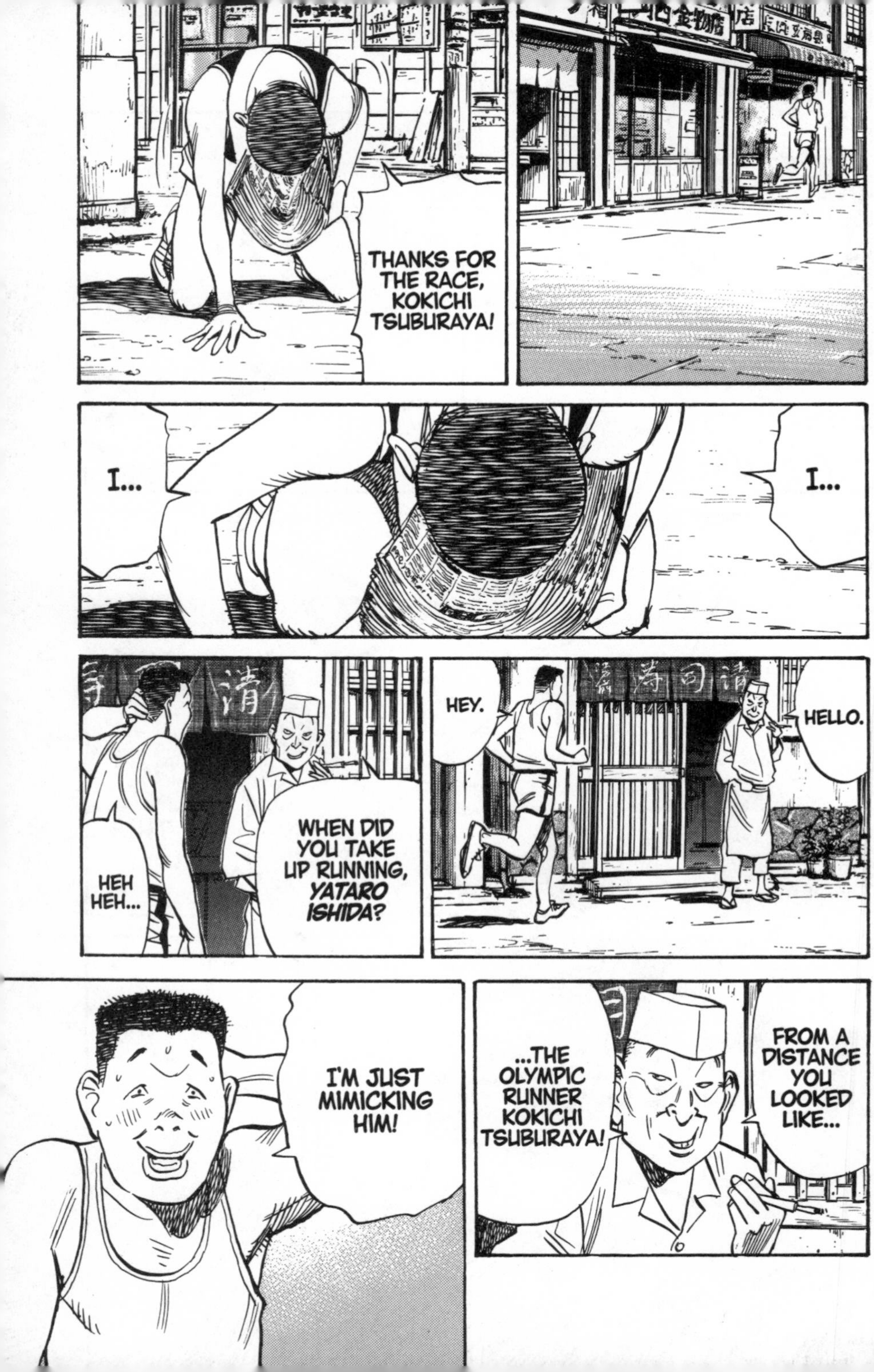
THANKS FOR THE RACE, KOKICHI TSUBURAYA!
I...
I...
HELLO.
HEY.
WHEN DID YOU TAKE UP RUNNING, *YATARO ISHIDA*?
HEH HEH...
FROM A DISTANCE YOU LOOKED LIKE...
...THE OLYMPIC RUNNER KOKICHI TSUBURAYA!
I'M JUST MIMICKING HIM!

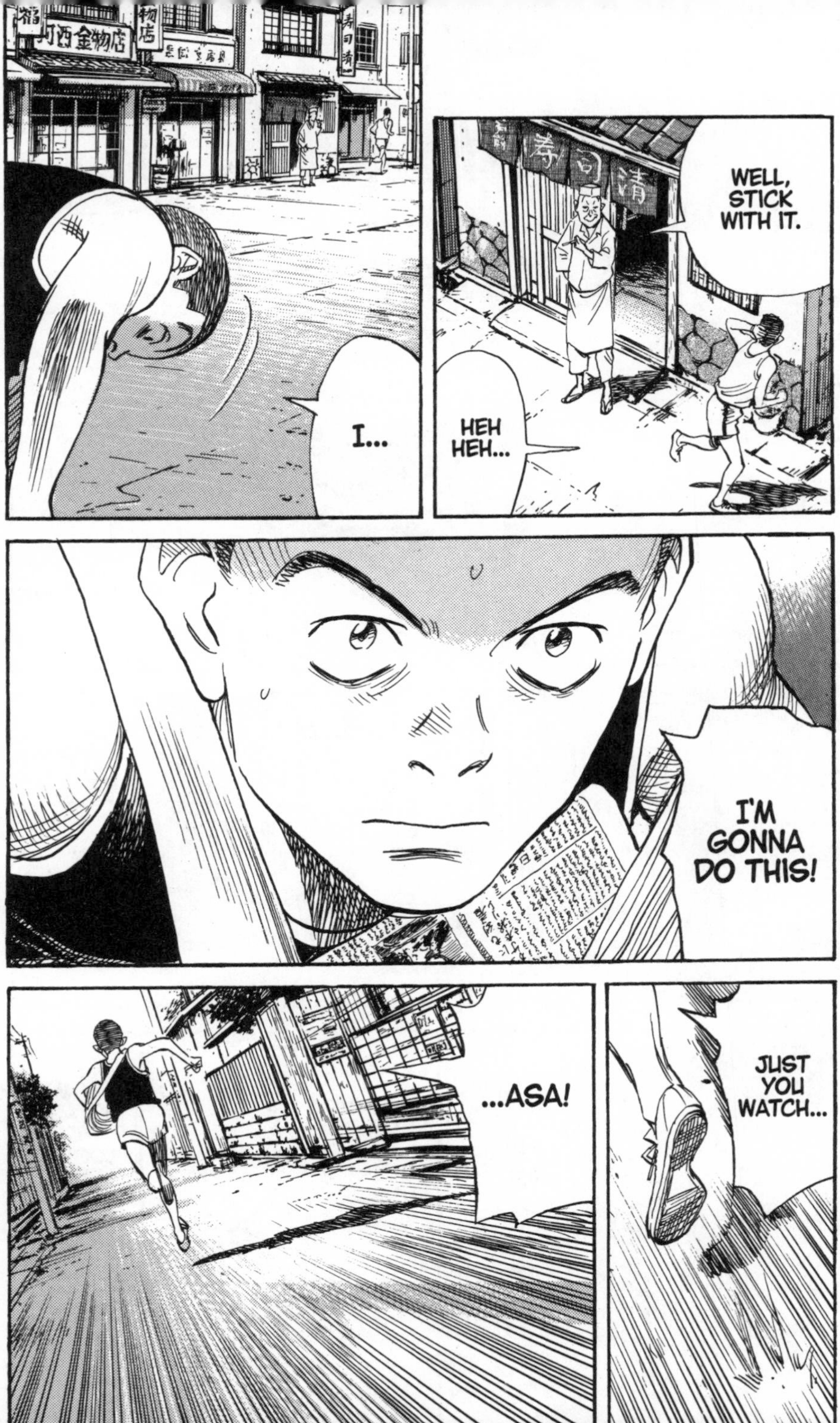
寿司清
WELL, STICK WITH IT.
HEH HEH...
I...
I'M GONNA DO THIS!
JUST YOU WATCH...
...ASA!

ASADORA!

ASADORA!

Chapter 22 ● Just a Fighter Plane

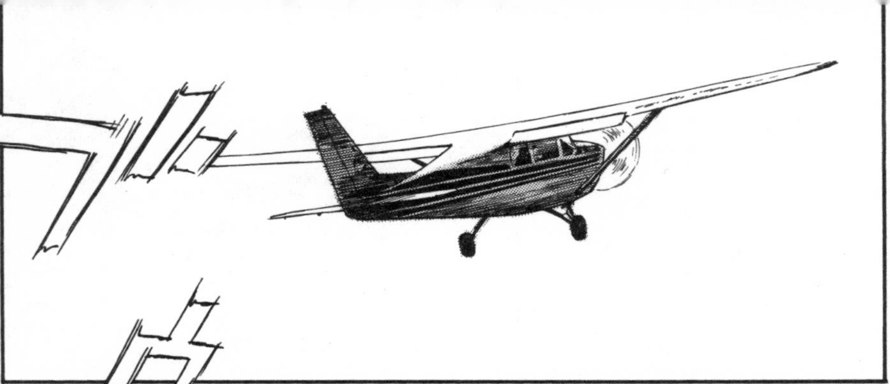

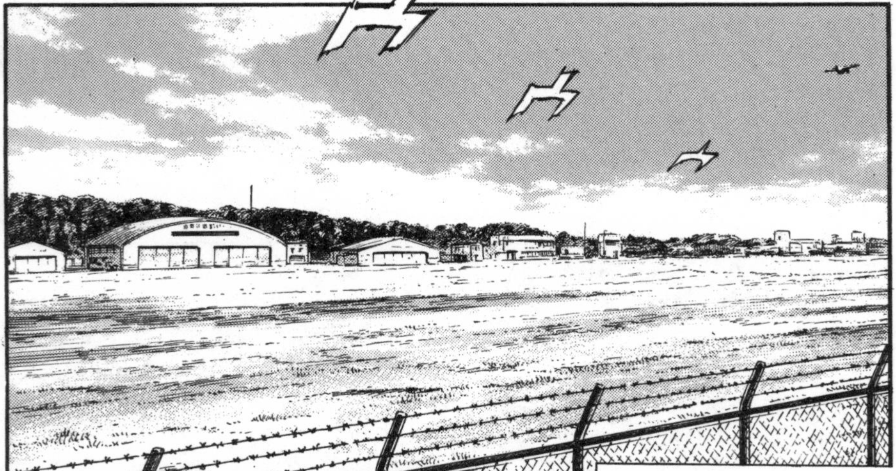
Chofu Airfield, Tokyo
October 6, 1964

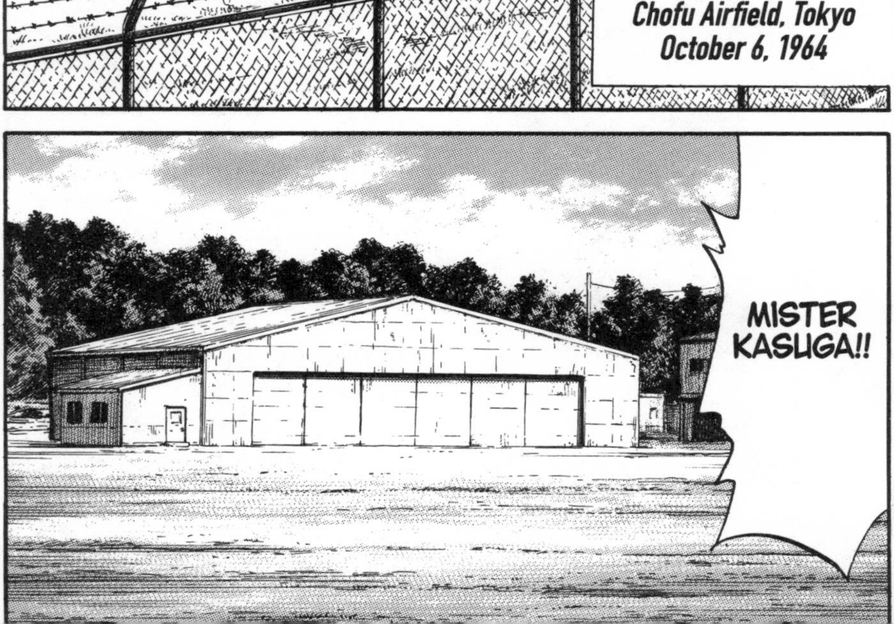
MISTER KASUGA!!

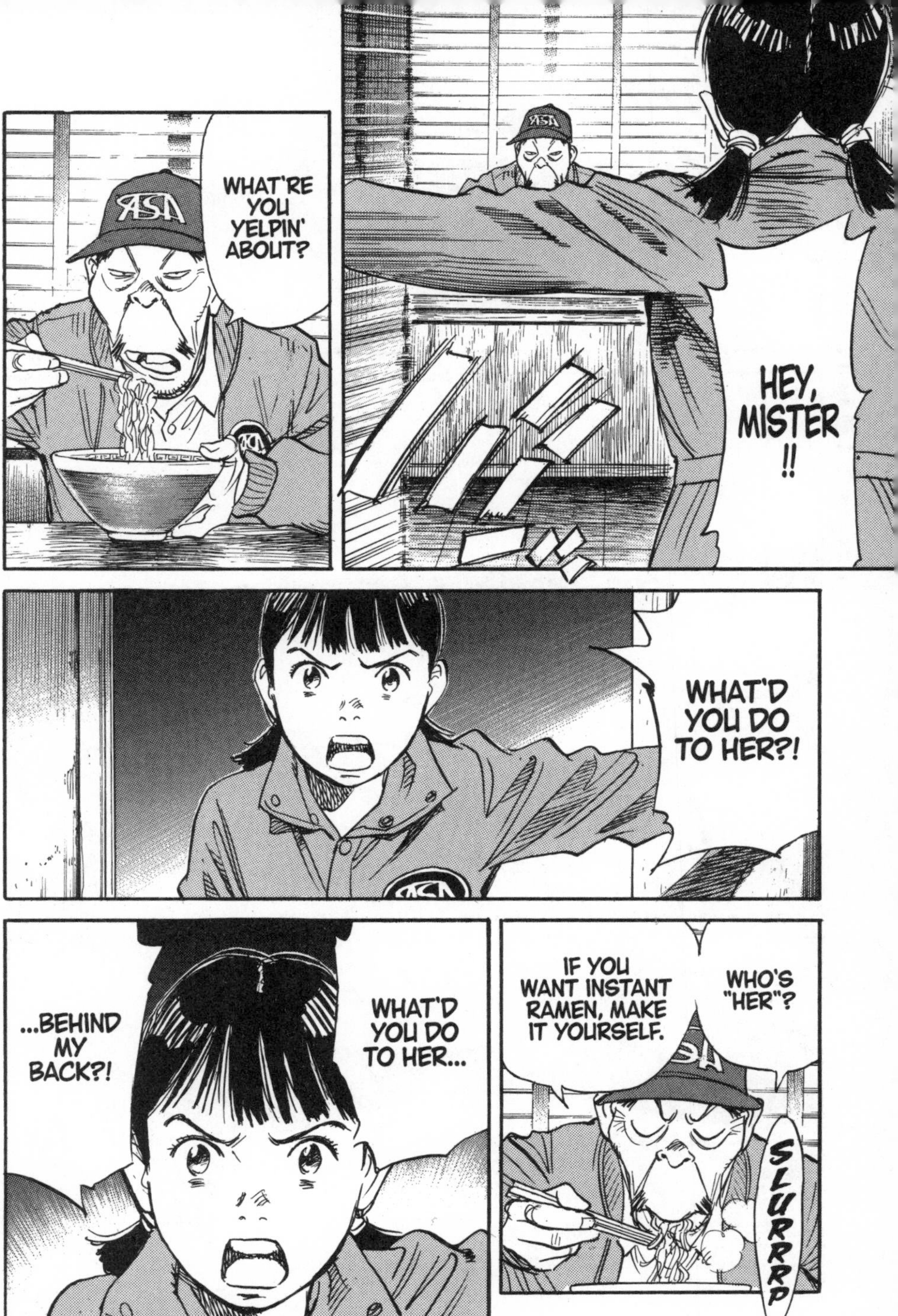
HEY, MISTER!!
WHAT'RE YOU YELPIN' ABOUT?
WHAT'D YOU DO TO HER?!
WHO'S "HER"?
IF YOU WANT INSTANT RAMEN, MAKE IT YOURSELF.
SLURRRP
WHAT'D YOU DO TO HER...
...BEHIND MY BACK?!

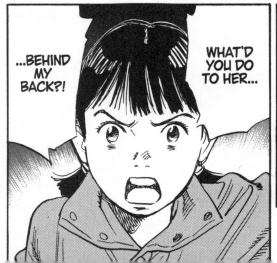

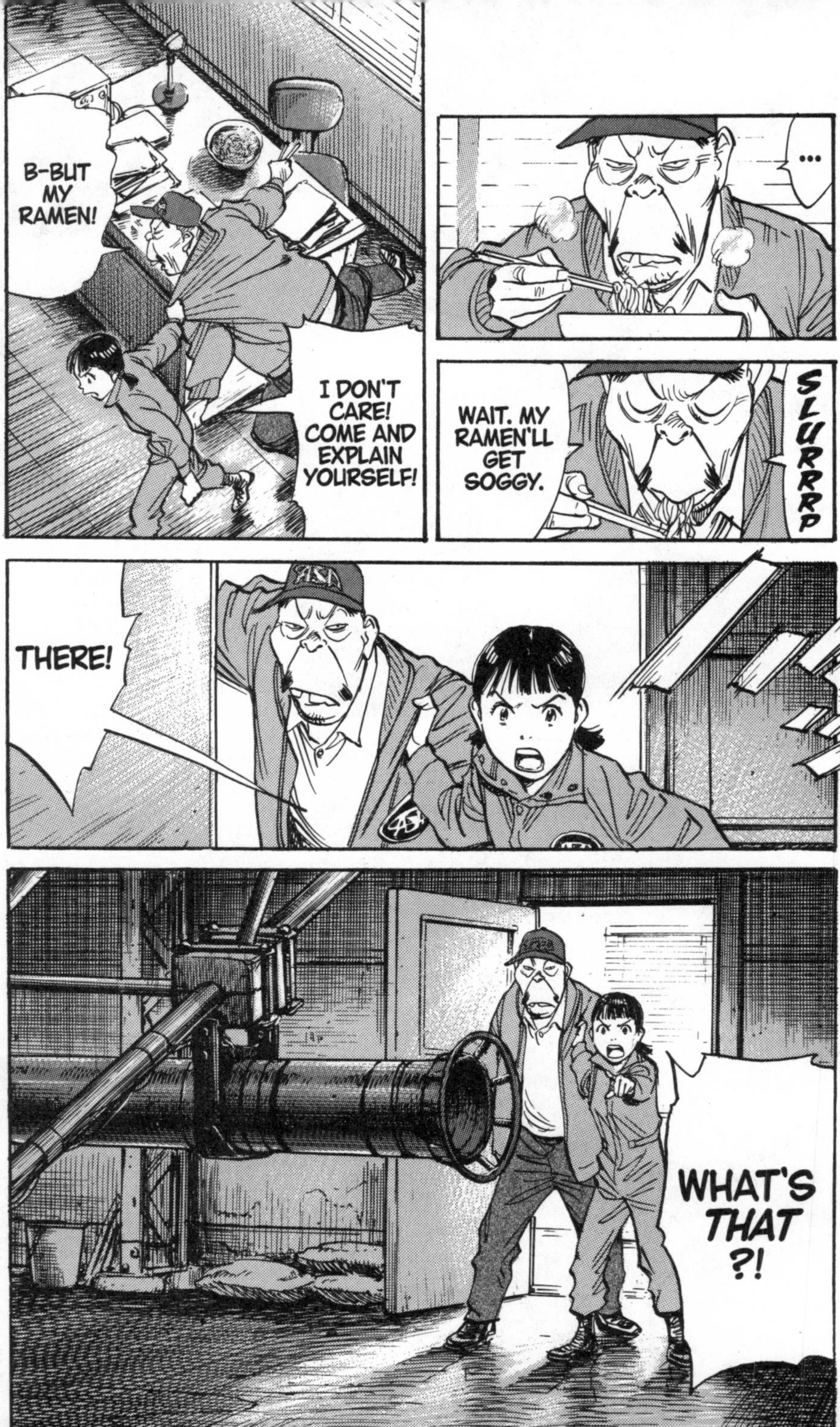
...
WAIT. MY RAMEN'LL GET SOGGY.
SLURRRP
I DON'T CARE! COME AND EXPLAIN YOURSELF!
B-BUT MY RAMEN!
THERE!
WHAT'S THAT ?!

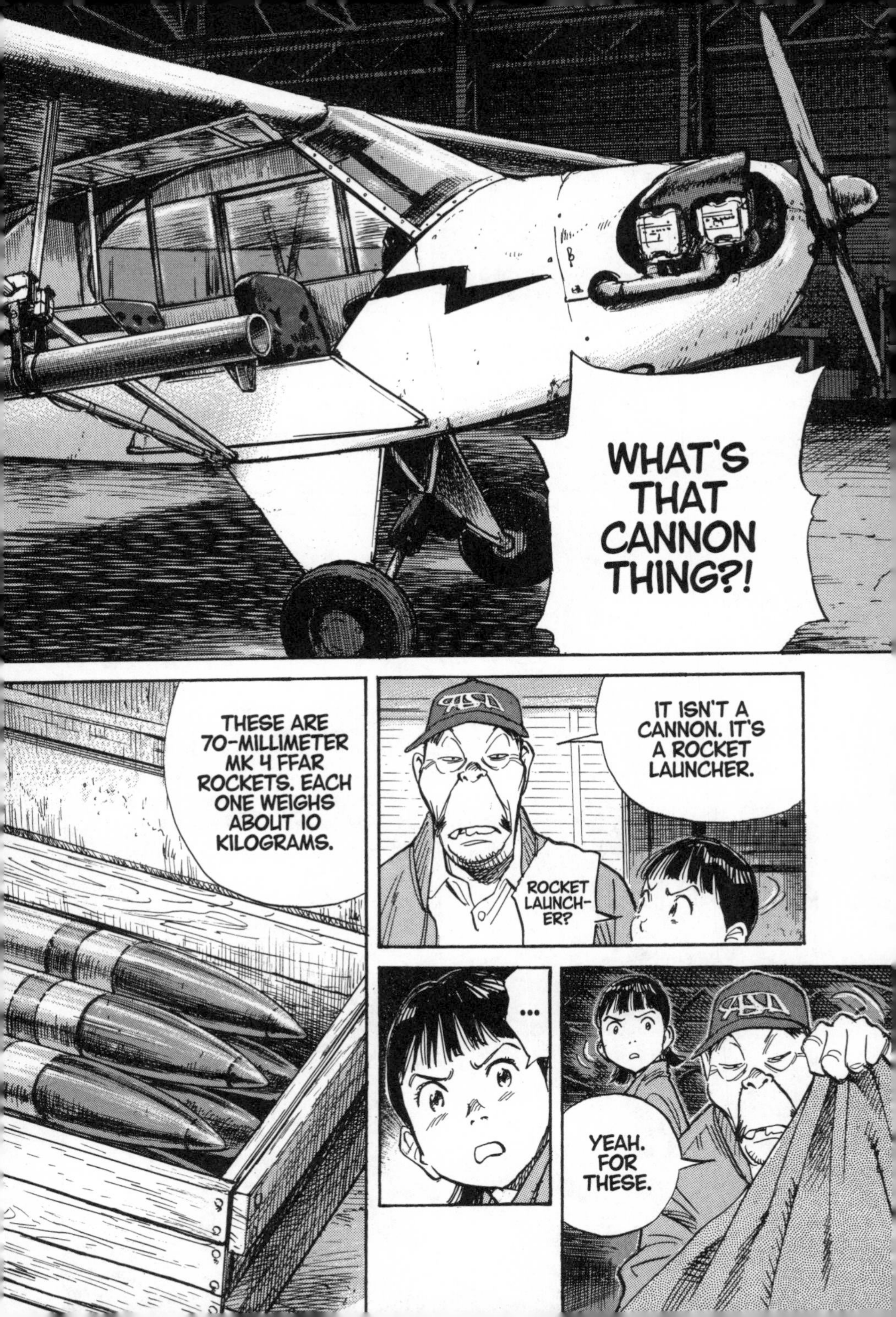
WHAT'S THAT CANNON THING?!
IT ISN'T A CANNON. IT'S A ROCKET LAUNCHER.
ROCKET LAUNCH-ER?
YEAH. FOR THESE.
...
THESE ARE 70-MILLIMETER MK 4 FFAR ROCKETS. EACH ONE WEIGHS ABOUT 10 KILOGRAMS.

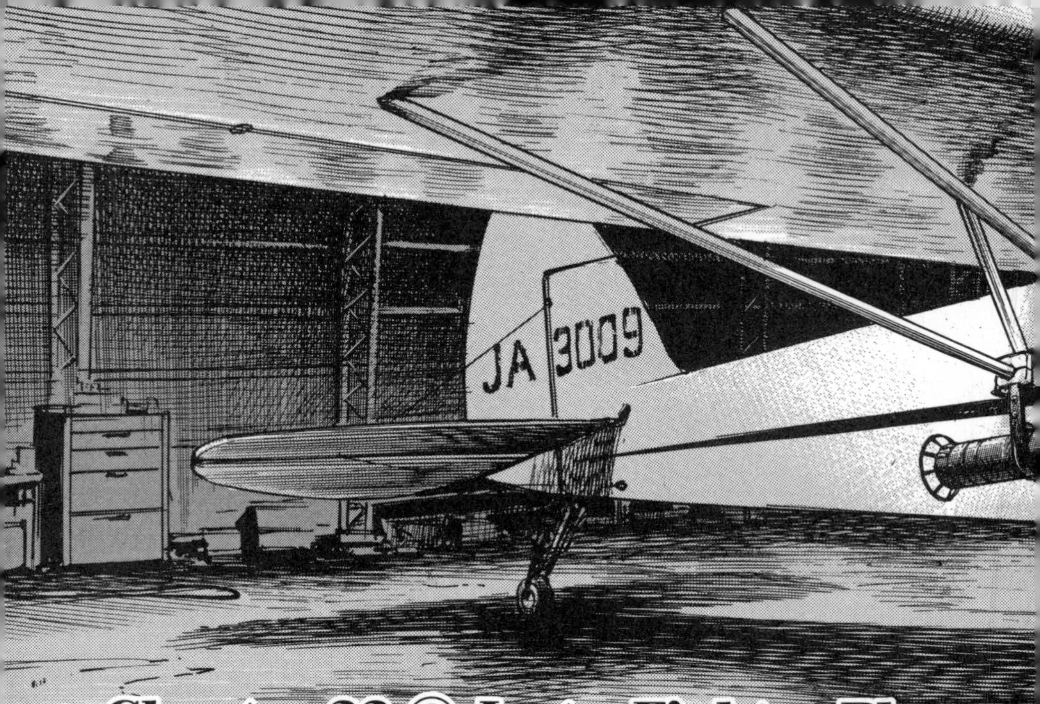

Chapter 22 ◉ Just a Fighter Plane

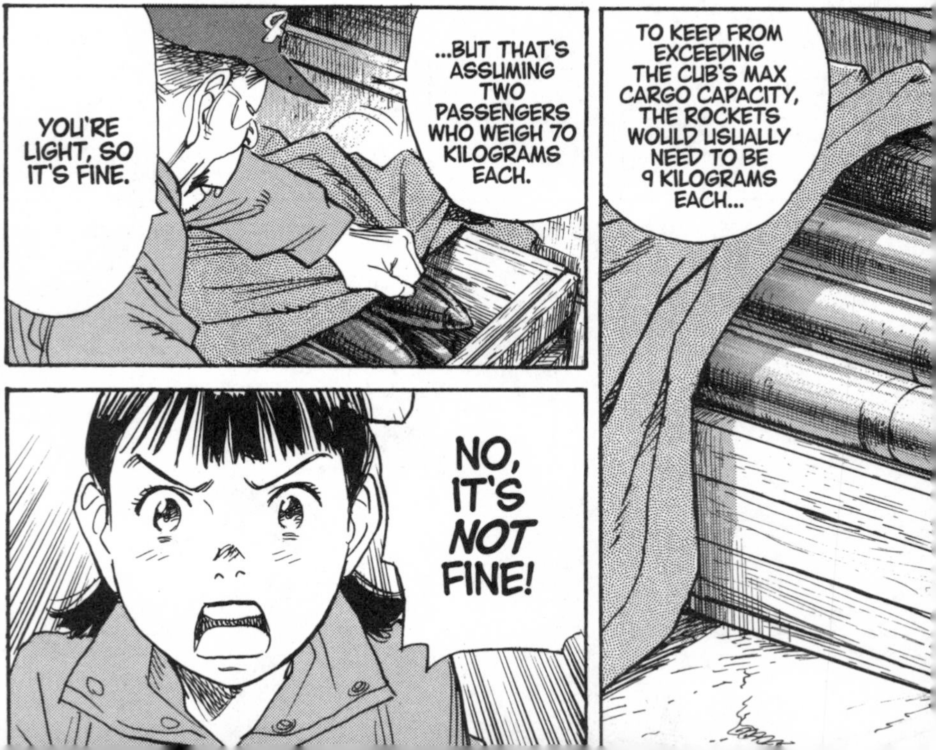
TO KEEP FROM EXCEEDING THE CUB'S MAX CARGO CAPACITY, THE ROCKETS WOULD USUALLY NEED TO BE 9 KILOGRAMS EACH...
...BUT THAT'S ASSUMING TWO PASSENGERS WHO WEIGH 70 KILOGRAMS EACH.
YOU'RE LIGHT, SO IT'S FINE.
NO, IT'S *NOT* FINE!

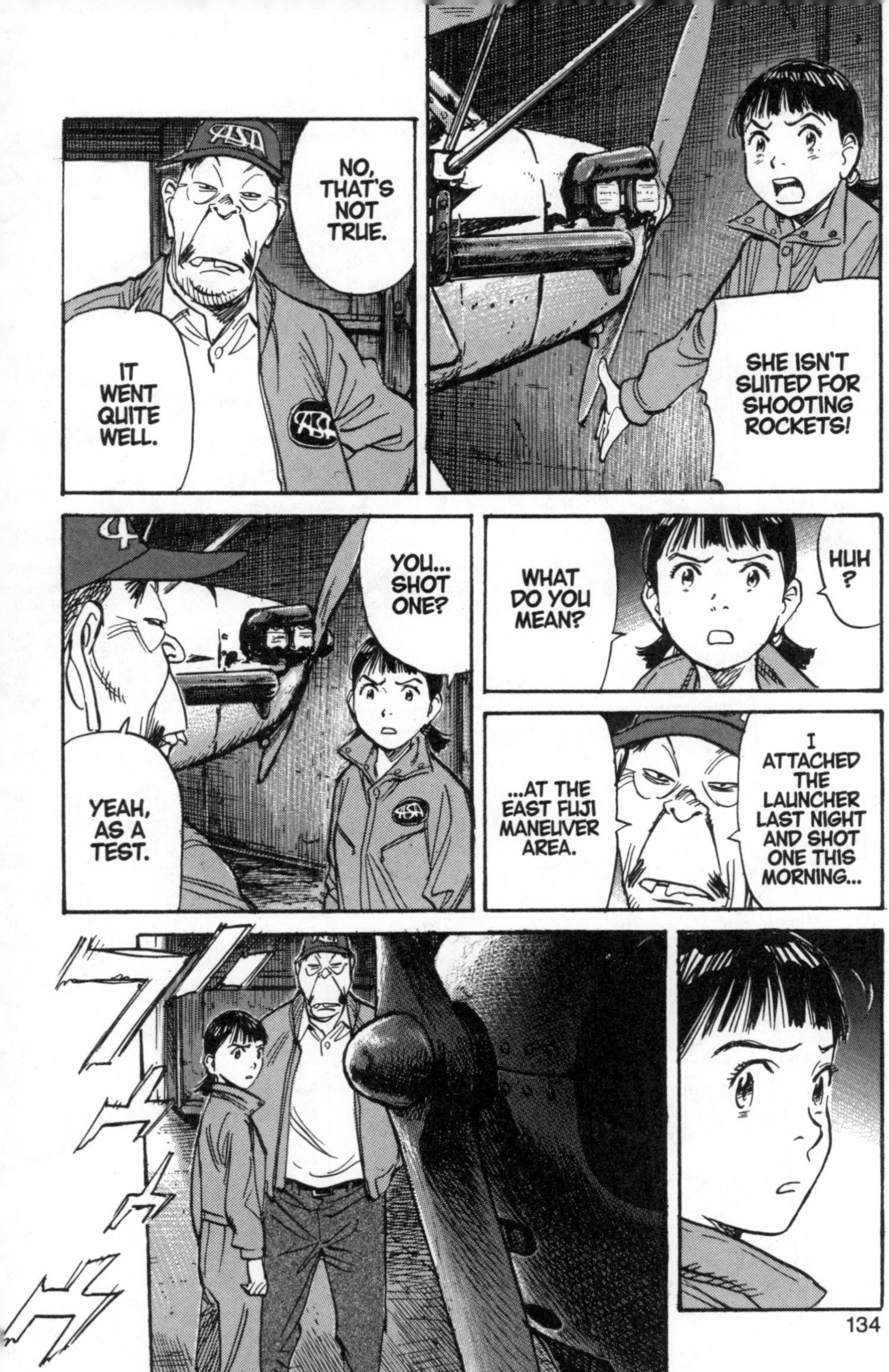
SHE ISN'T SUITED FOR SHOOTING ROCKETS!
NO, THAT'S NOT TRUE.
IT WENT QUITE WELL.
HUH?
WHAT DO YOU MEAN?
I ATTACHED THE LAUNCHER LAST NIGHT AND SHOT ONE THIS MORNING...
...AT THE EAST FUJI MANEUVER AREA.
YOU... SHOT ONE?
YEAH, AS A TEST.

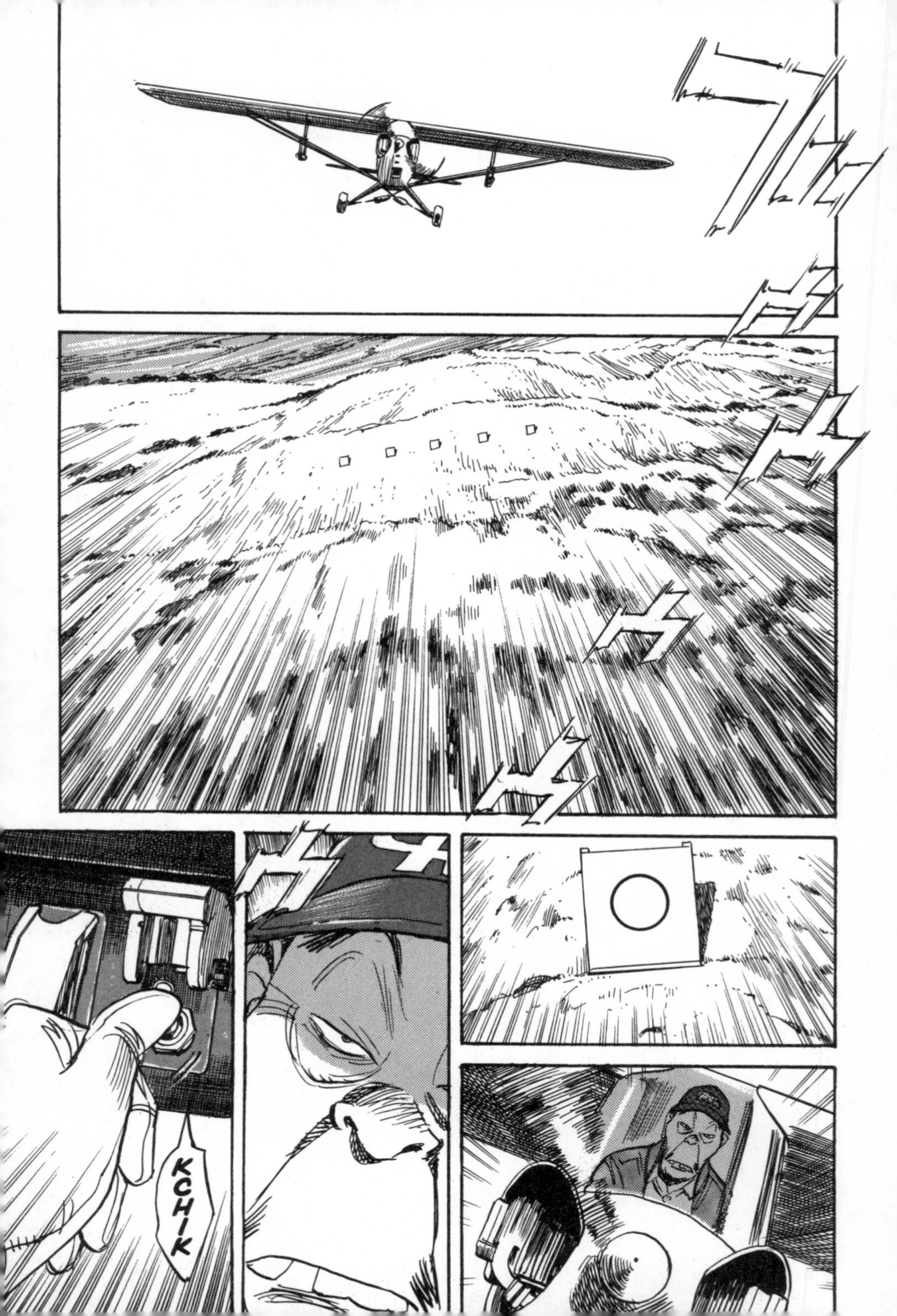
KCHIK

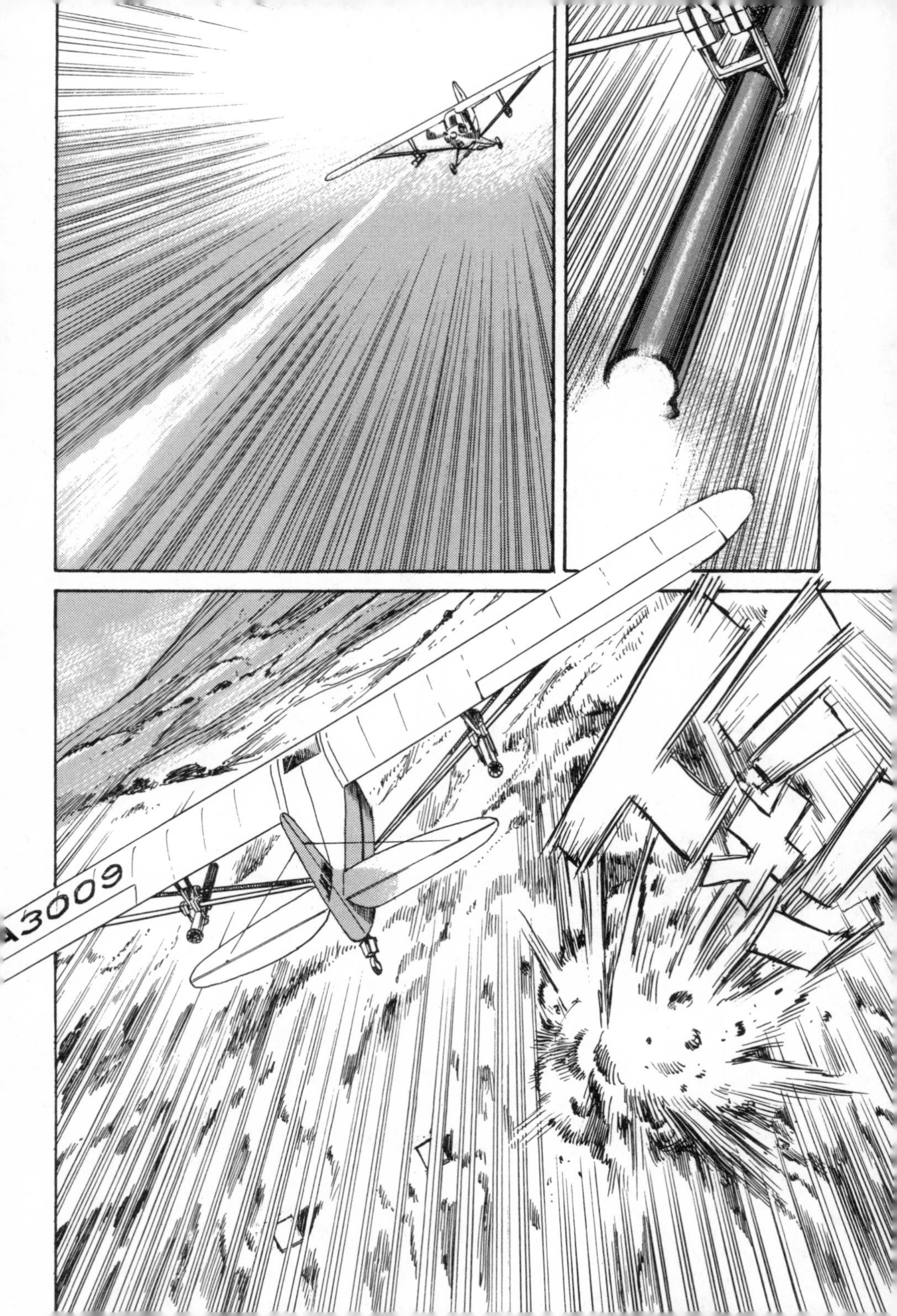
A3009

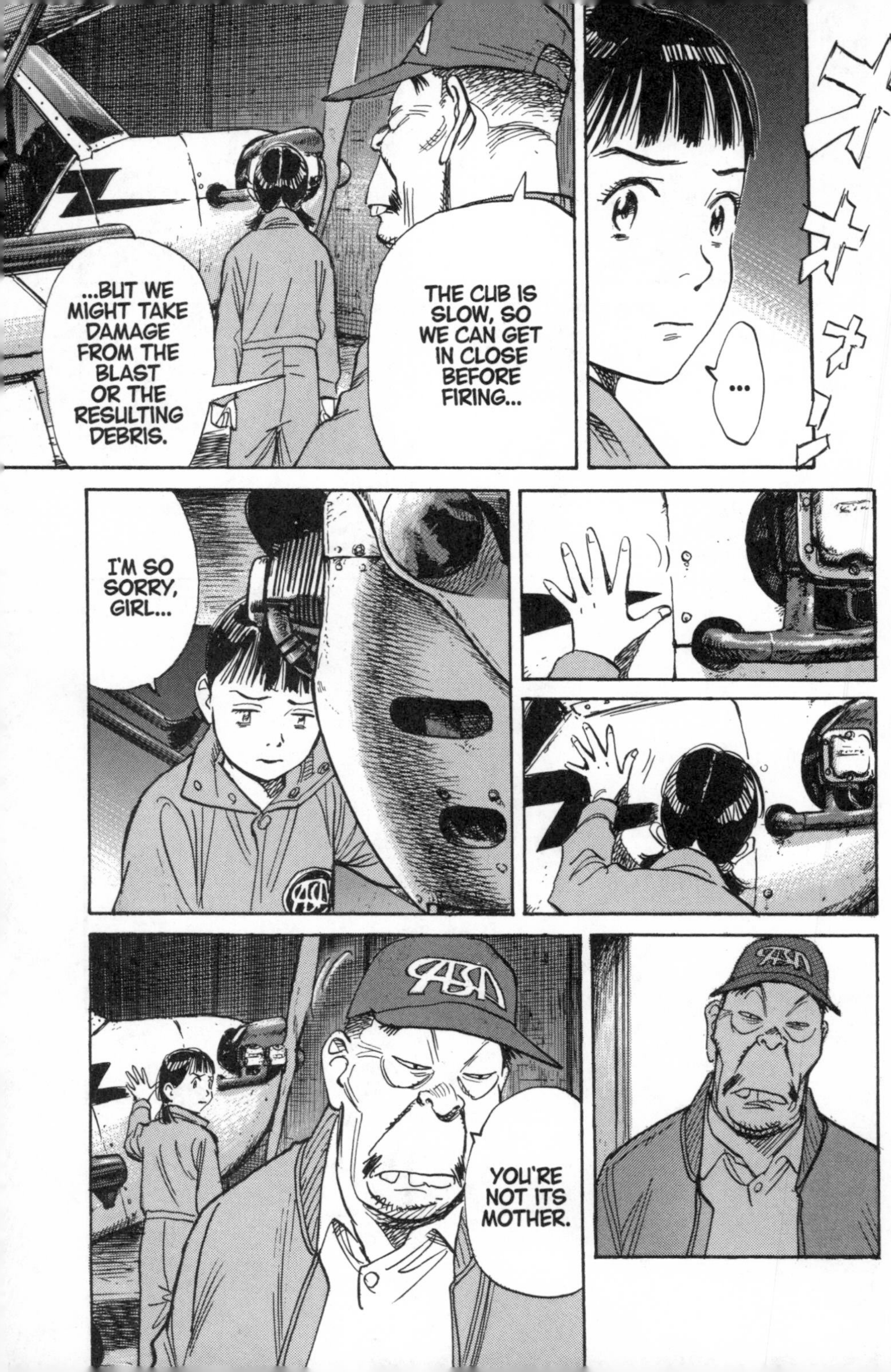
...
THE CUB IS SLOW, SO WE CAN GET IN CLOSE BEFORE FIRING...
...BUT WE MIGHT TAKE DAMAGE FROM THE BLAST OR THE RESULTING DEBRIS.
I'M SO SORRY, GIRL...
YOU'RE NOT ITS MOTHER.

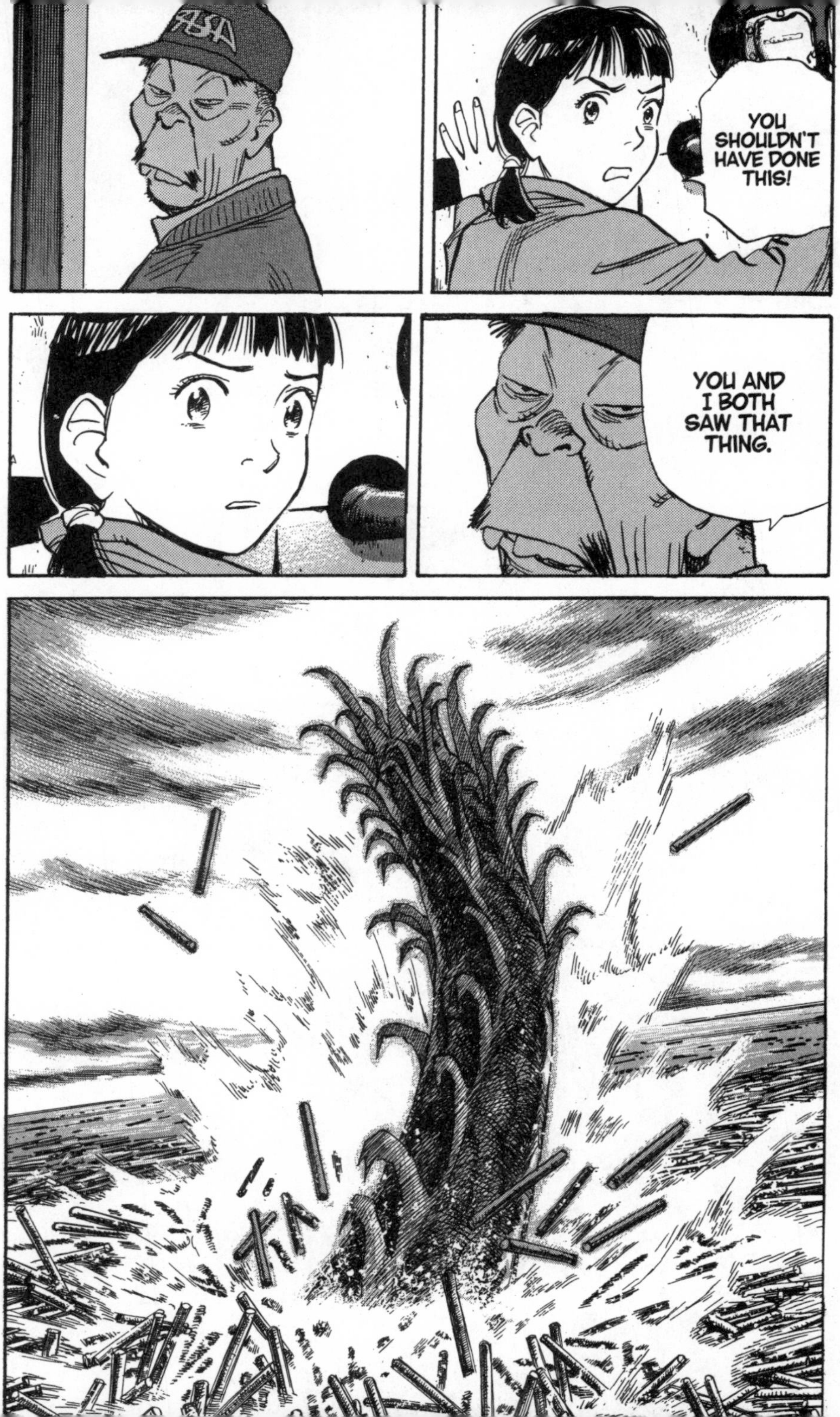
YOU SHOULDN'T HAVE DONE THIS!
YOU AND I BOTH SAW THAT THING.

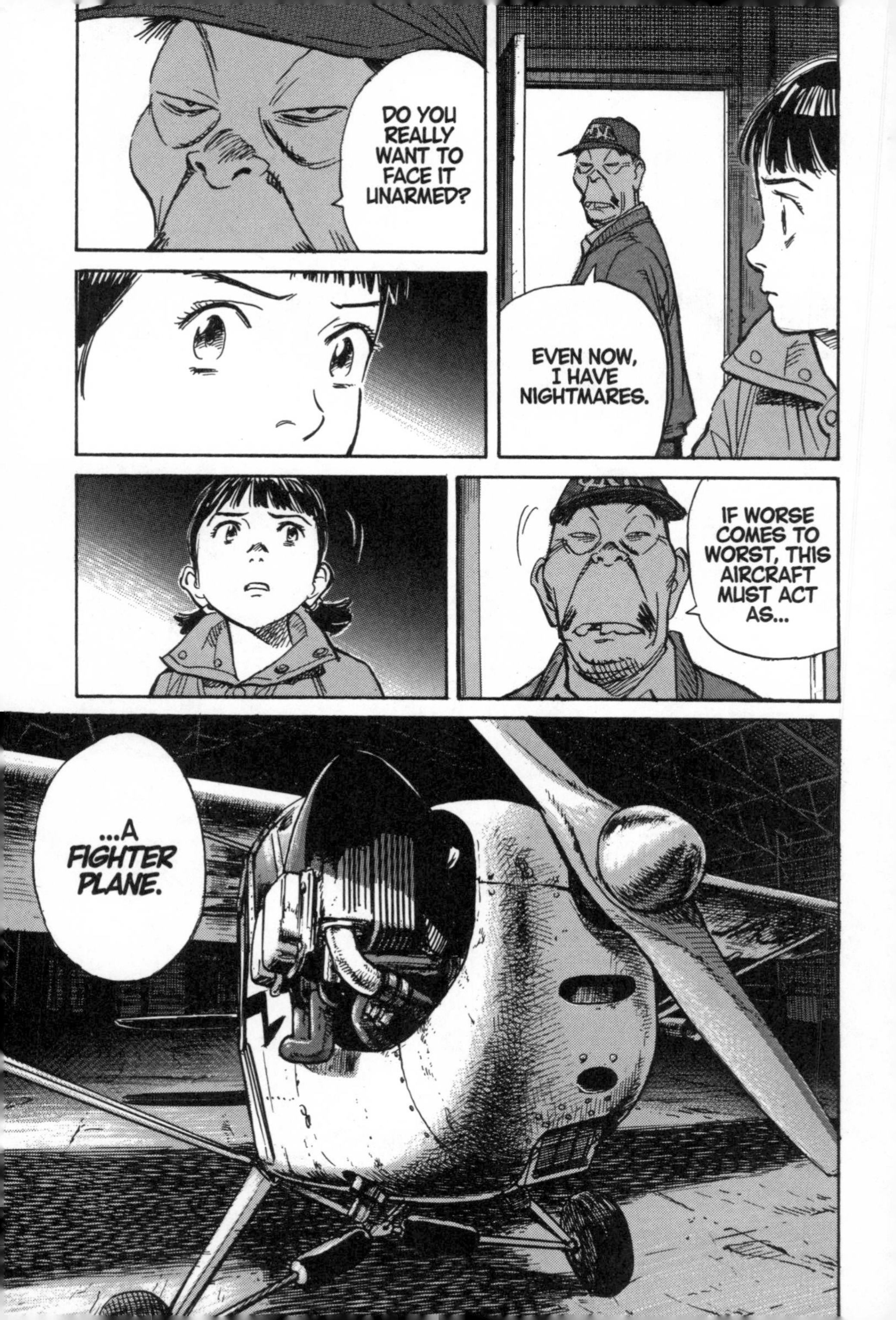
EVEN NOW, I HAVE NIGHTMARES.
DO YOU REALLY WANT TO FACE IT UNARMED?
IF WORSE COMES TO WORST, THIS AIRCRAFT MUST ACT AS...
...A FIGHTER PLANE.

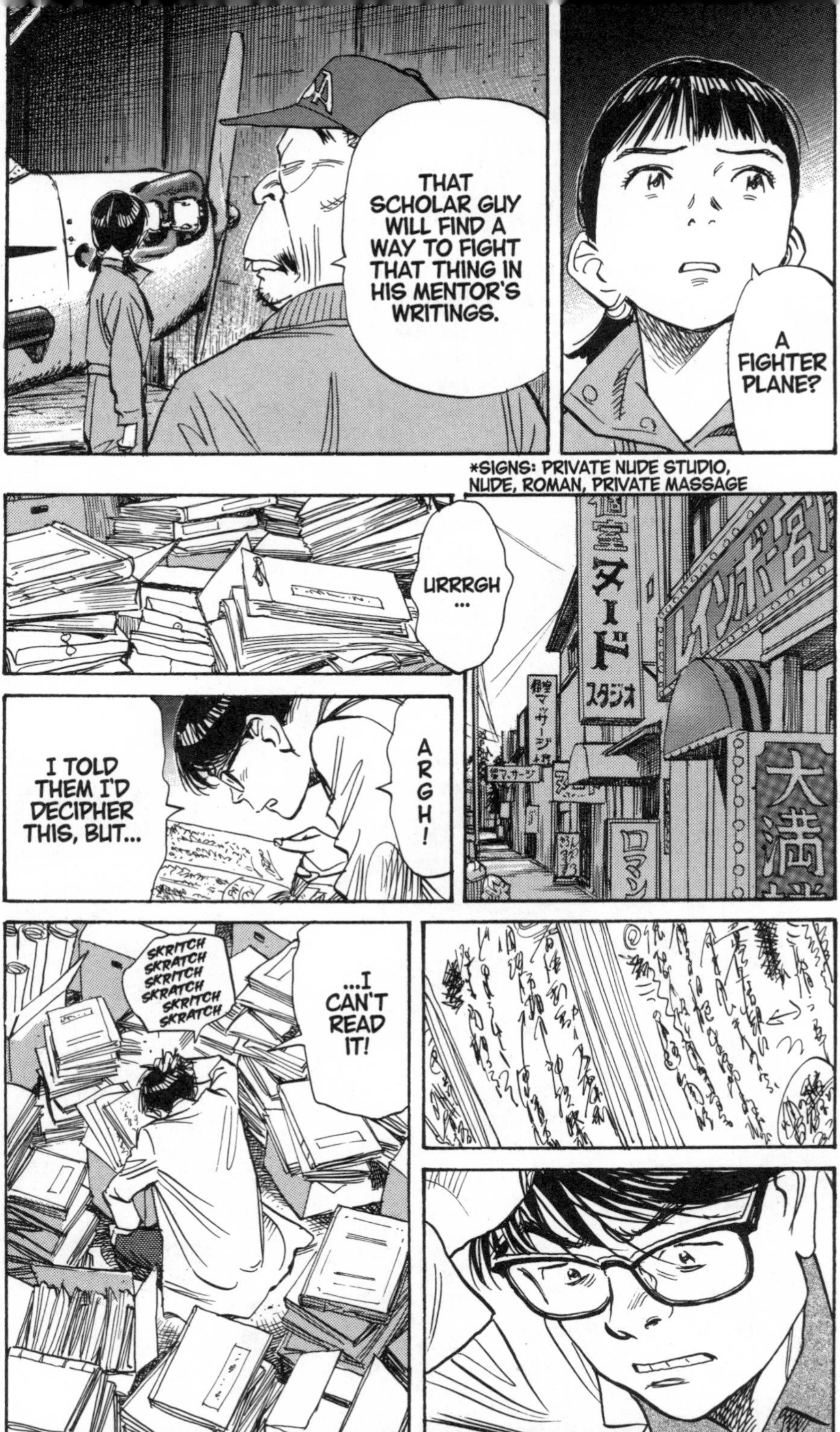
A FIGHTER PLANE?
THAT SCHOLAR GUY WILL FIND A WAY TO FIGHT THAT THING IN HIS MENTOR'S WRITINGS.
*SIGNS: PRIVATE NUDE STUDIO, NUDE, ROMAN, PRIVATE MASSAGE
個室
ヌード
スタジオ
ロマン
URRRGH...
ARGH!
I TOLD THEM I'D DECIPHER THIS, BUT...
...I CAN'T READ IT!
SKRITCH SKRATCH SKRITCH SKRATCH SKRITCH SKRATCH

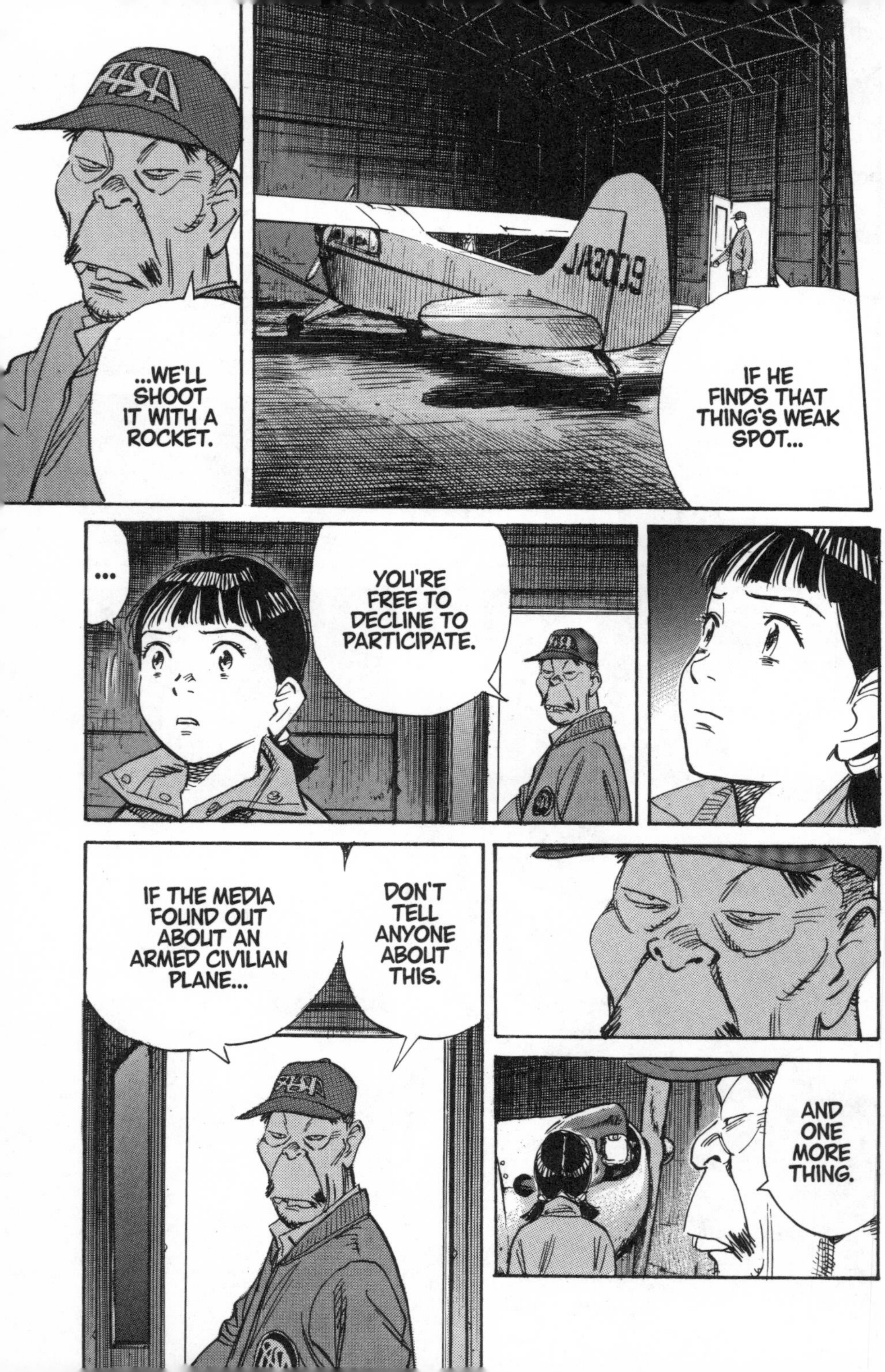
IF HE FINDS THAT THING'S WEAK SPOT...
...WE'LL SHOOT IT WITH A ROCKET.
YOU'RE FREE TO DECLINE TO PARTICIPATE.
...
AND ONE MORE THING.
DON'T TELL ANYONE ABOUT THIS.
IF THE MEDIA FOUND OUT ABOUT AN ARMED CIVILIAN PLANE...

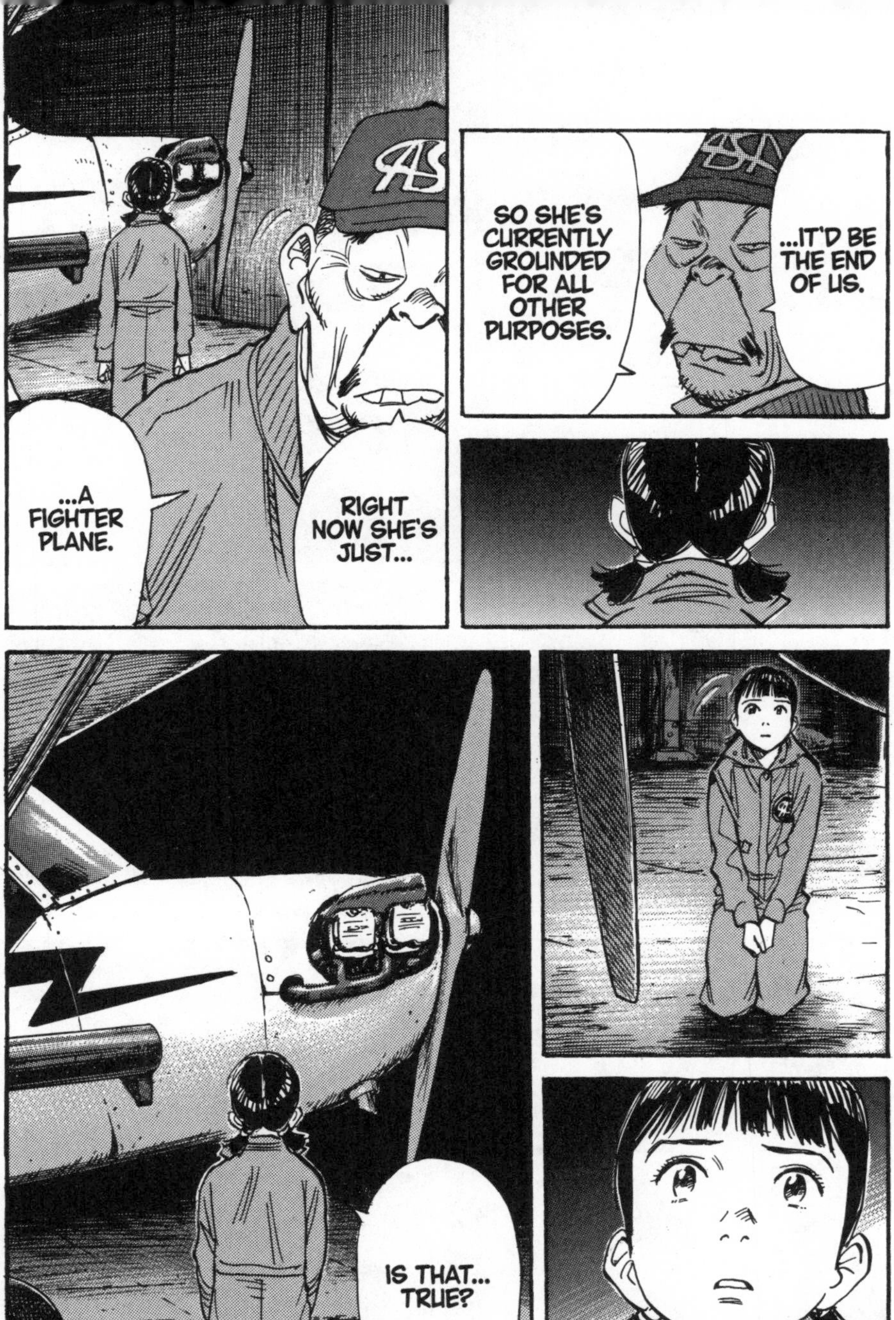
...IT'D BE THE END OF US.
SO SHE'S CURRENTLY GROUNDED FOR ALL OTHER PURPOSES.
RIGHT NOW SHE'S JUST...
...A FIGHTER PLANE.
IS THAT... TRUE?

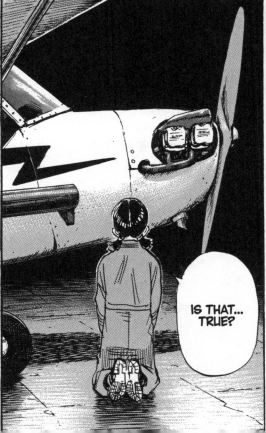

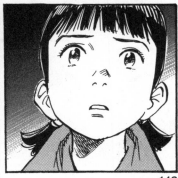

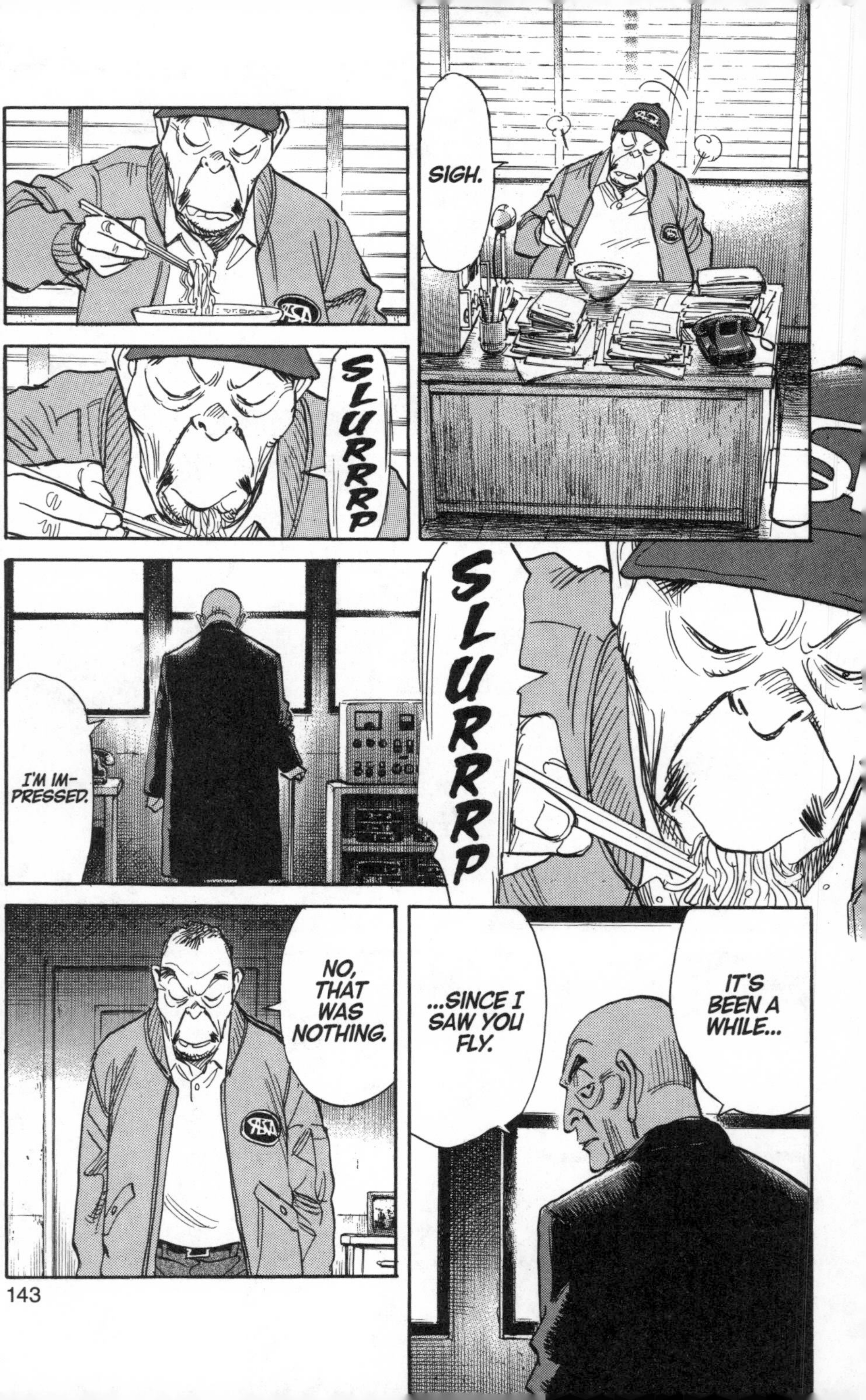
SIGH.
SLURRRP
SLURRRP
I'M IM-PRESSED.
IT'S BEEN A WHILE...
...SINCE I SAW YOU FLY.
NO, THAT WAS NOTHING.

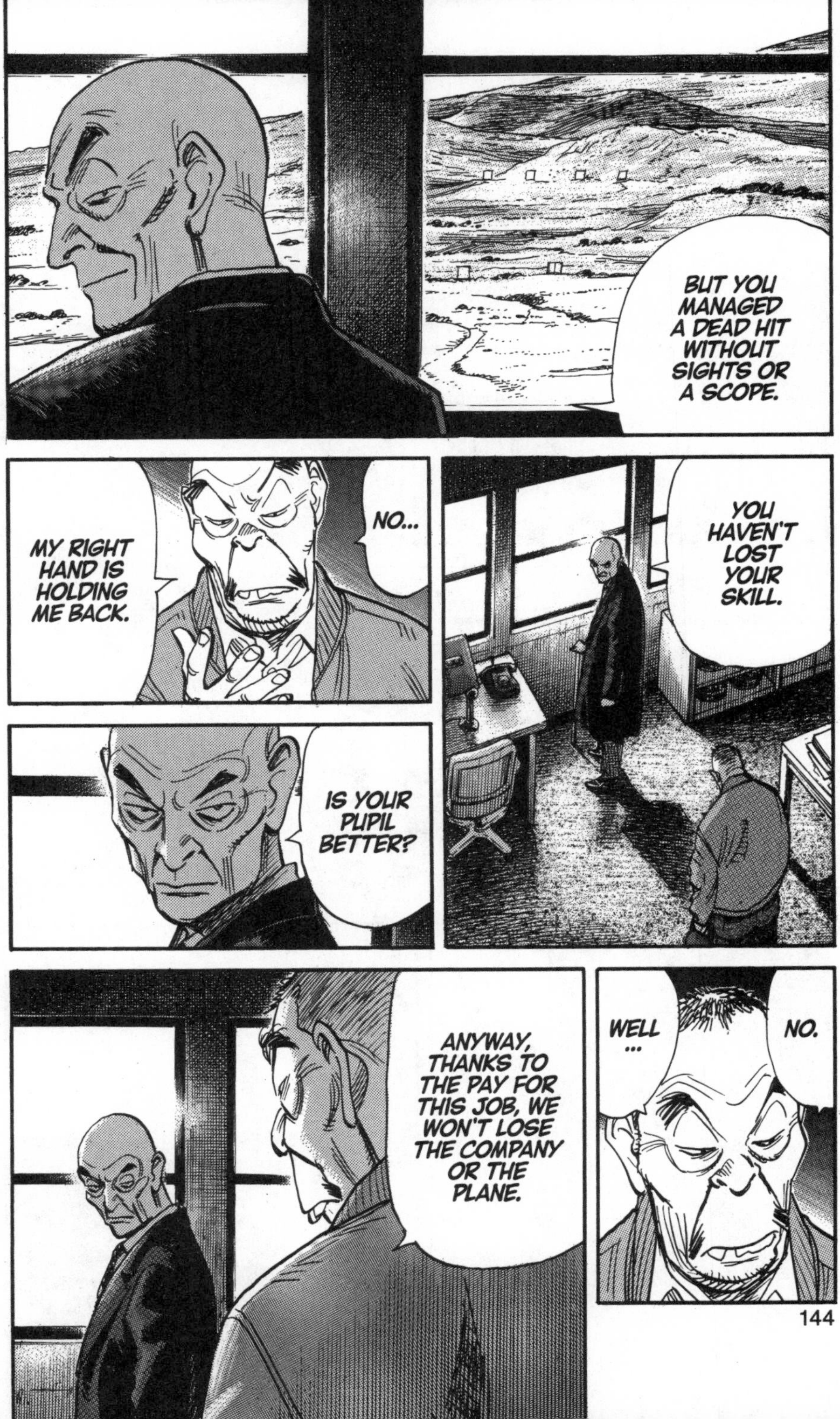
BUT YOU MANAGED A DEAD HIT WITHOUT SIGHTS OR A SCOPE.
YOU HAVEN'T LOST YOUR SKILL.
NO...
MY RIGHT HAND IS HOLDING ME BACK.
IS YOUR PUPIL BETTER?
NO.
WELL ...
ANYWAY, THANKS TO THE PAY FOR THIS JOB, WE WON'T LOSE THE COMPANY OR THE PLANE.

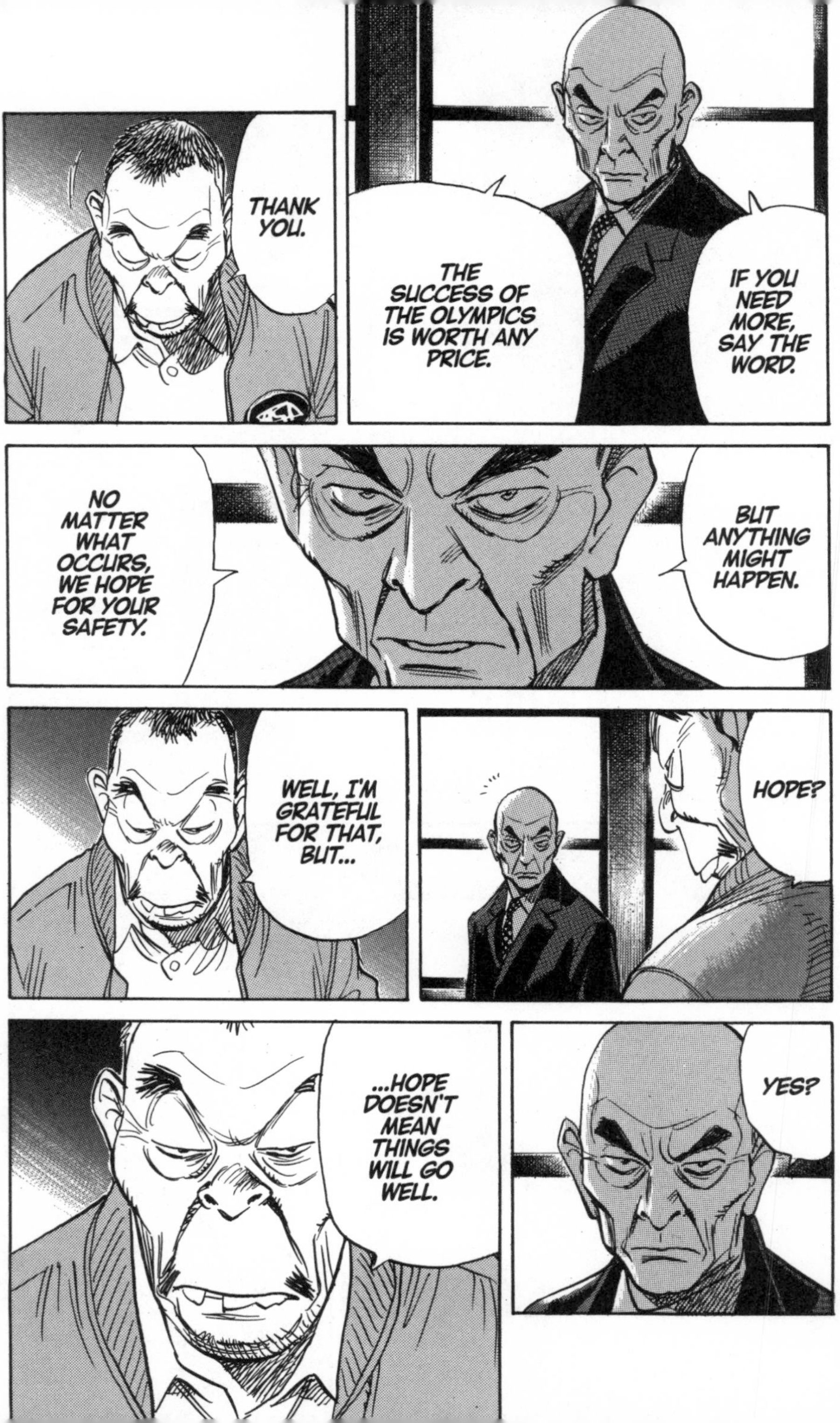
IF YOU NEED MORE, SAY THE WORD.
THE SUCCESS OF THE OLYMPICS IS WORTH ANY PRICE.
THANK YOU.
BUT ANYTHING MIGHT HAPPEN.
NO MATTER WHAT OCCURS, WE HOPE FOR YOUR SAFETY.
HOPE?
WELL, I'M GRATEFUL FOR THAT, BUT...
YES?
...HOPE DOESN'T MEAN THINGS WILL GO WELL.

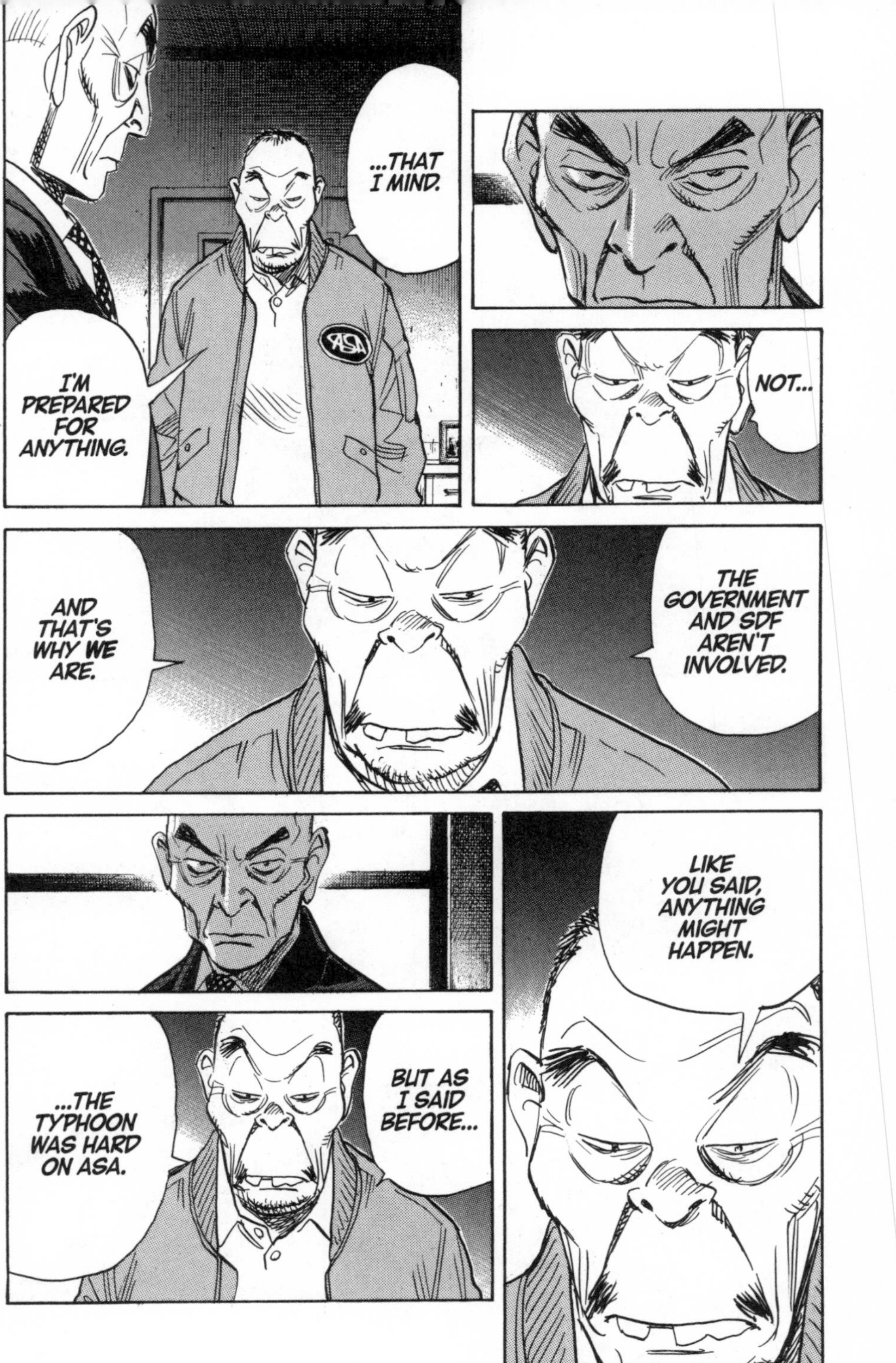
NOT...
...THAT I MIND.
I'M PREPARED FOR ANYTHING.
THE GOVERNMENT AND SDF AREN'T INVOLVED.
AND THAT'S WHY WE ARE.
LIKE YOU SAID, ANYTHING MIGHT HAPPEN.
BUT AS I SAID BEFORE...
...THE TYPHOON WAS HARD ON ASA.

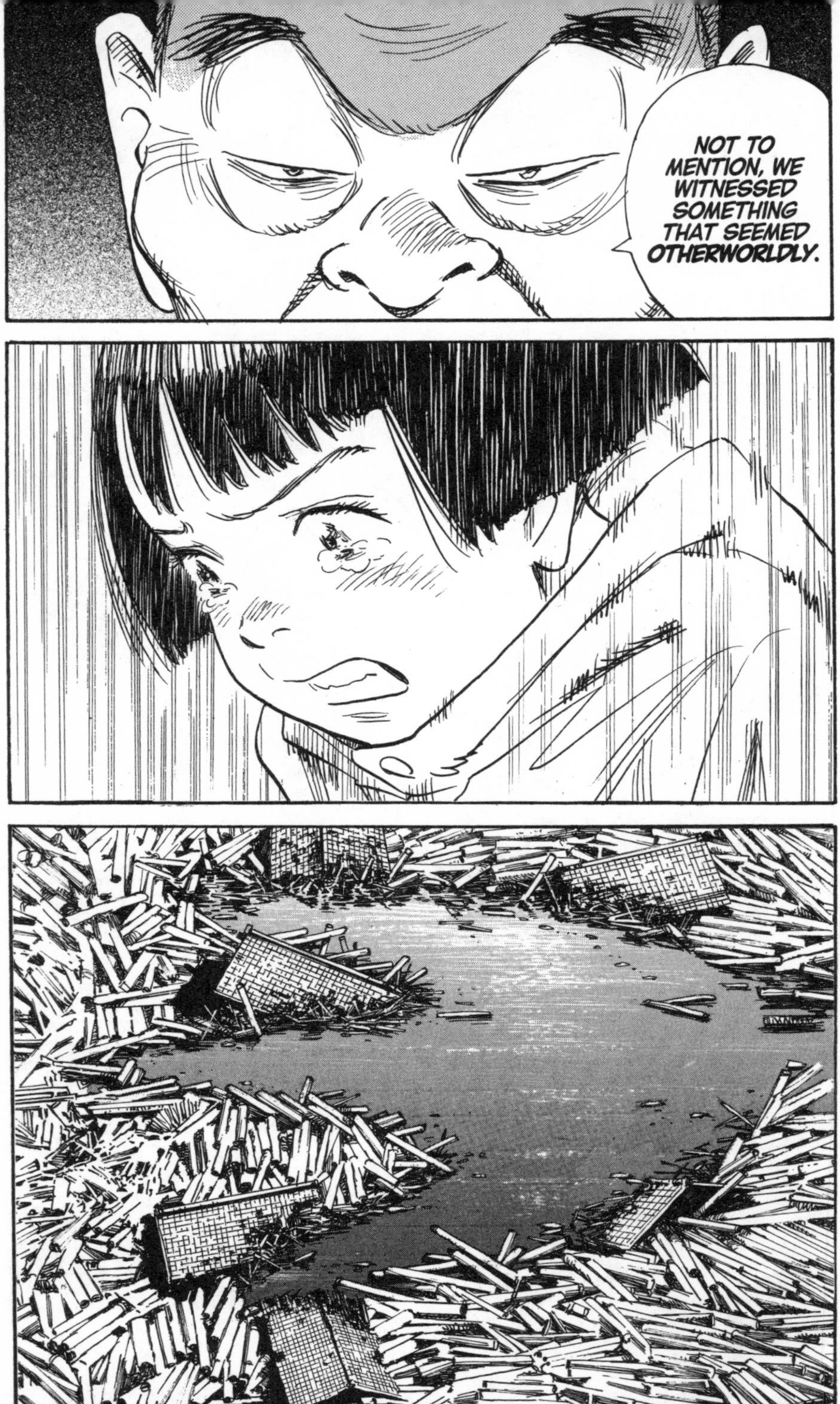
NOT TO MENTION, WE WITNESSED SOMETHING THAT SEEMED OTHERWORLDLY.

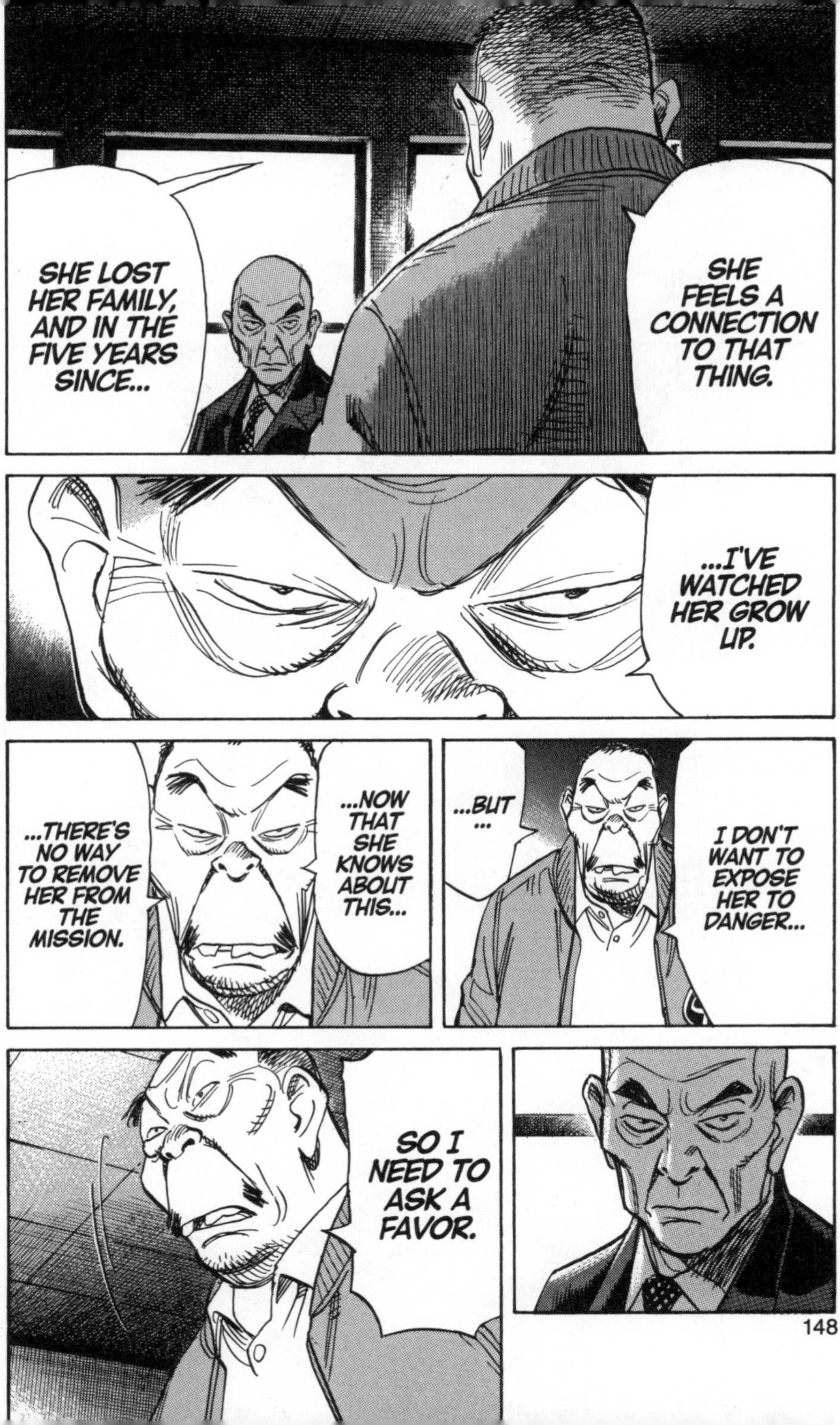
SHE FEELS A CONNECTION TO THAT THING.
SHE LOST HER FAMILY, AND IN THE FIVE YEARS SINCE...
...I'VE WATCHED HER GROW UP.
...BUT ...
I DON'T WANT TO EXPOSE HER TO DANGER...
...NOW THAT SHE KNOWS ABOUT THIS...
...THERE'S NO WAY TO REMOVE HER FROM THE MISSION.
SO I NEED TO ASK A FAVOR.

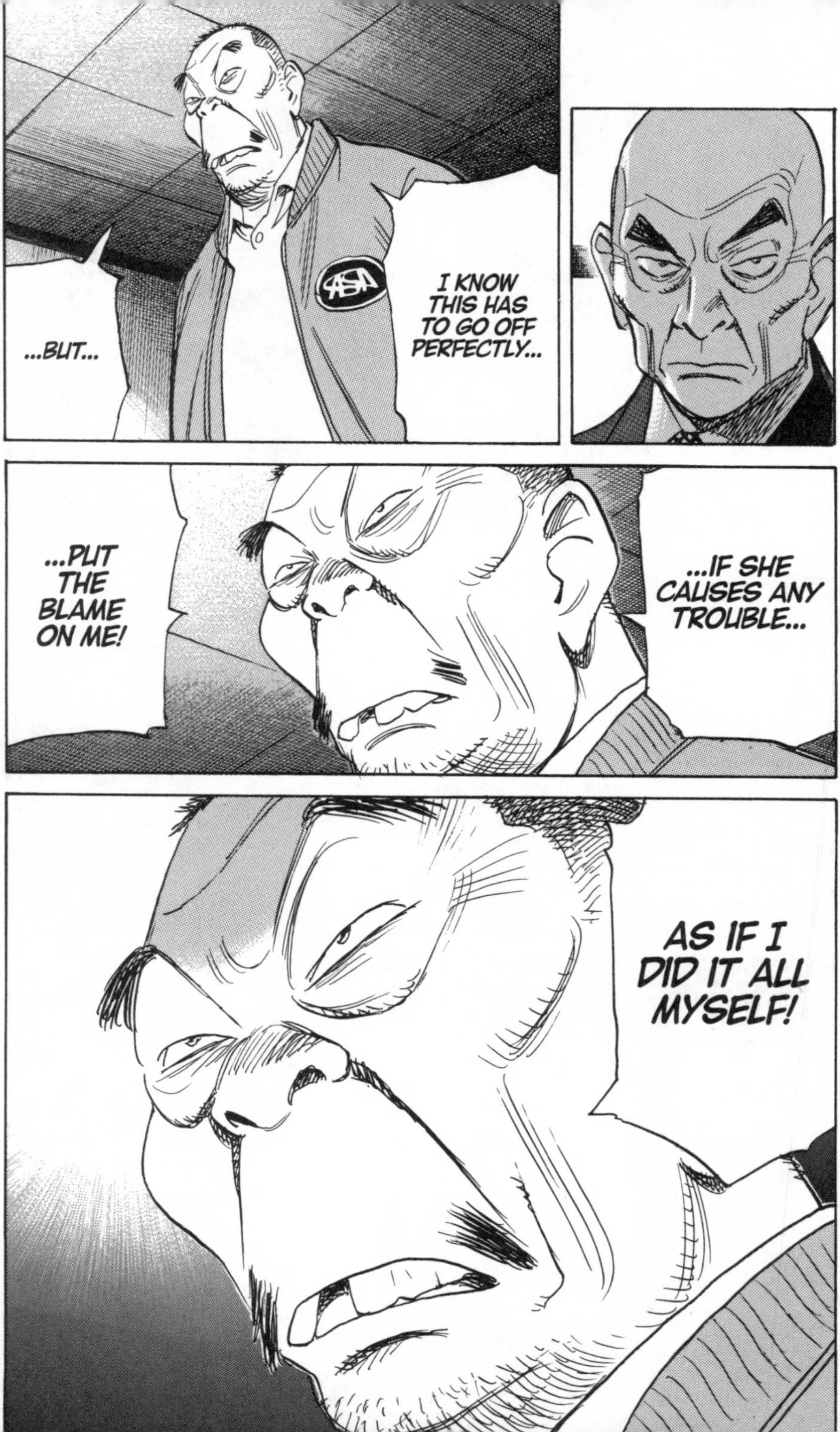
I KNOW THIS HAS TO GO OFF PERFECTLY...
...BUT...
...IF SHE CAUSES ANY TROUBLE...
...PUT THE BLAME ON ME!
AS IF I DID IT ALL MYSELF!

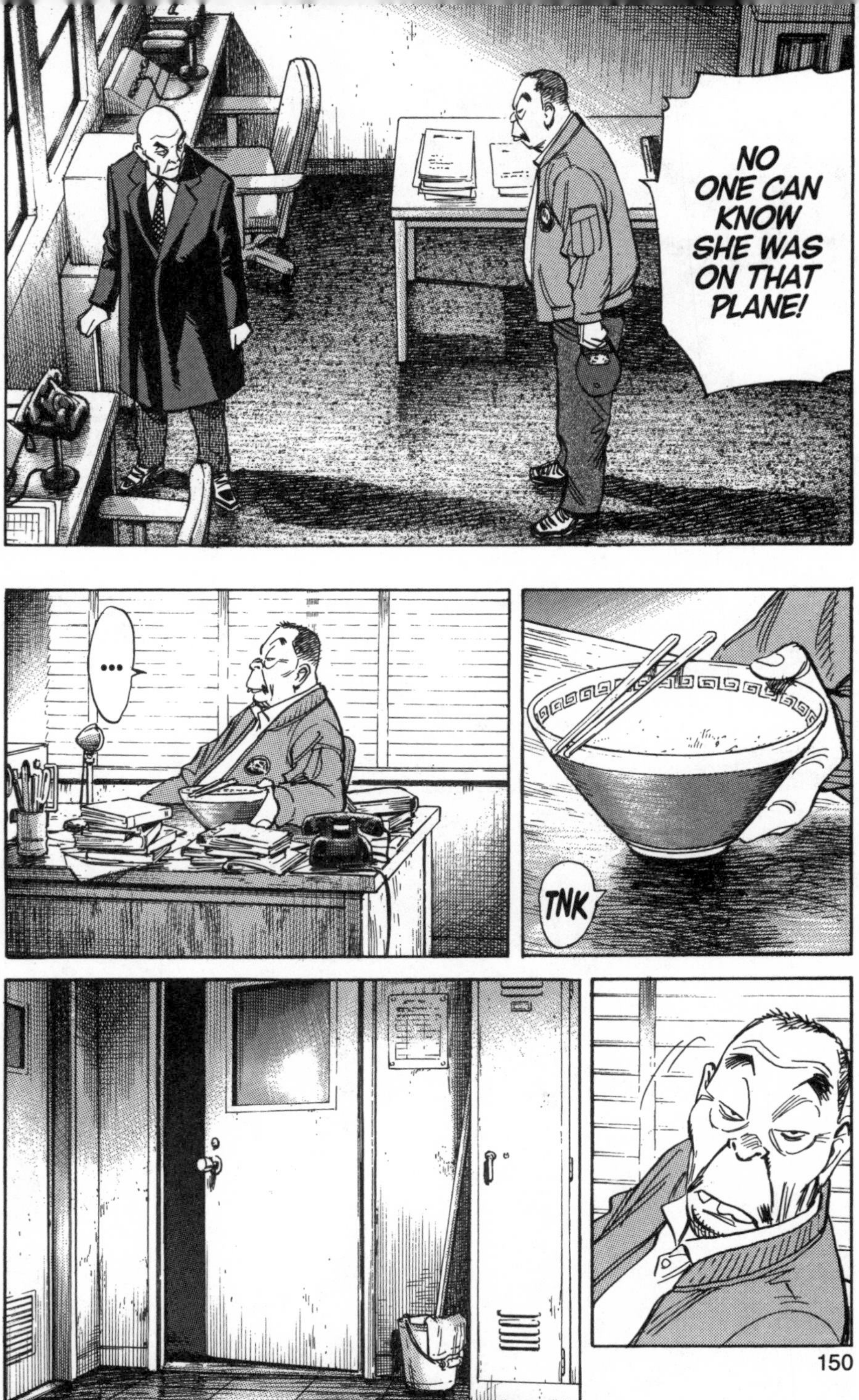
NO ONE CAN KNOW SHE WAS ON THAT PLANE!
TNK
...

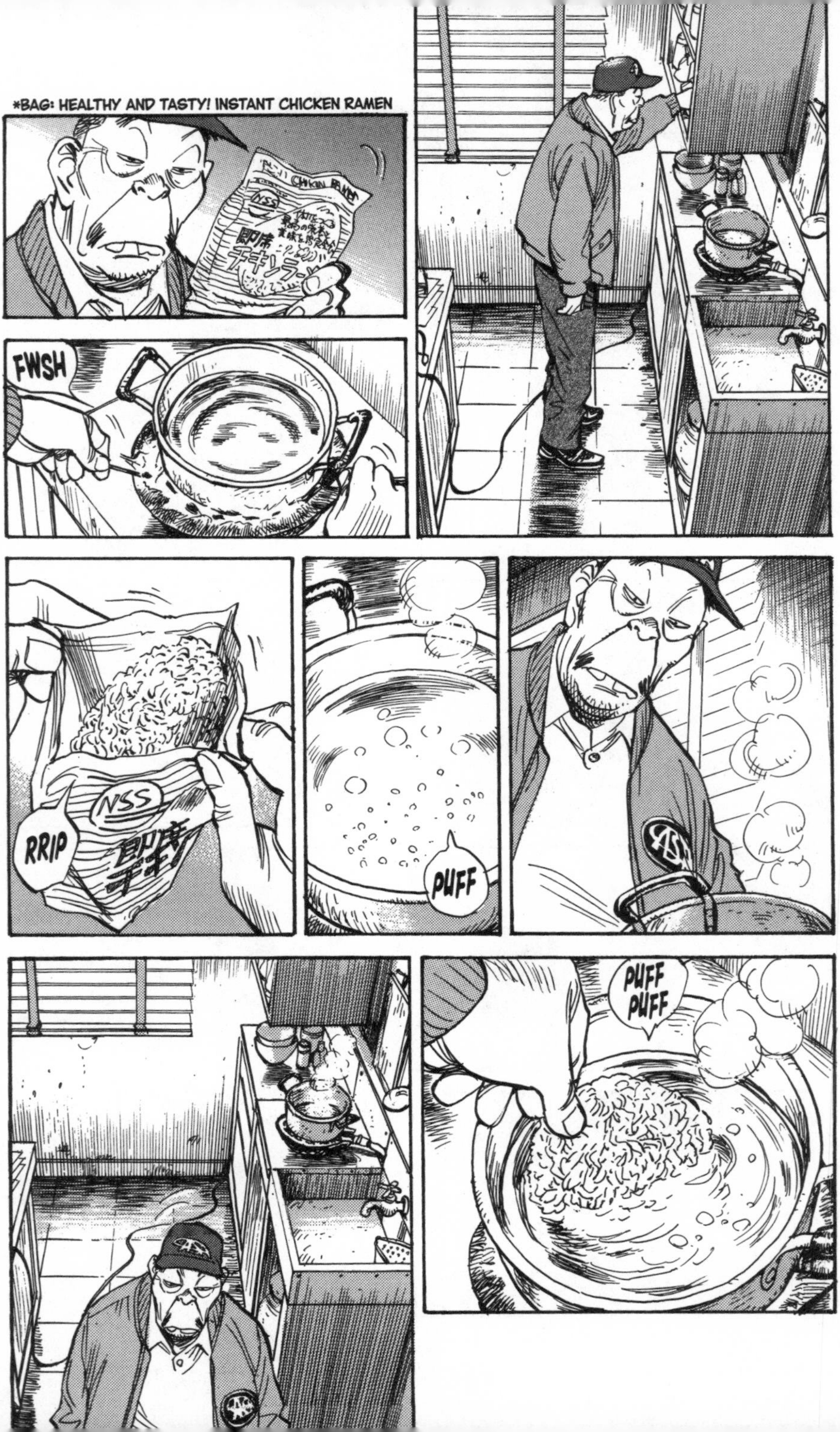
*BAG: HEALTHY AND TASTY! INSTANT CHICKEN RAMEN
FWSH
PUFF
RRIP
PUFF PUFF

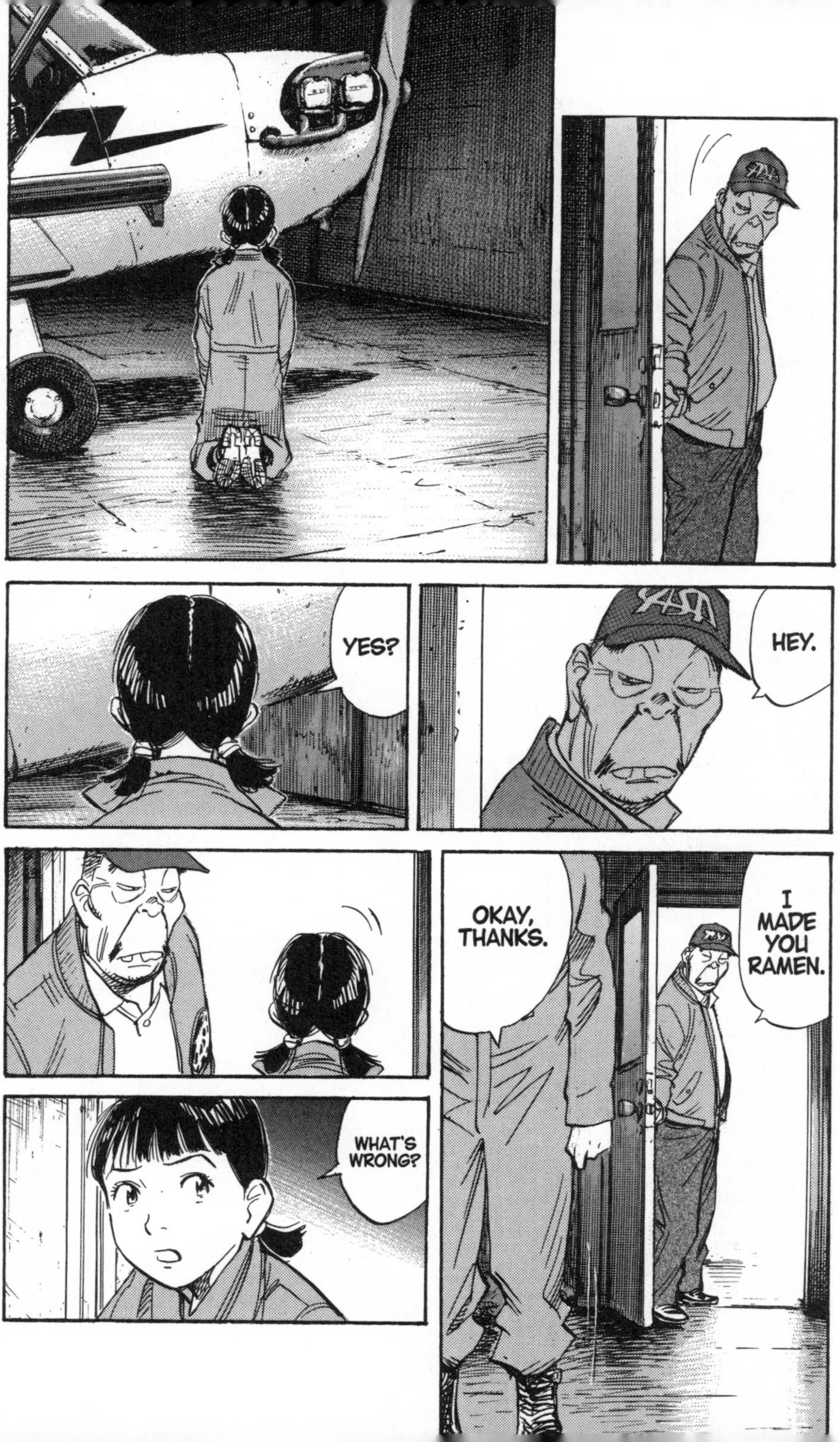
HEY.
YES?
I MADE YOU RAMEN.
OKAY, THANKS.
WHAT'S WRONG?

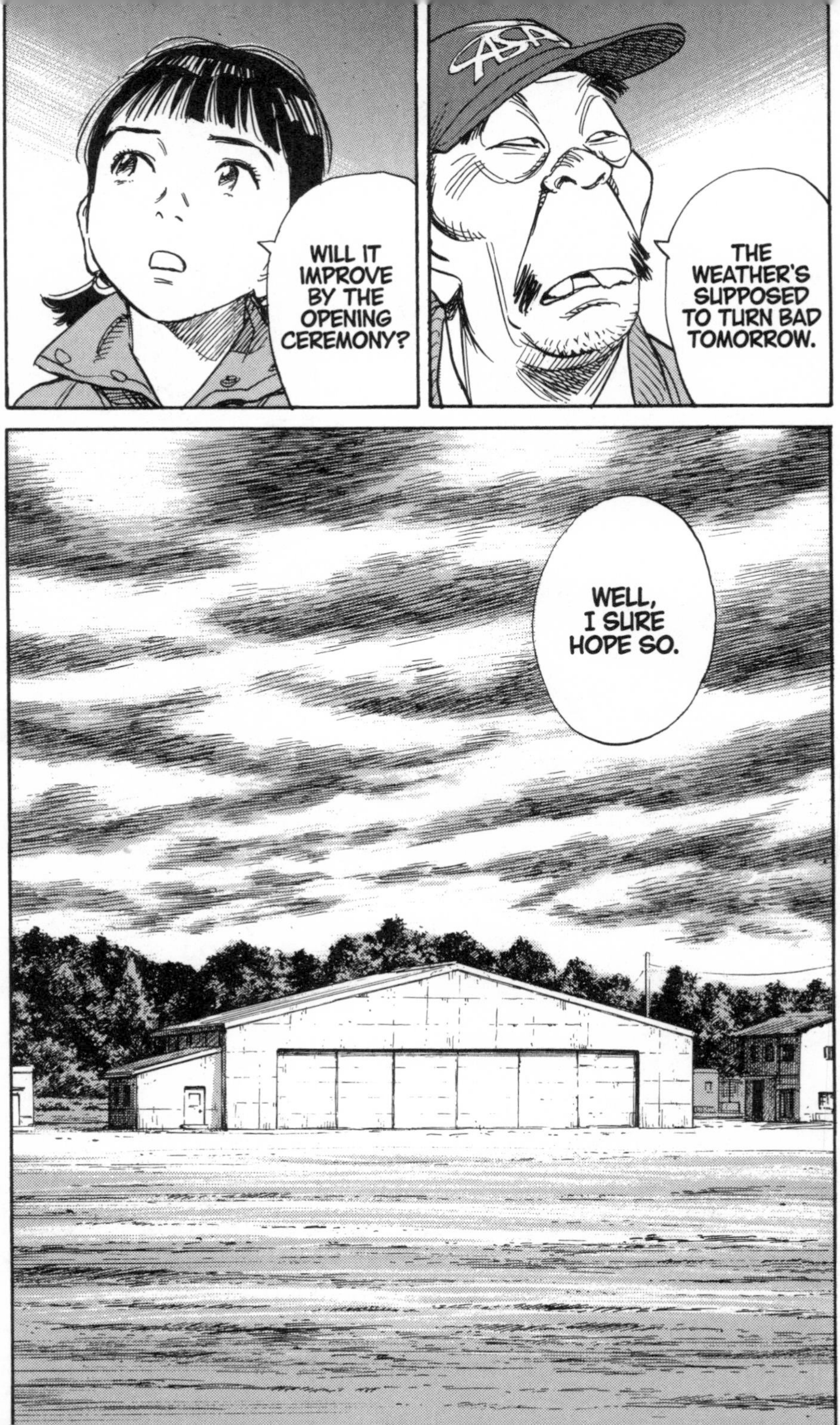
THE WEATHER'S SUPPOSED TO TURN BAD TOMORROW.
WILL IT IMPROVE BY THE OPENING CEREMONY?
WELL, I SURE HOPE SO.

ASADORA!

Chapter 23 ● Kinuyo's Wrath

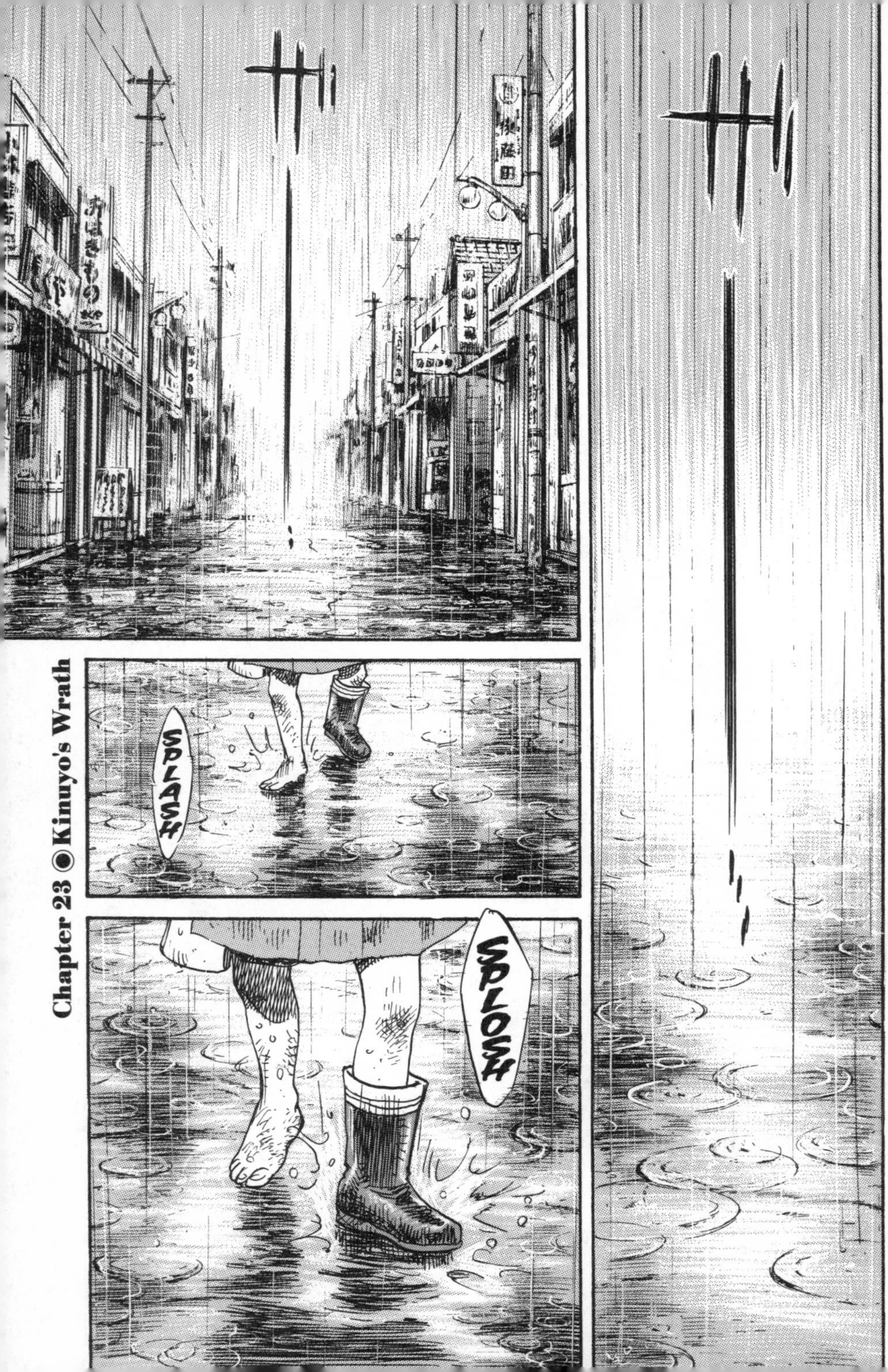
SPLASH
SPLOSH

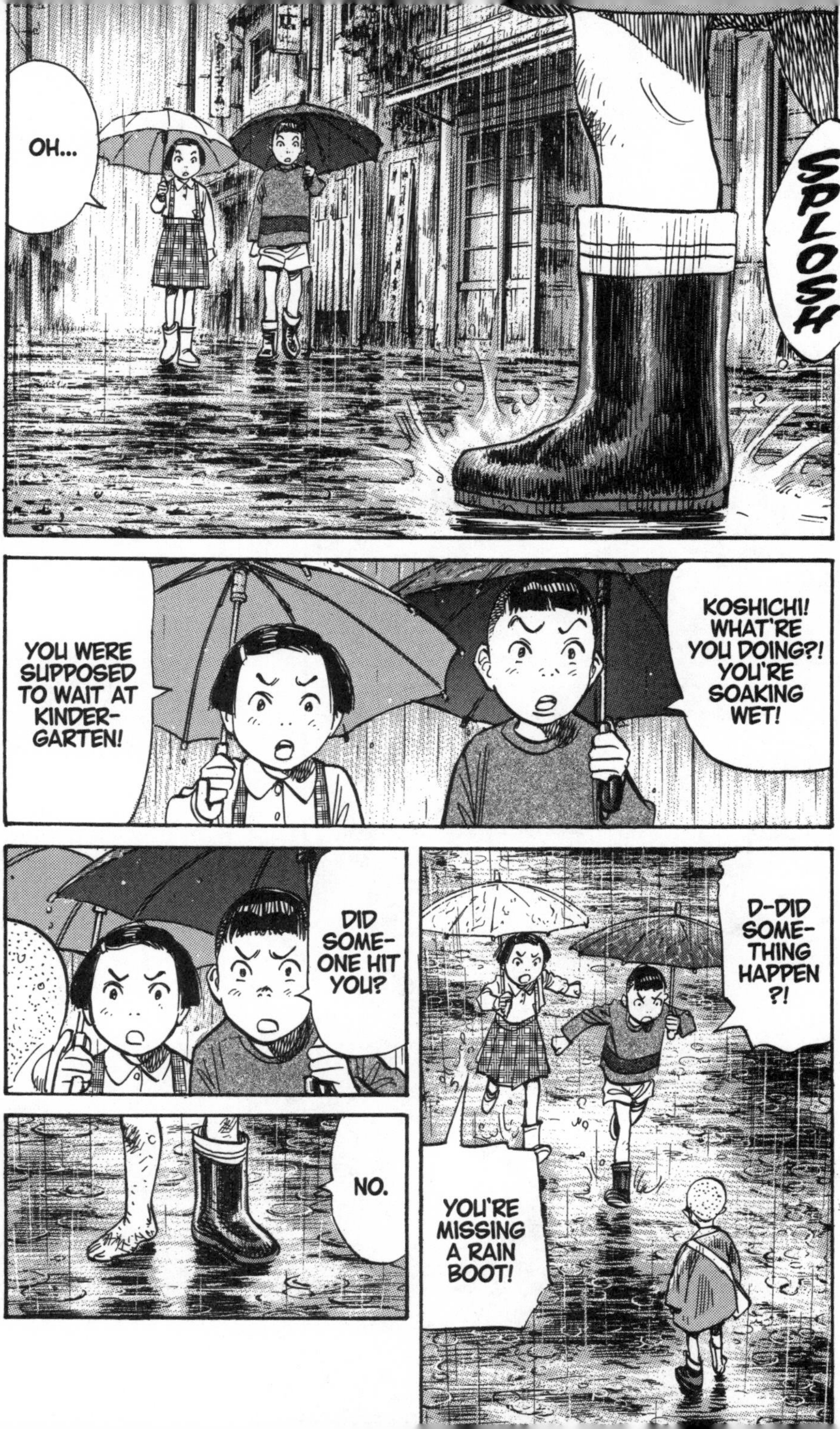
SPLOSH
OH...
KOSHICHI! WHAT'RE YOU DOING?! YOU'RE SOAKING WET!
YOU WERE SUPPOSED TO WAIT AT KINDER-GARTEN!
D-DID SOME-THING HAPPEN ?!
YOU'RE MISSING A RAIN BOOT!
DID SOME-ONE HIT YOU?
NO.

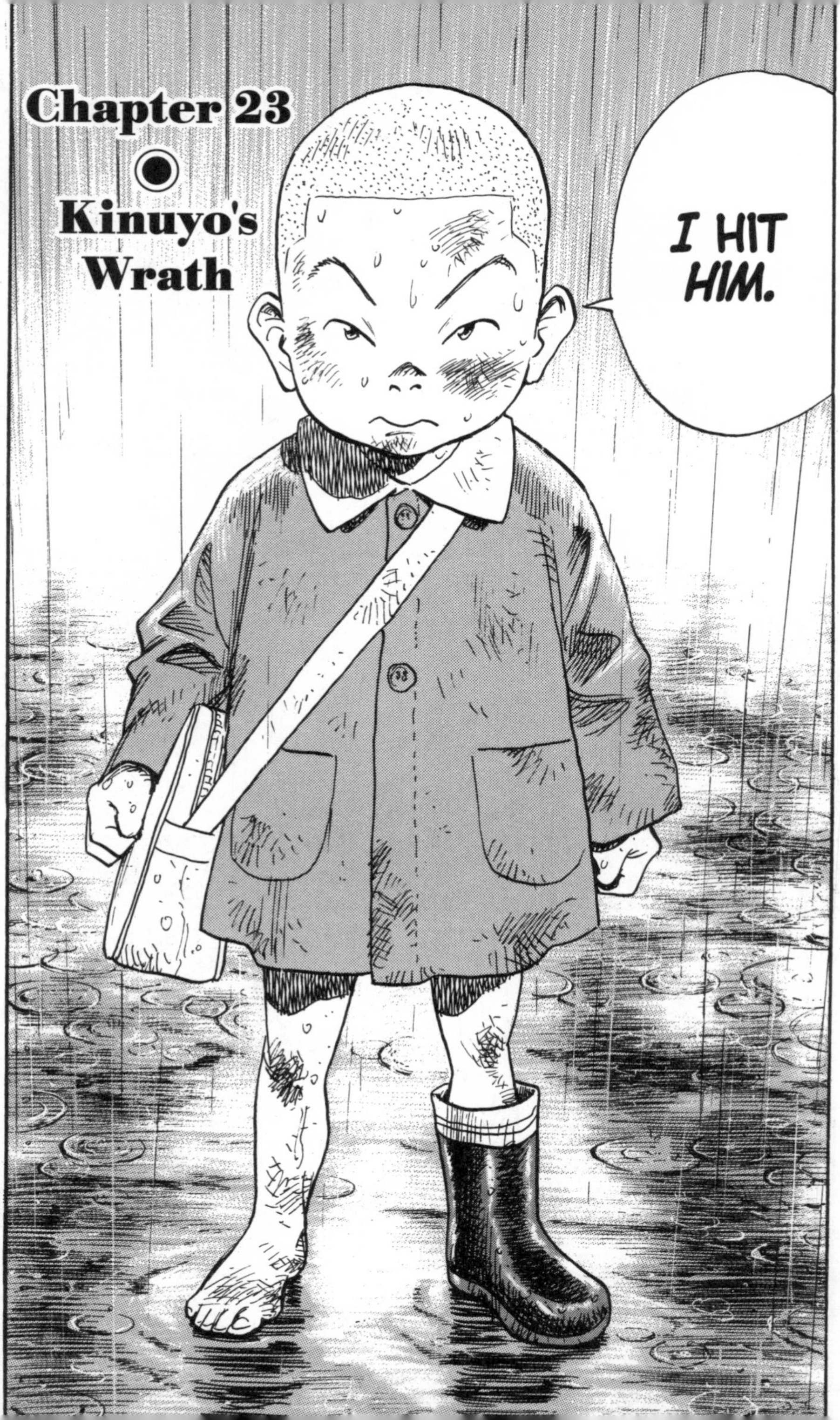
Chapter 23
Kinuyo's Wrath
I HIT HIM.

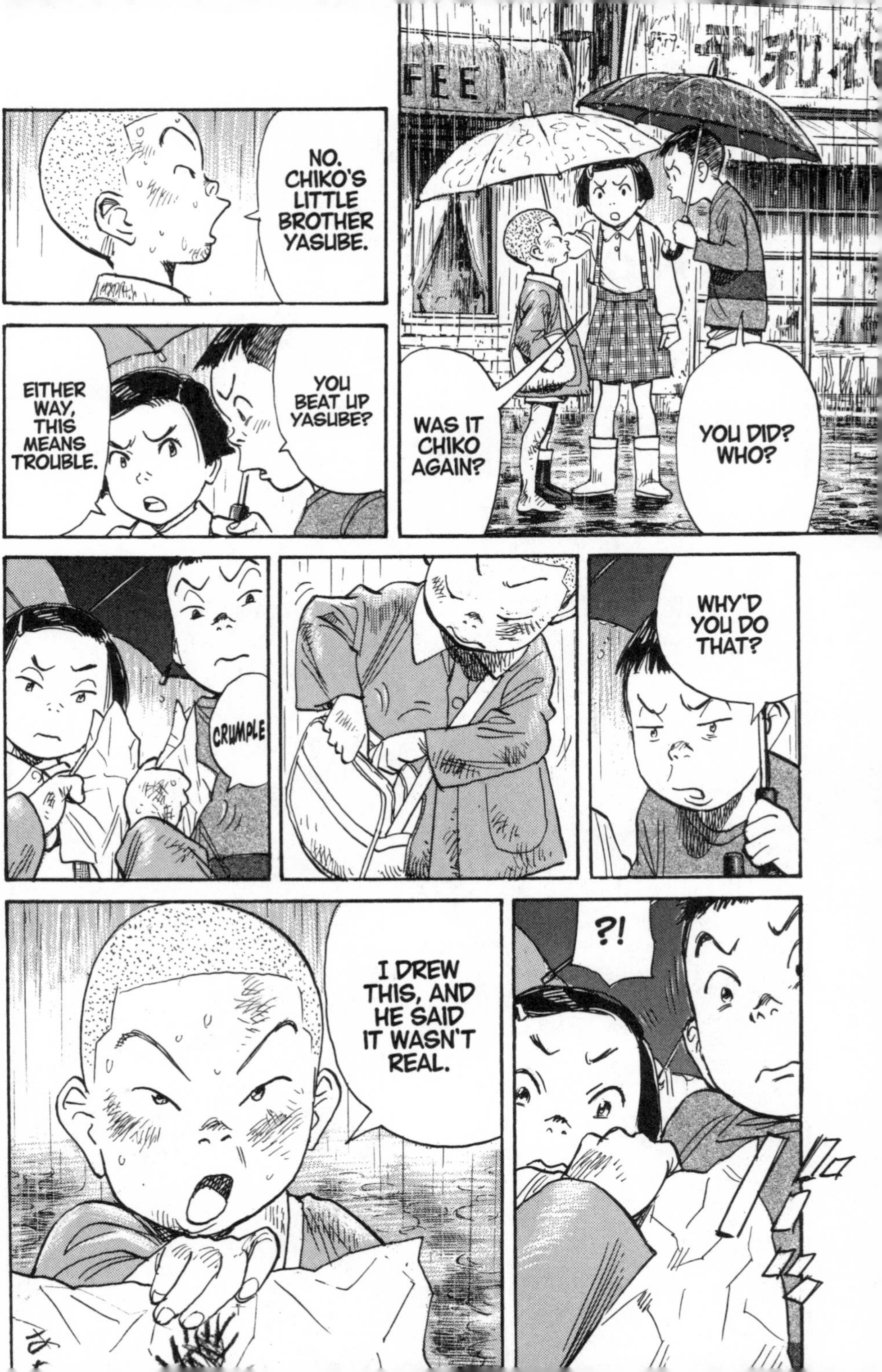
FEE
YOU DID? WHO?
WAS IT CHIKO AGAIN?
NO. CHIKO'S LITTLE BROTHER YASUBE.
YOU BEAT UP YASUBE?
EITHER WAY, THIS MEANS TROUBLE.
WHY'D YOU DO THAT?
CRUMPLE
?!
I DREW THIS, AND HE SAID IT WASN'T REAL.

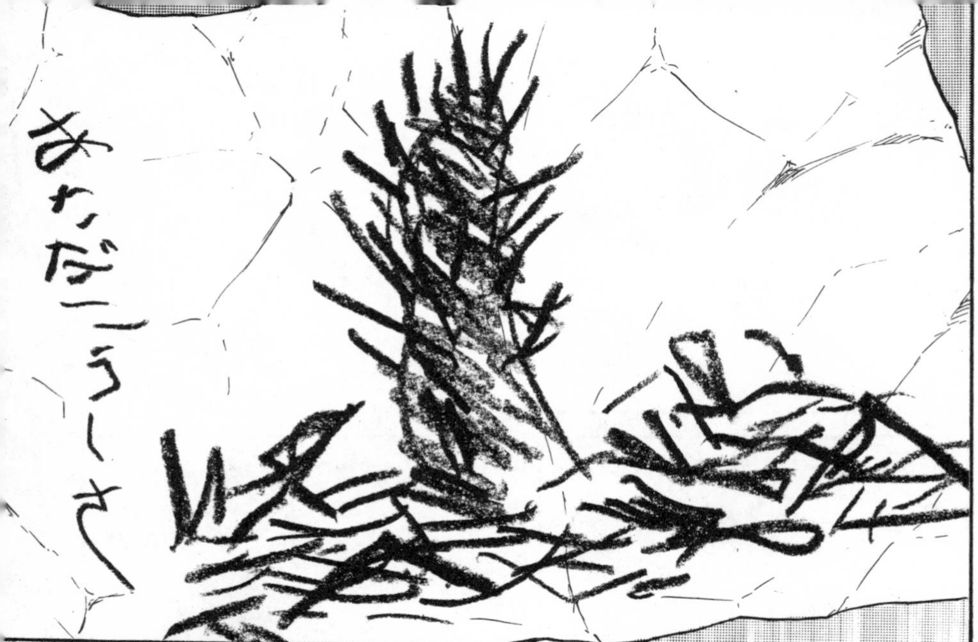

*PAPER: KOSHICHI ASADA

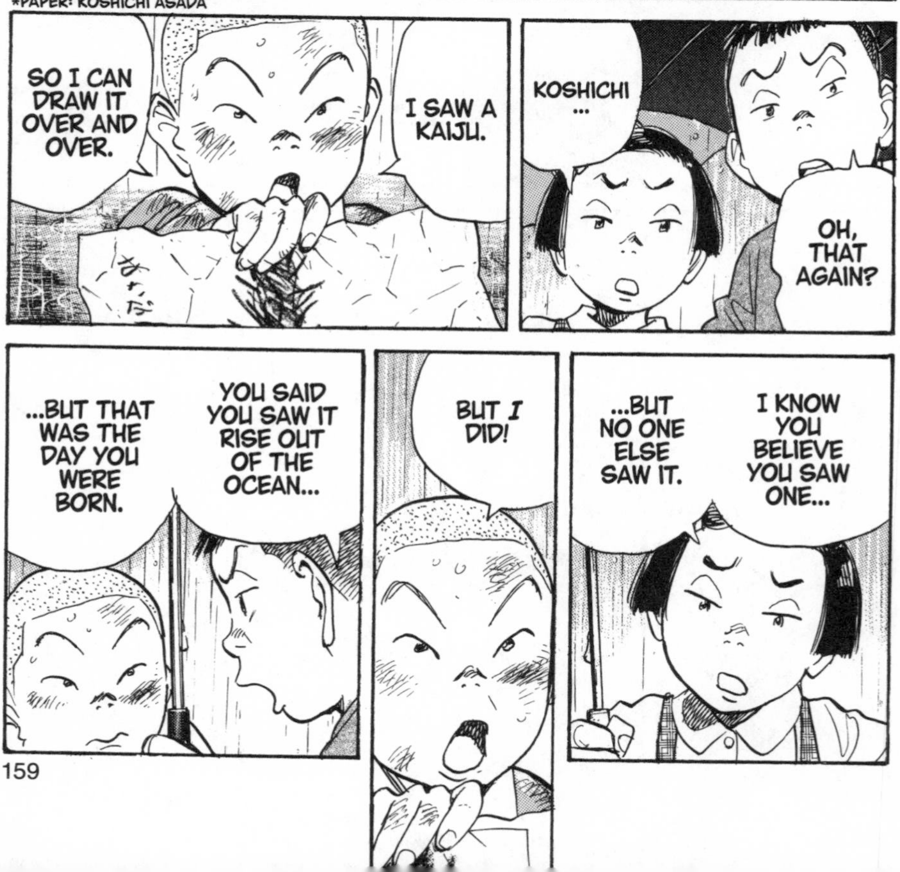
KOSHICHI ...
OH, THAT AGAIN?
I SAW A KAIJU.
SO I CAN DRAW IT OVER AND OVER.
I KNOW YOU BELIEVE YOU SAW ONE...
...BUT NO ONE ELSE SAW IT.
BUT *I* DID!
YOU SAID YOU SAW IT RISE OUT OF THE OCEAN...
...BUT THAT WAS THE DAY YOU WERE BORN.

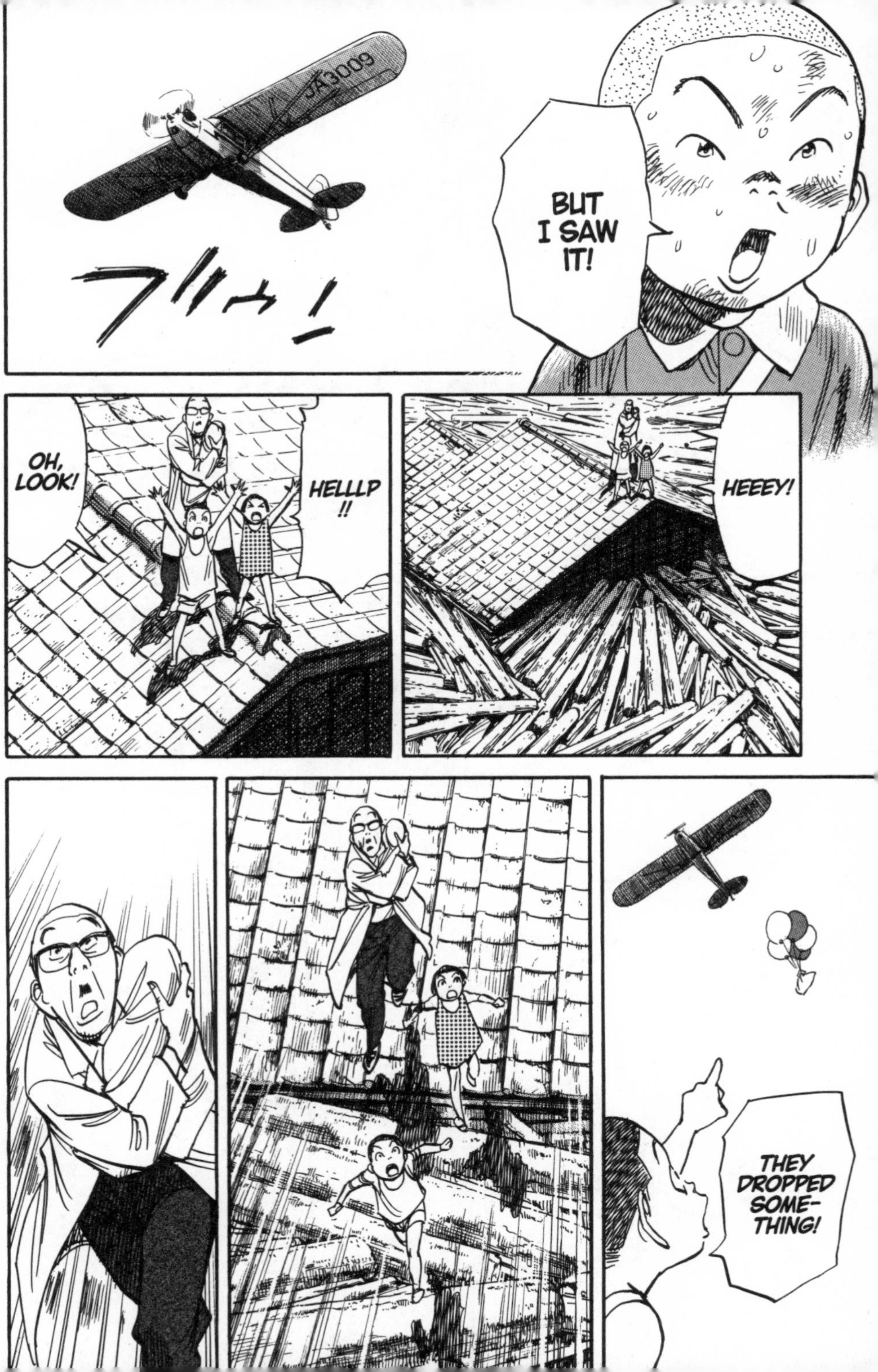
BUT I SAW IT!
JA3009
HEEEY!
HELLLP !!
OH, LOOK!
THEY DROPPED SOME-THING!

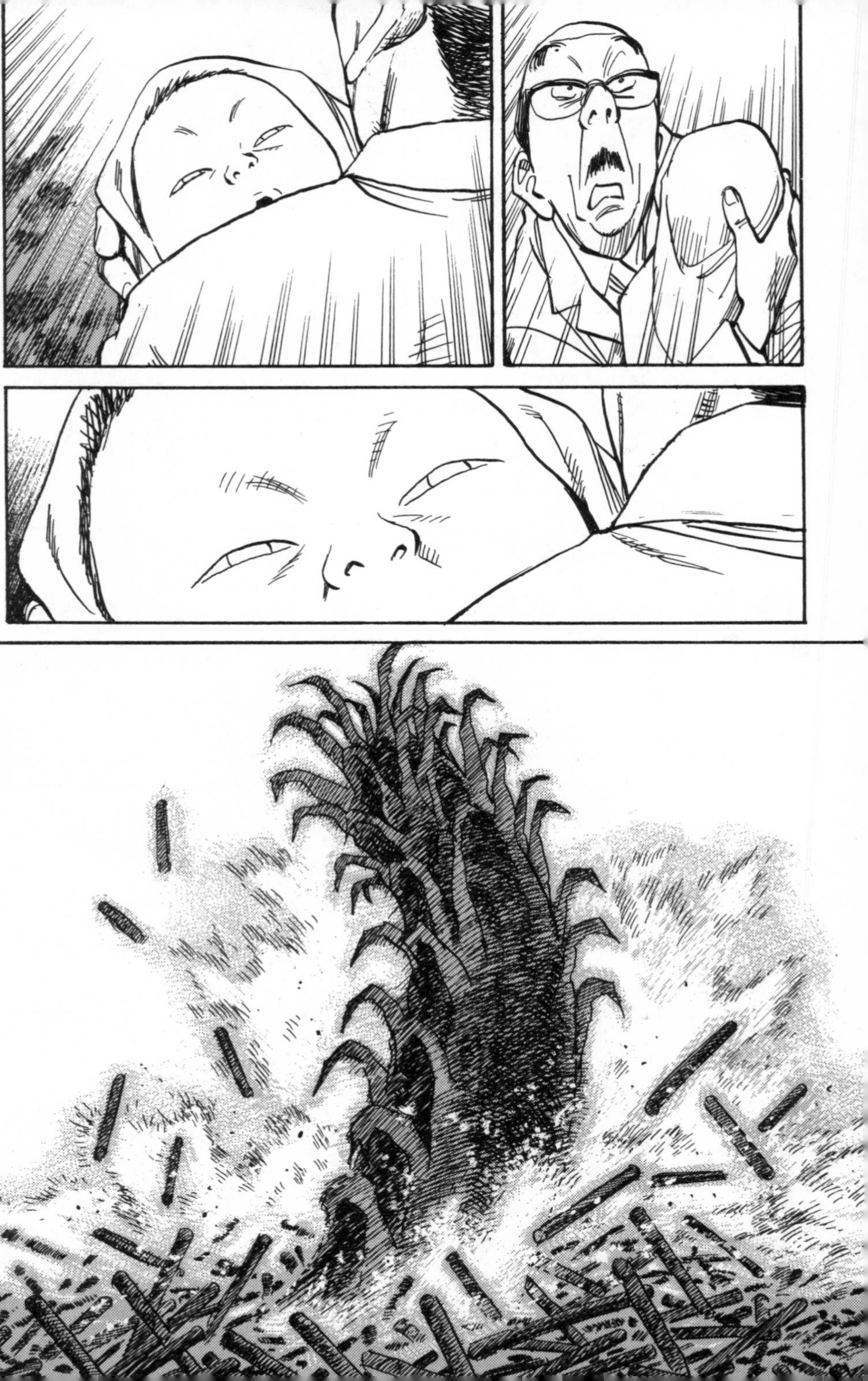

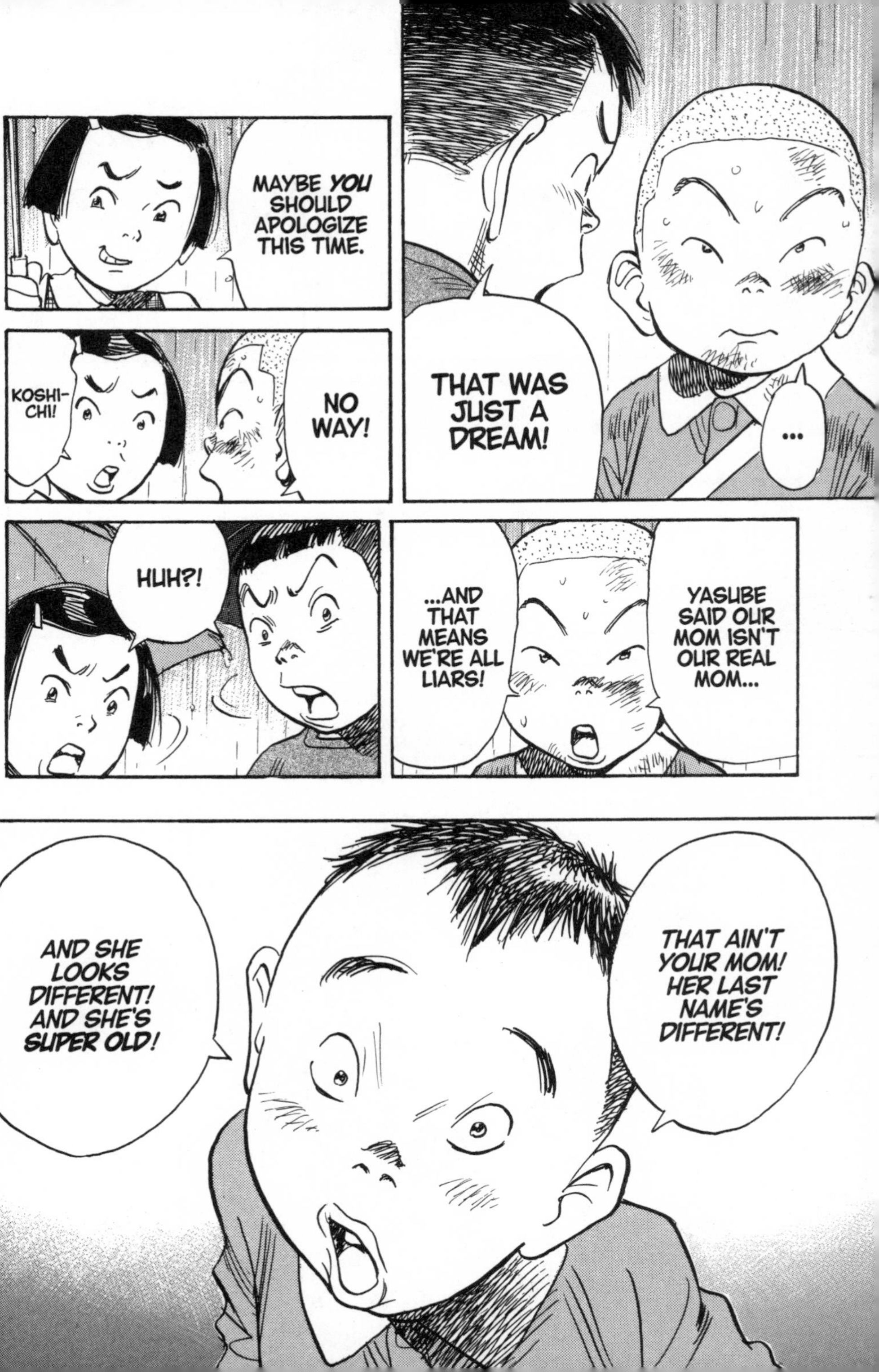
...
THAT WAS JUST A DREAM!
MAYBE YOU SHOULD APOLOGIZE THIS TIME.
NO WAY!
KOSHI-CHI!
YASUBE SAID OUR MOM ISN'T OUR REAL MOM...
...AND THAT MEANS WE'RE ALL LIARS!
HUH?!
THAT AIN'T YOUR MOM! HER LAST NAME'S DIFFERENT!
AND SHE LOOKS DIFFERENT! AND SHE'S SUPER OLD!

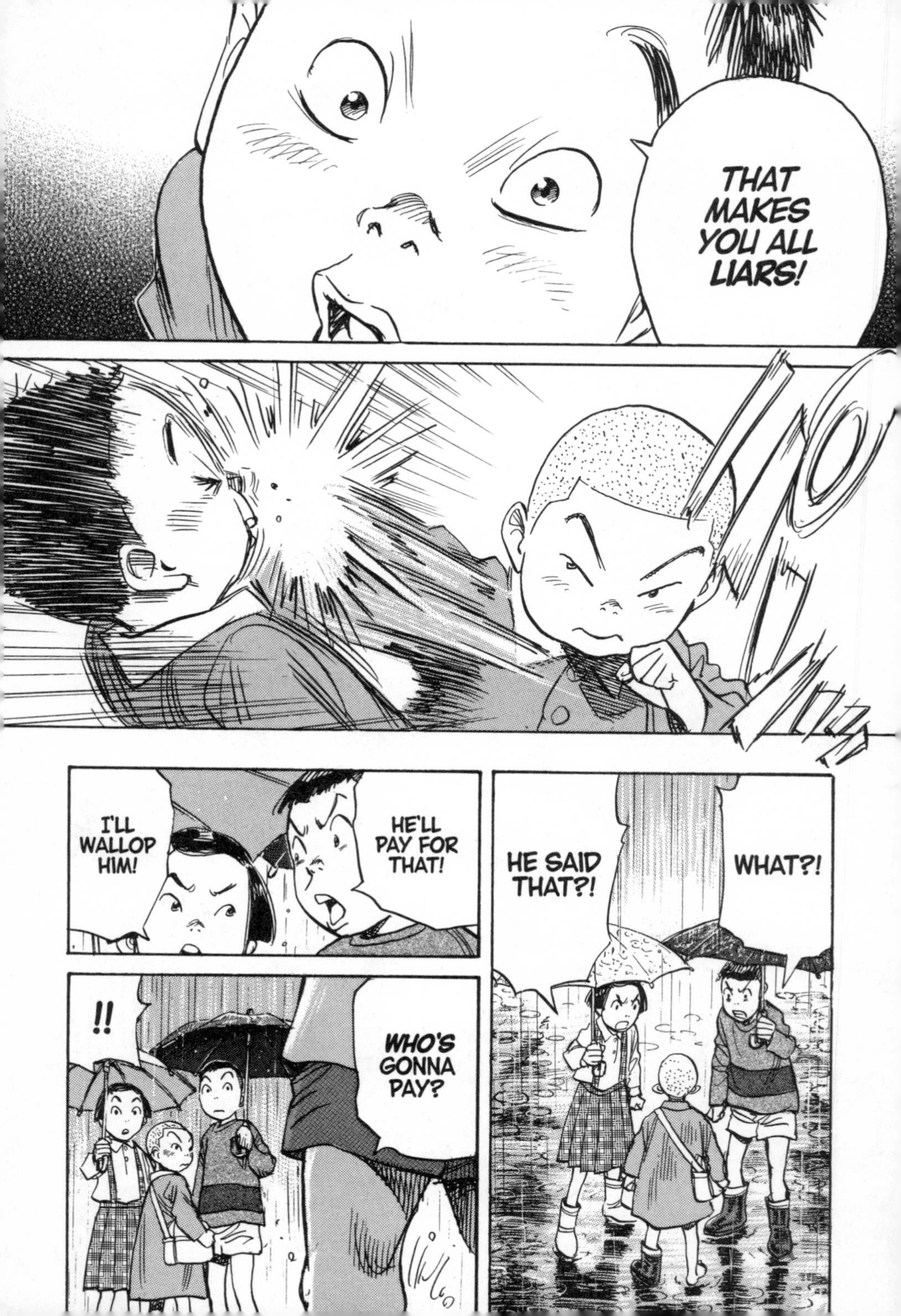
THAT MAKES YOU ALL LIARS!
WHAT?!
HE SAID THAT?!
HE'LL PAY FOR THAT!
I'LL WALLOP HIM!
WHO'S GONNA PAY?
!!

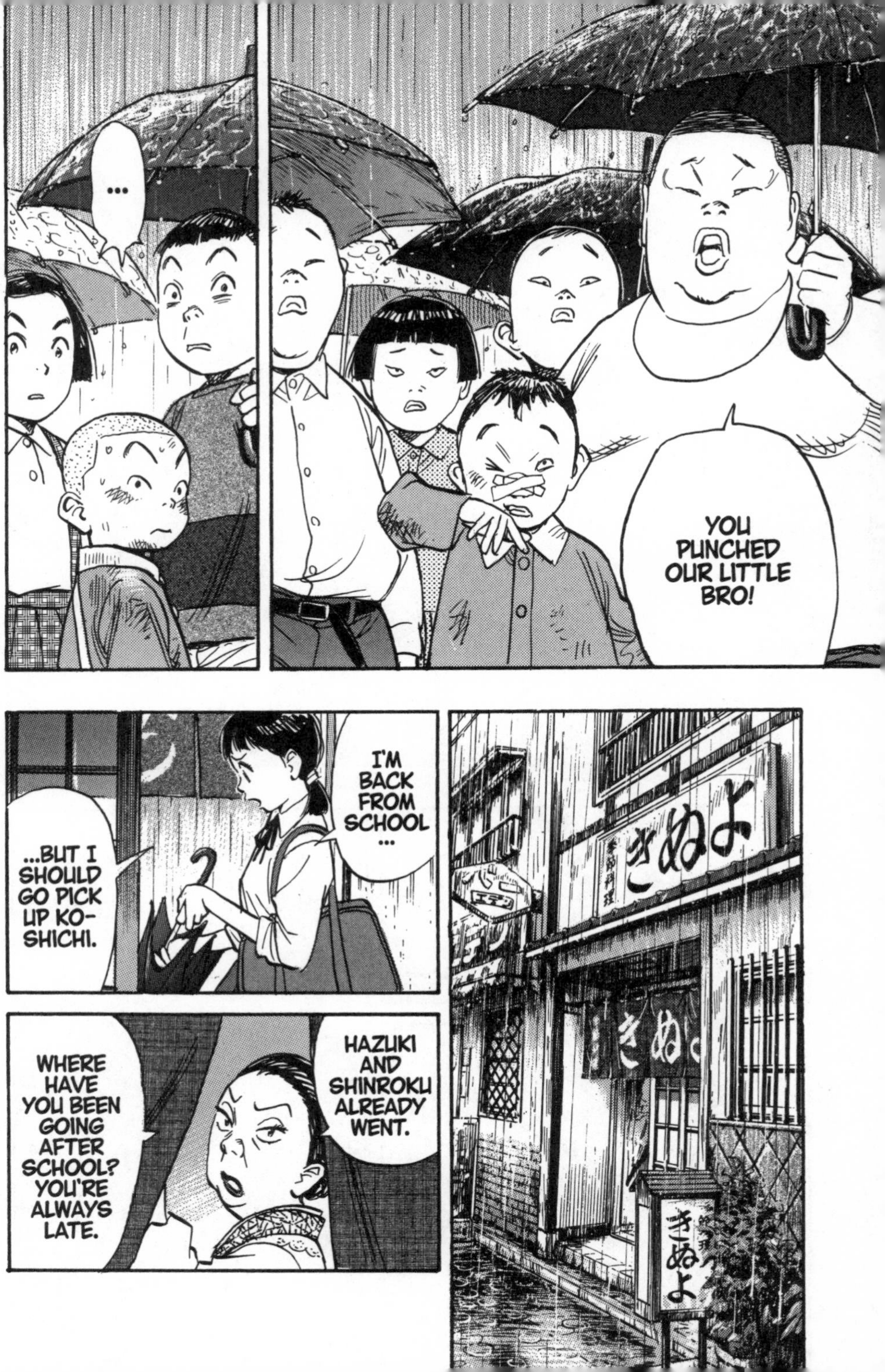
YOU PUNCHED OUR LITTLE BRO!
...
きぬよ
I'M BACK FROM SCHOOL ...
...BUT I SHOULD GO PICK UP KO-SHICHI.
HAZUKI AND SHINROKU ALREADY WENT.
WHERE HAVE YOU BEEN GOING AFTER SCHOOL? YOU'RE ALWAYS LATE.

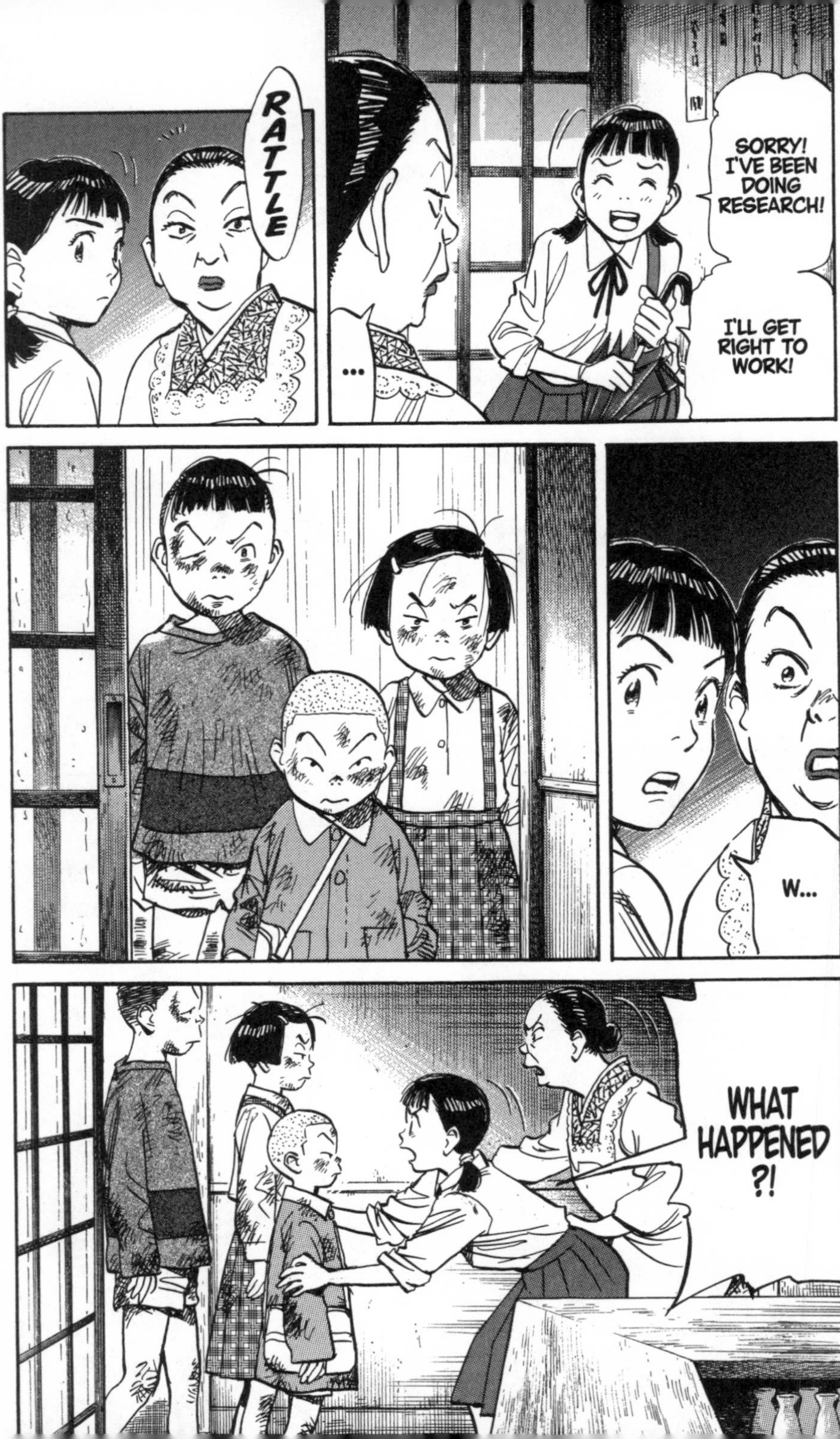
SORRY! I'VE BEEN DOING RESEARCH!
I'LL GET RIGHT TO WORK!
...
RATTLE
W...
WHAT HAPPENED?!

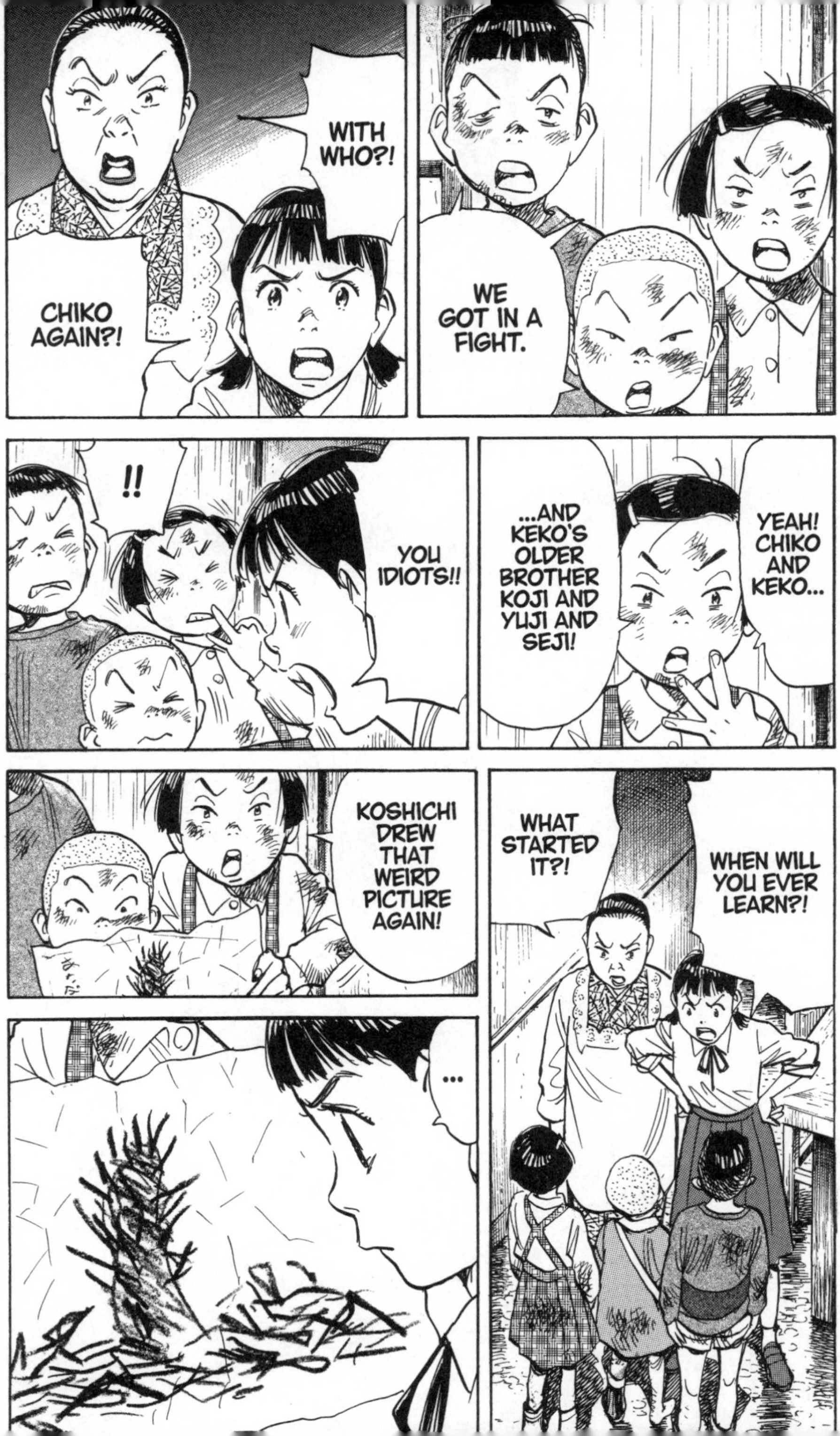
WE GOT IN A FIGHT.
WITH WHO?!
CHIKO AGAIN?!
YEAH! CHIKO AND KEKO...
...AND KEKO'S OLDER BROTHER KOJI AND YUJI AND SEJI!
YOU IDIOTS!!
!!
WHEN WILL YOU EVER LEARN?!
WHAT STARTED IT?!
KOSHICHI DREW THAT WEIRD PICTURE AGAIN!
...

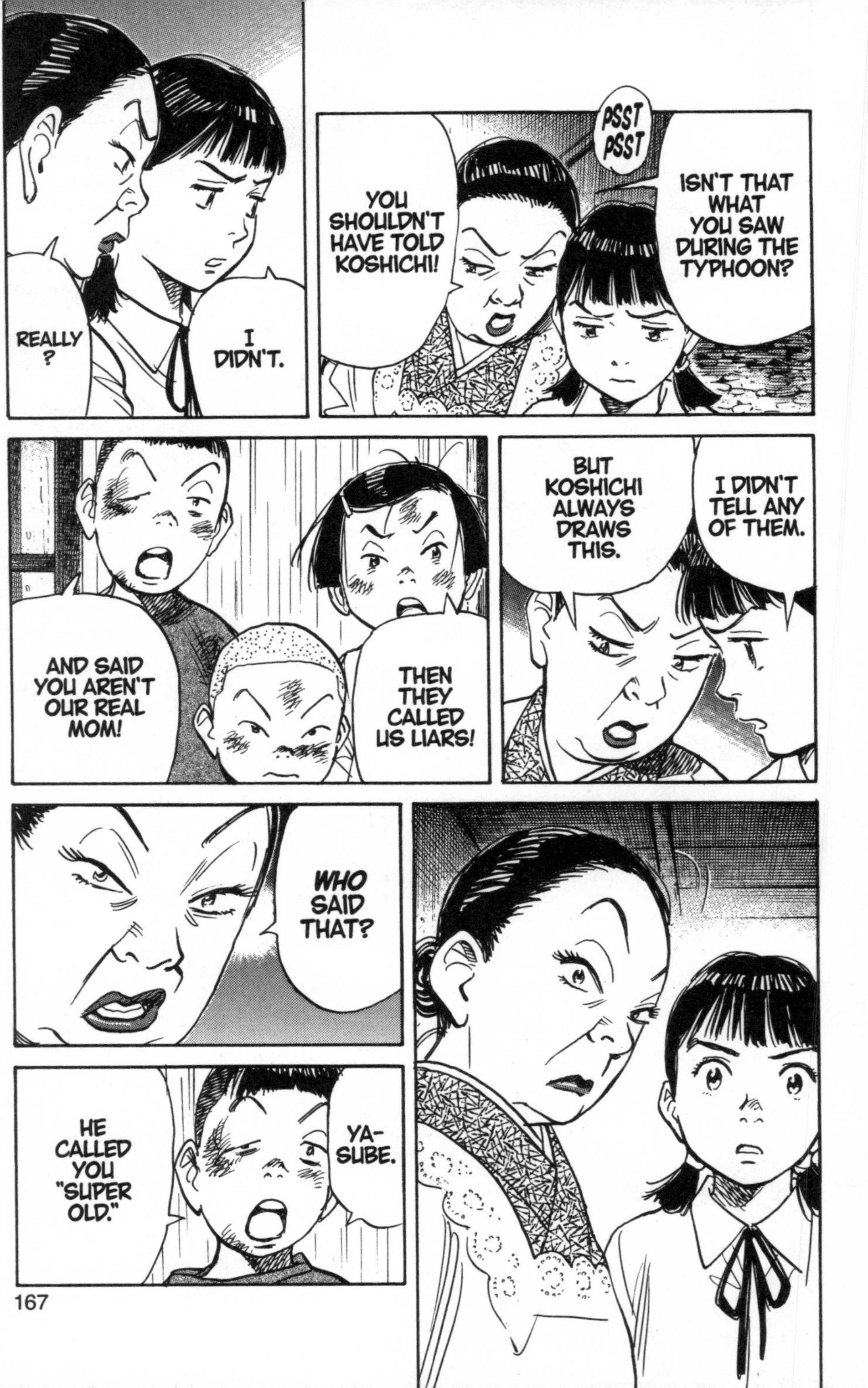
PSST PSST
ISN'T THAT WHAT YOU SAW DURING THE TYPHOON?
YOU SHOULDN'T HAVE TOLD KOSHICHI!
I DIDN'T.
REALLY?
I DIDN'T TELL ANY OF THEM.
BUT KOSHICHI ALWAYS DRAWS THIS.
THEN THEY CALLED US LIARS!
AND SAID YOU AREN'T OUR REAL MOM!
WHO SAID THAT?
YA-SUBE.
HE CALLED YOU "SUPER OLD."

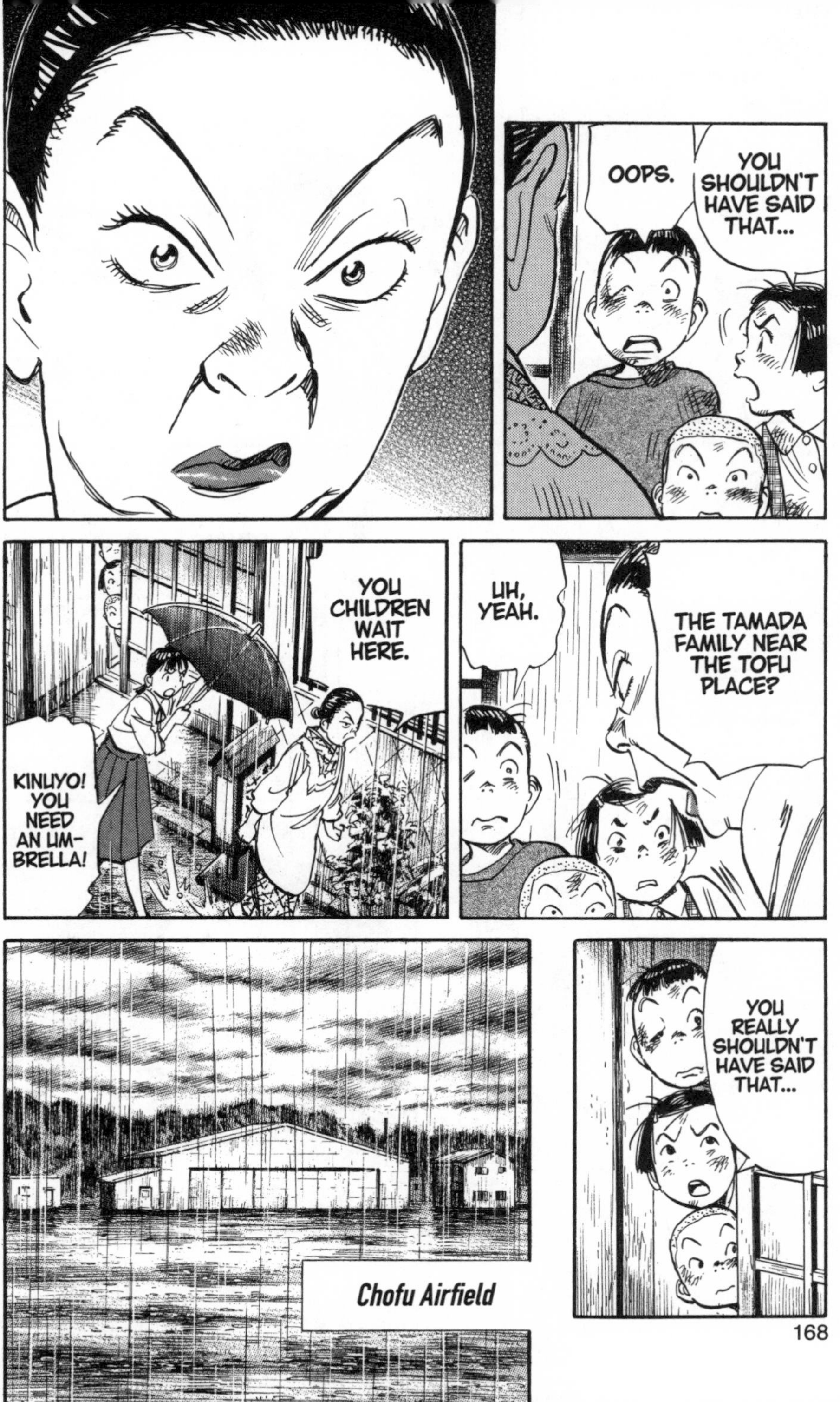
YOU SHOULDN'T HAVE SAID THAT...
OOPS.
THE TAMADA FAMILY NEAR THE TOFU PLACE?
UH, YEAH.
YOU CHILDREN WAIT HERE.
KINUYO! YOU NEED AN UM-BRELLA!
YOU REALLY SHOULDN'T HAVE SAID THAT...
Chofu Airfield

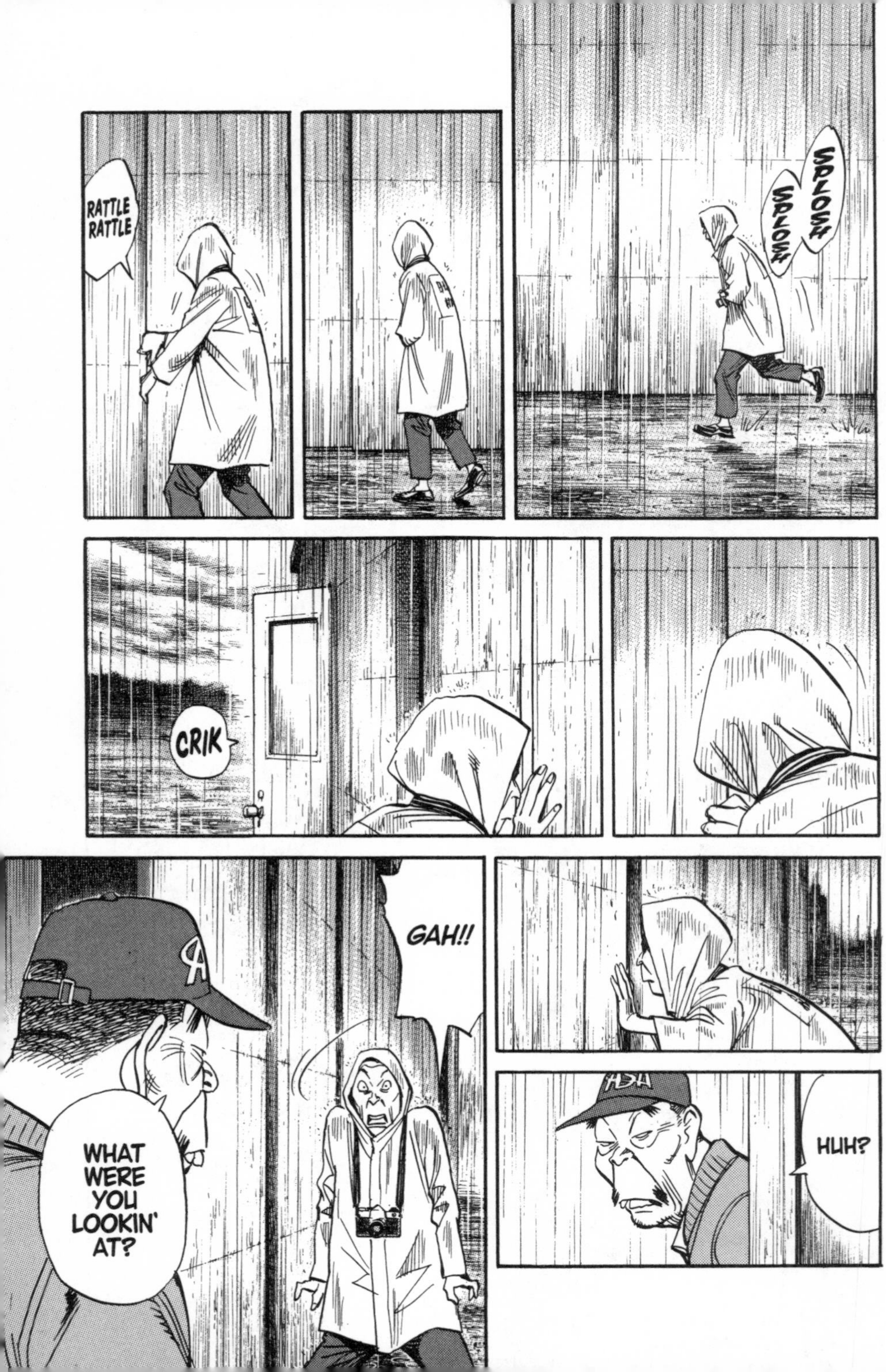
SPLOSH
SPLOSH
RATTLE RATTLE
CRIK
HUH?
GAH!!
WHAT WERE YOU LOOKIN' AT?

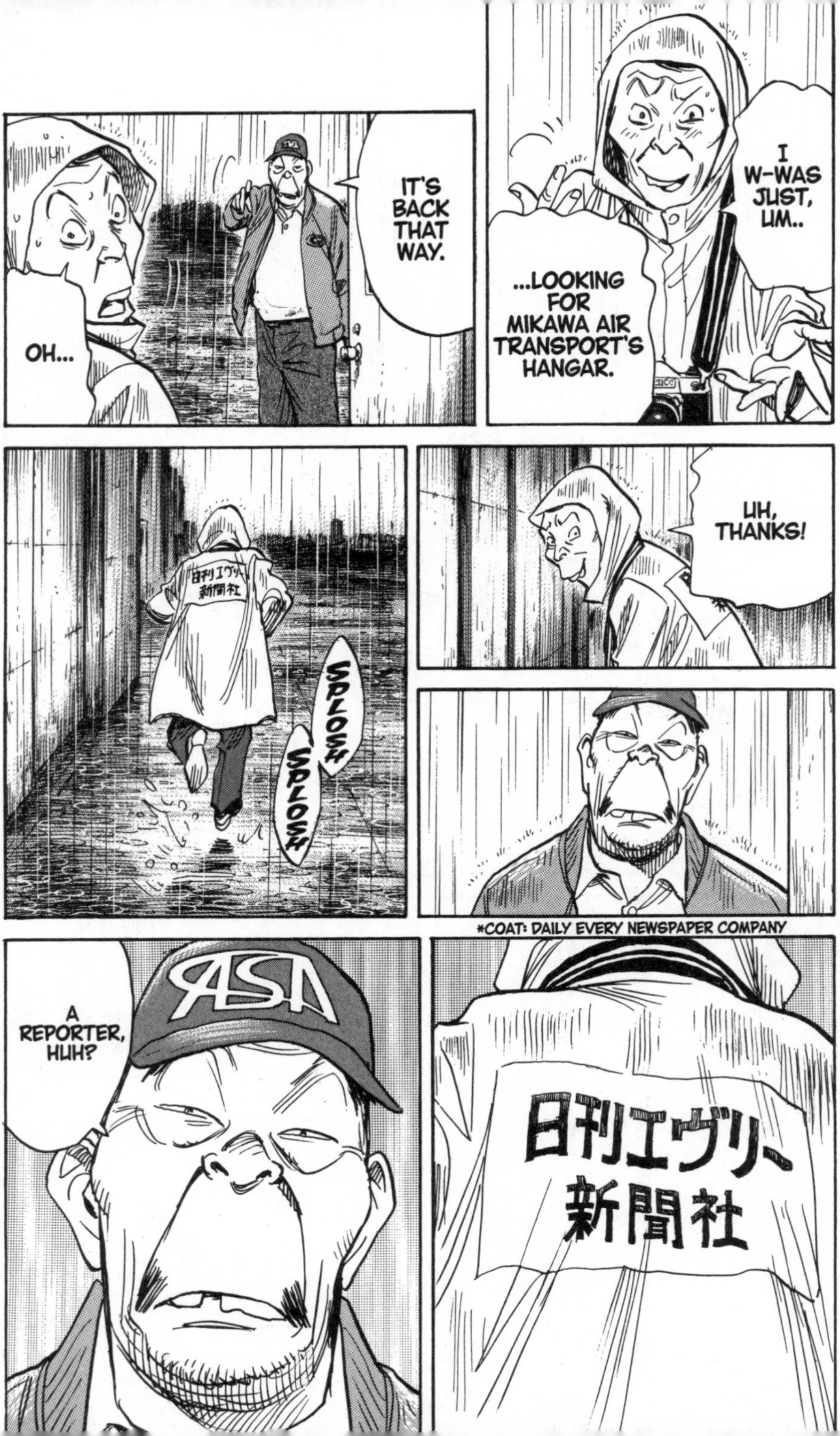
I W-WAS JUST, UM..
...LOOKING FOR MIKAWA AIR TRANSPORT'S HANGAR.
IT'S BACK THAT WAY.
OH...
UH, THANKS!
SPLOSH
SPLOSH
*COAT: DAILY EVERY NEWSPAPER COMPANY
日刊エヴリー新聞社
RASA
A REPORTER, HUH?

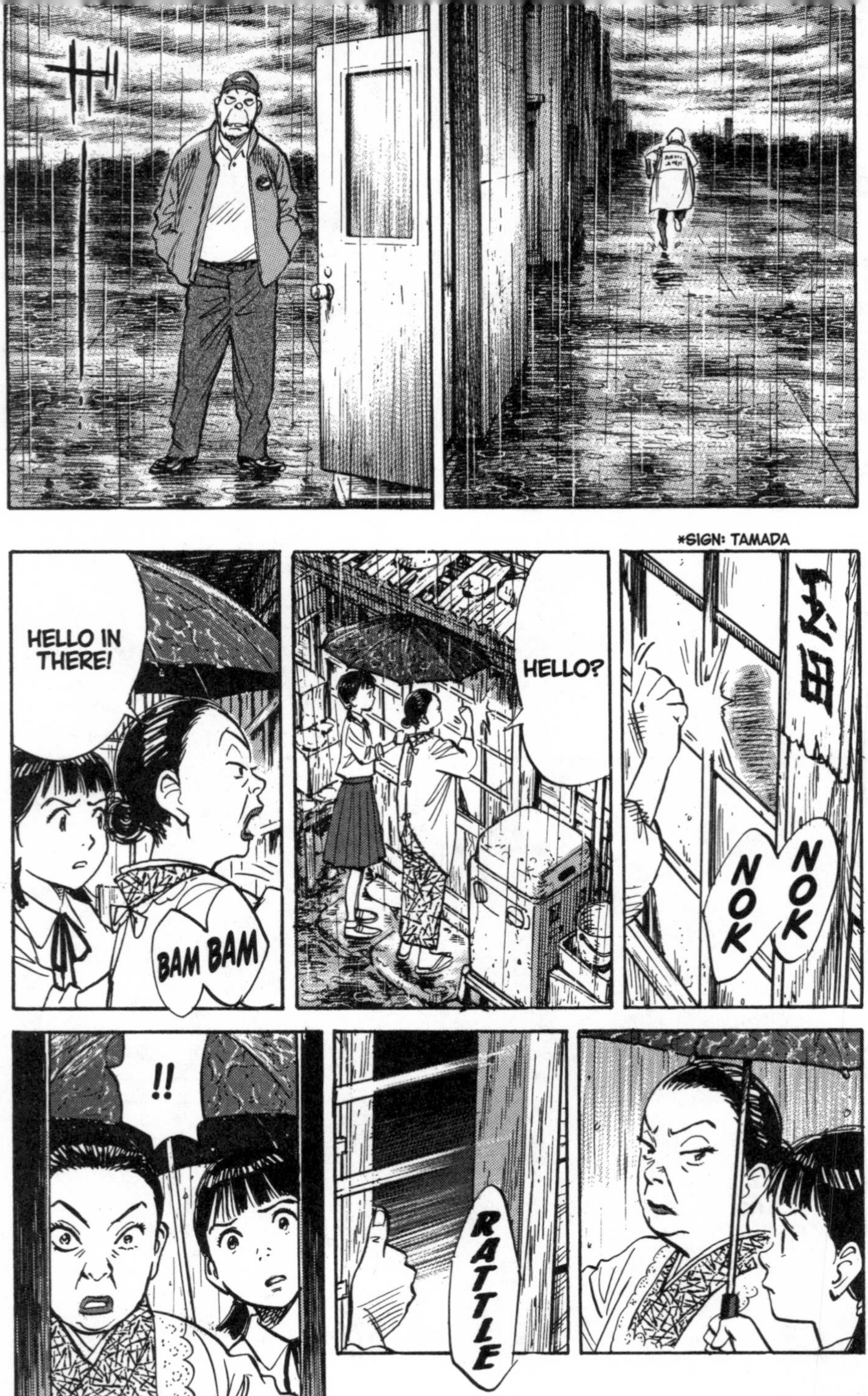
*SIGN: TAMADA
玉田
NOK NOK
HELLO?
HELLO IN THERE!
BAM BAM
RATTLE
!!

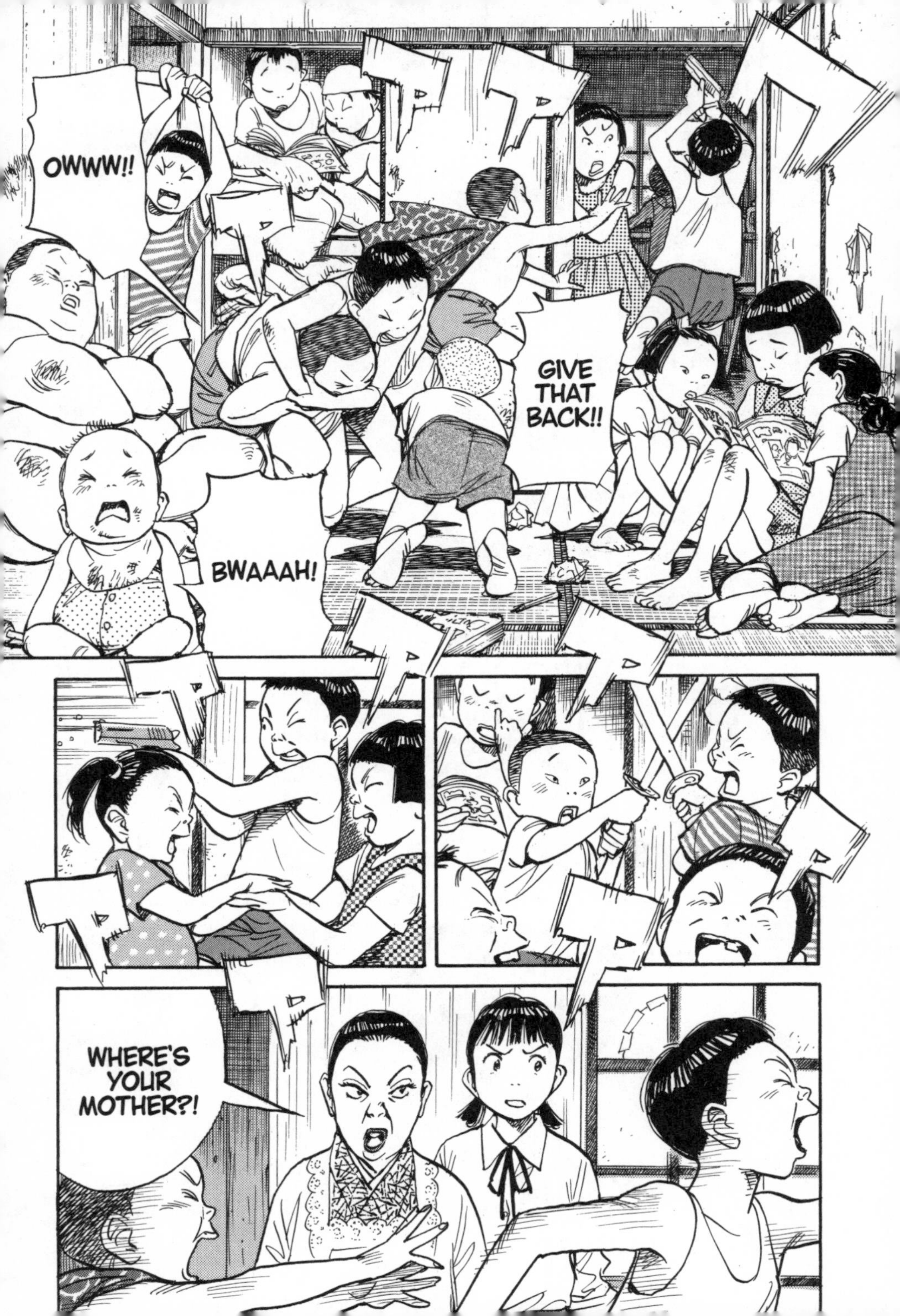
GIVE THAT BACK!!
OWWW!!
BWAAAH!
WHERE'S YOUR MOTHER?!

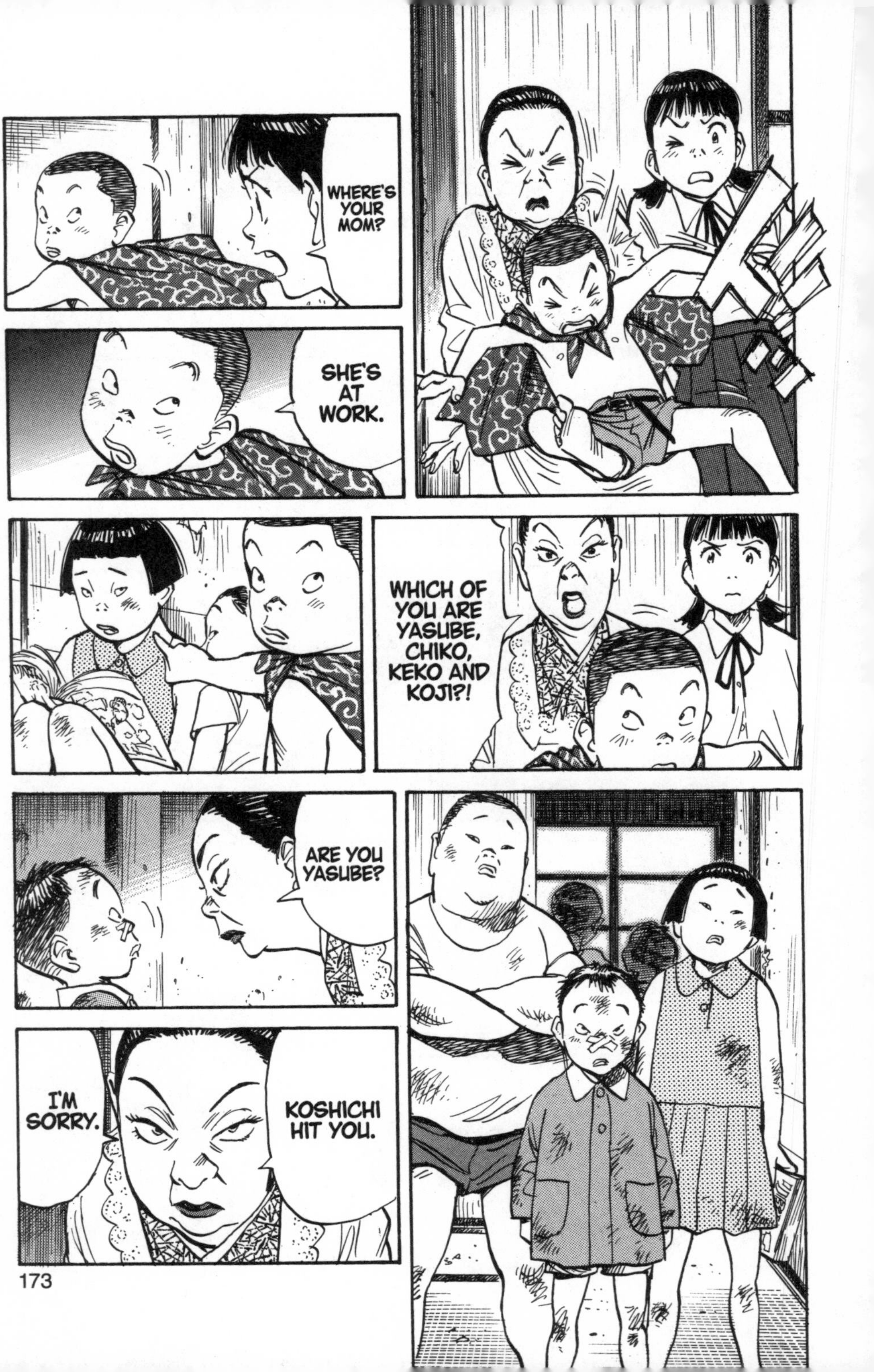

WHERE'S YOUR MOM?
SHE'S AT WORK.
WHICH OF YOU ARE YASUBE, CHIKO, KEKO AND KOJI?!
ARE YOU YASUBE?
KOSHICHI HIT YOU.
I'M SORRY.

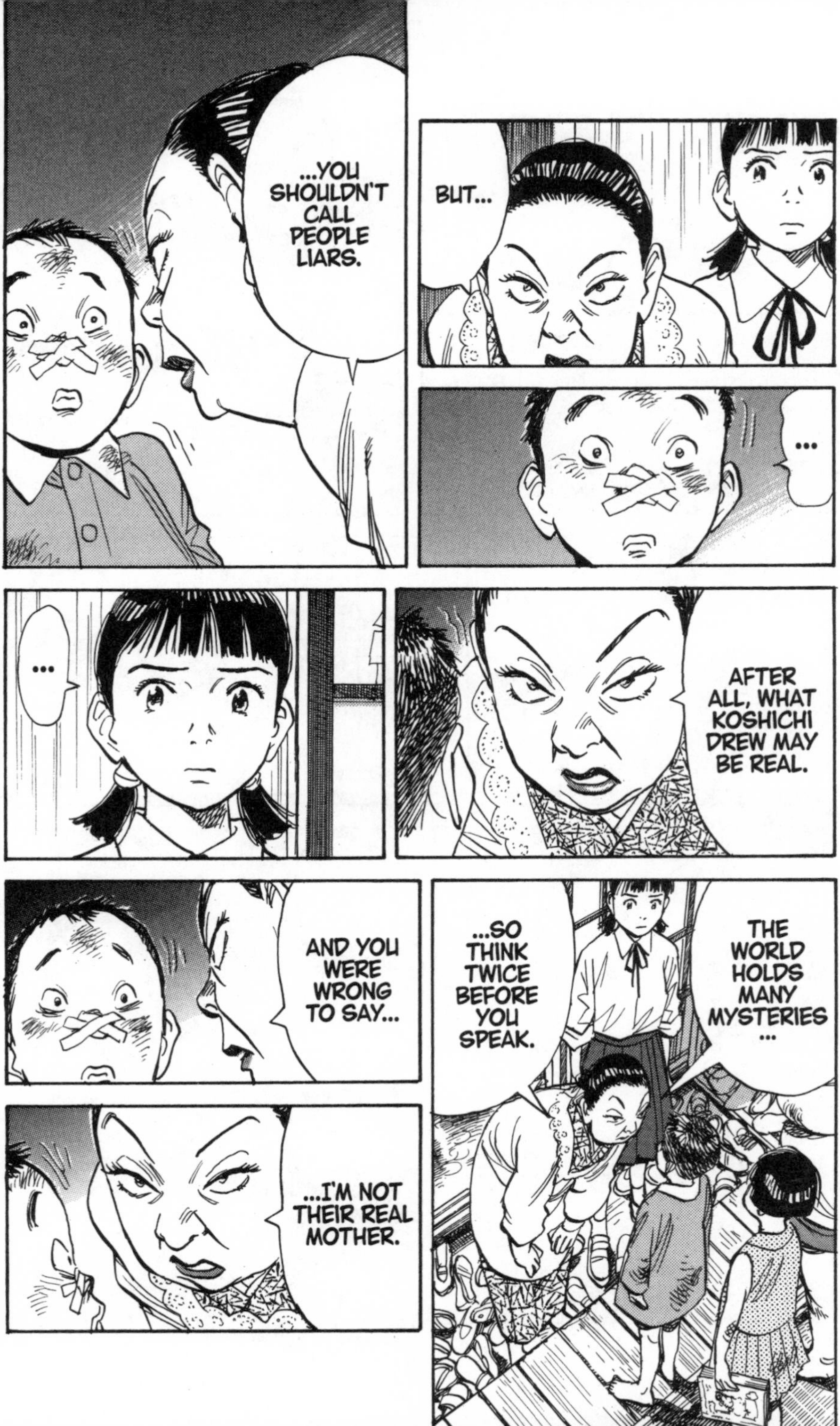
BUT...
...
...YOU SHOULDN'T CALL PEOPLE LIARS.
AFTER ALL, WHAT KOSHICHI DREW MAY BE REAL.
...
THE WORLD HOLDS MANY MYSTERIES...
...SO THINK TWICE BEFORE YOU SPEAK.
AND YOU WERE WRONG TO SAY...
...I'M NOT THEIR REAL MOTHER.

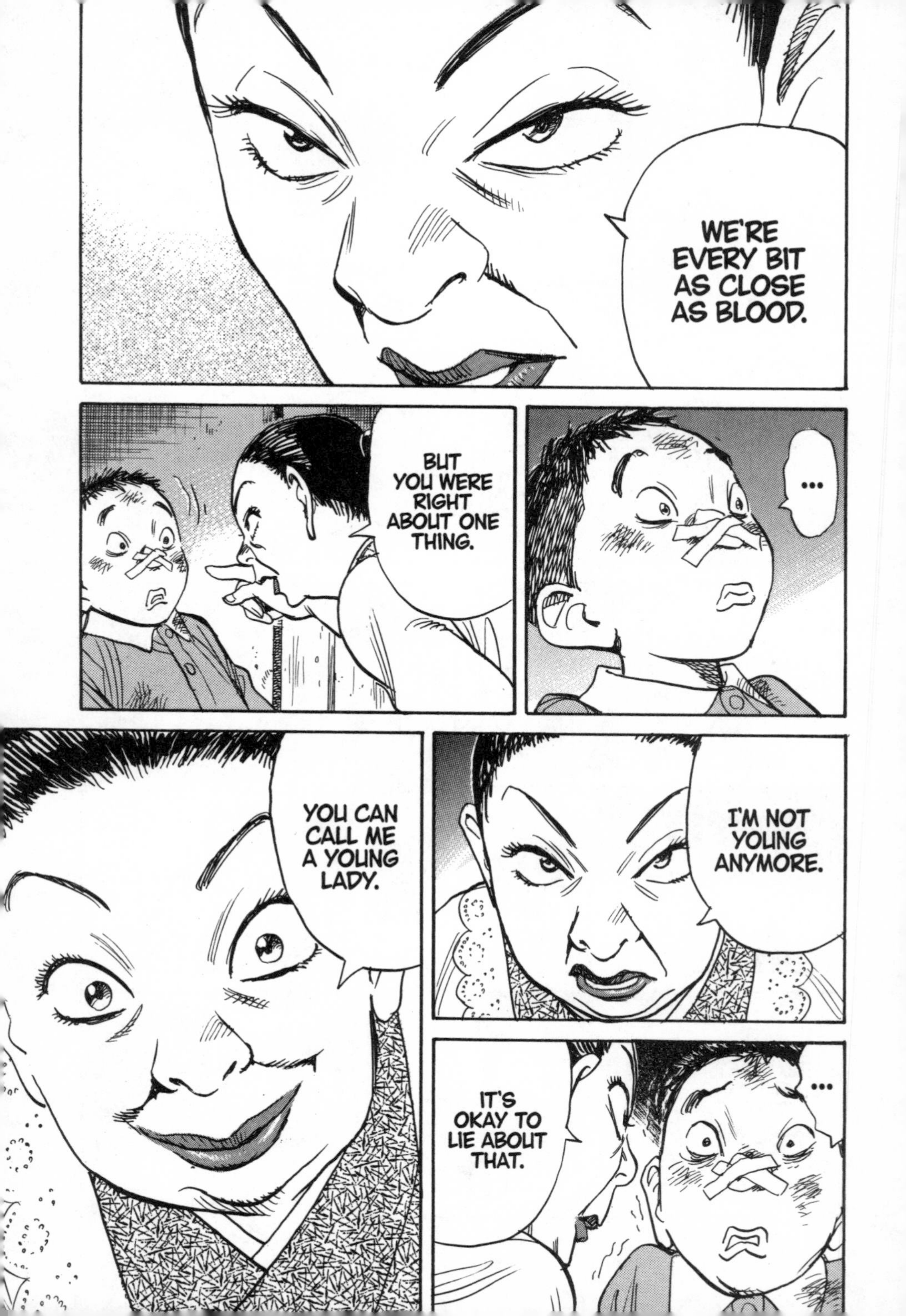
WE'RE EVERY BIT AS CLOSE AS BLOOD.
...
BUT YOU WERE RIGHT ABOUT ONE THING.
I'M NOT YOUNG ANYMORE.
IT'S OKAY TO LIE ABOUT THAT.
...
YOU CAN CALL ME A YOUNG LADY.

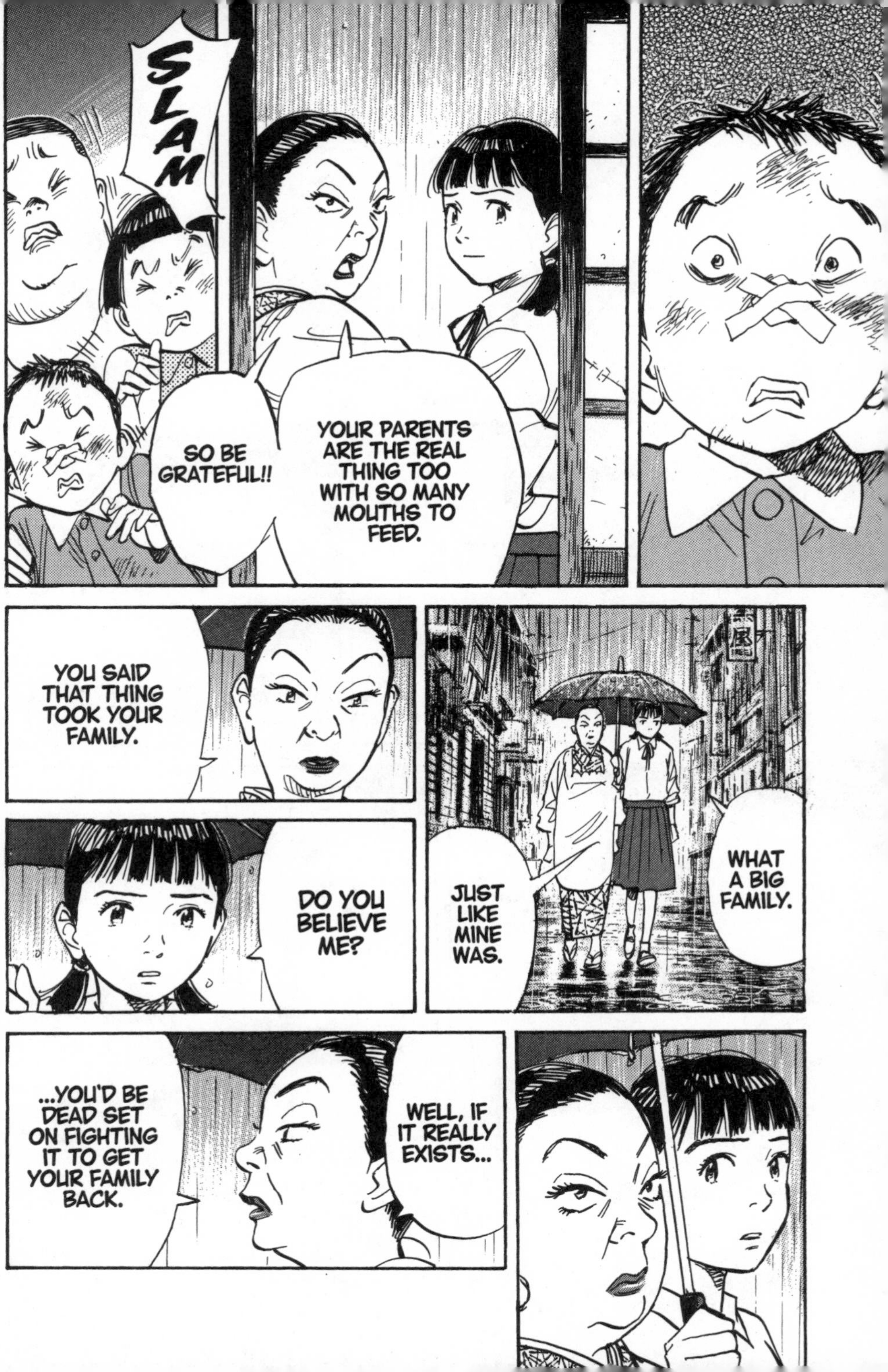
YOUR PARENTS ARE THE REAL THING TOO WITH SO MANY MOUTHS TO FEED.
SO BE GRATEFUL!!
SLAM
WHAT A BIG FAMILY.
JUST LIKE MINE WAS.
YOU SAID THAT THING TOOK YOUR FAMILY.
DO YOU BELIEVE ME?
WELL, IF IT REALLY EXISTS...
...YOU'D BE DEAD SET ON FIGHTING IT TO GET YOUR FAMILY BACK.

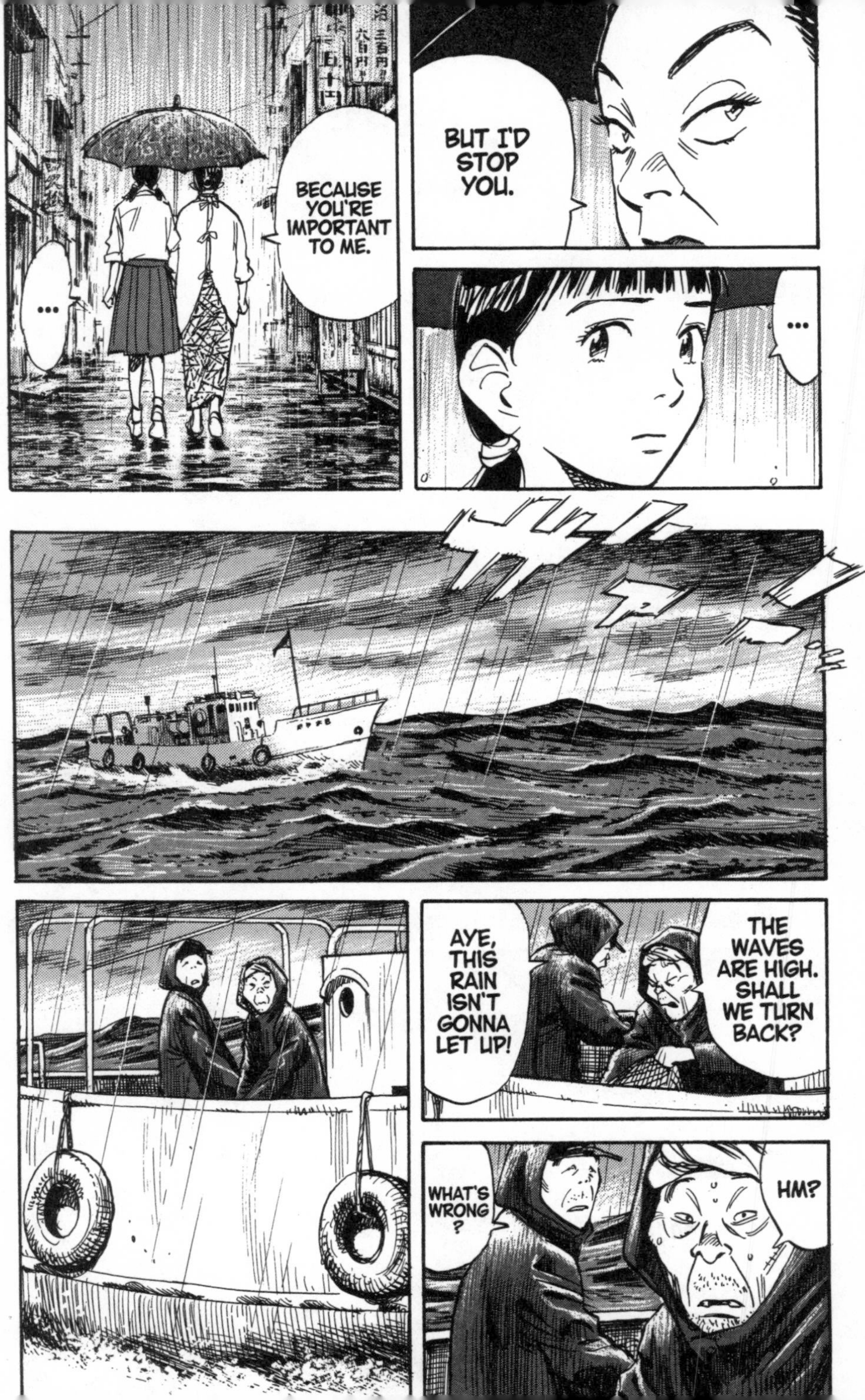
BUT I'D STOP YOU.
...
BECAUSE YOU'RE IMPORTANT TO ME.
...
THE WAVES ARE HIGH. SHALL WE TURN BACK?
AYE, THIS RAIN ISN'T GONNA LET UP!
HM?
WHAT'S WRONG?

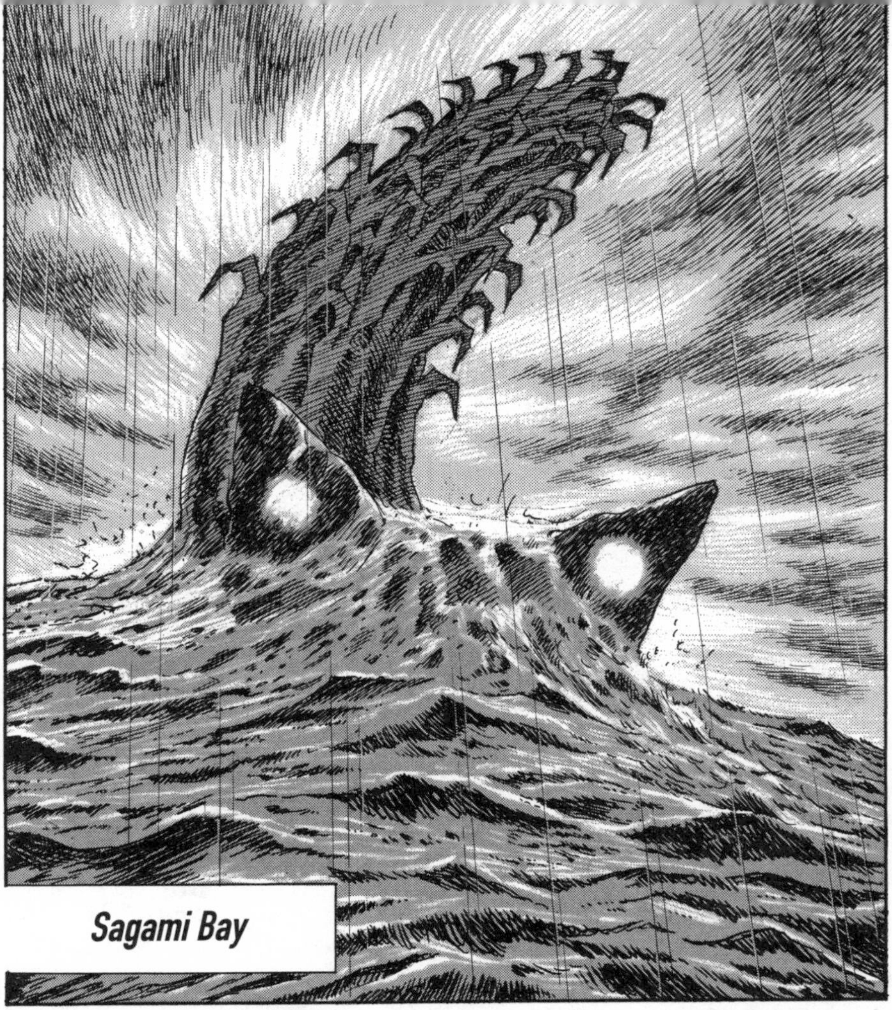
Sagami Bay

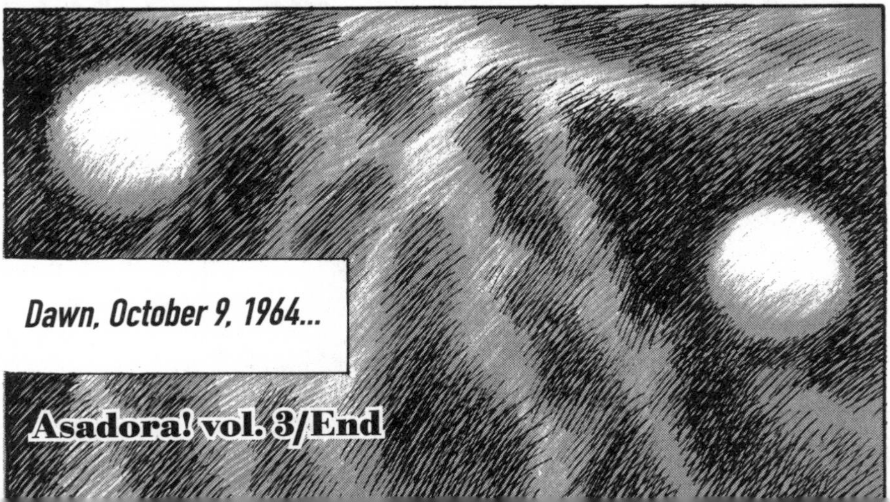
Dawn, October 9, 1964...
Asadora! vol. 3/End

ASADORA!

To be continued...

Production Staff:
Hideaki Urano
Tohru Sakata

Cooperation:
Satoshi Akatsuka (TAC Photography)
Jun Takahashi
Yorimasa Takeda
Hidetaka Shiba
Nagoya Times, Archives Committee
Japan Aeronautic Association, Aviation Library
Hajime Matsubara (The University Museum, The University of Tokyo)
National Museum of Nature and Science
Takeshi Ijichi (Ikaros Publications, Ltd.)
Akatsuka
Satomi Danno

Editor:
Haruka Ikegawa

References:
Takahashi, Jun. *Jun-san no Ozora Jinsei, Oreryu* (Jun's Life in the Skies, My Way).
Assisted by Masahiro Kaneda. Ikaros Publications, Ltd.

Takeda, Yorimasa. *Blue Impulse: Ozora o Kakeru Samurai-tachi*
(Blue Impulse: Samurai Who Fly Across the Sky). (Bungeishunju Ltd.)

Thank you to everyone else who offered help.

PAGE 107: *Uiro* is a chewy, subtly sweet Japanese steamed cake comprised of sugar and rice flour. It comes in a variety of flavors, such as red bean paste, strawberry, green tea, yuzu and chestnut. Nagoya, in particular, is famous for its uiro.

PAGE 112: Kokichi Tsuburaya was a Japanese athlete who competed in the marathon and the 10,000-meters event at the 1964 Tokyo Olympic Games. Tsuburaya took sixth place in the 10,000 meters and was in position to take second in the marathon until Britain's Basil Heatley overtook him suddenly in the final lap. Tsuburaya placed third in the event. Ashamed of his performance, Tsuburaya vowed to make amends to the people of Japan by running and hoisting his home country's flag in the next Olympic Games in Mexico. Unfortunately, after the Tokyo Games, Tsuburaya wound up suffering from lumbago, which made it nearly impossible for him to train. Tragically, in 1968, Tsuburaya died by suicide in his dorm room while training for the Mexico City Olympics. In his hand was his bronze medal from the Tokyo Games.

PAGE 116: Kenji Kimihara is a retired Japanese long-distance runner. He competed in the 1964 Olympics alongside Kokichi Tsuburaya, placing eighth. He also competed in the 1968 and 1972 Olympics, where he finished in second and fifth respectively. Kimihara had a number of first-place finishes outside of the Olympics, such as in the 1966 Boston Marathon and the 1966 and 1970 Asian Games. In 2016, to celebrate the 50th anniversary of his Boston Marathon win, Kimihara ran the marathon again, finishing with a time of 4:53:14.

PAGE 116: Toru Terasawa is a former Japanese long-distance runner who finished 15th in the marathon at the 1964 Olympics. On February 17, 1963, Terasawa set a marathon world record with a time of 2:15:16 at the Beppu Marathon.

PAGE 134: The East Fuji Maneuver Area serves as the major training grounds for the Japan Ground Self-Defense Force on the island of Honshu in Japan.

Translation Notes

PAGE 19: The bullet train railway project began in Japan in 1959. Just five years later, the Hikari bullet train opened to the public on October 1, 1964. The train, which traveled between Tokyo Station and Shin-Osaka Station, was the fastest on the line. It made fewer stops than the slower Kodama, making the Hikari the premier train of the time. These 0 series models remained in use until 1999. Today, the Hikari bullet trains operate on the Tokaido and Sanyo lines.

PAGE 34: Blue Impulse is the Japan Air Self-Defense Force's aerobatic demonstration team. The team's formation was inspired by the 1959 visit of the Thunderbirds, the United States Air Force's air demonstration squadron. The official Blue Impulse team was founded in 1960 at Hamamatsu Air Base as a team of five F-86 Sabres. In 1964, at the Tokyo Olympic Games, Blue Impulse successfully drew the Olympic rings in the air with colored smoke. The squadron continues to put on airshows for awestruck crowds to this day.

PAGE 64: Due to its affordability, simplicity and popularity, the Piper J-3 Cub is considered by many to be the Ford Model T of aircraft. The light American aircraft was produced by Piper Aircraft between 1938 and 1947. Despite being designed as a trainer, the Cub also gained popularity as a general aviation aircraft and proved well suited for a variety of military missions, including reconnaissance, liaison and ground control. In fact, during World War II, it was mass produced as the L-4 Grasshopper. Following the war, many L-4s were civilian-registered under the designation J-3.

PAGE 80: *Shabondama Holiday* (Soap Bubble Holiday) was a Japanese music variety show hosted by twin pop-sensation duo the Peanuts from 1961–1972. The Japanese jazz band and comedy group Hajime Hana and the Crazy Cats costarred on the show. A number of celebrities appeared on the show during its 11-year run.

PAGE 82: The Western Carnival was a rock music festival that began in Japan in the 1950s at Nihon Gekijo (also known as Nichigeki Theater) in Tokyo. The now-defunct rock festival was Japan's first.

Sound Effects Glossary

The sound effects in this edition of *Asadora!* have been preserved in their original Japanese format. To avoid additional lettering cluttering up the panels, a list of the sound effects is provided here. Each sound effect is listed by page and panel number; for example, "6.3" would mean the effect appears in panel 3 of page 6.

8.3 - hwip (bi: taking photograph)

11.2 - hwup (ba: taking documents)

11.6 - fwump (dosa: loading documents)

18.7 - honk honk honk
(paaa pappaa puaa: vehicles honking)

19.1 - honk honk (paaa pappaa:
vehicles honking)

20.6 - munch munch munch
(hagu hagu hagu: eating)

21.1 - hwonk (puan: train horn)

22.5 - skrik (zaa: jeep stopping)

24.3 - vreeeee (kiiiiin: jets flying)

25.1-3 - hwooosh (goooooooon: jets flying)

26.2 - swooosh (kiiiin: jets flying)

34.4 - hrooosh (kiiiin: jets flying)

38.1 - vreeen (kiiiin: jet landing)

38.2 - vrshhh (goo: jet landing)

39.5 - fwip (ba: saluting)

44.6 - fwap (pan: swatting)

59.6 - vroosh (kiiiin: jet flying)

60.1 - gwoosh (goooo: jets flying)

78.4 - slam (batan: closing car door)

86.8 - tunk (bamu: closing car door)

87.1 - vroom (vuo: car leaving)

87.4 - vroom (baa: car)

88.1 - vroom (vuoo: car)

90.6 - gwap (ga: grabbing)

100.1 - creak (gii: door opening)

103.1 - fump (dosa: setting down newspapers)

105.2 - hup (ta: starting to run)

109.3 - shtmp (da: stopping)

112.4 - whsh (da: running)

114.1 - woosh (da: running)

119.1 - whoosh (da: running)

124.1 - fwoosh (da: running)

124.2 - honk (paaa: truck horn)

124.5 - vroom (baa: truck leaving)

129.1-2 - vrrrr (buuuuu: airplane flying)

130.1 - bam (ban: bursting in)

131.4 - bam (ba: bursting in)

134.7 - vrrr (buuuu: airplane engine)

135.1-5 - vrrrrr (buuuuuu: airplane flying)

136.3 - boom (doon: explosion)

137.1 - bwoom (ooon: explosion)

155.1 - tshhhhh (zaaaaa: rain)

155.2 - tshhhhh (zaaaaa: rain)

158.7 - hwup (ba: raising paper)

160.1 - vrrr (buun: airplane flying)

163.2 - thok (pan: punching)

171.2 - tshhhhh (zaaaaa: rain)

172.1-4 - yaaaaaaah
(waaaaaaaaa: commotion)

173.1 - bump (do: colliding)

177.4 - sloosh (zaan: parting waves)

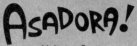

ASADORA!

Volume 3
VIZ Signature Edition

By Naoki URASAWA/N WOOD STUDIO

Translation & Adaptation John Werry
Touch-up Art & Lettering Steve Dutro
Design Jimmy Presler
Editor Karla Clark

ASADORA! Vol. 3
by Naoki URASAWA/N WOOD STUDIO
© 2019 Naoki URASAWA/N WOOD STUDIO
All rights reserved.
Original Japanese edition published by SHOGAKUKAN.
English translation rights in the United States of America, Canada,
the United Kingdom, Ireland, Australia and New Zealand arranged with SHOGAKUKAN.

Original Cover Design: Isao YOSHIMURA + Bay Bridge Studio

Printed in Canada

Published by VIZ Media, LLC
P.O. Box 77010
San Francisco, CA 94107

10 9 8 7 6 5 4 3 2 1
First printing, July 2021

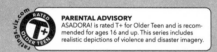

PARENTAL ADVISORY
ASADORA! is rated T+ for Older Teen and is recom-
mended for ages 16 and up. This series includes
realistic depictions of violence and disaster imagery.

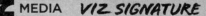

VIZ MEDIA
viz.com

VIZ SIGNATURE
vizsignature.com

This is the last page.

Asadora! has been printed in the original Japanese format
to preserve the orientation of the artwork.

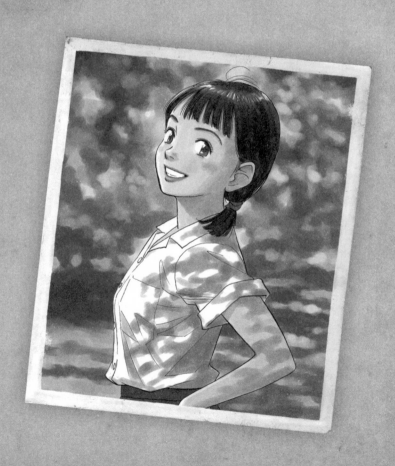